THEOLOGICAL
AND
RELIGIOUS
REFERENCE MATERIALS

THEOLOGICAL AND RELIGIOUS REFERENCE MATERIALS

Practical Theology

G. E. Gorman and Lyn Gorman

with the assistance of Donald N. Matthews

Bibliographies and Indexes in Religious Studies, Number 7

Greenwood Press
New York • Westport, Connecticut • London

Library of Congress Cataloging-in-Publication Data

Gorman, G. E.
   Theological and religious reference materials.

   (Bibliographies and indexes in religious studies,
ISSN 0742-6836 ; no. 7)
   Includes index.
   1. Theology, Practical—Bibliography.   I. Gorman,
Lyn.   II. Matthews, Donald Nathaniel, 1930-
III. Title.   IV. Series.
Z7825.4.G67 1986 [BV3]   016.26   86-380
ISBN 0-313-25397-8 (lib. bdg. : alk. paper)

Library of Congress Catalog Card Number: 86-380
ISBN: 0-313-25397-8
ISSN: 0742-6836

First published in 1986

Greenwood Press, Inc.
88 Post Road West, Westport, Connecticut 06881

Printed in the United States of America

The paper used in this book complies with the
Permanent Paper Standard issued by the National
Information Standards Organization (Z39.48-1984).

10 9 8 7 6 5 4 3 2 1

Contents

Preface

The first man I saw was of a meagre aspect,
with sooty hands and face, his hair and beard
long, ragged and singed in several places. His
clothes, shirt, and skin were all of the same
colour. He had been eight years upon a project
for extracting sun-beams out of cucumbers,
which were to be put into vials hermetically
sealed, and let out to warm the air in raw
inclement weather.

(Swift, Gulliver's Travels III/5)

Some years ago we embarked on a project which seemed simple enough,
the preparation of a basic guide to reference materials in theological and
religious studies. At that time our editor at Greenwood Press hoped that
we could expand the initial outline into a 450 page manuscript. In the end
the publisher sought some guarantee that the project could be kept to four
volumes. Gulliver's description of the Grand Academy of Lagado might well
have included a theological bibliographer among those engaged in futile enter-
prises, for the cucumber extractor is as likely to meet with definitive success
in his field as is the bibliographer of man's oldest discipline. Perhaps ironically
this situation is the very raison d'être for a work of the type now in hand.

As John Trotti indicates in his introductory chapter for the first volume
of this project, religious studies and theology are among the most complex
fields of human scholarship.[1] Certainly these disciplines have the longest
history of all scholarly endeavors, beginning with the earliest records of human
activity and continuing unabated to the present. Furthermore, religion and
theology as disciplines traditionally encompass far more than narrow definitions

would suggest, ranging from purely intellectual concerns of philosophical theory to the more concrete areas of history and literature and to the practical fields of social ethics, psychology, education and politics. Because religion covers such a wide range of man's interests and activities, the literature in this field is perhaps the most exhaustive of all subjects. Consequently, the sheer volume of material and the broad interests which it encompasses mean that any attempt to exercise bibliographic control requires a catholicity of knowledge and degree of stamina not usually associated with such activity. "To do his job properly, the bibliographer must first have a thorough acquaintance with his subject. He must know the primary texts well, and he must also have a command of the major reference works in the field. He should be well acquainted with previous bibliographic work on his author or subject and should have a solid understanding of previous trends in scholarship and criticism."[2] In addition to these requirements the bibliographer must have a clear grasp of the significance of theological bias. Because of the intensely subjective and personal nature of theological inquiry, there has developed over the centuries a very complex language in which each particular school defines terms according to its own views and requirements. As Jeannette Lynn has said, "A mere opinion may often be vested with importance in this field, when in another it would be of only a passing interest."[3]

Given these traits and consequent criteria required for effective theological bibliography, one is consistently amazed that scholars optimistically - or foolishly - devote time and effort to bibliographical activity at all, yet every year sees the appearance of still more guides to theological literature. Almost at random one can mention as examples such works as Kepple's Reference Works for Theological Research, Bollier's The Literature of Theology, Danker's Multipurpose Tools for Bible Study, McCabe's Critical Guide to Catholic Reference Works, Walsh's Religious Bibliographies in Serial Literature.[4] Guides of this type all share a common trait in limiting their coverage to specific traditions, topics or audiences in theology. Kepple and Bollier thus deal with basic reference works most often consulted by students and clergy; McCabe focuses on Roman Catholicism; Danker concentrates on the field of biblical studies; while Walsh covers a specific form division within religious studies.

The present series of volumes differs from these and similar works in several respects. First, the focus is international and interdenominational, including works in all Western languages and from all traditions which are likely to be consulted by students or scholars. While some users may look askance at the inclusion of general reference literature, as well as some material not generally regarded as theological in focus, we would remind them that works of this type can answer many basic questions which the more advanced and detailed reference books take for granted. Furthermore, students come to theology from a variety of disciplinary backgrounds, and what might seem unnecessarily repetitious to one will be totally new to another. Thus the student of sociology will know already about Sociological Abstracts, while the history graduate studying social issues for the first time will not. For these reasons we have included a broad range of general reference works under the appropriate subject divisions. The second distinguishing feature of importance in this series is its multidisciplinary approach, covering the literature of biblical studies, systematic and dogmatic theology, church history and practical or applied theology. Third, the target audience of the series is not just students or clergy or scholars but all three categories. Fourth, our definition of reference materials is purposely broad, encompassing bibliographies, indexes, abstracts, encyclopedias, dictionaries, handbooks, manuals and basic textbooks or major topical surveys. These last two categories are generally excluded from guides to reference literature, yet for students they can be particularly useful in providing concise information or the general background needed to place ideas and events in context. The one main category of literature specifically overlooked in this guide is periodical articles, for the adequate treatment of such material (bibliographical essays and literature surveys in particular) would require another set of volumes. Fifth, we have not limited our treatment to titles recently published or of recognized superiority. Most libraries of any size contain reference works which are often very dated and which, according to critical opinion, are clearly inferior. Since such works are available for consultation, it would be unfair to ignore their existence; rather we have tried to indicate the caution required in approaching works of this type.

The intention of this fairly generous categorization is to provide a work which introduces students to the full range of reference materials likely to be required in theological or religious studies and available in academic libraries. For this class of user John Trotti's introductory chapter in the first volume should be required reading, for it carefully sets forth the attributes of each type of reference material and places the literature within the broad context of academic research. More advanced users, including research students, clergy and scholars, are also catered to, for the survey is not limited to basic reference materials but also includes research tools required for a range of specific scholarly needs. This is particularly true of bibliographies, indexes and certain types of dictionaries, while the more general encyclopedias and basic textbooks are suitable primarily for the less advanced user.

Aiming to meet the rather different requirements embodied in such a broad range of users always poses certain organizational difficulties. The most suitable arrangement for advanced users, and the most satisfactory from a classificatory viewpoint, is one which follows a rather detailed classification of disciplines/subjects/topics. However, this presents a somewhat daunting prospect to the large body of student users unfamiliar with the niceties of theological and religious classification and may well discourage frequent use. In addition an intentionally broad subject arrangement encourages browsing by the neophyte theologian, and this is a prime consideration in a work which seeks to draw students into the maze rather than to reinforce barriers to understanding. Therefore, each volume follows a very broad subject division, with form subdivisions under each main subject. The more specific topical requirements of advanced students and scholars can be satisfied through the detailed author, title and subject indexes. A minor criticism of the first volume has been our use of broad subject divisions and detailed indexes; however, our experience with users of both the first and second volumes indicates that this arrangement is preferred to any other, and for this reason it has been used in the present volume.

The four volumes which comprise this set are obviously interrelated in the sense that they deal with the same general discipline. However, by following the traditional fourfold division of theology (with the addition of comparative religion) we have sought to provide volumes which can be used independently of one another. Each volume, therefore, is a separate entity, with self-contained introductory remarks, cross referencing and indexes. Since students new to theological study generally begin their work with biblical studies in one form or another, the introductory chapter by John Trotti has been attached more appropriately to the biblical studies volume than to any other. Volume 1, then, treats general reference materials and biblical studies; Volume 2 covers systematic/doctrinal/moral theology and church history; Volume 3 deals with practical theology and related subjects in the social sciences. These three discrete but related titles have been published within a two year period. The fourth and final volume, dealing with comparative and non-Christian religions, will appear somewhat later. Before then, however, it is likely that we shall see a supplement to Volumes 1-3, since the production of reference literature in theology has increased in both quantity and quality in recent years and therefore warrants continuing coverage of the type provided in this series.

In this third volume of the series we deal with the broad area of practical theology. As the alpha-numeric notation in Volume 2 ended with Section F, we have continued with a consecutive alphabetical indicator (G) in this volume in order to avoid the duplication of entry notations between subjects. Because disciplines overlap and are never mutually exclusive, users are likely to consult more than one volume in the series; and it is with this in mind that we wish to avoid any chance of confusion in notation.

Practical theology has been very broadly interpreted; the intention is to encourage student users to see the subject not as it is necessarily taught, as a series of discrete entities, but as a unified whole which relies heavily on the social sciences. The opening section on practical theology contains general reference literature of value in the study and professional practice of this field, while subsequent sections focus on particular aspects: liturgy and worship, homiletics, education, counseling, sociology. Outside the liturgical areas of practical theology, primarily worship and preaching, this discipline relies on work in the social sciences. Therefore, in such fields as education, counseling and sociology one will find numerous references to "secular" literature; given the indispensible role of such literature in a genuinely well rounded understanding of practical theology, we make no excuse for stepping outside traditional theological boundaries in this way.

In most instances the 1873 entries in this volume are divided into three form categories: bibliographies, dictionaries, handbooks. As in the preceding volumes, bibliographies are taken to include indexes and abstracting services; dictionaries encompass encyclopedic sets; while handbooks cover not only manuals and directories but also basic textbooks and a representative range of general studies. The exceptions to this general arrangement are in liturgy and worship, where handbooks for art and architecture and music have been separated into individual sections because of the large number of entries in each case. In addition homiletics has been given an extra division, quotations and illustrations, for the same reason. In all sections we have sought to include works from all traditions, from the most conservative to the most liberal. Items without annotations are those whose content we have been unable to verify or evaluate.

We are acutely aware that no volume devoted to the literature of practical theology and the social sciences can do justice to the subject because of the sheer volume of literature. While we trust that the relevant reference titles have been treated in this volume, we feel that there is a pressing need for similar bibliographical coverage of the monograph and serial literature in this field. Accordingly, the Greenwood Press series of which these three volumes form the initial component are to include a number of titles within the general area of practical theology and the social sciences. For example, Roger Homan of Brighton Polytechnic is preparing a volume on the sociology of religion; Daniel Breslauer of the University of Kansas, volumes on Jewish ethics and Jewish morality; Rabbi Jeffery Silberman, a volume on pastoral counseling; and Roger Wolcott and Dorita Bolger of Westminster College, a volume on the church and social action. We hope to treat other aspects of practical theology in due course.

The three indexes in this volume are intended to cater to those who wish to approach the field by author, title or specific subject. The author index includes not only all named authors but also editors and translators, while the title index lists all known titles under which a work has appeared (reprints, British and American variants, original foreign language titles of translations). In both of these indexes the computer has necessitated certain departures from normal indexing procedures, particularly the exclusion of diacritical marks and the adoption of short titles for many works. The results, however, are still detailed enough for anyone seeking a work through the title or author approach. In the subject index we have tried to select specific terms and cross references which provide an alternative to the very broad subject categorization adopted in the main bibliography, although it has not been possible to index specific parts of books. Nevertheless, individual titles are given as many subject entries as required to indicate the content relevant to all types of theological inquiry.

No matter how accurate and complete one seeks to be in preparing a work of this magnitude omissions and errors are bound to occur. We trust, however, that these are few and that they do not detract from the intended usefulness of the volumes. Some will disagree with our classification of materials and may find certain inconsistencies in the arrangement of entries. We hope that such infelicities will be brought to our attention so that they may be corrected in any supplementary volumes. More general omissions regarding topics in religion, of course, can never be overcome in a work which aims to cover the entire field of religious studies. In order to deal with some of the more important areas omitted from this guide Greenwood Press has agreed to institute a new collection of volumes, originally to be called Topics in Religion: A Bibliographic Series, but now entitled Bibliographies and Indexes in Religious Studies. This is intended to cover all aspects of religious studies which have as yet received inadequate bibliographic treatment. Initial volumes will deal with church and state in Eastern Europe, new religious movements, missions, the resurgence of Islam, pastoral counseling and other topics indicated above. We should be pleased to hear from those who believe that they have a subject worth including in the series. It is only by efforts of this kind that the many lacunae in theological and religious bibliography can be overcome effectively.

In preparing our own series of volumes we have had the extreme good fortune to secure the cooperation of several scholars and librarians and wish to acknowledge publicly our debt to them. Longest serving among our associates has been Donald N. Matthews of the Lutheran Theological Seminary in Gettysburg, who with consistent good humor and characteristic modesty has offered valuable advice on how to cope with the frustrations of broad classes of literature and over the years has provided several tons of photocopies (always within the law) for works not available to us. If anything can strain a friendship, this is it; however, we are happy to report that our relationship, now approaching its second decade, remains as close as ever. Marilyn Brownstein of Greenwood Press, having inherited this project from her predecessor, has provided a wealth of helpful insights nor only as an editor but also as one interested in religious studies. Over the years we have come to respect her wisdom and advice more than can be expressed in words. In addition library staff at the University of Sussex and the Ballarat College of Advanced Education have dealt, sometimes in puzzlement but always efficiently, with a bizarre range of requests arising from our search for some of the more elusive works in these volumes. Christ Wimlett, formerly of the University of Sussex Computing Centre and now of the University of St. Andrews, provided compassionate guidance and expert knowledge in our initially hesitant requests for computer assistance in compiling the author and title indexes. The tedious hours needed to put these indexes on tape were found by Barbara E. Degenhardt, who not only performed her task quickly and efficiently but also assisted us in correcting numerous errors and duplications in the text.

The invaluable assistance provided by these individuals has been largely responsible for the positive reception of Volumes 1 and 2, including the selection of the first volume as an Outstanding Academic Book by Choice and as an Outstanding Reference Book by the Reference Sources Committee of the American Library Association. We trust that this third volume will be regarded as equally useful by those scholars, students, clergy and librarians who are its intended audience. To all who seek to understand and communicate the wisdom embodied in our religious heritage we reiterate the warning of Qoheleth: "Of making many books there is no end, and much study is a weariness of the flesh."

Notes

1   John B. Trotti, "Introduction to the Study and Use of Theological Litera-ture," in G.E. Gorman and Lyn Gorman, Theological and Religious Refer-ence Materials: General Resources and Biblical Studies (Westport, Conn.: Greenwood Press, 1984), pp. 3-26; see also G.E. Gorman, "The Classifica-tion of Theological Literature: A Commentary and Annotated Bibliog-raphy," International Library Review 17 (1985): 203-231.

2   A.J. Colaianne, "The Aims and Methods of Annotated Bibliography," Scholarly Publishing 11 (1980): 324.

3   Jeannette Murphy Lynn, An Alternative Classification for Catholic Books (2nd rev. ed. by G.C. Peterson. Washington, D.C.: Catholic University of America Press, 1954), p. 17.

4   Robert J. Kepple, Reference Works for Theological Research: An An-notated Selective Bibliographical Guide (2nd ed. Lanham, Md.: University Press of America, 1981); John A. Bollier, The Literature of Theology: A Guide for Students and Pastors (Philadelphia, Pa.: Westminster Press, 1979); Frederick W. Danker, Multipurpose Tools for Bible Study (3rd ed. St. Louis, Mo.: Concordia Publishing House, 1970); James P. McCabe, Critical Guide to Catholic Reference Works (2nd ed. Littleton, Colo.: Libraries Unlimited, 1980); Michael J. Walsh, comp., Religious Bibliograph-ies in Serial Literature (Westport, Conn.: Greenwood Press; London: Mansell Publishing, 1981).

G.E. Gorman   L. Gorman
School of Information Studies   Creswick, Victoria
Riverina-Murray Institute of Higher Education
Wagga Wagga, New South Wales

Feast of St. Hugh of Lincoln, 1985

THEOLOGICAL
AND
RELIGIOUS
REFERENCE MATERIALS

G. Practical Theology

G0001 Apollinarius. Vol. 1- . Rome: Pontificia Universita Lateranense, Pontificio Istituto Utriusque Iuris, 1928- ; quarterly.

This scholarly journal devoted to canon law in the Roman Catholic tradition
includes systematic bibliographies at irregular intervals. These bibliographies are well organized and provide useful guidance on major works. However,
coverage is somewhat variable and often fails to treat the most current
titles and articles. A survey of periodicals in the field of canon law is
provided every few years. See also Monitor Ecclesiasticus (G0025).

G0002 Archiv für Katholisches Kirchenrecht; mit Besonderer Rücksicht auf
die Länder Deutscher Zunge. Vol. 1- . Mainz/Rhein: Verlag Kirchheim, 1857- ;
semi-annual.

Aimed primarily at a German Roman Catholic audience, this serial deals
with changes and developments in both ecclesiastical and civil law affecting
clergy in Germany. Legislation without particular significance to the
German church is not included, but despite this rather narrow approach
the coverage provided is both thorough and detailed. Of the several sections
in each issue those with reference value are the canon law chronicle,
reviews and notices, bibliography. Other sections usefully provide extracts
of relevant civil and ecclesiastical enactments, and these can serve as
helpful abstracts of the literature. In the bibliographical section entries
are arranged by subject, including canon law history, current law, Eastern
Christianity, Vatican II, church and state, Protestant churches. For those
interested in this very specialized field the Archiv is an indispensible
resource; inquiries of a more general nature will not be satisfied by this
compilation. The second issue of each volume includes indexes of contributors and of contents. See also Schulte (G0034, G0035).

G0003 Archives de Sciences Sociales des Religions. Vol. 1- . Paris: Editions
du Centre National de la Recherche Scientifique, 1956- ; quarterly, with
each volume being semi-annual.

Prepared by the Groupe de Sociologie des Religions of the Centre National de la Recherche Scientifique and originally entitled Archives de Sociologie des Religions, this scholarly journal contains in the second issue of each volume a Bulletin Bibliographique. Each bulletin includes an alphabetical author listing of periodical articles (Bulletin des Périodiques), some of which are annotated, and a book review section arranged by author. The lack of a subject index is partly overcome by the cumulative indexes for Volumes 31-42. The periodical entries in each issue are limited to items published in the preceding six months, while books are reviewed up to two years following the publication date. This gives the survey an up-to-date appearance particularly sought by social scientists. Approximately 500 items are indexed or reviewed in each volume, mostly from European and North American sources. Covering all religions from a social scientific perspective, this is an excellent guide which provides very up-to-date coverage of an exceedingly broad field. Without frequent subject indexing, however, ease of usage is less than it could be. See also Berkowitz (G0004) and Guide to Social Science and Religion (G0014).

G0004   Berkowitz, Morris I., and Johnson, J. Edmund. Social Scientific Studies of Religion: A Bibliography. Pittsburgh, Pa.: University of Pittsburgh Press, 1967.

This 258 page bibliography lists approximately 6000 books and articles dealing with the history and development of various religions, the relation of religion to other social institutions and to behavior, to education and communication, to social issues and social change. The scope is broad, and entries are representative rather than fully comprehensive. There is a detailed classification scheme and a complete author index. The fact that entries are not annotated and that the classification scheme is some-what unwieldy detracts from the usefulness of this compilation. See also Archives de Sciences Sociales des Religions (G0003).

G0005   Bibliographie Internationale sur le Sacerdoce et le Ministère/Inter-national Bibliography on the Priesthood and the Ministry. Vol. 1- . Montréal: Sacerdoce et Ministère, Centre de Documentation et de Recherche, 1969- .

Initially compiled by André Guitard and Marie-Georges Bulteau, this continuation of the earlier Bibliographie sur le Sacerdoce, 1966-1968 (G0015) lists books and articles on Roman Catholic, Protestant and Jewish clergy. Almost 7000 items are listed in the first issue, arranged in classified order under twenty-nine main headings. Author and subject indexes are provided. Roman Catholic literature tends to predominate. See also Il Sacerdote (G0032).

G0006   Byers, David M., and Quinn, Bernard. Readings for Town and Country Church Workers: An Annotated Bibliography. Washington, D.C.: Glenmary Research Center, 1974.

This 121 page bibliography contains 425 entries on books and essays drawn from sociology, anthropology, history, cultural studies, religious studies and literature. These works, mostly secular, provide information on rural America and the Christian mission there. The introductory chapter gives helpful suggestions on how the reader with limited time can get a quick overview of various aspects of rural studies. The annotations vary from a few lines to page-length. See also James and Wickens (G0018).

G0007   Canon Law Abstracts: A Half-Yearly Review of Periodical Literature in Canon Law. Vol. 1- . Edinburgh: Canon Law Society of Great Britain, Canon Law Abstracts, 1959- ; semi-annual.

Limited to Roman Catholic canon law, this service is arranged according to the Code of Canon Law and presents abstracts of periodical articles from more than eighty Roman Catholic sources published around the world. The abstracts are highly technical and thorough, reflecting the nature of this subject. Issues are not terribly up-to-date, and there are no indexes. Despite these drawbacks Canon Law Abstracts is an essential working tool for the scholarly community interested in this field. For bibliographies see Apollinarius (G0001) and Monitor Ecclesiasticus (G0025).

G0008   Chiesa Locale. Quaderni di Aggiornamento Bibliografica. Serie Teologia Pastorale, 4. Rome: Edizioni Pastorali, 1972.

See also Byers and Quinn (G0006) and James and Wickens (G0018).

G0009   Cunningham, Richard G. An Annotated Bibliography of the Work of the Canon Law Society of America, 1965-1980. Washington, D.C.: Canon Law Society of America, 1982.

Although severely limited in terms of dates, this is an important guide to publications by members of the Canon Law Society of America or works sponsored by the Society. Books, papers, workshop reports and symposium proceedings are all treated. Principal entries are listed under the names of 227 main authors with 348 descriptive annotations, and numerous cross references refer from joint authors and subjects to the main entry. This is a useful bibliography of an internationally respected group whose work in canon law reform and education cannot be overlooked. See also Ferreira-Ibarra (G0012) and Sheridan (G0036).

G0010   Current Contents: Behavioral, Social and Management Sciences. Vol. 1- . Philadelphia, Pa.: Institute of Scientific Information, 1969- ; weekly.

This listing reproduces weekly tables of contents from hundreds of foreign and domestic journals which report research in psychology, anthropology, sociology, economics, history, international and urban affairs, human development and management. Many are included in advance of publication date, and each issue contains a sheet for requesting any article listed. There is an author index and an address directory. More than 1000 journals are covered annually, and education receives particularly thorough treatment. See also Mukherjee (G0026) and White (G0040).

G0011   Duval, Frédéric Victor. Les Livres Qui S'Imposent: Vie Chrétienne, Vie Sociale, Vie Civique. 4e éd. Rev. et Augmentée. Paris: G. Beauchesne, 1913.

This well annotated Roman Catholic bibliography of the social sciences covers works in French, arranged by subject. Sociology receives good coverage. Author, title and subject indexes are provided. See also Laurent (G0020).

G0012   Ferreira-Ibarra, Dario C., comp. The Canon Law Collection of the Library of Congress: A General Bibliography with Selective Annotations. Washington, D.C.: Library of Congress, 1981.

Organized by subject, this bibliography of approximately 2500 items covers the code of canon law, historical foundations, other basic documents of the Roman Catholic Church and other subjects treated in the code itself (persons, things, procedural law, crimes and penalties). Within each topic entries are arranged alphabetically by author, and particularly important items include brief annotations. Name and subject indexes conclude the work, which is an up-to-date guide for the advanced student. See also Cunningham (G0009), Sheridan (G0036) and Zimmermann (G0042) for more limited bibliographies.

G0013 Ganghofer, Odilie. The Woman in the Church: International Bibliography, 1973-June 1975, Indexed by Computer/La Femme dans l'Eglise: Bibliographie Internationale, 1973-Juin 1975, Etablie par Ordinateur. RIC Supplément, no. 21. Strasbourg: CERDIC Publications, 1975.

This bibliography contains 688 citations in 45 pages.

G0014 Guide to Social Science and Religion in Periodical Literature. Vol. 1- . Flint, Mich.: National Periodical Library, 1964- ; quarterly, with annual and triennial cumulations.

Known initially as Guide to Religious Periodicals and then as Guide to Religious and Semi-Religious Periodicals, this guide indexes approximately 100 serials devoted to the social sciences, humanism and religion. Particular attention is paid to more popular serials not covered by the academic indexing services; furthermore, most of the titles carry only occasional articles devoted to religion, so this is a useful guide to generally elusive literature aimed at a general audience. The entries are arranged alphabetically by subject, although some of these are not especially helpful, particularly in view of the inadequate cross references. See also Archives de Sciences Sociales des Religions (G0003), Berkowitz (G0004) and Review of Religious Research (G0030).

G0015 Guitard, André, and Litalien, Rolland, comps. Bibliographies sur le Sacerdoce, 1966-1968. 9 vols. Montréal: Office National du Clergé, 1969.

This predecessor of Bibliographie Internationale sur le Sacerdoce et le Ministère (G0005) covers a specific topic in each volume: bibliographie sur la vocation et la formation sacerdotale; bibliographie sue l'épiscopat; bibliographie sur le sacerdoce et la vie des prêtres; bibliographie sur le ministère sacerdotale et la pastorale; bibliographie sur le célibat, l'obeissance et la pauvreté; bibliographie sur le diaconat. Each of these is arranged in classified order and includes an author index. Emphasis is on the Roman Catholic tradition, and many English language items, both books and articles, are included. This is a thorough and wide ranging compilation for students at various levels. See also Mierzwinski (G0024).

G0016 Hoselitz, Bert Frank, ed. A Reader's Guide to the Social Sciences. 2nd rev. ed. New York: Free Press; London: Collier-Macmillan, 1973.

In a series of chapters devoted to sociology, anthropology, psychology and other social sciences this guide explains the nature and development of the particular subject and provides a narrative commentary on the literature. The general bibliography (pp. 319-425) is arranged by major sections and presents a sound overview of the literature for beginners. See also White (G0040), which is both broader and more detailed in bibliographical coverage; see also Mukherjee (G0026), which has an Asian focus.

G0017   Institute on the Church in Urban-Industrial Society. <u>Abstract Service</u>. Vol. 1- . Chicago, Ill.: Institute on the Church in Urban-Industrial Society for the World Council of Churches, Commission on World Mission and Evangelism, Urban-Rural Mission Office, 1970- ; monthly.

Including an annual index (quarterly through 1977), this duplicated typescript compilation contains abstracts on the church in urban and industrial areas. It covers a wide range of social, economic and political topics within this broad field and treats books, articles, reports, conference papers and reprints. The subject headings are listed at the beginning together with a numerical index of entries for each category. Geographical coverage is very broad, and most entries are included within three months of publication. Copies of the 250-300 items abstracted each year can be obtained from the Institute. This is a useful guide to materials on Christian activism in an urban setting and is an excellent example of what can be done with limited financial resources.

G0018   James, Gilbert, and Wickens, Robert G., comps. <u>The Town and Country Church: A Topical Bibliography</u>. Wilmore, Ky.: Department of the Church in Society, Asbury Theological Seminary, 1968.

This topical bibliography of more than 1000 items comprising nearly 800 separate titles is designed to remedy relative neglect of problems of the rural church. Broad headings include rural society and town and country development, and there are subdivisions for each. The table of contents indicates how many books, articles and pamphlets are listed under each subdivision. See also Byers and Quinn (G0006).

G0019   Katt, Arthur. <u>Practical Theology: Bibliography for Graduate Studies in the Cincinnati Bible Seminary</u>. Cincinnati, Ohio: Cincinnati Bible Seminary, 1969.

See also Princeton Theological Seminary (G0028).

G0020   Laurent, Edouard. <u>Essai Bibliographique autour de "Rerum Novarum"</u>. Avec la collaboration de Laval Laurent. Québec: Editions de "Culture", 1942.

This 86 page classified bibliography is devoted to all aspects of Roman Catholic social thought. It treats both books and articles, providing critical notes for most entries. An author index is provided. For current requirements Laurent is now too dated but provides an interesting retrospective source of information on traditional Catholic approaches in the social sciences. See also Duval (G0011) and Utz (G0039).

G0021   Le Leannec, Bernard, and Schlick, Jean. <u>Authority in the Church: International Bibliography, 1972-1974, Indexed by Computer/Autorité dans l'Eglise: Bibliographie Internationale, 1972-1975, Etablie par Ordinateur</u>. RIC Supplément, no. 27. Strasbourg: CERDIC Publications, 1976.

G0022   Little, Lawrence Calvin. <u>Toward Understanding the Church and the Clergy: Contributions of Selected Doctoral Dissertations</u>. Pittsburgh, Pa.: Department of Religious Education, University of Pittsburgh, 1963.

This book offers an overview of doctoral dissertations on the church and the ministry prepared under the sponsorship of leading universities and theological seminaries. Some sixty dissertations are covered in four sections: toward understanding the church; toward understanding the minister; on preparing for the ministry; and on the work of the minister. The summary for each dissertation covers the main questions studied, methodology, and findings and conclusions. A bibliography is provided. This work provides a useful summary of otherwise not easily accessible material. See also Research in Ministry (G0029).

G0023   Messner, Francis, and Schlick, Jean. Participation in the Church: International Bibliography, 1968-June 1975, Indexed by Computer/Participation dans l'Eglise: Bibliographie Internationale, 1968-Juin 1975, Etablie par Ordinateur. RIC Supplément, no. 19. Strasbourg: CERDIC Publications, 1975.

This international bibliography contains 889 citations in 52 pages. See also World Council of Churches (G0041).

G0024   Mierzwinski, Theophil J., comp. and ed. What Do You Think of the Priest? A Bibliography of the Catholic Priesthood. New York: Exposition Press, 1972.

This 95 page bibliography of English language material on priest and the priesthood is a useful reference work on pastoral theology. Arrangement is by subject, with author and title indexes. See also Il Sacerdote (G0032).

G0025   Monitor Ecclesiasticus: Commentarius de Re Canonica et Pastorali post Vaticanum II. Vol. 1- . Naples: Agnesotti S.a.S., 1876- ; quarterly.

This canon law quarterly includes a substantial annual bibliography of current works in the field and provides useful coverage of an area which has seen much activity in recent years. Emphasis is on continental Roman Catholic publications. See also Apollinarius (G0001).

G0026   Mukherjee, Ajit Kumar. Annotated Guide to Reference Materials in the Human Sciences. New York: Asia Publishing House, 1962.

The 1164 annotated entries in this guide cover anthropology in Part One and sociology and allied topics in Part Two. Each subject field contains subdivisions for reference materials, journals and serials, source materials and standard treatises. The annotations are brief and not always informative. The author and subject indexes indicate the Asian focus of this work, which detracts from its usefulness for the sociology of religion and social welfare in a Western context. See also Hoselitz (G0016).

G0027   Noguez, Léon. Essai de Bibliographie Générale à l'Usage du Clergé. Nouvelle éd. Questions Pastorales, Ser. B. Paris: Union de Oeuvres Catholiques de France, [1953?].

G0028   Princeton Theological Seminary. Library. A Bibliography of Practical Theology. Princeton Seminary Pamphlets, no. 3. Princeton, N.J.: Theological Book Agency, 1949.

This brief (71pp.) bibliography, although dated, is a helpful compilation which indicates a range of titles still regarded as standard works by many. It is arranged in two divisions: homiletics and related subjects, Christian education and related subjects; under subheadings materials are arranged alphabetically, and there is a full table of contents but no index. See also Katt (G0019).

G0029   Research in Ministry: An Index. Vol. 1- . Chicago, Ill.: American
Theological Library Association, 1981- .

This index covers Doctor of Ministry project reports. See also Little
(G0022).

G0030   Review of Religious Research. Vol. 1- . New York: Religious Research
Association, 1959- ; triannual.

Although intended to cover all types of research on religion broadly defined,
this serial in its "Research and Planning Abstracts" exhibits a clear bias
towards the psychological and sociological aspects of religion. This abstract
section is based on a survey of professional journals and of Dissertation
Abstracts International, as well as of work by church agencies and individuals who provide the journal with summaries of their work. The coverage
of periodicals is not very comprehensive and has a clear North American
bias, and the abstracts themselves vary considerably in quality. However,
most items are listed within a year of their appearance, and this may
commend Review of Religious Research to those interested in the social
scientific aspects, of religion. There is a cumulative author and subject
index to the first twenty volumes. See also Berkowitz (G0004) and Guide
to Social Science and Religion (G0014).

G0031   Rzepecki, Arnold M., ed. Book Review Index to Social Science Periodicals. With the assistance of Paul Guenther. Ann Arbor, Mich.: Pierian Press,
1978.

Covering 1964-1970 in the first volume and then single years through
1973-1974 in each of the succeeding three volumes, this set is intended
to complement the Index to Book Reviews in the Humanities by providing
book review coverage of social science journals (including sociological
aspects of religion). All reviews in a given periodical are indexed, which
means that Rzepecki is broader in coverage than the title suggests. For
the period covered this is an important source of information.

G0032   Il Sacerdote. Quaderno di Aggiornamento Bibliografico. Serie Teologia
Pastorale, 1. Rome: Edizioni Pastorali, 1970.

See also Bibliographie Internationale sur le Sacerdoce (G0005) and Bibliographie sur le Sacerdoce (G0015).

G0033 Sankt-Benno-Verlag. Register des Pastoralen Schrifttums des St. Benno
Verlages 1952-1966. Pastoral-Katechetische Hefte. Leipzig: St. Benno-Verlag,
1967.

G0034 Schulte, Johann Friedrich von. Die Geschichte der Quellen und Literatur
des Canonischen Rechts von Gratian bis auf die Gegenwart. 3 vols. in 4.
Stuttgart: Ferdinand Enke, 1875-1880.

Detailed and comprehensive, this bibliography covers commentaries,
studies and other works on canon law published before the end of the
nineteenth century. Each volume is well indexed. See also the following
entry (G0035) and Archiv für Katholisches Kirchenrecht (G0002).

G0035 Schulte, Johann Friedrich von. Die Geschichte der Quellen und Literatur des Evangelischen Kirchenrechts in Deutschland und Osterreich und

die Evangelischen Kirchenrechtsschriftsteller. Stuttgart: Ferdinand Enke, 1880.

See also the previous entry on canon law (G0034).

G0036   Sheridan, Leslie W. Bibliography on Canon Law, 1965-1971. Tarlton Law Library Legal Bibliography, no. 6. Austin, Tex.: University of Texas, School of Law, 1971.

See also Cunningham (G0009) and Ferreira-Ibarra (G0012).

G0037   Social Sciences Citation Index. Philadelphia, Pa.: Institute for Scientific Information, 1972- ; three per annum with annual cumulations.

Exceeded in its scope of coverage only by its complexity in arrangement and use (even by social scientists), this service consists of three parts in each issue: a citation index arranged alphabetically by cited author with references to articles in which a work is cited, a source index (arranged alphabetically by author) giving full bibliographical details plus an author address wherever possible, a "permuterm" subject index. This work is thus extremely thorough and organized to provide maximum information; however, the underlying concept remains open to question, and it is unlikely that any but the most ardent researcher will find SSCI of value. See also Social Sciences Index (G0038).

G0038   Social Sciences Index. Vol. 1- . New York: H.W. Wilson Company, 1974- ; quarterly with annual cumulations.

This companion to the Humanities Index is a partial continuation of the Social Sciences and Humanities Index and International Index. It is an author and subject index in a single alphabetical sequence of articles on all social sciences culled from more than 260 serials. There is a separate book review index arranged by author at the end of each issue. The very specific subject headings and cross references include a number of religious topics within the social sciences. The bibliographical data provided for entries are quite full, and coverage in each issue is admirably up-to-date. For wide treatment of an area with significant religious content this is a very useful guide to primarily North American publications. The annual cumulations are especially suitable for retrospective searching but also list articles within two years of publication for more current requirements. See also Social Sciences Citation Index (G0037).

G0039   Utz, Arthur Fridolin. Grundsatzfragen des Offentlichen Lebens: Bibliographie (Darstellung und Kritik): Recht, Gesellschaft, Wirtschaft, Staat. Bases for Social Living: A Critical Bibliography Embracing Law, Society, Economics and Politics. Vol. 1- . Freiburg im Breisgau: Herder, 1960- .

This series of bibliographies in the social sciences is presented from the Catholic standpoint and includes works which seek to illuminate problems and questions in various areas of life. Divisions in each bibliography are given in German, French, English and Spanish. See also Laurent (G0020).

G0040   White, Carl Milton, et al. Sources of Information in the Social Sciences: A Guide to the Literature. 2nd ed. Chicago, Ill.: American Library Association, 1973.

The chapters in this detailed introductory guide cover the literature of social science generally, history, economics, sociology, anthropology, psychology, education and political science. In each chapter there is a bibliographical review of basic monographs for a collection of substantive materials, and this is followed by a list of reference works. Altogether more than 2700 items are listed and may be traced through the author and title indexes. There is no detailed list of contents and no subject index, which seriously detracts from a work which otherwise is more adequate than Hoselitz (G0016).

G0041   World Council of Churches. Department on the Laity. Laici in Ecclesia: An Ecumenical Bibliography on the Role of the Laity in the Life and Mission of the Church. Geneva: World Council of Churches, 1961.

This bibliography is an alphabetical author listing of 1422 books, articles, reports and pamphlets dealing with the laity in the church. Entries are devoted primarily to post-1945 Protestant materials, and many English language items are listed. Within this framework Laici in Ecclesia is a useful starting point for students, but it does include a fair number of more popular treatments as well. A subject index is provided. See also Messner and Schlick (G0023).

G0042   Zimmermann, Marie. Revision of Canon Law: International Bibliography, 1965-June 1977, Indexed by Computer/Revision de Droit Canonique: Bibliographie Internationale, 1965-Juin 1977, Etablie par Ordinateur. RIC Supplément, no. 29. Strasbourg: CERDIC Publications, 1977.

See also Monitor Ecclesiasticus (G0025).

PRACTICAL THEOLOGY: DICTIONARIES

G0043   Beckeroth, E., et al., eds. Handwörterbuch der Sozialwissenschaften. 13 vols. Tübingen, J.C.B. Mohr; Stuttgart: G. Fischer, 1951-1968.

This successor to Handwörterbuch der Staatswissenschaften (4. Aufl. 8 vols. Jena: G. Fischer, 1923-1929) is international in scope and covers all branches of the social sciences. The articles are lengthy and quite detailed, including extensive bibliographies with a largely European flavor. For readers of German this is a suitable alternative to Seligman (G0051) or Sills (G0052).

G0044   Cacciatore, Guiseppe, ed. Enciclopedia del Sacerdozio. 2. ed. Florence: Libraria Editrice Fiorentina, 1957.

This classified encyclopedia contains articles arranged under three main headings: the vocational formation of the priest; the theology of the priesthood; and works of the priest. Each article is followed by a brief bibliography and a classified and annotated general bibliography appears at the end of the book (pp. 1531-1636). Full indexing helps to compensate for the poor reference arrangement.

G0045   Gould, Julius, and Kolb, William Lester, eds. A Dictionary of the Social Sciences. New York: Free Press; New York: Macmillan Company; London: Tavistock Publications, 1964.

Including more than 1000 basic and general terms, this dictionary covers political science, sociology, social anthropology, social psychology and economics. Each term is given reasonably full and comprehensive treatment, which provides a concise definition, historical background and discussion of relevant controversies. There are bibliographical references in many articles, and the cross references are quite extensive. This is a sound guide for those unfamiliar with terminology in the social sciences, particularly those areas important in community studies and counseling. See also Reading (G0049) and Zadrozny (G0056).

G0046   Katholisches Soziallexikon. Hrsg. im Auftrag der Katholischen Sozial-akademie Osterreichs. Schriftleitung: Alfred Klose. Innsbruck: Tyrolia Verlag, 1964.

Covering all areas of the social sciences, this dictionary contains lengthy, signed articles with bibliographies and numerous cross references. Some biographical information is provided on important social scientists. For those seeking data and definitions in the social sciences from a Roman Catholic perspective, this is a useful volume. For more general treatment in German of the social sciences see Beckeroth (G0043).

G0047   Köstler, Rudolf. Wörterbuch zum "Codex Iuris Canonici". 3 pts. Munich: J. Kösel and F. Pustet, 1927-1929.

In 379 pages Köstler provides definitions in Latin and German of Latin terms in Roman Catholic canon law. Also included are references to canons in which the terms are used and a brief summary of each law. Because of the accurate references, this is a useful index to the code of canon law, as well as a sound dictionary for reference needs. See also Naz (G0048), Roussos (G0050) and Trudel (G0054).

G0048   Naz, R., ed.-in-chief. Dictionnaire de Droit Canonique, Contenant Tous les Termes du Droit Canonique, avec un Sommaire de l'Histoire et des Institutions et de l'Etat Actuel de la Discipline. Vol. 1- . Paris: Letouzey et Ané, 1935- .

Part of the Encyclopédie des Sciences Ecclésiastiques, this encyclopedic dictionary of canon law is issued in sections, each with a different editor. It includes signed articles on all aspects of canon law and biographical notes on individuals prominent in this field at various times. For historical purposes this is a useful reference work; otherwise it must be used with caution, as Vatican II reforms are not taken into consideration. See also Köstler (G0047), Roussos (G0050) and Trudel (G0054).

G0049   Reading, Hugo F. A Dictionary of the Social Sciences. London: Routledge and Kegan Paul, 1977.

This basic dictionary provides very brief definitions of more than 7500 terms used in all social sciences with the exception of economics and linguistics. There are numerous cross references. For beginning students and others requiring the briefest indication of a word's meaning this dictionary is a suitable work. See also Gould and Kolb (G0045) and Zadrozny (G0056).

G0050   Roussos, E. [Lexilogion Ekklēsiastikou Dikaiou]. 2 vols. Athens: n.p., 1948-1949.

This polyglot dictionary of the vocabulary of Eastern and Western canon law gives French, Latin and English definitions of Greek terms in volume 1 and of Latin terms in volume 2. It includes references to the canons in which the term appears. See also Köstler (G0047) and Pitra (G0196).

G0051   Seligman, Edwin Robert Anderson, ed.-in-chief. Encyclopaedia of the Social Sciences. Associate ed.: Alvin Saunders Johnson. 15 vols. New York: Macmillan Company, 1930-1935. Reprint. 15 vols. in 8. New York: Macmillan Company, 1951.

This comprehensive encyclopedia covering all of the social sciences is an international work which is widely respected for its broad historical perspective and judicious approach to the field. The articles are scholarly but readable and contain adequate cross references and bibliographies. The alphabetical arrangement of material is supplemented by the final volume, which contains a general index and a classification of articles in subject and biographical groups. See also Sills (G0052), which is a greatly updated encyclopedia but one without the historical awareness which gives Seligman its continuing value.

G0052   Sills, David L., ed.-in-chief. International Encyclopedia of the Social Sciences. 17 vols. New York: Macmillan Company and The Free Press, 1968.

Covering such fields as anthropology, economics, history, geography, law, politics, psychiatry, psychology, sociology, statistics and biography, this encyclopedia places strong emphasis on analytical and comparative aspects of the social sciences rather than on historical and descriptive aspects. These last two areas are much better covered by Seligman (G0051), to which Sills should be regarded as a complementary encyclopedia. The alphabetically arranged articles are detailed and scholarly, and there are many cross references and bibliographies. The complex amount of data in Sills means that the indexes in Volume 17 must be consulted in order to appreciate the broad coverage afforded. This volume also contains a list of contributors and a list of articles. For students of the social sciences and their role in religion and theology generally this is indisputably the prime encyclopedia for information at all levels.

G0053   Thinès, Georges, and Lempereur, Agnès. Dictionnaire Général des Sciences Humaines. Paris. Editions Universitaires, 1975.

Interpreting the human sciences very broadly, this 1033 page dictionary covers terms from such fields as anthropology, demography, esthetics, psychiatry, psychology and sociology among others. In cases where terms have specialized meanings in more than one field multiple definitions are provided. The entries are reasonably detailed and clearly presented for readers of French. There are some bibliographical citations, cross references and a few biographical entries. See also Gould and Kolb (G0045), Reading (G0049) and Zadrozny (G0056) for English dictionaries of the social sciences.

G0054   Trudel, P. A Dictionary of Canon Law. St. Louis, Mo.: B. Herder Book Company, 1919.

Arranged alphabetically by subject, this summary provides under each heading the provisions of the code together with the relevant reference numbers. It is suitable as a basic reference tool for students and others familiar with Roman Catholic canon law. For more detailed treatment see Naz (G0048).

G0055   Turnbull, Ralph G., ed. Baker's Dictionary of Practical Theology. Grand Rapids, Mich.: Baker Book House, 1967.

This evangelical Protestant compilation is a source book of practical theology classified under ten headings: preaching, homiletics, hermeneutics, evangelism/missions, counseling, administration, pastoral matters, stewardship, worship and education. Access to data is through the table of contents, index of subjects and individuals. Within its tradition this is a useful but nonacademic work. The bibliographies at the end of each section reflect a North American bias.

G0056   Zadrozny, John Thomas. Dictionary of Social Science. Washington, D.C.: Public Affairs Press, 1959.

This dictionary of social science terms is intended to meet the needs of both specialists and laymen. It contains clear and concise definitions of some 4000 terms, concentrating on current usage of the more important terms, especially in sociology, political science and economics. Terminology of psychology, psychiatry, jurisprudence and statistics is also covered. There are useful cross references.   See also Gould and Kolb (G0045) and Reading (G0049).

PRACTICAL THEOLOGY: HANDBOOKS

G0057   Abbo, John A., and Hannon, Jerome D. The Sacred Canons: A Concise Presentation of the Current Disciplinary Norms of the Church. 2nd ed. 2 vols. St. Louis, Mo.: Herder, 1960.

This lucid commentary explains each canon in numerical order.   The texts themselves are not reproduced, but background data, historical notes and bibliographical references are provided for each canon. Volume 2 includes a general bibliography (pp. 873-890) and an index. See also Bouscaren (G0069), Mathis and Meyer (G0171) and Rocca (G0204).

G0058   Adams, Arthur Merrihew. Pastoral Administration. Philadelphia, Pa.: Westminster Press, 1964.

This compact handbook covers the whole field of the minister's responsibilities as church administrator. It is practical, and is intended for the pastor. The first part sets out various principles and deals with major administrative categories. The second is a reference section concerned with worship, nurture, witness and supporting activities. The third is concerned with success and failure. A bibliography and index are provided. See also Ditzen (G0097) and Guffin (G0118).

G0059   Althoff, Leona Lavender. The Church Library Manual. Nashville, Tenn.: Southern Baptist Convention, Sunday School Board, 1937.

Although dated and written in extremely simplistic style, this 137 page manual for beginners is a moderately useful guide on organizing and operating a church library. The nine chapters include physical considerations, book selection, processing and miscellaneous topics. Larger and more complete than Foote (G0103), this work contains useful examples and review questions. See also Methodist Publishing House (G0174).

G0060   American Jewish Archives. Your Congregational Archives. Cincinnati, Ohio: American Jewish Archives, 1961.

G0061   Anderson, James Desmond, and Jones, Ezra Earl. The Management of Ministry. San Francisco, Calif.: Harper and Row, 1978.

This basic, practical guide to church management discusses ways to achieve goals most effectively. Working with boards, managing time, motivation, the church as a system and other topics are dealt with in detail. Each chapter includes excellent case studies. See also Bonar (G0068), Deegan (G0095) and Gray (G0117).

G0062   Arnold, Franz Xaver, and Rahner, Karl, eds. Handbuch der Pastoraltheologie: Praktische Theologie der Kirche in Ihrer Gegenwart. 5 vols. in 6. Freiburg im Breisgau: Herder, 1964-1972.

This comprehensive treatise covers the entire history of pastoral theology together with its principles and their application in modern situations. It includes bibliographies of almost exclusively German publications for each chapter, and in every case the topical treatment is full, detailed and analytical. Although Roman Catholic in origin, this survey analyzes pastoral theology as it appears throughout the Christian tradition, and is the most detailed work of its kind. See also Haendler (G0119).

G0063   Atkinson, Charles Harry. How to Get Your Church Built. Garden City, N.Y.: Doubleday and Company, 1964.

For a work on more general aspects of church administration see Leach (G0156).

G0064   Beatty, Frank M. The Office of the Clerk of Session. [Rev. ed.] Richmond, Va.: John Knox Press, 1963.

See also Jumper (G0146) and Wright (G0247).

G0065   Beck, Linda. A Handbook for Church Librarians. Ed. by Miriam Johnson. Resources for Parish Leaders. Philadelphia, Pa.: Parish Life Press, 1982.

This basic volume of 64 pages provides practical suggestions for the selection, organization and circulation of library materials. It also covers library publicity, nonprint media and other topics often overlooked in similar library guides. There are illustrations of card formats and filing aids, while appendixes provide basic subject headings and Dewey numbers for a wide ranging church library collection. Included are lists of jobbers and suppliers of library materials and their addresses. This is a very useful, easy to follow and up-to-date guide which should be of interest to parish librarians regardless of denomination. See also Newton (G0183) and Towns (G0230).

G0066   Blake, Eugene Carson, and Shaw, Edward Burns. Presbyterian Law for the Presbytery: A Manual for Ministers and Ruling Elders. Philadelphia, Pa.: Division of Publication of the Board of Christian Education of the Presbyterian Church in the United States of America for the Office of the General Assembly, 1958.

See also Garrison (G0109) and Presbyterian Church (G0198, G0199).

G0067   Bockelman, Wilfred. Toward Better Church Committees. Minneapolis, Minn.: Augsburg Publishing House, 1962.

This brief work contains seven chapters on qualifications for church committee membership, organizational structure for committees, and basic attitudes of committees. Questions for discussion are included at the end of each chapter. See also Foshee (G0107) and Harkins (G0120).

G0068   Bonar, James Charles. Management Education for Churchmen: A Source-Book; Selected Documents and Personal Papers. 4 vols. Montreal: n.p., 1968.

See also Anderson and Jones (G0061), Deegan (G0095) and Gray (G0117).

G0069   Bouscaren, Timothy; Ellis, Adam Charles; and North, Francis K. Canon Law: A Text and Commentary. 4th ed. Milwaukee, Wisc.: Bruce Publishing Company, 1966.

This basic textbook of canon law provides the text of canons together with background and commentary. Also included are sample cases and questions plus bibliographies for each section. See also Abbo (G0057), Mathis and Meyer (G0171), Rocca (G0204) and Woywood (G0246).

G0070   Bowen, V.S. A Vestryman's Guide. New York: Seabury Press, 1972.

See also Clark (G0086), Harper (G0121), Lawrence (G0155) and Luffberry (G0160).

G0071   Bramer, John C., Jr. Personal Finance for Clergymen. Church Business Management Series. Englewood Cliffs, N.J.: Prentice-Hall, 1964.

See also Gilbert (G0112).

G0072   Brandon, Owen. The Pastor and His Ministry. The Library of Pastoral Care. London: SPCK, 1972.

See also Oates (G0186) and Perry and Lias (G0194).

G0073   Broadman Press. The Church Media Center Development Plan. 3 pts. Nashville, Tenn.: Broadman Press, 1973.

This useful series consists of three basic booklets on administration, processing, classification and maintenance of media. See also Corrigan (G0089) and McMichael (G0167).

G0074   Broholm, Richard R. Strategic Planning for Church Organizations. Valley Forge, Pa.: Judson Press, 1969.

See also Gangel (G0108).

G0075   Buder, Christine. How to Build a Church Library. St. Louis, Mo.:

Bethany Press, 1955.

> This practical guide deals in seven very basic chapters with planning a church library, procedures regarding finance, physical facilities and equipment, the selection and ordering of books and other materials, and with record keeping and promoting use of the library. There is a detailed table of contents, but no index is provided. Buder is too basic for all but beginners and need not be consulted where more detailed manuals are available. See also Johnson (G0139).

G0076 Bunker, Barbara Benedict; Pearlson, Howard B.; and Schulz, Justin W. A Student's Guide to Conducting Social Science Research. New York: Human Science Press, 1975.

> This very basic guide of 120 pages introduces the beginner to research methods and related activities as practised in the social sciences. It is useful for theological students without training in the social sciences but who wish to understand the essentials behind parish surveys and similar undertakings. See also Miller (G0175) and Mullins (G0179).

G0077 Caemmerer, Richard R., et al. The Pastor at Work. St. Louis, Mo.: Concordia Publishing House, 1960.

> This collection of twenty-three signed articles by members of the Lutheran Church is intended to acquaint the reader with the wide scope of the pastor's duties and opportunities as well as with ways and means of meeting them. Topics include the pastor and the public, the pastor and parish education, the pastor and holy baptism, communion and marriage. There is no index, but the table of contents provides an adequate guide to the collection of articles. See also Hovey (G0135) and Perry and Lias (G0194).

G0078 The Canon Law Digest: Officially Published Documents Affecting the Code of Canon Law. Vol. 1- . Milwaukee, Wisc.: Bruce Publishing Company, 1934- .

> Published at irregular intervals, the volumes in this series provide English translations of documents on Roman Catholic canon law together with bibliographical references and some commentary. Also included are references to the 1917 code of canon law to which each document relates. See also Sartori (G0206) and Stickler (G0223).

G0079 Catholic Church. Codex Iuris Canonici Pii X Pontificis Maximi Iussu Digestus, Benedicti Papae XV Auctoritate Promulgatus. Praefatione, fontium annotatione et indice analytico-alphabetico ab Emo Petro Gasparri auctus. Rome: Typis Polyglottis Vaticanis, 1917.

> Containing the official text of the 1917 revision of canon law, this key collection contains the canons in numbered sequence plus a detailed analytical index and extensive notes on sources. See also the following entry (G0080) and Gasparri and Sevedi (G0110).

G0080 Catholic Church. Corpus Iuris Canonici. Editio Lipsiensis Secunda: Post Aemilii Ludovici Richteri Curas ad Liborum Manu Scriptorum et Editionis Romanae Fidem Recognuit et Adnotatione Critica Instruxit Aemilius Friedberg. 2 vols. Leipzig: Bernard Tauchnitz, 1879-1881. Reprint. Graz: Akademisch Druck- und Verlagsanstalt, 1955.

This thorough compilation contains the six major collections of laws on which the 1917 canon law code is based. As such, it is an indispensible reference collection for students of historical and legal aspects of Roman Catholic canon law. See also the preceding entry (G0079) and Gasparri and Sevedi (G0110).

G0081   Catholic Library Association. Handbook and Membership Directory. Haverford, Pa.: Catholic Library Association, 1940- ; annual.

This directory sets out the Association's constitutions and bylaws, describes committees, councils and other bodies, provides a directory of supplies and services, and lists individual and institutional members with addresses and a geographical index.

G0082   Center for Parish Development. The Denominational Executive's Handbook. Naperville, Ill.: Center for Parish Development, 1971.

See also Owensby (G0188).

G0083   Church of England. The Canons of the Church of England: Canons Ecclesiastical Promulgated by the Convocations of Canterbury and York in 1964 and 1969. London: SPCK, 1969.

This collection sets forth the canons of the Church of England as approved in law, and in seven sections presents statutes dealing with all aspects of ecclesiastical life: worship, clergy, officers, church fabric, courts. There is a detailed index. Moore (G0177) should be consulted for explanations of the meaning of the various canons.

G0084 Church of England. Central Council of Diocesan Advisory Committees for the Care of Churches. The Churchyards Handbook: Advice on the Care and Maintenance of Churchyards. London: Church Information Office, 1962.

For more general treatment of church property see Graves (G0115).

G0085   Church of the Nazarene. Manual of the Church of the Nazarene: History, Government, Ritual. Kansas City, Mo.: Nazarene Publishing House, 1964.

G0086   Clark, Howard Gordon. A Handbook for Vestrymen: A Lay Vocation in the Service of the Church. New York: Morehouse-Barlow Company, 1962.

See also Bowen (G0070), Harper (G0121), Lawrence (G0155) and Luffberry (G0160).

G0087   The Clergyman's Fact Book.   New York: M. Evans, 1963- ; annual.

Prepared especially for parish clergy, this guide provides basic religious and general information likely to be of value in daily work. Statistics, facts and figures, dates and names are provided on a wide range of topics, especially those relevant to Roman Catholic clergy. This is a useful almanac-like compilation which serves as a handy reference volume on a wide range of material.

G0088   Cooke, Bernard J. Ministry to Word and Sacrament. Philadelphia, Pa.: Fortress Press, 1976.

This valuable source book draws together material on scriptural, historical and theological sources on ministry in the church. It examines ministry as an element in the formation of community, and in relation to God's word in community, the issue of judgment and authority in the church, etc. There are extensive footnotes, a selected bibliography for each chapter and subject and name indexes. See also Segler (G0214).

G0089   Corrigan, John T., ed. Guide for the Organization and Operation of a Religious Resource Center. Haverford, Pa.: Catholic Library Association, 1977.

This is a comprehensive and up-to-date handbook for religious resource center staff, covering organization of media and the planning for media use. Corrigan discusses in detail media acquisition, handling, administration, services and activities of the center. A glossary and directory of publishers are included. See also Broadman Press (G0073), McMichael (G0167) and Schneider (G0213).

G0090   Corwin, Edward Tanjore. A Digest of Constitutional and Synodical Legislation of the Reformed Church in America. Prepared by order of General Synod. New York: Board of Publication of the Reformed Church in America, 1906.

This digest attempts to cover all topics of importance in the legislation of the Reformed Church of America up to the date of publication. Topics are arranged in alphabetical order and are treated in narrative form, with reference to the Minutes of the General Synod. Individuals are referred to only in relation to prominent official positions.

G0091   Craig, Floyd A. Christian Communicator's Handbook: A Practical Guide for Church Public Relations. Rev. ed. Nashville, Tenn.: Broadman Press, 1977.

First published in 1969, this practical guide to Christian communication and public relations is designed for church leaders. See also Dolloff (G0098) and Hess (G0125).

G0092   Dana, Harvey Eugene. A Manual of Ecclesiology. 2nd ed. Rev. in collaboration with L.M. Sipes. Kansas City, Kans.: Central Seminary Press, 1944.

First published in 1941, this 358 page compendium is a summary of Baptist polity. It contains much material from Dana's 1926 work, Christ's Ecclesia. See also Graves (G0114), Hiscox (G0127, G0128), McCoy (G0163), McNutt (G0168), Maring and Hudson (G0169) and Pendleton (G0191).

G0093   Davis, James Lucien. Church Treasurer's Manual. New York: Greenwich Book Publishers, 1965.

See also Gibbs (G0111), Peterson (G0195) and Thompson (G0229).

G0094   DeBoer, John C. Let's Plan: A Guide to the Planning Process for Voluntary Organizations. Philadelphia, Pa.: Pilgrim Press, 1970.

This planning guide analyzes the process clearly and in some detail (182pp.), suggesting why and how it should be done. It is an excellent manual for group leaders and clergy not familiar with detailed planning. Included is a full table of exhibits. See also McDonough (G0164).

G0095   Deegan, James, Jr. The Priest As Manager. Glencoe, Ill.: Glencoe Press, 1969.

This book of guidelines for the priest discusses the process of management, the development of management theory, and specific aspects such as use of time, the art of delegation, leadership styles, management by objectives, and problem-solving and decision-making. A chapter on management of the parish and a case study conclude the volume. There is a detailed table of contents but no index. See also Anderson and Jones (G0061), Bonar (G0095) and Powell (G0197).

G0096   Ditzen, Lowell Russell. Handbook for the Church Secretary. Englewood Cliffs, N.J.: Prentice-Hall, 1963.

Addressed primarily to the church secretary, but with the minister who supervises the secretary's work also in mind, this handbook deals with appropriate qualifications for the church secretary, duties, relationship to church officers, filing, statistics, records and papers, correspondence, planning, publications and similar topics. There is a full table of contents as well as an index. There is much practical information in this useful handbook. For specific aspects of the secretary's work see Harrall (G0122) and Jones (G0143).

G0097   Ditzen, Lowell Russell. Handbook of Church Administration. New York: Macmillan Company, 1962.

Although designed for metropolitan churches this handbook contains much of use in any administrative setting. It deals with parish organization, activities and personnel, the church fabric, furnishings, grounds, records, etc., civil matters, publicity and public relations. An index is provided. see also Adams (G0058) and Nygaard (G0185).

G0098   Dolloff, Eugene Dinsmore. The Pastor's Public Relations. Philadelphia, Pa.: Judson Press, 1959.

This work is in two parts, one concerned with the minister's relations with his own congregation, and one with his contacts with individuals and groups in the community. Its aim is to be practical rather than theoretical. There is no index, but a bibliography is provided. See also Craig (G0091) and Hess (G0125).

G0099   Donaldson, Margaret F. How to Put Church Members to Work. Westwood, N.J.: Fleming H. Revell Company, 1963.

See also Judy (G0144) and Wiest (G0244).

G0100   Engstrom, Theodore Wilhelm, and Dayton, Edward R. The Art of Management for Christian Leaders. Waco, Tex.: Word Books, 1976.

See also Ford (G0104) and White (G0243).

G0101   Episcopal Church. Constitution and Canons for the Government of the Protestant Episcopal Church in the United States of America, Otherwise

Known as the Episcopal Church, Adopted in General Conventions, 1789-1967. New York: printed for the General Convention, 1967.

G0102   Feldman, Julian, and Richert, G. Henry. Church Purchasing Procedures. Church Business Management Series. Englewood Cliffs, N.J.: Prentice Hall, 1964.

See also Walz (G0238).

G0103   Foote, Elizabeth Louisa. The Church Library: A Manual. New York: Abingdon Press, 1931.

This was one of the early predecessors of works by John (G0137), Schneider (G0213) and others on building a parish library. Foote discusses the role of the library, acquisition procedures, classification and cataloging and related areas. This should be supplemented with newer manuals such as Beck (G0065), Newton (G0183) and Towns and Barber (G0230).

G0104   Ford, George Lonnie. Manual on Management for Christian Workers. Grand Rapids, Mich.: Zondervan Publishing House, 1964.

See also Engstrom (G0100) and White (G0243).

G0105   Foshee, Howard B. Broadman Church Manual. Nashville, Tenn.: Broadman Press, 1973.

This practical manual on various matters of church activity, organization, etc. is useful for students, clergy and libraries. It reflects a Baptist viewpoint. See also Goulooze (G0113) and Hobbs (G0129).

G0106   Foshee, Howard B. The Ministry of the Deacon. Nashville, Tenn.: Convention Press, 1968.

See also Naylor (G0181).

G0107   Foshee, Howard B.; McDonough, Reginald M.; and Sheffield, James A. The Work of Church Officers and Committees. Nashville, Tenn.: Convention Press, 1968.

See also Bockelman (G0067) and Harkins (G0120).

G0108   Gangel, Kenneth O. Competent to Lead: A Guide to Management in Christian Organizations. Chicago, Ill.: Moody Press, 1974.

See also Broholm (G0074).

G0109   Garrison, Pinkney J. Presbyterian Polity and Procedures: The Presbyterian Church, U.S. Richmond, Va.: John Knox Press, 1953.

See also Blake and Shaw (G0066) and Presbyterian Church (G0198, G0199).

G0110   Gasparri, Pietro, and Sevédi, Jusztinián György, eds. Codicis Iuris Canonici Fontes. 9 vols. Rome: Typis Polyglottis Vaticanis, 1923-1939. Reprint. Rome: Typis Polyglottis Vaticanis, 1930-1951.

This extensive collection of documents contains conciliar materials, papal and curial documents which form the basis for Catholicism's code of canon law. The wide range of material reproduced and the thorough indexing make Gasparri a valuable resource for students and scholars. See also Catholic Church (G0079, G0080).

G0111   Gibbs, George. Manual for Mission Treasurers. 3rd ed. Los Angeles, Calif.: Episcopal Church, Los Angeles Diocese, 1963.

See also Davis (G0093), Peterson (G0195) and Thompson (G0229).

G0112   Gilbert, John Edwin. Income Tax for Clergy: A Practical Guide. London: SPCK, 1962.

This work will be of limited interest to North American readers as it was prepared for clergy in Britain. See also Bramer (G0071).

G0113   Goulooze, William. The Christian Worker's Handbook. Grand Rapids, Mich.: Baker Book House, 1953.

This manual is intended for pastors and other church officers, as a guide and source of relevant scriptural references.   Four sections cover the biblical basis for Christian service and Bible passages for personal workers, for special problems and biblical forms for special services. Scriptural quotations, with the reference, are grouped under subheadings. See also Foshee (G0105), Hobbs (G0129) and The Minister's Manual (G0176).

G0114   Graves, Allen Willis. A Church at Work: A Handbook of Church Policy. Nashville, Tenn.: Convention Press, 1972.

Concerned with Baptist church polity, this guide covers a similar area to McCoy (G0163), McNutt (G0168) and Maring and Hudson (G0169).

G0115   Graves, Allen Willis. Maintaining and Using Church Property. Church Business Management Series. Englewood Cliffs, N.J.: Prentice-Hall, 1965.

See also Stiles (G0224).

G0116   Graves, Allen Willis. Principles of Administration for a Baptist Association. Nashville, Tenn.: Broadman Press, 1978.

G0117   Gray, Gary M. The Church Management Profession: A Descriptive Analysis. Minneapolis, Minn.: National Association of Church Business Administration, 1970.

See also Anderson and Jones (G0061), Bonar (G0068) and Deegan (G0095).

G0118   Guffin, Gilbert Lee. Pastor and Church: A Manual for Pastoral Leadership. 4th ed. Birmingham, Ala.: Banner Press, 1963.

Intended particularly for pastors and church leaders in smaller churches, this manual deals with church organization and officers, activities such as the Sunday school, church publicity and public relations, a constitution and bylaws for the church. A bibliography is included. There is no index, but the detailed table of contents facilitates access. See also Ditzen (G0097) and Lawrence (G0155).

G0119   Haendler, Otto. Grundriss der Praktischen Theologie. Sammlung Töpelmann, 1. Reihe: Die Theologie im Abriss, Bd. 6. Berlin: Alfred Töpelmann, 1957.

See also Arnold and Rahner (G0062) and Otto (G0187).

G0120   Harkins, George F. Handbook for Committees of Congregations of
the Lutheran Church of America. Philadelphia, Pa.: Lutheran Church of
America, Board of Publications, 1967.

This handbook provides a guide to the committees called for in the Approved Constitution for Congregations of the Lutheran Church in America.
Seven committees are discussed, including those on education, finance,
social ministry and worship and music. A directory of various Lutheran
agencies and church supply stores is included. See also Bockelman (G0067)
and Foshee (G0107).

G0121   Harper, Howard V. The Vestryman's Manual. New York: Seabury
Press, 1964.

This handbook examines aspects such as vestrymen's qualifications, relationships with the rector, with parishioners, with the diocese and with the
national church, vestrymen and parish finances and parish meetings.
Appendixes contain a glossary of useful terms, an admission service for
wardens and vestrymen, and an office for a vestry meeting. An index
is included.   See also Bowen (G0070), Clark (G0086), Lawrence (G0155)
and Luffberry (G0160).

G0122   Harrall, Steward. Handbook of Effective Church Letters. New York:
Abingdon Press, 1965.

See also Jones (G0143).

G0123   Harrison, George W. Church Fund Raising. Contributing authors:
Howell Farnworth and Chester A. Myrom. Church Business Management
Series. Englewood Cliffs, N.J.: Prentice-Hall, 1964.

See also Knudsen (G0153) and Page (G0189).

G0124   Harvey, John F., ed. Church and Synagogue Libraries. Metuchen, N.J.:
Scarecrow Press, 1980.

This collection of twenty papers is organized in five categories: an overview, Jewish libraries, Catholic libraries, Protestant and other Christian
libraries, religious library associations. The essays cover historical antecedents, finance, architecture, collection building and professional associations. For those employed in libraries of this type and for others interested
in such libraries this is a useful introductory collection. Particularly
interesting is the coverage of professional associations, denominational
concern with libraries, compilation of bibliographies and the preparation
of manuals of procedure. For a work on Catholic libraries only see Martin
(G0170).

G0125   Hess, Geraldine. Planning the Church Bulletin for Effective Worship.
New York: Exposition Press, 1962.

This brief work deals with basic questions about what to include in and how to arrange materials for a worship folder. Appendixes list publishers and supply companies, sources for worship folders for special days and sources of stationery. An index is included. See also Craig (G0091) and Dolloff (G0098).

G0126   Hiltner,   Seward. Theological Dynamics. Nashville, Tenn.: Abingdon Press, 1972.

This work on the theological dimensions of the pastoral ministry considers what light theological doctrines and personal dynamics can throw on each other. Themes such as freedom, grace, the sacraments and sin are examined. Bibliographical references are included. See also Rahner (G0200), Segler (G0214) and Vinet (G0235).

G0127 Hiscox, Edward Thurston. The Hiscox Guide for Baptist Churches. Valley Forge, Pa.: Judson Press, [1964].

This 253 page revision of The New Directory for Baptist Churches (Philadelphia, Pa.: American Baptist Publication Society, 1894. Reprint. Grand Rapids, Mich.: Kregel Publications, 1970), itself first published in 1859 as The Baptist Church Directory, covers church government, discipline, ordinances, membership, confession of faith, baptism, local councils. It is well organized for easy reference and includes an index. The eight main chapters are also available as The Hiscox Standard Baptist Manual (Valley Forge, Pa.: Judson Press, 1965). See also Graves (G0114) and Maring and Hudson (G0169).

G0128   Hiscox, Edward Thurston. The Star Book on Baptist Church Polity. New York: Ward and Drummond, 1880.

See also Dana (G0128) and McCoy (G0163).

G0129   Hobbs, James Randolph. The Pastor's Manual. Nashville, Tenn.: Sunday School Board, Southern Baptist Convention, 1924. Reprint. Nashville,   Tenn.: Sunday School Board, Southern Baptist Convention, 1934.

This guide contains useful information on business sessions, meetings and liturgical events in which Baptist and other clergy are expected to participate. See also Foshee (G0105) and Goulooze (G0113).

G0130   Hoh, Paul Jacob. Parish Practice: A Manual of Church Administration. Rev. ed. Philadelphia, Pa.: Muhlenberg Press, 1956.

This work on practical parish administration is intended for students of theology, pastors and interested laymen. Thirteen chapters treat aspects such as church property, finance, publicity, organizations, records and reports. references and notes are included (pp. 189-199), publications mentioned in the text and notes are listed (pp. 200-204) and an index is provided. See also Ditzen (G0097), Nygaard (G0185) and Schaller (G0210).

G0131 Holck, Manfred. Accounting Methods for the Small Church. Minneapolis, Minn.: Augsburg Publishing House, 1961.

This manual provides information for the church officer on the best way to keep accurate financial records, illustrating various accounting methods and suggesting ways of achieving uniformity and accuracy. It is intended especially for the pastor, the church treasurer, the financial secretary and congregation leaders. A brief bibliography and a glossary are included, and there are almost thirty useful illustrations of budgets, various forms, ledgers, etc. See also Walker (G0237) and Walz (G0238).

G0132   Holt, David R. Handbook of Church Finance. New York: Macmillan Company, 1960.

This handbook attempts to provide the church officer with a spiritually oriented source book on church finance. It deals with budgetary control, financial records, church credit and borrowing, the finances of real estate, insurance coverage, legal aspects of church finance, and related topics. A selected bibliography is provided (pp. 173-176), and there is an index. A selection of tables adds to the usefulness of this practical book. It is similar in many respects to John C. Bramer, Jr., Efficient Church Business Management (Philadelphia, Pa.: Westminster Press, 1960). See also Walker (G0237) and Walz (G0238).

G0133   Hough, H.D. Churchmanship: A Primer for Presbyterian Churchmen. Charleroi, Pa.: Courier and Digest, 1955.

G0134   Hove, Alphonse van. Commentarium Lovaniense in Codicem Iuris Canonici. 5 vols. Mechlin: Dessain, 1928-1939.

This valuable commentary on the code of canon law covers a specific section in each volume and provides substantial information on the history of each canon together with numerous bibliographical references. It is well indexed and serves as a most detailed handbook for advanced students and scholars of Roman Catholic canon law. See also Vermeersch (G0233) and Wernz (G0240).

G0135   Hovey, Byron P. The Minister's Work: An Outline of His Duties and Obligations. New York: Exposition Press, 1961.

See also Caemmerer (G0077) and Perry and Lias (G0194).

G0136   Hyles, Jack. The Hyles Church Manual. Murfreesbobo, Tenn.: Sword of the Lord Publishers, 1968.

This practical manual written from a conservative Protestant viewpoint covers every aspect of pastoral life from ordination to church business. It is highly concrete in approach and well outlined. See also Foshee (G0105), Goulooze (G0113) and Hobbs (G0129).

G0137   John, Erwin E. The Key to a Successful Church Library. Minneapolis, Minn.: Augsburg Publishing House, 1958.

This is a brief (44pp.) but practical guide to the establishment and operation of an effective parish library and is directed particularly to those without any experience in this field. See also Beck (G0065), Johnson (G0140) and Straughan (G0226).

G0138   Johnson, Douglas W. Managing Change in the Church. New York: Friendship Press, 1974.

This brief work analyzes factors that make change in the church necessary and ways of participating in constructive change. It deals with aspects such as pluralism, decisions, and conflict. Bibliographical references are included, but there is no index. See also Jones (G0142) and Judy (G0145).

G0139   Johnson, Marian S. Planning and Furnishing the Church Library. Minneapolis, Minn.: Augsburg Publishing House, 1966.

See also Buder (G0075).

G0140   Johnson, Marian S. Promoting Your Church Library. Minneapolis, Minn.: Augsburg Publishing House, 1968.

This 48 page guide is essentially a collection of ideas on how to promote a parish library throughout the church year. It includes a basic list of resources and helpful illustrations. This is a useful complement to John (G0137) or Straughan (G0226) and should prove helpful in stimulating ideas of a fairly simple and inexpensive type. See also Smith (G0216).

G0141   Jones, Eli Stanley. The Reconstruction of the Church - on What Pattern? Nashville, Tenn.: Abingdon Press, 1970.

See also Vaughan (G0232).

G0142   Jones, Ezra E. Strategies for New Churches. New York: Harper and Row, 1976.

Concerned especially with new church development, this work also discusses the renewal of existing congregations and the societal context for organizing new congregations. It is a useful manual for those involved in this area and concerned with institutional aspects. See also Johnson (G0138) and Rusbuldt (G0205).

G0143   Jones, George Curtis. Handbook of Church Correspondence. New York: Macmillan Press, 1962.

This handbook sets out guidelines of various types of church correspondence (administrative letters, family correspondence, invitations, acceptances, resignations, inquiries, employment letters, etc.). It is clearly presented and written in a straightforward style. An index and footnote references are included. See also Harrall (G0122).

G0144   Judy, Marvin T. Multiple Staff Ministry. With the cooperation of Murlene O. Judy. Nashville, Tenn.: Abingdon Press, 1969.

This work provides material on the relation of laymen and employees in the church, and on staff function in terms of specialization, reviews of current literature on leadership, personnel management and group activity, and suggestions for developing creativity in staff activity. Profiles of 1349 staff members in large churches of eight major denominations are given, and material covers job descriptions of the senior minister, assistant minister, educator, musician, business administrator, and secretary. See also Donaldson (G0099) and Parrott (G0190).

G0145   Judy, Marvin T. The Parish Development Process. New York: Abingdon Press, 1973.

Based on the concept of the cooperative parish, this volume examines aspects such as parish structures, establishing the cooperative parish, and leadership and human relations. A study guide, an appendix on parish development aids (pp. 189-196), a bibliography (pp. 201-204), and an index are provided. See also Kemp (G0147), Markens (G0172) and Rusbuldt (G0205).

G0146 Jumper, Andrew A. Chosen to Serve: The Deacon; a Practical Manual for the Operation of the Board of Deacons in the Presbyterian Church in the United States. Richmond, Va.: John Knox Press, 1961.

See also Beatty (G0064) and Wright (G0247).

G0147 Kemp, Charles F. The Pastor and Community Resources. St. Louis, Mo.: Bethany Press, 1960.

This manual was prepared as a guide to pastors, providing a brief statement of basic principles underlying the pastor's relationship with social agencies and other professional workers, information on helpful resources (lists of local and national agencies regarding health, housing, minority groups, various church-related, government and voluntary bodies), and an index of local resources where the pastor can fill in names and addresses of people and agencies in his own community. The National Council of the Churches of Christ in the USA collaborated in publishing the manual.

G0148 Kerfoot, Franklin Howard. Parliamentary Law: A Text-Book and Manual. Nashville, Tenn.: Broadman Press, 1899.

See also Stevenson (G0222).

G0149 Kerr, William F., gen. ed. Ministers' Research Service. Wheaton, Ill.: Tyndale House Publishers, 1970.

G0150 Kersten, Dorothy Barbara. Classifying Church or Synagogue Library Materials. CSLA Guides, no. 7. Bryn Mawr, Pa.: Church and Synagogue Library Association, 1977.

See also the following entry (G0151) and Southern Baptist Convention (G0219).

G0151 Kersten, Dorothy Barbara. Subject Headings for Church or Synagogue Libraries. CSLA Guides, no. 8. Bryn Mawr, Pa.: Church and Synagogue Library Association, 1978.

This 22 page work is limited to those subjects most likely to be found in a standard church or synagogue library. It includes Dewey classification numbers taken from Kersten (G0150). Cross references and scope notes are provided, and there is a bibliography on p.22.

G0152 Kilinski, Kenneth K., and Wofford, Jery C. Organization and Leadership in the Local Church. Grand Rapids, Mich.: Zondervan Publishing House, 1973.

This three part work provides guidance on spiritual maturity, on the role and function of church leaders in equipping others, and on orderly and systematic organization in planning for the local church. Practical suggestions for leadership and organization are provided, with many useful diagrams and charts. Written from an evangelical viewpoint, this work will appeal to leaders of evangelical churches. See also Guffin (G0118) and Merkens (G0173).

G0153   Knudsen, Raymond B. New Models for Financing the Local Church: Fresh Approaches to Giving in the Computer Age. New York: Association Press, 1974.

This book gives some new insights into church financing in modern technological society. See also Harrison (G0123) and Page (G0189).

G0154   Lauer, Artur. Index Verborum Codicis Iuris Canonici. Rome. Typis Polyglottis Vaticanis, 1941.

This concordance to the 1917 code of canon law (see Catholic Church (G0079)) is arranged in sections by parts of speech, thereby departing from the usual alphabetical listing in works of this sort. Each entry employs a very complicated set of symbols to indicate grammatical and syntactical usage, and no attempt is made to quote entries in context. Because of these features, Lauer is far less useful than it might have been.

G0155 Lawrence, William Appleton. Parsons, Vestries and Parishes: A Manual. Greenwich, Conn.: Seabury Press, 1961.

This manual is intended particularly for clergymen and vestries of smaller parishes and missions of the Episcopal Church. It deals with topics such as the ministry, the parish, the laity, various church officials, principles and practices of parish administration, administering the sacraments, etc. A bibliography is included. See also Clark (G0086), Guffin (G0118) and Luffberry (G0160).

G0156   Leach, William Herman. Handbook of Church Management. Englewood Cliffs, N.J.: Prentice-Hall, 1958.

This substantial handbook of 504 pages covers all aspects of church management, from physical location and construction to administration and worship, in twenty-seven detailed chapters. Basic concepts of management are presented clearly and unpretentiously, and various alternatives are offered for dealing with specific situations. A detailed table of contents and an index are provided. Leach presents a wealth of practical information in considerable detail, as well as covering such tangential topics as pastoral ethics. See also Linger (G0159) and White (G0243).

G0157   Liebard, Odile M., comp. Clergy and Laity. Official Catholic Teachings, vol. 5. Wilmington, N.C.: Consortium Books, 1978.

Containing more than 200 documents from papal, conciliar and other Roman Catholic sources, Liebard provides a useful collection for students of clerical attitudes and laicization in the Roman Catholic Church. The texts are numbered in sections, and a subject index is included.

G0158   Lierde, Petrus Canisius van. The Holy See at Work: How the Catholic Church I s Governed. Trans. by James Tucek. New York: Hawthorn Books, 1962.

This volume examines basic principles relevant to the government of the Roman Catholic Church before discussing the central government as it exists: the Pope, the cardinals, the Roman curia, the permanent commissions, and international Catholic organizations. Notes, a bibliography (pp. 221-222), a glossary, and an index are included. See also Scharp (G0211).

G0159   Linger, O. Afton. Church Management Guidelines. Hendersonville, N.C.: Fruitland Baptist Bible Institute, 1972.

See also Anderson and Jones (G0061) and Gray (G0117).

G0160   Luffberry, Henry Benner. Manual for Vestrymen. Philadelphia, Pa.: Muhlenberg Press, 1960.

Written in a popular, anecdotal manner for the Protestant layman involved in parochial government, this work covers the obvious areas briefly but clearly: stewardship, evangelism, education, worship, parliamentary procedure. This is not a manual but an introduction; it should be used in conjunction with more substantial works. See also Bowen (G0070), Clark (G0086), Harper (G0121) and Lawrence (G0155).

G0161   Lutheran Church - Missouri Synod. Guidelines for the Constitution and Bylaws of a Lutheran Church, Revised as of December 15, 1963. St. Louis, Mo.: Concordia Publishing House, 1964.

See also Harkins (G0120).

G0162   [no entry]

G0163   McCoy, Lee H. Understanding Baptist Polity. Nashville, Tenn.: Convention Press, 1964.

See also Dana (G0092), Graves (G0114), McNutt (G0168) and Maring and Hudson (G0169).

G0164   McDonough, Reginald M. Working with Volunteer Leaders in the Church. Nashville, Tenn.: Broadman Press, 1976.

See also DeBoer (G0094), Kilinski and Wofford (G0152) and Merkens (G0173).

G0165   McGrath, John Joseph. Catholic Institutions in the United States: Canonical and Civil Law Status. Washington, D.C.: Catholic University of America Press, 1968.

This handbook for administrators of Catholic hospitals, schools and similar institutions explains the civil and canon laws applicable to them and provides a bibliography of practical works for further reference.

G0166   McInnis, Raymond G., and Scott, James William. Social Science Research Handbook. The Barnes and Noble Outline Series, C05140. New York: Barnes and Noble, 1975.

This substantial bibliography of 1500 reference works is arranged in two sections: the first defines the various social science disciplines and discusses relevant reference sources by type and materials on specialized subdivisions; the second uses a similar arrangement in discussing geographical regions. A bibliographical section provides full information for all titles dealt with in the first two parts.   This is a sound starting point for students new to the field. See also Bunker (G0076) and Mullins (G0179).

G0167   McMichael, Betty. The Library and Resource Center in Christian Education. Chicago, Ill.: Moody Press, 1977.

Intended primarily for pastors and Christian education workers, as well as for church librarians, this volume provides detailed guidance on starting a church library, choosing library staff, selecting books and audio-visual material, determining library policies, preparing books and nonbook materials for library use, promoting the library, financing, housing and equipping the library as a resource center. Appendixes include a sample questionnaire from a library survey conducted as part of research for the volume; a directory of suppliers; a classification system for church libraries; and subject headings for church libraries. A bibliography (pp. 247-251) and an index are provided. See also Broadman Press (G0073) and Corrigan (G0089).

G0168   McNutt, William Roy. Polity and Practice in Baptist Churches. Rev. ed. Chicago, Ill.: Judson Press, 1959.

See also Dana (G0092), Graves (G0114), McCoy (G0163) and Maring and Hudson (G0169).

G0169   Maring, Norman Hill, and Hudson, Winthrop Still. A Baptist Manual of Polity and Practice. Valley Forge, Pa.: Judson Press, 1963.

Also available as A Short Baptist Manual of Polity and Practice (Valley Forge, Pa.: Judson Press, 1965), this 237 page manual provides descriptive information as well as stimulating basic questions about issues such as Baptist church membership. See also Dana (G0092), Graves (G0114), Hiscox (G0127, G0128), McCoy (G0163), McNutt (G0168) and Pendleton (G0191).

G0170   Martin, David. Catholic Library Practice. 2 vols. Miscellaneous Publications, no. 1. Portland, Oreg.: University of Portland Press, 1947-1952.

This excellent work consists of a series of essays by various authorities on Catholic bibliography, library education, publishing, role of the library and similar topics.   This is the most detailed and wide ranging work of its kind, which retains particular value (despite its age) for the treatment of bibliography in volume 1 and reference tools in volume 2. For narrower treatment of church library matters see Schneider (G0213) and Trezza (G0231).

G0171   Mathis, Marcian Joseph, and Meyer, Nicholas W. The Pastoral Companion: A Handbook of Canon Law. 12th ed. Chicago, Ill.: Franciscan Herald Press, 1961.

See also Abbo (G0057), Bouscaren (G0069), Rocca (G0204) and Woywood (G0246).

G0172   Merkens, Guido A. Organized for Action: How to Build a Successful Parish and Its Program. St. Louis, Mo.: Concordia Publishing House, 1959.

This manual "for pastor and people" sets out the theological and scriptural basis for sound practice, then provides practical advice on matters such as congregational organization, stewardship, the Sunday school, records, and keeping the membership informed. It contains neither bibliography nor index. See also the following entry (G0173), Rusbuldt (G0205) and Schaller (G0208).

G0173   Merkens, Guido A. Organized for Action: Training Lay Leadership; Supplement. St. Louis, Mo.: Concordia Publishing House, 1961.

This work supplements Merkens' previous publication (G0172). See also Kilinski and Wofford (G0152) and McDonough (G0164).

G0174   Methodist Publishing House. Your Church Library: A Manual of Instruction. Nashville, Tenn.: Methodist Publishing House, 1960.

This manual provides practical guidance on how to establish a church library (location, equipment, finance, staffing, book selection and ordering, etc.), organization of the book collection, collection of nonbook materials, and how to make the church library service effective. Appendixes suggest a classification system, a subject heading index and how to use catalog cards. There is no index, but the table of contents is sufficiently detailed to allow easy access. See also Althoff (G0059) and Foote (G0103).

G0175   Miller, Delbert Charles. Handbook of Research Design and Social Measurement. 3rd ed. New York: David McKay, 1977.

This standard handbook is geared primarily to the needs of advanced students and other researchers requiring detailed information on research grant proposals, social science data libraries and research centers, guides to statistical analysis, sociometric scales and indexes, research funding and budgeting. A personal name index concludes the work, which has value for those conducting social science research in religion. See also Mullins (G0179) for information on writing and publishing in this field.

G0176   The Minister's Manual. San Francisco, Calif.: Harper and Row, 1926- ; annual.

Originally known as Doran's Ministers Manual, this handbook provides study, teaching and preaching suggestions for clergy, teachers and other church leaders. Sections include sermon outlines, prayers and services for special occasions, resources for evangelism and missions. It is widely used among free churches. See also Goulooze (G0113).

G0177   Moore, Evelyn Gerth. An Introduction to English Canon Law. Oxford: Clarendon Press, 1967.

Although dated in view of the canons revised in 1969 (G0083), Moore is an excellent introduction which treats the subject thoroughly and concisely. It deals in turn with each major area of canon law, explaining the meaning and intention of the relevant canons in clear and nontechnical language. Tables of statutes, measures and cases are provided, and there is a basic index for reference purposes.

G0178   Moyer, Elgin Sylvester. The Pastor and His Library. Chicago, Ill.: Moody Press, 1953.

A much expanded version of the same author's Building a Minister's

Library, this book focuses primarily on the personal library but covers much material of use in larger collections as well. Moyer treats classification, cataloging, files, indexes, book selection and repair with clarity and simplicity. It is however, dated and would benefit from revision. Emphasis is on the Dewey classification in condensed form. See also Kersten (G0150).

G0179   Mullins, Carolyn J. A Guide to Writing and Publishing in the Social and Behavioral Sciences. New York: John Wiley and Sons, 1977.

Intended primarily for students and professional researchers, this useful practical guide contains sections on outlines, first drafts, revisions, submitting scholarly articles for publication, preparing book manuscripts and information on contracts. There is a bibliography and an index. See also Bunker (G0076), Miller (G0175) and Noland (G0184).

G0180   National Conference of Catholic Charities. Committee on Personnel Practices and Salary Scales. Guidelines to Personnel Practices and Salary Scales. Washington, D.C.: National Conference of Catholic Charities, 1966.

This is a useful administrative guide and bibliography to this specific area.

G0181   Naylor, Robert E. The Baptist Deacon. Nashville, Tenn.: Broadman Press, 1955.

See also Foshee (G0106).

G0182   Newhall, Jannette E. A Theological Library Manual. London: Theological Education Fund, 1970.

This handbook of 162 pages was written particularly for theological librarians, seminary administrators and staff in seminaries in developing countries. It is designed to assist in the firm establishment and good organization of seminary libraries. A guide to use of the manual indicates which sections are most likely to be relevant to particular groups of users. The fifteen chapters each cover an aspect such as cataloging, administration, handling periodicals, and the library building. Three appendixes include a glossary and bibliographies (pp. 151-156). An index is provided.

G0183   Newton, LaVose. Church Library Handbook. Rev. ed. Portland, Oreg.: Multinomah Press, 1972.

This brief work contains a manual covering aspects such as beginning a church library, preparing books for circulation, library aims and policies, and library publicity. Sections on book suggestions, a classification system, library supplies, accession sheets and a financial record follow the manual. See also Beck (G0065) and Scheer (G0212).

G0184   Noland, Robert L. Research and Report Writing in the Behavioral Sciences: Psychiatry, Psychology, Sociology, Educational Psychology, Cultural Anthropology, Managerial Psychology. Springfield, Ill.: C.C. Thomas, 1970.

This undergraduate guide to library research and report writing is succinct, brief (98pp.) and to the point. It offers concrete suggestions and examples for students writing papers and reports in the behavioral sciences for the first time. It includes a list of representative references on scientific methods and research design (pp. 66-82). See also Mullins (G0179).

G0185   Nygaard, Norman Eugene. A Practical Church Administration Handbook. Grand Rapids, Mich.: Baker Book House, 1962.

This handbook deals with such aspects of church administration as integrating new members, an effective worship service, pulpit attire, publicizing the church, etc. It offers much practical advice for those involved in various parts of the church's program. It is brief, and there is no index. See also Adams (G0058) and Ditzen (G0097).

G0186   Oates, Wayne Edward. The Christian Pastor. Rev. and enlarged ed. Philadelphia, Pa.: Westminster Press, 1964.

This volume contains useful material on the work of the pastor, the life of the church, and the ministerial profession. It includes reviews of recent research and a helpful bibliography. The appendixes contain a list of criteria and a scale for evaluating the effectiveness of pastoral care and suggestions on keeping records of pastoral work. The distinctive work of the pastor in pastoral counseling is emphasized. See also Caemmerer (G0077) and Hovey (G0135).

G0187   Otto, Gert, ed. Praktisch-Theologisches Handbuch. Hamburg: Furche Verlag, 1970.

Focusing on social and psychological issues in particular, this handbook covers a broad range of topics from worship and funerals to grief and use of the mass media. While some attention is devoted to formal and theological issues within topics, most emphasis is given to contextual, practical aspects. This 532 page compendium is a reasonably compact, if sometimes uneven, guide to many perennial issues and topics in practical theology. See also Haendler (G0119).

G0188   Owensby, Idus V. Church Custodians Manual. Nashville, Tenn.: Convention Press, [1974].

See also Center for Parish Development (G0082).

G0189   Page, Harry Robert. Church Budget Development. Church Business Management Series. Englewood Cliffs, N.J.: Prentice-Hall, 1964.

See also Harrison (G0123) and Knudsen (G0153).

G0190   Parrott, Leslie. Building Today's Church: How Pastors and Laymen Work Together. Grand Rapids, Mich.: Baker Book House, 1973.

This work, by a pastor of the Nazarene Church, is concerned with the professional skills and abilities of the local minister to run an effective church program. Aspects such as educational programs, dealing with committees, counseling and ushering are covered. Although written from a particular denominational background, the book contains much generally useful, practical information. See also Schaller (G0209).

G0191   Pendleton, James Madison. Baptist Church Manual. [Rev. ed.] Nashville, Tenn.: Broadman Press, [1966].

This 182 page handbook was originally published in 1912 as Church Manual Designed for the Use of Baptist Churches. See also Graves (G0114) and Maring and Hudson (G0169).

G0192   Pendleton, Othniel Alsop. Fund Raising: A Guide for Non-Profit Organizations. Englewood Cliffs, N.J.: Prentice-Hall, 1981.

In 207 pages this guide examines operating procedure under sixteen headings, providing practical advice for those involved in fund raising. Churches are included among the institutions which can usefully employ the techniques discussed. A bibliography is included (pp. 195-203). For church fund raising see Harrison (G0123).

G0193   Pendorf, James G., and Lundquist, Helmer C. Church Organization: A Manual for Effective Local Church Administration. Wilton, Conn.: Morehouse-Barlow, 1977.

See also Rusbuldt (G0205) and Schaller (G0208).

G0194   Perry, Lloyd Merle, and Lias, Edward John. A Manual of Pastoral Problems and Procedures. Grand Rapids, Mich.: Baker Book House, 1962. Reprint. Grand Rapids, Mich.: Baker Book House, 1964.

This comprehensive handbook contains detailed and practical information on the full range of pastoral work, including the pastor as leader of worship, as Christian educator, as church administrator, etc. Presentation is concise, and a general bibliography of pastoral theology is provided. See also Caemmerer (G0077) and Hovey (G0135).

G0195   Peterson, Robert E. Handling the Church's Money: A Handbook for Church Treasurers, Financial Secretaries, Stewardship Leaders. St. Louis, Mo.: Bethany Press, 1965.

See also Davis (G0093), Gibbs (G0111) and Thompson (G0229).

G0196   Pitra, Jean Baptiste, ed. Iuris Ecclesiastici Graecorum Historia et Monumenta Iussu Pii IX Pont. Max. 2 vols. Rome: Typis Collegii Urbani, 1864-1868.

Pitra contains the texts and commentaries on Greek canon law. Texts are provided in Greek and Latin, and the historical/explanatory commentaries include bibliographies. Both canons and subjects are indexed in Volume 2. See also Roussos (G0050).

G0197   Powell, Robert Richard. Managing Church Business through Group Procedures. Church Business Management Series. Englewood Cliffs, N.J.: Prentice-Hall, 1964.

Intended for those responsible for effective management of church business affairs, this work treats group dynamics and church business management side by side. Ten chapters cover aspects such as group goals, participation, and problem-solving, leadership and membership, and analyzing and evaluating a group. A bibliography (pp. 164-166) and an index are provided. See also Deegan (G0095).

G0198   Presbyterian Church in the U.S. General Assembly. The Book of

Church Order of the Presbyterian Church in the United States. Rev. ed. Richmond, Va.: Board of Christian Education for the General Assembly of the Presbyterian Church in the United States, 1963.

See also Blake and Shaw (G0066), Garrison (G0109) and the following entry (G0199).

G0199 Presbyterian Church in the U.S.A. The Constitution of the Presbyterian Church in the United States of America, Being Its Standards Subordinate to the Word of God; viz., the Confession of Faith, the Larger and Shorter Catechisms, the Form of Government, the Book of Discipline, and the Directory for Worship of God, As Ratified and Adopted by the Synod of New York and Philadelphia in the Year of Our Lord 1788 and As Amended, Together with the General Rules for Judicatories. [Rev. ed.] Philadelphia, Pa.: Board of Christian Education of the Presbyterian Church in the U.S.A. for the Office of the General Assembly, 1956.

See also Blake and Shaw (G0066), Garrison (G0109) and the previous entry (G0198).

G0200 Rahner, Karl. Theology of Pastoral Action. Trans. by W.J. O'Hara and adapted by Daniel Morrissey. Studies in Pastoral Theology, vol. 1. New York: Herder and Herder, 1968.

This translation of Grundlegung der Pastoraltheologie als Praktische Theologie considers the basis for pastoral action as well as practical problems regarding pastoral questions. It is a useful contribution, combining the theological approach with practical insights. See also Hiltner (G0126), Segler (G0214) and Vinet (G0235).

G0201 Reorganized Church of Jesus Christ of Latter-Day Saints. Pastor's Handbook. Independence, Mo.: Herald Publishing House, 1971.

See also the following entry (G0202).

G0202 Reorganized Church of Jesus Christ of Latter-Day Saints. The Priesthood Manual. Prepared by Alfred H. Yale. Rev. ed. Independence, Mo.: Herald Press, 1972.

See also the preceding entry (G0201).

G0203 Robinson, Godfrey Clive, and Winward, Stephen F. Church Workers Handbook. Valley Forge, Pa.: Judson Press, 1973.

This work was originally published in 1957 as The King's Business. See also McDonough (G0164).

G0204 Rocca, Fernando della. Manual of Canon Law. Trans. by Anselm Thatcher. Milwaukee, Wisc.: Bruce Publishing Company, 1959.

This 624 page manual includes a history of the sources of canon law plus a numerically arranged explanation of each law in the code. An index is included. See also Abbo (G0057), Bouscaren (G0069), Mathis and Meyer (G0171) and Woywood (G0246).

G0205 Rusbuldt, Richard E.; Gladden, Richard K.; and Green, Norman M., Jr.

Local Church Planning Manual. Contains all needed instructions and worksheets. Valley Forge, Pa.: Judson Press, 1977.

Containing practical, basic and easily adapted ideas, this manual provides comprehensive instructions for every phase of church planning. It is particularly useful in new parishes or for review in existing situations. See also Pendorf (G0193) and Schaller (G0208).

G0206   Sartori, Cosmas. Enchiridion Canonicum seu Sanctae Sedis Responsiones. 11th ed. Bibliotheca Pontificii Athenaei Antonianum, 2. Rome: Pontificium Athenaeum Antonianum, 1963.

This compendium of Vatican decisions concerning canon law from 1917 to 1963 is arranged by canon number, which makes consultation much faster than with the Canon Law Digest (G0078). For those less familiar with the canons a subject index is provided. See also Rocca (G0204).

G0207   Schaller, Lyle E. The Decision Makers: How to Improve the Quality of Decision-Making in the Churches. Nashville, Tenn.: Abingdon Press, 1974.

Designed for both religious organizations and voluntary associations, this study deals with ways to improve decision-making. Specific suggestions are offered in the areas of budgeting, evaluation and accountability. This is a useful work for clergy, church administrators and students.

G0208   Schaller, Lyle E. Parish Planning. Nashville, Tenn.: Abingdon Press, 1971.

This manual deals clearly and concisely with ways to accomplish various tasks in the parish, including evangelism, finance and administration. It offers practical suggestions, particularly on the process of implementing programs, for local congregations. This is a useful work for clergy and laymen. See also Pendorf (G0193) and Rusbuldt (G0205).

G0209   Schaller, Lyle E. The Pastor and the People: Building a New Partnership for Effective Ministry. Nashville, Tenn.: Abingdon Press, 1973.

This work is intended for congregations seeking a new pastor, for pastors moving to a new parish, for local church leaders and others concerned with relations between pastor and congregation. It includes discussion of such aspects as pastoral priorities, financial matters, choosing a new pastor or choosing a new parish. It is written in a straightforward, popular style. See also Parrott (G0190).

G0210   Schaller, Lyle E., and Tidwell, Charles A. Creative Church Administration. Nashville, Tenn.: Abingdon Press, 1975.

This is a useful work for clergy and laymen, with many practical suggestions regarding parish life and management, and emphasis on creativity in the organizational structure of the church. Aspects such as planning models, membership recruitment, financing, lay leadership, and motivation are treated. See also Adams (G0058) and Hoh (G0130).

G0211   Scharp, Heinrich. How the Catholic Church is Governed. [Trans. by Annelise Derrick]. New York: Herder and Herder, [1960].

See also Lierde (G0158).

G0212   Scheer, Gladys E. The Church Library: Tips and Tools. St. Louis, Mo.:
Bethany Press, 1973.

Intended primarily as a guide to church librarians on the processes of
starting and developing a church library, as well as promoting its use,
this work covers physical aspects, selection and preparation of books,
circulation, library promotion, nonbook materials, etc. Appendixes list
relevant sources, library supply and equipment companies, and denominational services to libraries. A bibliography is provided; there is no index,
but the detailed table of contents facilitates access to the work. See
also Newton (G0183) and Smith (G0217).

G0213   Schneider, Vincent P., ed. The Parish and Catholic Lending Library
Manual. 2nd ed. Haverford, Pa.: Catholic Library Association, 1965.

First published in 1959 as Parish Library Manual, this useful guide of
ten chapters on organizing and maintaining a parish library covers book
selection, classification, subject headings, cataloging and publicity. As in
the original edition, there are helpful appendixes; an adequate index
is provided. For a newer guide in the same vein see Corrigan (G0089);
see also Trezza (G0231).

G0214   Segler, Franklin M. A Theology of Church and Ministry. Nashville,
Tenn.: Broadman Press, 1960.

This study sets out to interpret the church's ideal ministry and to relate
this to its functional ministry; to interpret the office of pastor; to aid
the pastor in self-understanding and in interpersonal relations; and to
provide a bibliography on the church and its ministry. Four parts examine
the church and its ministry; leadership in ministry; person and ministry;
and ministry in function. The bibliography (pp. 238-248) and an index
conclude the volume. See also Hiltner (G0126), Rahner (G0209) and Vinet
(G0235).

G0215   Short, Roy Hunter. Evangelism through the Local Church. New York:
Abingdon Press, 1956.

For a global perspective see Vaughan (G0232).

G0216   Smith,   Ruth S. Publicity for a Church Library. Washington, D.C.:
Church Library Council, 1962.

This brief publication explains various aspects of publicity and promotion
relevant to the development and effective use of church libraries. Advertis-
ing requirements, sponsoring activities, coordinating with other programs,
patterns and purposes of publicity are among the aspects discussed. This
is a useful approach to the specific topic covered. See also Johnson (G0140).

G0217   Smith, Ruth S. Running a Library: Managing the Congregation's Library
with Care, Confidence and Common Sense. New York: Seabury Press, 1982.

This 120 page guide begins with a description of how to create a parish
library geared to the needs of a specific community. It then deals fairly
generally with ways to maintain and make popular the library, offering

useful ideas and procedures suitable for a wide range of situations. See also Newton (G0183) and Scheer (G0212).

G0218   Southern Baptist Convention. Brotherhood Commission. Church Program Guidebook. Nashville, Tenn.: Convention Press, 1964/1965- ; annual.

G0219   Southern Baptist Convention. Church Library Department. Church Library Classification and Cataloging Guide: Books, Filmstrips, Recordings, Slides; Technical Information to Help the Church Librarian Classify and Catalog Titles in These Four Categories. Nashville, Tenn.: Broadman Supplies, 1967.

See also Kersten (G0150).

G0220   Spaan, Howard B. Christian Reformed Church Government. Grand Rapids, Mich.: Kregel Publications, 1968.

G0221   Spencer, Harold, and Finch, Edwin. Constitutional Practice and Discipline of the Methodist Church. Prepared by order of the Methodist Conference. 5th ed. Prepared by Bernard Sheldon. London: Methodist Publishing House, 1969.

G0222   Stevenson, Fred Gray. Pocket Primer of Parliamentary Procedure. 4th ed. Boston, Mass.: Houghton Mifflin Company, 1952.

This well outlined and clearly arranged guide supplies simple and concise answers to problems confronting those responsible for the conduct of meetings. See also Kerfoot (G0148).

G0223   Stickler, Alfonso Maria. Historia Iuris Canonici Latini Institutiones Academicae. Vol. 1- . Turin: Libreria Pontif. Athenaei Salesiani, 1950- .

The initial volume in this incomplete series treats the history of canon law compilations, including descriptions of contents and role in later developments. See also Canon Law Digest (G0078).

G0224   Stiles, Joseph. Acquiring and Developing Church Real Estate. Church Business Management Series. Englewood Cliffs, N.J.: Prentice-Hall, 1965.

See also Graves (G0115).

G0225   [no entry]

G0226   Straughan, Alice. How to Organize Your Church Library. Revell's Better Church Series.   Westwood, N.J.: Fleming H. Revell Company, 1962.

Straughan is essentially a guide to staffing and book processing, providing clear and simple guidelines for these important areas of library work. Because it does not cover cataloging or classification, this work must be used in conjunction with more comprehensive treatments of parish libraries, especially Schneider (G0213) and Towns and Barber (G0230).

G0227   Strommen, Merton P., ed. Research on Religious Development: A Comprehensive Handbook. A project of the Religious Education Association. New York: Hawthorn Books, 1971.

This volume summarizes what is known from research about religious development in the Judeo-Christian tradition. Comprehensive reviews, prepared by specialists, are presented in six main sections: religion and research; personal and religious factors in religious development; religion, personality and psychological health; dimensions of religious development; religious development by age grouping; and research in religious education. Catholic, Protestant and Jewish scholars contributed to the project. An index is provided. This work provides a useful compendium for those reviewing social scientific research in religion, and the extensive bibliographies, some carefully annotated, provided by each contributor add to its value as a source.

G0228   Suelflow, August R. Religious Archives: An Introduction. Chicago, Ill.: Society of American Archivists, 1980.

This 55 page manual is intended to provide helpful, practical suggestions for those who work with religious records of all kinds. The topics covered include the history and nature of religious archives, defining the scope of a collection, basic requirements, acquisition policies, processing procedures, reference services, photoduplication and microfilming. An appendix provides examples of forms used in Suelflow's own collection (Concordia Historical Institute of St. Louis, Mo.), and there is a helpful bibliography. This is a concise and valuable survey of the nature of religious archives and of their value to various fields of research.

G0229   Thompson, Thomas K. Handbook of Stewardship Procedures. Library of Christian Stewardship, LCS-1. Englewood Cliffs, N.J.: Prentice-Hall, 1964.

This handbook is intended for pastors and leaders of the congregation, and provides a kind of checklist by which a stewardship program may be judged. It includes references to other sources (books, films, etc.). The introductory chapter examines a biblical theology of stewardship; subsequent chapters deal with topics such as program budget building, capital funds for the congregation and Christian stewardship education. An annotated bibliography is provided (pp. 59-72), and appendixes include capital funds services and sermon themes. See also Davis (G0093), Gibbs (G0111) and Peterson (G0195).

G0230   Towns, Elmer L., and Barber, Cyril J. Successful Church Libraries. Grand Rapids, Mich.: Baker Book House, 1971.

This excellent text deals with cataloging, classification and book processing in general, and is useful for developing new libraries or strengthening existing ones. It fails to touch on staffing or publicity so should be used in conjunction with Johnson (G0140) or Straughan (G0226).

G0231   Trezza, Alphonse F., ed. Parish Library Manual. Villanova, Pa.: Catholic Library Association, 1959.

Similar to Buder (G0075) in audience and content, this basic manual of thirteen chapters covers all aspects of parish library organization and management for the beginner. Appendixes include main Dewey numbers, subject headings, a list of books and periodicals and other useful items. A basic index is provided. For Roman Catholics and others this is one of the more useful basic guides. See also Schneider (G0213).

G0232   Vaughan, Benjamin Noel Young. Structures for Renewal: A Search for the Renewal of the Church's Mission to the World. London: A.R. Mowbray and Company, 1967.

Concerned with overcoming divisions which hinder the renewal of the church for its service and mission to men, this work includes discussion of the work of clergy and laity, of the meaning of fellowship, liturgy and service. The style has been criticized as rather heavy.

G0233   Vermeersch, Arthur, and Creusen, Joseph. Epitome Iuris Canonici cum Commentariis ab Scholas et ad Usum Privatum. Vol. 1- . Rome: H. Dessain, 1962- ?

This revision of the three volume edition of 1940 is a useful updating of a classic manual. Text, commentary and bibliography are provided for each section of the code. There are also numerous bibliographical footnotes. Indexes of canons are included in each volume. See also Hove (G0134) and Wernz (G0240).

G0234   Veuillot, Pierre, ed. The Catholic Priesthood According to the Teaching of the Church: Papal Documents from Pius X to Pius XII. 2 vols. in 1. Dublin: Gill, 1957; Westminster, Md.: Newman Press, 1958.

This work contains a collection of reprints of papal documents dealing with the priesthood from Pius X to Pius XII. A brief introduction accompanies each document. Arrangement is by chronological order, with indexes for scripture, canon law and subjects.

G0235   Vinet, Alexandre Rodolphe. Théologie Pastorale, [ou] Théorie du Ministère Evangélique. 3e éd., rev. Paris: Fischbacher, 1889.

See also Hiltner (G0126), Rahner (G0200) and Segler (G0214).

G0236   Wages, Orland. A Handbook for Church Librarians. [Commerce, Tex.: n.p., 1961].

See also Beck (G0065) and White (G0241).

G0237   Walker, Arthur Lee. Church Accounting Methods. Church Business Management Series. Englewood Cliffs, N.J.: Prentice-Hall, 1964.

This handbook is addressed to those who make and maintain financial records for churches and related organizations. It is arranged so that those who have had little or no formal training in church accounting may become reasonably proficient by studying the text and illustrations. Much of the material is applicable to smaller as well as larger churches and to all denominations, although examples are drawn from the Methodist Church. This is a very practical work, clearly presented and usefully illustrated, with a glossary, bibliography, appendixes including study and teaching suggestions, and an index. See also Holck (G0131) and Walz (G0238).

G0238   Walz, Edgar. Church Business Methods: A Handbook for Pastors and Leaders of the Congregation. St. Louis, Mo.: Concordia Publishing House, 1970.

This handbook was written to help clergymen see the importance of church business methods as a part of their ministry and to help laymen see the special stewardship nature of church business. The twelve chapters discuss aspects of church organization from filing to budget control, building maintenance and public relations aspects of church business. The presentation is clear and straightforward, with helpful diagrams supplementing the text. There is no index, but each chapter deals with a clearly defined topic. See also Holck (G0131) and Walker (G0237).

G0239   Weld, Wayne, and McGavran, Donald Anderson. Principles of Church Growth. 2nd ed. South Pasadena, Calif.: William Carey Library, 1974.

This is a translation of Principios del Crecimiento de la Iglesia. See also Johnson (G0138) and Worrell (G0245).

G0240   Wernz, Franz Xaver. Ius Decretalium ad Usum Praelectionum in Scholis Textus Canonici sive Iuris Decretalium. 8 vols. Prati: Libraria Giachetti, 1908-1913.

Because it focuses on the pre-codification canons, this massive commentary is valuable as an historical guide to the various areas and subjects treated in canon law. Each volume is thoroughly indexed. See also Hove (G0134) and Vermeersch (G0233).

G0241   White, Joyce L., and Parr, Mary Y., eds. Church Library Guide: Proceedings from the Third Church Library Conference. Drexel Library School Series, no. 12. Philadelphia, Pa.: Drexel Press, 1965.

This 50 page guide comprises thirteen conference papers on topics such as church library organization and administration, book selection, audio-visual material, and cataloging and classification practice. A list of Protestant church-owned publishers and a bibliography of church library manuals are included. See also Althoff (G0059) and Beck (G0065).

G0242   White, Reginald E.O. A Guide to Pastoral Care: A Practical Primer of Pastoral Theology. London: Pickering and Inglis, 1976.

For a much more substantial work in German see Arnold and Rahner (G0062). For a survey of the history of pastoral theology in action see McNeill, John Thomas. A History of the Cure of Souls (New York: Harper and Brothers, [1951]; London: SCM Press, [1952, c. 1951]. Reprint. New York: Harper and Row, [1965]).

G0243   White, Robert N., ed. Managing Today's Church. Valley Forge, Pa.: Judson Press, [1981].

This 192 page guidebook provides useful material on aspects of organizational management relevant to the pastor and lay leader. Financial management, responsible use of human resources, making an administrative audit and time management are among the topics covered. A bibliography (pp. 183-185) and an index are included. See also Engstrom and Dayton (G0100).

G0244   Wiest, Elam G. How to Organize Your Church Staff. Westwood, N.J.: Fleming H. Revell Company, 1962.

See also Donaldson (G0099) and Judy (G0144).

G0245   Worrell, George E., ed. <u>Resources for Renewal.</u> Nashville, Tenn.: Broadman Press, 1976.

See also Judy (G0145) and Weld (G0239).

G0246   Woywood, Stanislaus. <u>A Practical Commentary on the Code of Canon Law.</u> Rev. by Callistus C. Smith. 2 vols. in 1. New York: J.F. Wagner, 1957.

This standard commentary on the Roman Catholic code of canon law is particularly useful for its emphasis on books 4 and 5, which are not so well covered in other English language commentaries. A bibliography and an index are provided. Despite its reliance on the older text, Woywood is a suitable reference volume. See also Abbo (G0057), Bouscaren (G0069), Mathis and Meyer (G0171) and Rocca (G0204).

G0247   Wright, Paul S. <u>The Duties of the Ruling Elder.</u> Philadelphia, Pa.: Westminster Press, 1957.

See also Beatty (G0064) and Jumper (G0146).

Liturgy and Worship

LITURGY AND WORSHIP: BIBLIOGRAPHIES

G0248   Adkins, Cecil, and Dickinson, Alis. International Index of Dissertations and Musicological Works in Progress. Philadelphia, Pa.: American Musicological Society and International Musicological Society, 1977.

Combining Doctoral Dissertations in Musicology and Musicological Works in Progress, this index of 4641 titles is arranged by period and then by topic within each period. Both American and foreign work is included, making Adkins an important reference work for postgraduate students and scholars.

G0249   Allen, Jelisaveta S., ed. Literature on Byzantine Art, 1892-1967. 2 vols. in 3. Dumbarton Oaks Bibliographies, Series 1. London: Mansell Publishing for Dumbarton Oaks Center for Byzantine Studies, 1973-1976.

Based on entries from the first sixty volumes of Byzantinische Zeitschrift, this collection is arranged under two main categories: location and art form. The first covers the Byzantine art of specific places, while the second treats individual art forms and historical periods. Entries are reproduced from Byzantinische Zeitschrift and include full bibliographical details, citations and critical annotations. However, not all relevant items are included in the second volume if they have appeared in the first, which can confuse the user. Each volume is well indexed by both subject and author. For students of iconography in particular this is a most valuable source of information. For an encyclopedia on Byzantine art see Wessel (G0466).

G0250   Anderson, Frank J., comp. and ed. Hymns and Hymnody. Wofford College Library. Special Collections Checklists, no. 1. Spartanburg, S.C.: Wofford Library Press, 1970.

See also Clark (G0274) and Voigt and Porter (G0372).

G0251   Architectural Periodicals Index. Vol. 1- . London: RIBA Publications for the British Architectural Library, 1972- ; quarterly with annual cumulations.

This successor to the RIBA Annual Review of Periodical Articles is arranged alphabetically by subject, with entries repeated under as many headings as necessary. A list of subject headings is provided in each issue together with a name index; the cumulations include a topographical index, but the names of buildings are not indexed. Each issue also provides a list of periodical titles and issues treated, which is a particularly valuable service. Many of the subjects covered are of specific interest to theological and liturgical studies, including cathedrals, chapels, churches and church halls, synagogues, Islamic architecture. Historical themes, current usage and the architectural arts are particularly well represented in this guide to approximately 300 journals from around the world. Each entry includes title, author, architect if relevant, illustration types, periodical title and essential bibliographical data. Coverage is reasonably current, helping to make this a valuable reference tool for those interested in the design, planning and history of religious buildings.

G0252   Archiv für Liturgiewissenschaft. Vol. 1- . Regensburg: Verlag Friedrich Pustet, 1950- ; annual.

This continuation of the Jahrbuch für Liturgiewissenschaft (vols. 1-15, 1921-1941) generally contains four sections: articles, miscellanea, literature bulletin, indexes. The literature bulletin is the largest and, from a reference viewpoint, most valuable part of each volume. This is arranged by subject, including liturgy in the Bible, monastic liturgy, pastoral liturgy, liturgy and architecture and similar topics. Each main subject is subdivided into specific fields. Although German Roman Catholic in orientation, this compilation includes materials on Protestantism, liturgical history and non-Christian liturgies. Well over 1000 items from some 200 journals are listed in each volume, making this the most thorough bibliography of serial literature in its field. Those with a knowledge of German and willing to accept the five to six year spread of articles in each compilation will find the Archiv an indispensible mine of information on all aspects of the liturgy. Each volume is indexed, and there is a cumulative index to volumes 1-19. See also Ephemerides Liturgicae (G0287), Jahrbuch für Liturgik und Hymnologie (G0306), Questions Liturgiques (G0343) and Rupke (G0357).

G0253   Art Index: An Author and Subject Index to Domestic and Foreign Art Periodicals and Museum Bulletins Covering Archaeology, Architecture, Art History, Arts and Crafts, City Planning, Fine Arts, Graphic Arts, Industrial Design, etc. Vol. 1- . New York: H.W. Wilson Company, 1929- ; quarterly with annual and biennial or triennial cumulations.

Focusing on North American and British output, this compilation indexes more than 140 fine arts journals and bulletins, providing about 60,000 author and subject entries annually. Entries are arranged according to broad headings and subdivisions, which makes use of the cumulations essential when tracing materials on a given topic. Ecclesiastical art is given some treatment, although this is not a significant aspect of Art Index. See also Art/Kunst (G0254).

G0254   Art/Kunst: International Bibliography of Art Books/Internationale Bibliographie des Kunstbuchs. Vol. 1- . Basel: W. Jaeggi, 1972- ; annual.

The only publication of its kind which brings together art material on an annual basis, Art/Kunst is a classified bibliography of titles published throughout the world. Each volume contains more than 1500 entries arranged in seven sections, and there is an author index. This is an important service for those who wish to be kept informed of current art publications. See also Artbibliographies (G0255) and RILA (G0349).

G0255   Artbibliographies: Current Titles. Vol. 1- . Santa Barbara, Calif.: ABC-Clio Press, 1972- ; bimonthly.

This guide reproduces the tables of contents from approximately seventy-five journals, museum publications, annual and irregular serials in each issue. The serials selected cover a broad range of art topics and are to be indexed in Artbibliographies Modern. As a current awareness tool, Current Titles is useful for researchers and scholars wishing to keep abreast of publications which may include articles on ecclesiastical art. See also Art/Kunst (G0254) and RILA (G0349).

G0256   Augsburg Publishing House. A Guide to Music for the Church Year. 4th ed. Minneapolis, Minn.: Augsburg Publishing House, 1975.

First published in 1962, this guide is designed to encourage preparation of a unified service. Anthems are suggested which contain texts based on or related to the Propers for the day, and the organ music is based on a tune for the appropriate Sunday. The listing is arranged chronologically beginning with the first Sunday of Advent. Information provided includes hymn title, composer, voice parts, grade, publisher and price for the choral works, with similar details for the organ music. A title page provides easy access. See also Royal School of Church Music (G0356).

G0257   Becker, Carl Ferdinand. Die Choralsammlungen der Verschiedenen Christlichen Kirchen. Leipzig: F. Fleischer, 1845. Reprint. Hildesheim: H.A. Gerstenberg, 1972.

See also Wackernagel (G0373).

G0258   Benton, Josiah Henry. The Book of Common Prayer and Books Connected with Its Origin and Growth; Catalogue of the Collection of Josiah Henry Benton. 2nd ed. Prepared by William Muss-Arnolt. Boston, Mass.: privately printed (D.B. Updike), 1914.

This collection covers prayer books of various Anglican churches, including those of England, Scotland, Ireland and the United States.

G0259 Bibliographie zur Symbolik, Ikonographie und Mythologie: Internationales Referateorgan. Vol. 1- . Baden-Baden: Verlag Valentin Koerner, 1968- ; annual.

Each volume, in addition to a substantial article on a single topic, includes a lengthy collection of reviews prepared by an international group of compilers. These short, factual reviews are arranged alphabetically by author but contain inadequate bibliographical information. The survey covers both books and articles, but there is no list of periodicals scanned. The annual subject index includes a number of useful headings for students of religious symbolism and related topics. This bibliography lists more than 600 items annually, many from three or four years earlier, and despite its many drawbacks must be regarded as a unique guide to a very specialized field. There is a cumulative index to the first ten volumes. See also Lurker (G0315).

G0260   Bibliotheca Catholica Neerlandica, Impressa 1500-1727. The Hague: Martinus Nijhoff, 1954.

This 669 page bibliography is a chronological listing of devotional literature published in Holland during the period indicated. More than 18,000 works are treated, but the bibliographical descriptions are not accompanied by abstracts. There is an index. See also Dols (G0282), Sáenz de Tejada (G0358) and Sinclair (G0362).

G0261   Blume, Clemens. Repertorium Repertorii: Kritischer Wegweiser durch U. Chevalier's Repertorium Hymnologicum. Alphabetisches Register Falscher, Mangelhafter oder Irreleitender Hymnanfänge und Nachweise mit Erörterung über Plan und Methode des Repertoriums. Leipzig: O.R. Reisland, 1901.

This is a supplement of additions and corrections to Chevalier (G0273).

G0262   Bohatta, Hanns. Bibliographie der Brevière, 1501-1850. 2. Aufl. Stuttgart: A. Hiersemann; Nieuwkoop: B. De Graaf, 1963.

First published in 1937, this bibliography contains 2891 numbered items with locations. The main sections are Breviarium Romanorum, Orden, Diozesen. A chronology, a list of sources quoted, and title and country (subdivided by town) indexes are included. This is a very full listing of breviaries and focuses on the period when work in this area was at its height of productivity.

G0263   Bohatta, Hanns. Bibliographie der Livres d'Heures (Horae B.M.V.) Officia, Hortuli Animae, Coronae B.M.V., Rosaria und Cursus B.M.V. des XV. und XVI. Jahrhunderts. 2. Aufl. Vienna: Gilhofer und Rauschburg, 1924.

This is a catalog of 1582 books of hours and 236 offices of the Blessed Virgin Mary. Focusing on the fifteenth and sixteenth centuries, it is of both historical and liturgical interest. Annotations are concise but full and provide valuable insights into a significant area in the history of worship.

G0264   Bohatta, Hanns. Liturgische Bibliographie des XV. Jahrhunderts mit Ausname der Missale und Livres d'Heures. Vienna: Gilhofer und Rauschburg, 1911. Reprint. Hildesheim: Georg Olms, 1961.

This provides a useful supplement to Bohatta's other bibliographies (G0262, G0263) and to Weale (G0375). See also Hoskins (G0300) and Lacombe (G0309).

G0265   Brambach, Wilhelm. Gregorianisch: Bibliographische Lösung der Streitfrage über den Ursprung des Gregorianischen Gesanges. Sammlung Bibliothekswissenschaftlicher Arbeiten, Heft 7. Leipzig: M. Spirgatis, 1895. Reprint. Weisbaden: O. Harrassowitz, 1969.

See also Bryden and Hughes (G0269).

G0266   Brambach, Wilhelm. Psalterium: Bibliographischer Versuch über die Liturgischen Bücher des Christlichen Abendlandes. Sammlung Bibliothekswissenschaftlicher Arbeiten, Heft 1. Berlin: A. Asher and Company, 1887. Reprint. Nedeln: Kraus; Weisbaden: O. Harrassowitz, 1969.

G0267   British Museum. Department of Printed Books. General Catalogue

of Printed Books. Liturgies. Photo-offset ed. London: Trustees of the British
Museum, 1962.

Reprinted from volumes 138 and 139 of the General Catalogue of Printed
Books, this detailed bibliography consists of three main parts, covering
Latin, Greek and other Eastern rites; Anglicanism, primarily the Church
of England; Lutheran, Calvinistic, Zwinglian and other Reformed bodies.
A very detailed index (from volume 139) adds significantly to the value
of this bibliography.

G0268   Brooke, William Thomas. Bibliotheca Hymnologica. London: Charles
Higham, 1890.

This extensive catalog is an important source of information on English
hymnals produced between 1750 and 1850 in particular. Full indexes
of dates, principal subjects, authors, composers and editors, places of
publication and/or use of the 2000 items are provided. For students of
English hymnody this bibliography is an important reference guide. See
also Perry (G0337).

G0269   Bryden, John Rennie, and Hughes, David G., comps. An Index of
Gregorian Chant. 2 vols. Cambridge, Mass.: Harvard University Press, 1969.

Volume 1 contains an alphabetical index, while volume 2 presents a thematic
index of Gregorian chant. The chants thus indexed are drawn from nineteen
generally available sources (including modern chant books and manuscript
facsimiles). The first volume lists textual incipits, and the second volume
uses a system of melodic equivalents for numerical incipits for items
listed in the first volume. This is a useful reference tool for specialist
collections of music and liturgy. See also Brambach (G0265).

G0270   Burnsworth, Charles C. Choral Music for Women's Voices: An Annotated Bibliography of Recommended Works. Metuchen, N.J.: Scarecrow Press, 1968.

This bibliography of approximately 350 works is arranged by composer
and indexed by title, number of parts, grade of difficulty and similar
approaches. This is an exceptionally well prepared compilation with the
requirements of performers clearly in mind. See also Locke (G0314).

G0271   Buszin, Walter, et al. A Bibliography of Music and the Church. Pre-
pared for the Commission on Music, Department of Worship and the Arts,
National Council of Churches of Christ in the United States of America.
New York: National Council of Churches of Christ, 1958.

See also J.W. Pepper (G0304).

G0272   Chamberlin, Mary W. Guide to Art Reference Books. Chicago, Ill.:
American Library Association, 1959.

This authoritative, although dated, bibliography contains 2565 numbered
items organized in nineteen chapters. These include types of publication
(bibliographies, dictionaries, indexes, etc.) and topics (architecture, painting, sculpture, etc.). Items are annotated and some evaluation is included.
Standard books and periodicals covered by indexing services are also
noted. The work is international in scope. Areas such as book arts, cal-
ligraphy, photography and the theatre are not covered. For a partial

continuation see Ehresmann (G0286).

G0273   Chevalier, Cyr Ulysse Joseph. Repertorium Hymnologicum: Catalogue des Chants, Hymnes, Proses, Séquences, Tropes en Usage dans l'Eglise Latine depuis les Origines jusqu'à Nos Jours. 6 vols. Subsidia Hagiographica, no. 4. Louvain: Imprimerie Lefever; Brussels: Société des Bollandistes, 1892-1921. Reprint. 6 vols. [Brussels: Société des Bollandistes?, 1959].

Originally published in parts as a separately paginated supplement to Analecta Bollandiana, 1889-1920, this is the standard bibliography of Latin rhymed texts for liturgical use. For each hymn it gives first line, saint or feast day to which it belongs and its place in the office, number of strophes, author's name, date of composition if known, and reference to manuscripts of printed sources where the hymn is to be found. The main sequence appears in the first two volumes, with supplementary listing in volumes 3 and 4. Corrigenda and addenda are found in volume 5, and the indexes appear in volume 6. The first four volumes were published in Louvain under various imprints, while the final two volumes were published in Brussels by the Bollandists. For a very helpful supplement see Blume (G0261).

G0274   Clark, Keith C. A Selective Bibliography for the Study of Hymns. Papers of the Hymn Society of America, no. 33. Springfield, Ohio: Hymn Society of America, 1980.

First published as A Short Bibliography for the Study of Hymns (Papers of the Hymn Society of America, no. 25. New York: Hymn Society of America, 1964), this revision includes both major older works plus recent publications. The six sections cover hymnology, individual biographies, psalmody, Afro-American religious music, carols and church music; there are further subdivisions as necessary. Within each subsection entries are arranged alphabetically by author (or biographee in the case of biography). For each entry full bibliographical details are provided, although some of the citations are inaccurate. Coverage is limited to English language items but includes translations from other languages. There is no index, which means that cross references should have been far more prolific. Otherwise Clark is a suitable 45 page compilation for those new to the study of hymnology. See also Anderson (G0250) and Voigt and Porter (G0372).

G0275   Cornish, Graham P., comp. Inter-Action between Modern Drama and the Church: A Selective Bibliography. Theological and Religious Bibliographies, vol. 3. Harrogate, North Yorkshire: G.P. Cornish, 1981.

Part of a series which continues the two volumes of Theological and Religious Index, this typescript production contains 162 entries for mainly English language periodical articles, books and dissertations issued since 1950 on the church and drama. Most of the publications have appeared in the last twenty years. Arrangement is alphabetical by author; full bibliographical citations are provided, but there are no abstracts.

G0276   Council for the Care of Churches. The Conservation of Churches and Their Treasures: A Bibliography. London: Council for the Care of Churches, 1970.

This brief bibliography of approximately 500 entries is arranged in twenty-seven sections, covering materials, internal fittings and equipment, sculpture, wall paintings and similar features. A few of the entries are annotated, but there is no index. The intention is to provide a practical guide to sources relevant to church maintenance.

G0277 Coussemaker, Charles Edmond Henri de, ed. Scriptorum de Musica Medii Aevi Novam Seriem a Gerbertina Alteram Collegit. 4 vols. Paris: Apud A. Durand, 1864-1876. Reprint. 4 vols. Milan: Bolletino Bibliografico Musicale, 1931.

This work is a continuation of Gerbert (G0295).

G0278 Daniel, Ralph T., and Le Huray, Peter, comps. The Sources of English Church Music, 1549-1660. Early English Church Music, Supplementary Vol. 1. London: Stainer and Bell for the British Academy, 1972.

Arranged in two parts, this guide treats musical incipits of anonymous compositions and anonymous compositions themselves with sources and editions. Both parts cover services as well as anthems. Part 1 includes a first line index of anthems and a key to sources; part 2 lists anthems and services alphabetically by composer with sources and editions provided. See also Wilkes (G0377) and Yeats-Edwards (G0378).

G0279 Davies, J.H. Musicalia: Sources of Information in Music. 2nd ed. The Commonwealth and International Library. Libraries and Technical Information Division. Oxford: Pergamon Press, 1969.

This 184 page bibliographical survey treats basic sources of information from a beginner's standpoint. It is suitable for those without any background in music or knowledge of the relevant reference tools. For a more detailed guide see Duckles (G0283).

G0280 Dearmer, Percy. A Subject Index of Hymns in "The English Hymnal" and "Songs of Praise". London: Oxford University Press, 1926.

See also Rogers (G0353).

G0281 Diehl, Katherine Smith. Hymns and Tunes: An Index. New York: Scarecrow Press, 1966.

This publication provides five basic indexes based on seventy-eight hymnals using first lines, authors, tune names, composers, melodies. The hymnals are mainly in English, representing British and North American institutions, and are listed. A useful introduction, cross references, historical information and comprehensive appendixes are included. A bibliography is provided, and hymns are located in the hymnals used. See also McDormand and Crossman (G0318).

G0282 Dols, Jean Michel Emile. Bibliographie der Moderne Devotie. 2 vols. Nijmegen: N.V. Centrale Drukkerij, 1936-1941.

This is a selected, unannotated bibliography of international devotional literature with material on the history of the literature and biographies of authors. Some periodical literature is included. See also Bibliotheca Catholica Neerlandica (G0260), Sáenz de Tejada (G0358) and Sinclair (G0362).

G0283   Duckles, Vincent Harris, comp. Music Reference and Research Materials: An Annotated Bibliography. 3rd ed. New York: Free Press; London: Collier-Macmillan, 1974.

First published in 1964 with a second edition in 1967, this bibliography contains more than 1900 entries which are briefly but clearly annotated. The eleven main sections include dictionaries and encyclopedias, histories, bibliographies, discographies, directories and similar resources. The tools listed are selected for their usefulness as reference materials, and the thorough coverage has made Duckles a standard reference guide. There are detailed indexes of authors and editors, subjects, titles. Reviewers are included with authors and editors. See Marco (G0319) for a guide to foreign rather than English language materials.

G0284   Edson, Jean Slater. Organ Preludes: An Index to Compositions on Hymn Tunes, Chorales, Plainsong Melodies, Gregorian Tunes and Carols. 2 vols. Metuchen, N.J.: Scarecrow Press, 1970.

These volumes and the Supplement (G0285) provide an excellent and thorough guide to organ preludes of a wide range of types suitable for sacred programs. Volume 1 contains the composer index, while volume 2 contains the tune name index; the latter includes the first few measures of the tune in musical notation. See also Nardone (G0329).

G0285   Edson, Jean Slater. Organ Preludes: An Index to Compositions on Hymn Tunes, Chorales, Plainsong Melodies, Gregorian Tunes and Carols. Supplement. Metuchen, N.J.: Scarecrow Press, 1974.

This volume corrects, supplements and updates the main work (G0284); particularly thorough is the coverage of French and Scandinavian organ compositions.

G0286   Ehresmann, Donald L. Fine Arts: A Bibliographic Guide to Basic Reference Works, Histories and Handbooks. Littleton, Colo.: Libraries Unlimited, 1975.

This work continues Chamberlin (G0272) to some extent, although the 1200 entries only cover painting and books on sculpture and architecture published after 1958. Part 1 covers reference works; part 2 histories and handbooks of world art history. The bibliography has been criticized for omissions, errors and poor indexes. However, the topical arrangement, good annotations and author/title and subject indexes make Ehresmann easy to use and suitable for basic information required by beginners. See also Muehsam (G0327).

G0287   Ephemerides Liturgicae. Vol. 1- . Rome: Edizioni Liturgiche, 1887- ; bimonthly.

This review journal includes a bibliography of liturgical studies which is particularly valuable for its coverage of works on the history of the liturgy. It also regularly treats modern works, focusing primarily on the Roman Catholic tradition. See also Rivista Liturgica (G0351).

G0288   Episcopal Church. Joint Commission on Church Music. Service Music and Anthems for the Nonprofessional Choir. New York: H.W. Gray Company, 1963.

See also Royal School of Church Music (G0356).

G0289 Espina, Noni. Repertoire for the Solo Voice: A Fully Annotated Guide to Works for the Solo Voice Published in Modern Editions and Covering Material from the 13th Century to the Present. 2 vols. Metuchen, N.J.: Scarecrow Press, 1977.

> The solos cited in this interesting compilation are based primarily on voice-piano editions available through 1975 and are arranged by nationality and form, including spirituals. Most sections are further divided by type of voice. There are indexes of sources and of composers. Espina is a helpful guide for those seeking new solo pieces, and there are a number of religious entries. See also the following entry (G0290) and Moore (G0326).

G0290 Espina, Noni. Vocal Solos for Protestant Services: A Descriptive Reference of Solo Music for the Church Year, Including a Bibliographical Supplement of Choral Works; Sacred Repertoire for Concert and Teaching. 2nd ed. New York: Vita d'Arte, 1974.

> This annotated listing of recommended solo music for Protestant churches provides basic information about each work, as a guide for musicians in search of materials to perform. Information includes title, publisher, compass or range of the song, type of voice, comments on difficulty of the accompaniment, and on basic essentials of the musical style, as well as suggested occasions on which a song may be performed. A short supplement of more frequently performed choral works is appended to the sacred solo list. See also the preceding entry (G0289) and Moore (G0326).

G0291 Fichier Bibliographique de Liturgie. Louvain: Abbaye du Mont-César, Institut Bibliographique de Liturgie, 1964- .

> This card index service provides coverage of journals, producing on average about 100 cards per week. Full bibliographical details are provided, as well as a descriptive note if the title is not indicative of contents. Author and subject classifications are indicated. One may subscribe to the index in various ways: for a particular subject, for past years, etc.

G0292 Follieri, Enrica. Initia Hymnorum Ecclesiae Graecae. 5 vols. in 6. Studi e Testi, 211-215 bis. Vatican City: Biblioteca Apostolica Vaticana, 1960-1966.

G0293 Ford, Wyn Kelson. Music in England before 1800: A Select Bibliography. Library Association Bibliographies, no. 7. London: Library Association, 1967.

> This 128 page bibliography is a detailed guide to English music, both secular and sacred, and provides especially good coverage of ecclesiastical aspects. See also Frere (G0294) and Hughes (G0301).

G0294 Frere, Walter Howard. Bibliotheca Musico-Liturgica: A Descriptive Handlist of the Musical and Latin-Liturgical Manuscripts of the Middle Ages Preserved in the Libraries of Great Britain and Ireland. 2 vols. London: Bernard Quaritch for the Plainsong and Mediaeval Music Society. Reprint. 2 vols. Hildesheim: Georg Olms, 1967.

G0295 Gerbert, Martin. Scriptores Ecclesiastici de Musica Sacra Potissimum.

Ex Variis Italiae, Galliae et Germaniae Codicibus Manuscriptis Collecti. 3 vols. n.p.: Typis San-Blasianis, 1784. Reprint. 3 vols. Milan: Bolletino Bibliografico Musicale, 1931.

See also Coussemaker (G0277) for a continuation.

G0296   Gombosi, Marilyn, comp. Catalog of the Johannes Herbst Collection. Chapel Hill, N.C.: University of North Carolina Press, 1970.

This work provides a thematic catalog of Moravian church music. See also Rau and David (G0344).

G0297   Harrah, Barbara K., and Harrah, David F. Funeral Service: A Bibliography of Literature on Its Past, Present and Future, the Various Means of Disposition and Memorialization. Metuchen, N.J.: Scarecrow Press, 1976.

This lengthy bibliography, with indexes, also contains appendixes on professional funeral organizations, memorial societies and trade journals.

G0298   Hartley, Kenneth R. Bibliography of Theses and Dissertations in Sacred Music. Detroit Studies in Music Bibliography, no. 9. Detroit, Mich.: Information Coordinators, 1966 [c. 1967].

Based on a thesis presented at New Orleans Baptist Theological Seminary, this bibliography contains 1525 numbered entries arranged alphabetically by university. Coverage is limited to research at American universities. There is an author index, an index of composers and a subject index.

G0299   Herrero, Salgado Felix. Aportación Bibliográfica a la Oratoria Sagrada Española. Anejos de Revista de Literatura, 30. Madrid: Consejo Superior de Investigaciones Científicas, [Instituto Miguel de Cervantes de Filología Hispánica, 1971].

G0300   Hoskins, Edgar. Horae Beatae Mariae Virginis; or, Sarum and York Primers, with Kindred Books and Primers of the Reformed Roman Usage together with an Introduction. London: Longmans, Green and Company, 1901.

This publication lists 297 liturgical books printed in England from 1778 to 1817 with descriptive annotations. A directory of printers and booksellers as well as indexes are provided. See also Bohatta (G0263, G0264) and Lacombe (G0309).

G0301   Hughes, Andrew. Medieval Music: The Sixth Liberal Art. Toronto Medieval Bibliographies, no. 4. Toronto: University of Toronto Press, 1974.

This bibliography lists 2003 books, articles and essays on all aspects of medieval music. It is intended for students without formal training in music and for others with a general interest in the subject. The arrangement of entries is topical and geographical, and brief annotations are included. There is a subject index and an index of authors and editors. For studies of medieval church music this is an important listing. See also Ford (G0293) and Frere (G0294).

G0302   International Catholic Association for Radio and Television. Catalogue du Disque de Musique Religieuse. Fribourg: International Catholic Association for Radio and Television, 1956.

See also Royal School of Church Music (G0355).

G0303   Irwin, John C. American Protestantism's Self-Understanding of Its Worship: A Selected Bibliography. Bibliographical Lecture Series, no. 4. Evanston, Ill.: Garrett Theological Seminary Library, 1969.

G0304   J.W. Pepper. Complete Pepper Guide to the Sacred Music of All Publishers. Philadelphia, Pa.: J.W. Pepper, n.d.

See also Buszin (G0271).

G0305   Jackson, Irene V., comp. Afro-American Religious Music: A Bibliography and a Catalogue of Gospel Music. Westport, Conn.: Greenwood Press, 1979.

This bibliography offers systematically organized materials as a basis for comprehensive study of Afro-American religious music. It covers music of established Black churches or denominations in the United States and the Caribbean, and Afro-Christian cults in the Caribbean and South America, as well as West African music. Thematic chapters cover such topics as religious folksongs (spirituals, blues, gospel, etc.), Black church/ Black religion (primarily on the United States) and Afro-Christian religion, music, culture, folklore and history in the Caribbean. Two indexes are provided. The bibliography is especially concerned with the impact of Christianity on traditional worship patterns.

G0306   Jahrbuch für Liturgik und Hymnologie. Vol. 1- . Kassel: Johannes Stauda Verlag for the International Fellowship for Research in Hymnology, 1955- ; annual.

Following a collection of articles in each annual issue, this yearbook lists scholarly, primarily German, books and articles on liturgy and hymnology, each subject being treated separately. Within each of the two subject areas entries are arranged by topic and chronology and subdivided by country. Coverage is up-to-date for most materials but does not extend to either the more esoteric or lesser known publications. The Jahrbuch is particularly useful for researchers with an interest in German writings related to these two fields, although some attention is given to works in other languages as well. See also Questions Liturgiques (G0343) and Rivista Liturgica (G0351). For the English language counterpart see Yearbook of Liturgical Studies (Vol. 1-6. Notre Dame, Ind.: Fides Publishing Association, 1960-1967).

G0307   Kapsner, Oliver Leonard. Benedictine Liturgical Books in American Benedictine Libraries: A Progress Checklist Prepared for the Library Science Section of the American Benedictine Academy. Latrobe, Pa.: St. Vincent College Library, 1960.

G0308   Krummel, Donald William, ed. Bibliographical Inventory of the Early Music in the Newberry Library, Chicago, Illinois. Boston, Mass.: G.K. Hall and Company, 1977.

This compilation reproduces catalog entries on music from the Newberry Library, which is noted for its collection of medieval, Renaissance and American musical material. Sections devoted to manuscripts, printed music and treatises are followed by eight geographical sections with chronologically arranged subdivisions. There is an index of composers, editors and musical subjects plus an index of printers, engravers, artists, copyists and publishers. For those interested in early church music Krummel is an important bibliographical guide. See also the New York Public Library catalogs (G0332-G0335).

G0309   Lacombe, Paul. Livres d'Heures Imprimés au XV et XVIe Siècle, Conservés dans les Bibliothèques Publiques de Paris. Paris: Imprimerie Nationale, 1907.

This publication lists 598 items, arranged by publisher, with complete transcriptions of title pages, descriptive notes and locations. An index is provided. See also Bohatta (G0263, G0264) and Hoskins (G0300).

G0310   Leaver, Robin A., comp. English Hymns and Hymn Books: Catalogue of an Exhibition Held at the Bodleian Library, Oxford. Oxford: Bodleian Library, 1981.

This descriptive exhibition catalog is a useful bibliographical tool which surveys the major sources of English hymnody to the year 1930. Although its use as a bibliography is hampered by arrangement according to the exhibition, this is a useful work for those interested in the history of hymnody in England. See also Leaver's Hymn Book Survey (G0311).

G0311   Leaver, Robin A. Hymn Book Survey, 1962-80. Grove Worship Series, no. 71. Bramcote, Nottinghamshire: Grove Books, 1980.

Limited to Trinitarian denominations in Britain which have revised or supplemented their hymnals since 1962, this 24 page listing begins with coverage of twelve standard hymn books. This is followed by a listing of five supplements which are to be used until the parent works are revised, then a list of fifteen additional supplements, and finally a guide to thirteen Roman Catholic collections. For each item Leaver provides full bibliographical details plus references to companion volumes and detailed critical annotations. This is an extremely useful guide for students of modern hymnology. See also Leaver's English Hymns and Hymn Books (G0310).

G0312   Leaver, Robin A. Hymns with the New Lectionary. Bramcote, Nottinghamshire: Grove Books, 1980.

In many ways a sequel to the same author's Thematic Guide to the Anglican Hymn Book (G0313), this compilation is intended as an accompaniment to the revised lectionary of the Church of England's Alternative Service Book. As such, it contains a list of suitable hymns drawn from twenty-five hymnals; these are geared to the new order of eucharistic readings and provide excellent guidance for planning services in the Anglican tradition.

G0313   Leaver, Robin A., ed. A Thematic Guide to the Anglican Hymn Book. London: Church Book Room Press, 1975.

This 65 page guide is arranged in two parts. The first is a topical index of hymns in numerical order. The second is a listing of lectionary themes for Series 3 with hymns appropriate for the Sundays of the church year. The latter part has been incorporated into the Alternative Service Book.

See also Leaver's Hymns with the New Lectionary (G0312).

G0314 Locke, Arthur Ware, and Fassett, Charles K. Selected List of Choruses for Women's Voices. 3rd ed. Northampton, Mass.: Smith College, 1964.

This work is broader in coverage but less detailed in analysis than Burnsworth (G0270).

G0315 Lurker, Manfred. Bibliographie zue Symbolkunde. Unter Mitarbeit von Ferdinand Hermann et al. Vol. 1- . Bibliotheca Bibliographica Aureliana, 12. Baden-Baden: Verlag Heitz, 1964- .

This extensive bibliography projected in three volumes consists of systematically arranged entries under a wide range of form and subject headings, including Christliche Liturgik, Bibelwissenschaft, etc. The third volume of this international compilation contains author and subject indexes. As a guide to publications on symbolism, and especially symbols relevant to the Christian tradition, Lurker is an indispensible compilation. See also Bibliographie zur Symbolik (G0259).

G0316 Lutheran Church in America. Indexes Based on the "Service Book and Hymnal". Philadelphia, Pa.: Lutheran Church in America, Board of Publication, 1968.

See also the following entry (G0317).

G0317 Lutheran Church in America. Commission on Worship. Index of Free Accompaniments for Hymn Tunes of the "Service Book and Hymnal". New York: Lutheran Church in America, 1965.

See also the preceding entry (G0316).

G0318 McDormand, Thomas Bruce, and Crossman, Frederic S. Judson Concordance to Hymns. Valley Forge, Pa.: Judson Press, 1965.

This valuable reference work indexes 2342 hymns from twenty-seven hymnals of major North American denominations. The user is referred from the keyword in any line to the line index and then to the first line of the hymn. It is useful for discovering the title of a hymn when only a phrase from one stanza is known. This work should be used in conjunction with Diehl (D0281) for identifying the hymnal that contains a particular hymn.

G0319 Marco, Guy A. Information on Music: A Handbook of Reference Sources in European Languages. With the assistance of Sharon Paugh Ferris. Vol. 1- . Littleton, Colo.: Libraries Unlimited, 1975- .

Projected in eight volumes, this annotated bibliography is intended to supplement and expand Duckles (G0283). The entries are chosen on the basis of their usefulness to students of music, and this makes Marco a particularly helpful guide for those without detailed knowledge of the field. The first volume covers basic and universal sources, while succeeding volumes treat the literature dealing with specific regions.

G0320 May, James D. Avant-Garde Choral Music: An Annotated Selected Bibliography. Metuchen, N.J.: Scarecrow Press, 1977.

This annotated bibliography of choral music available from American music publishers focuses entirely on innovative modern works. Each entry includes full publishing information, voice requirements, accompaniment and various supplementary requirements. There is an index. May is intended for use by choral directors of schools, colleges and churches, although in the last case it is not entirely satisfactory in its choice of material. See also the bibliographical supplement in Espina (G0290).

G0321 Mearns, James. Early Latin Hymnaries: An Index of Hymns and Hymnaries before 1100, with an Appendix from Later Sources. Cambridge: Cambridge University Press, 1913.

The texts referred to are those reprinted in Dreves and Blume (G0916) and other sources. Arrangement is alphabetical by first line, and subjects and authors are indicated.

G0322 Meggett, Joan M. Musical Periodical Literature: An Annotated Bibliography of Indexes and Bibliographies. Metuchen, N.J.: Scarecrow Press, 1978.

Intended primarily for college and university students unfamiliar with the scope of periodical literature available in music, this annotated list of periodical indexes and bibliographies covers both music itself and music related topics. There are indexes of authors, editors and compilers (one sequence), of subjects and of titles. This is a valuable guide to periodical reference indexes and should not be overlooked by students of sacred music. See also Music Index (G0328) and RISM (G0345).

G0323 Metcalf, Frank Johnson, comp. American Psalmody; or , Titles of Books Containing Tunes Printed in America from 1721 to 1820. New York: C.F. Heartman, 1917. Reprint. Da Capo Press Music Reprint Series. New York: Da Capo Press, 1968.

See also Warrington (G0374).

G0324 Methodist Church. Subject, Textual and Lineal Indexes to the Methodist Hymn Book. London: Methodist Conference Office [Epworth Press], 1934. Reprint. London: Methodist Publishing House, 1978.

Reprinted on various occasions, this set of indexes to the Methodist Hymn-Book of 1933 (G0961) is an indispensible guide for preachers, choir directors and others involved in planning worship within this tradition. One list arranges hymns under a very wide range of subject headings; another list treats biblical texts which are referred to or illustrated in specific hymns. Most of the work, however, consists of an index to every line in the hymns included in the Methodist Hymn-Book; and it is this section which gives the compilation its particular value, as very few guides aim to index hymns so thoroughly. Since Methodist hymnody draws on many traditions and is used in a wide range of other denominations, this is an exceedingly useful guide far beyond the bounds of British Methodism. See also Perry (G0337).

G0325 Meyer-Baer, Kathi. Liturgical Music Incunabula: A Descriptive Catalogue. London: Bibliographical Society, 1962.

This list of 450 items is arranged alphabetically and gives both locations of copies and citations in such major catalogs as Weale (G0375). There is a chronological list of entries (pp. 48-61), a bibliography, an index of printers and an index of places. Twelve facsimiles accompany the listing.

G0326   Moore, Edgar J. A Guide to Music in Worship: A Comprehensive, Current Index of Sacred Solos in Print. Great Neck, N.Y.: Channel Press, 1959.

Intended for clergy, choir directors, organists, singers and music committees, this is a comprehensive listing of sacred solos available in the United States. Keys and ranges are indicated; texts are analyzed; the songs are indexed according to appropriateness to special days; and the availability of suitable accompaniments is shown. See also Espina (G0289, G0290).

G0327   Muehsam, Gerd. Guide to Basic Information Sources in the Visual Arts. Information Resources Series. Santa Barbara, Calif.: ABC-Clio Press, 1978.

This guide consists of a series of bibliographical essays followed by an alphabetical listing of publications cited. The essays are aimed primarily at students of art and art history and treat techniques of art research, general art reference materials, primary sources, materials for research on specific periods and art forms, national schools of art. There is a combined author, title and subject index. For students of ecclesiastical or religious art this is a useful compendium. See also Ehresmann (G0286).

G0328   Music Index: A Subject-Author Guide to over 300 Current International Periodicals. Vol. 1- . Detroit, Mich.: Information Coordinators, 1949- ; monthly with annual cumulations.

This useful compilation indexes by author and subject a wide range of serials dealing with all aspects of music. Periodicals devoted specifically to music are indexed fully, while more general periodicals are scanned for relevant articles to be indexed as well. Reviews and obituaries are included in this important service. See also Meggett (G0322) and RILM (G0350).

G0329   Nardone, Thomas R. Organ Music in Print. Music-in-Print Series, vol. 3. Philadelphia, Pa.: Musicdata, 1975.

Intended to provide a comprehensive catalog of international music publishers with a listing of the complete organ work issues of each one, this is an important reference work for librarians, music directors and organists. Both traditional and contemporary works of secular and sacred interest are listed. Composers, titles, cross references all appear in a single alphabetical sequence. See also Edson (G0284, G0285).

G0330   Nardone, Thomas R.; Nye, James H.; and Resnick, Mark. Choral Music in Print. 2 vols. Music-in-Print Series, vols. 1-2. Philadelphia, Pa.: Musicdata, 1974.

These two volumes and the Supplement (G0331) attempt to be an exhaustive listing of music publishers throughout the world and of choral compositions found in their catalogs. Volume 1 treats sacred choral music in 656 pages; volume 2 deals with secular choral music. In each volume the musical works are listed in a single alphabetical sequence by title and composer, with full information under the author's name or under title in the case of anonymous works. See also May (G0320) and Steere (G0365).

G0331   Nardone, Thomas R.; Nye, James H.; and Resnick, Mark. Choral Music in Print. Supplement. Philadelphia, Pa.: Musicdata, 1976.

Like the main volume (G0330), this additional compilation lists sacred and secular compositions in separate sections.

G0332   New York Public Library. Music Division. Bibliographic Guide to Music. Vol. 1- . Boston, Mass.: G.K. Hall and Company, 1976- ; annual.

This ongoing supplement to the Dictionary Catalog of the Music Collection (G0333) includes all music materials catalogued by the Library's Research Libraries. In addition it incorporates entries from the Library of Congress MARC tapes in the fields of music history, bibliography, criticism, philosophy, composition, orchestration, singing and voice. Each annual volume covers items catalogued in the preceding year, which makes it a reasonably current publication of importance to those seeking material on all aspects of music.

G0333   New York Public Library. Research Libraries. Dictionary Catalog of the Music Collection. 33 vols. Boston, Mass.: G.K. Hall and Company, 1964.

This catalog of a very important music collection provides detailed entries for books, pamphlets, periodical articles, essays, scores and librettos. The dictionary arrangement and frequent cross references make the work very easy to use, although some of the catalog card reproductions are somewhat illegible. Together with the two supplements (G0334, G0335) and ongoing Bibliographic Guide (G0332) this is an indispensible tool for advanced students and scholars of all aspects of religious music. See also Krummel (G0308).

G0334   New York Public Library. Research Libraries. Dictionary Catalog of the Music Collection. Supplement 1974. Boston, Mass.: G.K. Hall and Company, 1976.

This 559 page continuation of Supplement II (G0335) reproduces additions to the catalog made from January 1972 to September 1974. It follows the same format as the main set (G0333) and brings coverage up to the first year treated by the Bibliographic Guide to Music (G0332).

G0335   New York Public LIbrary. Research Libraries. Dictionary Catalog of the Music Collection. Supplement II. 10 vols. Boston, Mass.: G.K. Hall and Company, 1973.

Incorporating all material included in Supplement I, this catalog covers all additions to the collection from 1964 to 1971. It is an essential complement to the basic catalog (G0333) and follows the same arrangement.

G0336   Parks, Edna D. Early English Hymns: An Index. Metuchen, N.J.: Scarecrow Press, 1972.

This publication lists over 900 hymns alphabetically by first line, including many which do not appear in Julian (G0427). Publication dates are mainly seventeenth century. Metre, number of stanzas, author's name, publication date, page reference in a collection, composer's name and tune are indicated. A bibliography and author, composer and tune indexes are provided.

See also Rogers (G0353).

G0337 Perry, David W. Hymns and Tunes Indexed by First Lines, Tune Names and Metres. Croydon: Hymn Society of Great Britain and Ireland and Royal School of Church Music, 1980.

Based on the contents of approximately forty British hymnals, including Anglican, Roman Catholic, Protestant and interdenominational collections, this index consists of three main parts. The index of first lines contains about 6800 entries; the index of tune names, including alternative names, contains more than 5000 entries; the index of metres classifies tunes under some 900 metres and also provides a popularity rating based on the number of hymnals in which each tune is found. Variant forms of the same first lines are cross indexed, and alternative versions of translated hymns are shown, while for some translations the original first lines are also given. The introduction includes a classified listing of hymnals indexed (although not always correctly classified); this list is repeated on the endpaper in alphabetical order of abbreviations used. This is a helpful and time saving guide to hymns from a broad range of sources and traditions. See also Parks (G0336) and Rogers (G0353).

G0338 Pigault, Gérard, and Schlick, Jean. Baptism/Baptême: International Bibliography, 1971-1973, Indexed by Computer. RIC Supplément, no. 9. Strasbourg: CERDIC Publications, 1974.

With 387 citations of books and articles, this unannotated bibliography contains nine sections (baptism celebration, baptism theology, baptism ecumenism, infant baptism, adult baptism, etc.), each arranged alphabetically by author. The material listed is primarily European but is broadly representative of materials produced during 1971-1973, with some emphasis on the Roman Catholic tradition.

G0339 Pigault, Gérard, and Schlick, Jean. Eucharist and Eucharistic Hospitality/Euchariste et Hospitalité Eucharistique: International Bibliography, 1971-1973, Indexed by Computer. RIC Supplément, no. 10. Strasbourg: CERDIC Publications, 1974.

The 490 entries in this bibliography, although overlapping somewhat with Pigault's later guide to the eucharist in general (G0340) focus on theological problems and ecumenism in relation to the eucharist, and intercommunion and eucharistic hospitality. Unannotated, numbered entries are arranged alphabetically by author in three sections. Books and articles are included, with the bulk of the material being European.

G0340 Pigault, Gérard, and Schlick, Jean. Eucharist: International Bibliography, 1971-1974, Indexed by Computer/Euchariste: Bibliographie Internationale, 1971-1974, Etablie par Ordinateur. RIC Supplement, no. 17. Strasbourg: CERDIC Publications, 1975.

This compilation contains references to 561 books and journal articles. See also the preceding entry (G0339).

G0341 Poscharsky, Veronika. Bibliographie des Kirchenbaues und der Kirchlichen Kunst der Gegenwart. Im Auftrag des Institutes für Kirchenbau und Kirchliche Kunst der Gegenwart. 4 vols. Marburg/Lahn: Institut für Kirchenbau und Kirchliche Kunst der Gegenwart, 1963-1964.

See also Princeton University (G0342).

G0342   Princeton University. Department of Art and Archaeology. Index of Christian Art, Princeton University. [Princeton, N.J.: Princeton University, 1963].

See also Poscharsky (G0341).

G0343   Questions Liturgiques. Vol. 1- . Louvain: Questions Liturgiques, 1910- ; quarterly.

Originally entitled Questions Liturgiques et Paroissiales, this scholarly journal is devoted to the Roman Catholic liturgy in both historical and practical terms, including theological and catechetical matters in its coverage. The bibliographical section, "Bulletin de Littérature Liturgique", is arranged by subject and provides both bibliographical information and brief abstracts of entries. Coverage is limited to books in European languages (with litte attention to English), and there is an annual author index. In terms of up-to-date coverage and representative treatment of its field this is a reasonably useful tool which is best consulted when full summaries of books are sought. See also Ephemerides Theologicae (G0287) and Rivista Liturgica (G0351).

G0344   Rau, Albert George, and David, Hans Theodore, comps. Catalogue of Music by American Moravians, 1742-1842, from the Archives of the Moravian Church of Bethlehem, Pa. Bethlehem, Pa.: The Moravian Seminary and College for Women, 1938. Reprint. New York: AMS Press, 1970.

See also Gombosi (G0296).

G0345   Repertoire Internationale des Sources Musicales. Vol. 1- . Munich: G. Henle, 1960- .

Issued in parts, RISM is an extensive catalog of all available bibliographical works on music, writings about music, textbooks on music and similar publications from all countries and all periods up to 1800. Bibliographical descriptions are very full and extremely accurate. Indexes are provided for each volume or group of volumes. For advanced students of all aspects of music in its earlier periods this is an indispensible reference tool. The main difficulty lies in the arrangement of materials into a série alphabetique (volumes designated by the letter "A") and a série systematique (designated "B") and lack of a detailed content outline for the series. See also Meggett (G0322).

G0346   Revitt, Paul Joseph, comp. The George Pullen Jackson Collection of Southern Hymnody: A Bibliography. UCLA Library Occasional Papers, no. 13. Los Angeles, Calif.: University of California Library, 1964.

See also Rhodes University (G0347).

G0347   Rhodes University. Library. James Rodger Hymnological Collection. Catalogue. Rhodes University Library, 1966.

See also Revitt (G0346).

G0348   Richardson, Alice Marion. Index to Stories of Hymns: An Analytical

Catalog of Twelve Much-Used Books. Yardley, Pa.: F.S. Cook, 1929. Reprint. New York: AMS Press, 1975.

G0349   RILA, Répertoire International de la Littérature de l'Art/RILA, International Repertory of the Literature of Art. Vol. 1- . New York: College Art Association of America, 1975- ; semi-annual.

Each issue of this service contains abstracts and an index of books, dissertations, periodicals and other publications. The abstracts are arranged topically under broad subject headings, including reference works, medieval art, Renaissance and baroque art. The detailed author and subject index allows users to retrieve information quickly and accurately. Coverage is international and fairly up-to-date. See also Art/Kunst (G0254) and Artbibliographies (G0255).

G0350   RILM Abstracts of Music Literature. Vol. 1- . New York: International Association of Music Literature, 1967- ; quarterly.

This service attempts to include abstracts of all significant music literature, including books, articles, reviews, dissertations, iconographies and catalogs. Entries are presented in a classified arrangement with an annual author-subject index produced by computer. Coverage is extremely thorough and reasonably up-to-date, providing for scholars and others a valuable international summary of the literature. See also Music Index (G0328).

G0351   Rivista Liturgica. Vol. 1- . Turin: Centro Catechistico Salesiano, 1914- ; bimonthly.

Devoted largely to practical aspects of the Roman Catholic liturgy, this review regularly includes a "Rivista delle Riviste", as well as a bibliography occupying all of the final issue each year. The first of these contains lengthy abstracts of material from approximately 150 less well known serials, while the annual bibliography provides abstracts of books for the most part. This bibliographical section is arranged by subject according to the requirements of the literature for a given year. Although this journal is rather narrow in focus, it does provide very detailed notes on the literature and is especially valuable in its treatment of obscure periodicals. The very dated coverage is a serious failing, but the bibliography is indexed by author and subject to assist users. Overall Rivista Liturgica can be recommended largely to those engaged in detailed study of the liturgy from a pastoral or practical standpoint within the Roman Catholic tradition. See also Ephemerides Liturgicae (G0287) and Questions Liturgiques (G0343).

G0352   Robertson, Festus G., Jr. Church Music for Adults. Nashville, Tenn.: Convention Press, 1969.

See also Episcopal Church (G0288).

G0353   Rogers, Kirby. English and Scottish Psalm and Hymn Tunes: An Index. MLA Index Series, no. 8. Ann Arbor, Mich.: Music Library Association, 1967.

This compilation indexes material in the work by Frost (G0926), providing a valuable guide to tunes of the sixteenth and seventeenth centuries. See also Parks (G0336) and Perry (G0337).

G0354   Rowell, Lois, comp. American Organ Music on Records. Braintree, Mass.: Organ Literature Foundation, 1976.

This listing by composer of works issued between 1941 and 1975 concentrates on music written originally for the organ or transcribed for the organ by the composer. It is limited to American born composers and those permanently resident in the United States. There are numerous indexes catering to a variety of reference needs: performer, organ builder and instrument location; album title, record label and number; author of program notes, series. See also Nardone (G0329).

G0355   Royal School of Church Music. A Selected List of Church Music Recordings. Croydon: Royal School of Church Music, 1967.

See also International Catholic Association for Radio and Television (G0302).

G0356   Royal School of Church Music. Musical Advisory Board. Church Music Recommended by the Musical Advisory Board. Rev. ed. Croydon: Royal School of Church Music, 1967.

See also Episcopal Church (G0288).

G0357   Rupke, Ursula Irene. Liturgische Zeitschriften und Reihen des Deutschen Sprachgebiets im 20 Jahrhundert unter Berücks. d. Liturg. Bewegung u. Reform im Kath. Raum. Veröffentlichungen der Arbeitsgemeinschaft Katholisch-Theologischer Bibliotheken, 2. Paderborn: Arbeitsgemeinschaft Katholisch-Theologischer Bibliotheken, 1974.

This 166 page bibliography deals exclusively with German language literature on liturgical reform. It is a useful complement to Vixmans (G0371) and other Roman Catholic works which tend to overlook German liturgical thinking. See also Archiv für Liturgiewissenschaft (G0252).

G0358   Sáenz de Tejada, José Maria. Bibliografía de la Devoción al Corazón de Jesús (Ensayo). Bilbao: Mensajero del Corazón de Jesús, 1952.

This 434 page bibliography covers books in all languages on devotion to the Sacred Heart. Most items have full bibliographical references and descriptive annotations. Arrangement is alphabetical by author, and a subject index is provided. See also Bibliotheca Catholica Neerlandica (G0260), Dols (G0282) and Sinclair (G0362).

G0359   Sauget, Joseph Marie. Bibliographie des Liturgies Orientales (1900-1960). Rome: Pontificum Institutum Orientalium Studiorum, 1962.

G0360   Schaal, Richard. Die Musikhandschriften des Ansbacher Inventars von 1686. Quellenkataloge zur Musikgeschichte, Bd. 1. Wilhelmshaven: Heinrichshofen, 1966.

G0361   Sendrey, Alfred, comp. Bibliography of Jewish Music. New York: Columbia University Press, 1951.

This comprehensive bibliography contains some 10,000 entries in two sections: literature on the subject, the music itself from all periods and of all types. There are author indexes for both sections. Although somewhat dated, Sendrey is an indispensible bibliography of Jewish music. See also

Weisser (G0376), which is less comprehensive but more up-to-date.

G0362   Sinclair, Keith Val. French Devotional Texts of the Middle Ages: A Bibliographic Manuscript Guide. Westport, Conn.: Greenwood Press, 1979.

This bibliography of 1500 prose and verse compositions in manuscript form covers holdings in European and American libraries. All of the entries deal with praise, adoration, veneration, supplication or gratitude, as well as benediction, exhortation, meditation, lamentation, contrition or penance. Each item is listed according to the text's opening words and includes identifying information, manuscripts, editions and critical opinion. The six indexes cover cited texts by manuscript and location, individual owners, authors and translators, saints and biblical personalities referred to, subject and title. See also Bibliotheca Catholica Neerlandica (G0260), Dols (G0282) and Sáenz de Tejada (G0358).

G0363   [no entry]

G0364   Spencer, Donald Amos, comp. Hymn and Scripture Selection Guide: A Cross Reference of Scripture and Hymns with over 12000 References for 380 Hymns and Gospel Songs. Valley Forge, Pa.: Judson Press, 1977.

G0365   Steere, Dwight. Music for the Protestant Church Choir: A Descriptive and Classified List of Worship Material. Richmond, Va.: John Knox Press, 1955.

This 229 page listing covers works for Protestant services of worship, including those for mixed voices but excluding junior and youth choir music and works for men's or women's voices only. The listing is selective and does not claim to be authoritative. Guidance on how to use the listings is provided, and there are four useful indexes. See also May (G0320) and Nardone (G0330, G0331).

G0366   Studia Liturgica: An International Ecumenical Quarterly for Liturgical Research and Renewal. Vol. 1- . Rotterdam: Liturgical Ecumenical Center Trust, 1962- ; quarterly.

Although not primarily a bibliographical review, this journal devoted to liturgiology and liturgical renewal primarily in the Protestant and Orthodox traditions does include bibliographical material in most issues. This is presented in the form of index cards, and for each item there is a citation plus brief abstract. Both books and articles are treated, and emphasis is on recently published material. Although this section does not appear as regularly as it might, it does provide a wide ranging coverage of liturgical publications of both scholarly and pastoral value. See also Rupke (G0357) and Tiller (G0367).

G0367   Tiller, John Eric. A Modern Liturgical Bibliography. Grove Booklet on Ministry and Worship, no. 23. Bramcote: Grove Books, 1974.

This 24 page bibliography lists 472 books and articles in English, covering both theory and practice of worship in four sections. It is limited to works published or reprinted between 1960 and 1974. Annotations are not provided. Tiller is suitable for the beginner interested in Anglican and Protestant worship. See also Rupke (G0357) and Studia Liturgica (G0366).

G0368   Travis, Stephen. Audio-Visual Media: A Guide to Sources of Materials for Christian Education and Worship. Bramcote, Nottinghamshire: Grove Press, 1972.

This 16 page work is an accompaniment to Lloyd's Informal Liturgy (G0646).

G0369   Turner-Evans, H. A Bibliography of Welsh Hymnology to 1960. London: Library Association, 1964; Ann Arbor, Mich.: University Microfilms, 1969.

Arranged alphabetically by composer, this interesting bibliography includes brief biographical sketches, lists of published works, first lines of hymns composed and lists of references to each hymn writer. Hymns appearing in periodicals are omitted. A list of bardic names is prefixed to the work, and a bibliography of books, articles and manuscripts on hymnology is included.

G0370   Verret, Mary Camilla. A Preliminary Survey of Roman Catholic Hymnals Published in the United States of America. Washington, D.C.: Catholic University of America Press, 1964.

This work lists over 300 hymnals with locations and descriptive annotations which include editions and number of hymns. Arrangement is chronological, covering the period 1788-1961, with an author index.

G0371   Vismans, Thomas Antonius, and Brinkhoff, Lucas, comps. Critical Bibliography of Liturgical Literature. Trans. by Raymund W. Fitzpatrick and Clifford Howell. Bibliographia ad Usum Seminariorum; Annotated Basic Bibliography, vol. E.1. Nijmegen: Bestelcentrale der VSKB Publishers, 1961.

This classified listing of 278 liturgical sources, commentaries, handbooks, monographs and periodicals is mainly Roman Catholic but includes a brief section on Eastern and Protestant liturgy. An index of authors and of anonymous works is provided. See also Tiller (G0367).

G0372   Voigt, Louis, and Porter, Ellen Jane. Hymnbook Collections of North America. New York: Hymn Society of America, 1980.

See also Anderson (G0250) and Clark (G0274).

G0373   Wackernagel, Philipp. Bibliographie zur Geschichte des Deutschen Kirchenliedes im XVI. Jahrhundert. Frankfurt am Main: Heyder und Zimmer, 1855. Reprint. Hildsheim: Georg Olms Verlagsbuchhandlung, 1961.

See also Becker (G0257).

G0374   Warrington, James. Short Titles of Books, Relating to or Illustrating the History and Practice of Psalmody in the United States, 1620-1820. Philadelphia, Pa.: privately printed, 1878. Reprint. Ed. by Theodore M. Finney. Bibliographia Tripotamopolitana, no. 1. Pittsburgh, Pa.: Pittsburgh Theological Seminary, Clifford E. Barbour Library, 1970.

Also available in a reprint as Burt Franklin Bibliography and Reprint Series, vo. 438 (New York: Burt Franklin, 1971), this pamphlet was originally prepared by Warrington as a means of inducing others to provide him with full bibliographical details of relevant works for a projected history of American psalmody. This never materialized, and Short Titles is simply a chronological listing of works on psalmody; as a rule, each entry provides title, place of publication and date. For the serious scholar or bibliographer this is a useful starting point but does contain a number of inaccuracies, as many of the items listed were not actually seen by the compiler. Nevertheless, for the 200 years in question this remains an important early guide to psalmody. See also Metcalf (G0323).

G0375   Weale, William Henry James, comp. Bibliographia Liturgica: Catalogus Missalium Ritus Latini ab Anno MCCCCLXXXIV Impressorum. Ed. by Hanns Bohatta. London: Bernard Quaritch, 1928.

This bibliography lists 1931 Roman missals printed between 1474 and about 1655 by place name and by religious orders. Locations in libraries and complete bibliographical descriptions are given, and typographical and chronological indexes are provided. See also Bohatta (G0264).

G0376   Weisser, Albert, comp. Bibliography of Publications and Other Resources on Jewish Music. New York: National Jewish Music   Council, 1969.

Based in part on Joseph Yasser's The Bibliography of Books and Articles on Jewish Music published in 1955, Weisser is a revised and expanded compilation which treats publications of all types which appeared through 1967. It is much less comprehensive than Sendrey (G0361) but has the advantage of including more recent works.

G0377   Wilkes, Roger. English Cathedrals and Collegiate Churches and Chapels: Their Music, Musicians and Musical Establishments; A Select Bibliography. London: Friends of Cathedral Music, 1968.

Containing only 12 pages, this bibliography of approximately fifty annotated entries is arranged in five major sections. Areas covered include cathedral music, church music, music and worship, choral foundations, composers and musicians. For a less limited compilation see Yeats-Edwards (G0378); see also Daniel and Le Huray (G0278).

G0378   Yeats-Edwards, Paul. English Church Music: A Bibliography. London: White Lion Publishers, 1975.

Based on the author's Library Association Fellowship thesis entitled "The History and Development of English Church Music: A Select Bibliography", this compilation of items published in England from 1500 to 1973 contains some 1500 citations in seven sections. Bibliographies, history, biography, choral music, theological and theoretical considerations, liturgical aspects, musical elements, practical and fictional areas are all considered. There is a substantial index (pp. 301-375) to this survey of music in English choral worship. Yeats-Edwards is a valuable compilation which deserves wider use than it enjoys at present. See also Daniel and Le Huray (G0278) and Wilkes (G0377).

G0379   Zaccaria, Francesco Antonio. Bibliotheca Ritualis, Concinnatum Opus. 2 vols. in 3. Rome: Octavii Puccinella, 1776-1781. Reprint. 2 vols. in 3. Burt Franklin Bibliography and Reference Series, vol. 58. New York: Burt Franklin, 1964.

LITURGY AND WORSHIP: DICTIONARIES

G0380 Adeline, Jules. The Adeline Art Dictionary, Including Terms in Architecture, Heraldry and Archaeology. With a supplement of new terms by Hugo G. Beigel. New York: Frederick Ungar Publishing Company, 1966.

Incorporating much information from F.W. Fairholt's Dictionary of Terms in Art (London: Virtus, 1854), this standard translation of a French classic has appeared in many English editions since its first publication in 1891. This reprinting is the most useful one, as it includes a section of new terms (pp. 423-459). The work is reasonably comprehensive, containing more than 4000 terms and some 2000 illustrations. See also Mollett (G0439).

G0381 Aigrain, René, ed. Liturgia: Encyclopédie Populaire des Connaissances Liturgiques. Paris: Bloud et Gay, 1930. Reprint. Paris: Bloud et Gay, 1947.

This substantial dictionary of 1141 pages has been reprinted on various occasions, indicating its popularity. See also Lesage (G0434).

G0382 Alscher, Ludger, et al., eds. Lexikon der Kunst: Architektur, Bildende Kunst, Angewandte Kunst, Industrieformgestaltung, Kunsttheorie. Vol. 1- . Leipzig: Seemann, 1968- .

This extensive dictionary covers a very wide range of topics in art and architecture generally. Some of the articles are quite substantial and relatively technical, and bibliographical references are found at the end of many articles. Coverage is international but with a strong European focus, and the biographical articles are particularly useful. For students with knowledge of German who require an advanced and detailed encyclopedia, Alscher is a useful reference work. See also Jahn (G0426) and Thieme and Becker (G0459).

G0383 Ammer, Christine. Harper's Dictionary of Music. New York: Harper and Row, 1972.

This 414 page dictionary contains entries for musical terms and for composers, in many cases providing brief historical notes in addition to definitions. The content is geared to a basic level of inquiry and is suitable for quick reference needs. See also Picerno (G0449).

G0384 Apel, Willi. Harvard Dictionary of Music. 2nd ed. Cambridge, Mass.: Belknap Press of Harvard University Press, 1969.

This dictionary covers musical topics, not including biographical articles, and provides useful bibliographies. Apel is particularly valuable for those who wish to understand the basic science of musicology, for the excellent summaries of both technical and historical fields are clearly written in nontechnical language and are supported by numerous examples and bibliographical references. See also Blom (G0393) and Jacobs (G0425).

G0385 Appleton, LeRoy H., and Bridges, Stephen. Symbolism in Liturgical Art. New York: Charles Scribner's Sons, 1959.

Arranged alphabetically, this brief compendium provides basic descriptions, bibliographies and illustrations of key symbols found in Christian churches. It is useful as a starting point for inquiries of a basic nature, particularly where a Roman Catholic emphasis is sought. For a far more substantial treatment see Aurenhammer (G0386); see also Cirlot (G0405) and Vries (G0464).

G0386   Aurenhammer, Hans. Lexikon der Christlichen Ikonographie. Vol. 1- . Vienna: Hollinek, 1959- .

This scholarly dictionary of Christian iconography is a very detailed encyclopedic treatment which under each subject treats sources, symbols and attributes.   References to representations in art are included, and most articles have bibliographies as well. Biblical personalities, saints, objects and concepts are listed in a single alphabetical sequence, which makes this much easier to consult than the less comprehensive work by Kirschbaum (G0429). When completed, Aurenhammer will undoubtedly be the most wide ranging work of its kind.

G0387   Baker, Theodore. Biographical Dictionary of Musicians. 5th ed. Rev. by Nicolas Slonimsky. New York: G. Schirmer, 1958.

First published in 1900, this useful compendium provides compact biographies of varying length of musicians from all periods and countries. Bibliographies of the subject's own works and of works about him are included, and pronunciation of foreign names is indicated. The fifth edition is thoroughly revised and includes 2300 new biographies of past and present musical personalities.   See also Sadie (G0453) and Thompson (G0460).

G0388   Bell, David, ed. Pall Mall Encyclopaedia of Art. 5 vols. London: Pall Mall Press, 1971.

Based on R. Maillard's Dictionnaire Universal de l'Art et des Artistes (3 vols. Paris: Hazan, 1967-1968), this comprehensive and authoritative reference publication contains nearly 4000 alphabetically arranged entries. Bell contains fewer but much longer entries than Myers (G0442), and the bibliographies are also rather fuller. Particular attention is paid to contemporary artists and architects, which gives the work marginal value for ecclesiastical needs.   There is an index in the final volume (pp. 2103-2131). See also Champlin (G0403) and Harper's Encyclopedia of Art (G0420).

G0389   Bénézit, Emmanuel. Dictionnaire Critique et Documentaire des Peintres, Sculpteurs, Dessinateurs et Graveurs de Tous les Temps et de Tous les Pays. Nouvelle éd. 8 vols. Paris: Gründ, 1948-1955.

This excellent biographical guide is a comprehensive listing which covers artists in all fields from the fifth century B.C. to the mid-twentieth century. Both major and minor figures are included regardless of their geographical location. The 25,000 entries usually include a list of chief works, museums where displayed and prices paid for works. Symbols and signatures are reproduced in facsimile. This is a valuable guide for those requiring basic information on artists. See also Enciclopedia dell'Arte (G0414) and Encyclopedia of World Art (G0416).

G0390   Berger, Rupert. Kleines Liturgisches Wörterbuch. Herder-Bücherei, Bd. 339/340/341. Freiburg im Breisgau, 1969.

This 495 page liturgical lexicon is particularly useful as a guide to post-Vatican II changes in the Roman Catholic liturgy but also covers the full range of terms, concepts and historical developments in Roman Catholic worship. In addition there is broad treatment of Eastern and non-Catholic rites. Music, sacraments, liturgical books, rubrics and ceremonial are all treated briefly but objectively. Berger is suitable as a reference volume for anyone interested in liturgical matters. See also Brinkhoff (G0398); for a German liturgical dictionary written from a Protestant viewpoint see Jung (G0428).

G0391   Bernen, Satia, and Bernen, Robert. Myth and Religion in European Painting, 1270-1700: The Stories As the Artists Knew Them. New York: George Braziller; London: Constable, 1973.

This dictionary outlines the stories of 850 common subjects of painting, including mythology, ancient history, Italian poetry, lives of saints and the Bible. The stories are summarized briefly and usually include references to the biblical or classical sources.   See also Daniel (G0406) and Seyn (G0455).

G0392   Blaise, Albert. Le Vocabulaire Latin des Principaux Thèmes Liturgiques. Rev. by Antoine Dumas. Turnhout: Brepols, 1966.

The two parts of this dictionary consist of a glossary of approximately 6000 liturgical terms plus detailed discussion of principal liturgical themes in the Roman Catholic tradition. The work also serves as a liturgical index to the Fathers by giving quotations along with detailed definitions. A bibliography is included. See also Diamond (G0410).

G0393   Blom, Eric. Everyman's Dictionary of Music. 5th ed. Rev. by Jack Allan Westrup. London: J.M. Dent, 1971; New York: St.   Martin's Press, [1972].

First published in 1947, this essential dictionary for quick reference needs contains approximately 10,000 brief, factual entries on all aspects of music, musicology, history, composers, performers, techniques, etc. The biographical sketches cover many personalities not mentioned in larger works, and there are numerous cross references. As a general dictionary, Blom is more satisfactory than most of the other works prepared for a nonspecialist audience. See also Apel (G0384) and Jacobs (G0425).

G0394   Blume, Friedrich, ed. Die Musik in Geschichte und Gegenwart: Allgemeine Enzyklopädie der Musik. Vol. 1- . Kassel: Bärenreiter Verlag, 1949- .

This comprehensive international work is similar to Sadie (G0453) in seeking to provide a thorough and detailed guide to music. As a reference work, Blume is an excellent compendium; the articles are long and factual, including illustrations, bibliographies and references to other entries. For readers of German this is a valuable alternative to Sadie and presents a great deal of information of interest to students of church music. A general index will be provided upon completion of the main volumes.

G0395   Bobillier, Marie. Dictionnaire Pratique et Historique de la Musique. 2e éd. Paris: A. Colin, 1930.

This standard French dictionary of musical terms contains, in addition to the definitions, many figures and music examples. There are entries for forms of music (e.g., "Messe"), instruments, technical terms and concepts. There are many cross references in the clear and concise definitions. Bobillier is useful for readers of French requiring brief notes on a wide range of topics. For a larger French work see Honegger (G0422).

G0396   Braun, Joseph. Liturgisches Handlexicon. 2. Aufl. Regensburg: J. Kösel, 1924.

This small dictionary of the liturgy covers history, ceremonies, technical terms, national liturgies, etc. It does not include any bibliography. See also Brinkhoff (G0398).

G0397   Briggs, Martin Shaw. Everyman's Concise Encyclopaedia of Architecture. New York: E.P. Dutton Company; London: J.M. Dent, 1959.

This work contains alphabetically arranged terms and biographies relevant to architecture. Line drawings and a section of thirty-two plates accompany the text. See also Peusner (G0447) and Saylor (G0454).

G0398   Brinkhoff, Lucas, et al. Liturgisch Woordenboek. 2 vols. Roermond: J.J. Romen, 1962.

This Dutch Roman Catholic lexicon covers a wide variety of liturgical topics of historical, doctrinal and cultural significance. Also treated are pastoral aspects of the liturgy, but minor rubrical matters subject to change are ignored. The information provided is detailed and scholarly, giving particularly sound guidance on practical matters related to liturgical practice. The views expressed are those of a liberal European Catholic tradition. See also Berger (G0390) and Braun (G0396).

G0399   Britt, Matthew, ed. A Dictionary of the Psalter, Containing the Vocabulary of the Psalms, Hymns, Canticles and Miscellaneous Prayers of the Breviary Psalter. New York: Benziger Brothers, 1923. Reprint. New York: Benziger Brothers, 1928.

Based on the Vulgate, this dictionary of Latin terms includes English equivalents and representative quotations. In some cases translations of the Hebrew text are also provided. Although dated, Britt remains adequate as a basic reference tool for Roman Catholic students. See also Konus (G0430).

G0400   Bryant, Al. Encyclopedia of Devotional Programs for Women's Groups. Vol. 1- . Grand Rapids, Mich.: Zondervan Publishing House, 1956- .

G0401   Cabrol, Fernand, et al. Dictionnaire d'Archéologie Chrétienne et de Liturgie. 15 vols. in 30. Paris: Letouzey et Ané, 1907-1953.

This complete and scholarly work covers pre-Carolingian social and religious life as well as liturgical art, architecture, music, rites and related topics in lengthy, signed articles with copious bibliographies. Line drawings and plans accompany the text. As part of the Encyclopédie des Sciences Ecclésiastiques, Cabrol reflects the thorough Roman Catholic scholarship of this series but also suffers from the drawback of dated early volumes.

G0402   Carroll, Joseph Robert. Compendium of Liturgical Music Terms.

Toledo, Ohio: Gregorian Institute of America, 1964.

See also Hughes (G0423).

G0403   Champlin, John Denison, Jr., ed. Cyclopedia of Painters and Paintings. Critical editor: Charles Callahan Perkins. 4 vols. New York: Charles Scribner's Sons, 1885-1887. Reprint. 4 vols. Port Washington, N.Y.: Kennicat Press, 1969.

This dated guide contains material arranged alphabetically by both titles of paintings and names of artists. For each painter there is substantial biographical data and a list and location of paintings. Volume 1 includes an extensive bibliography, and there are nearly 200 portrait reproductions of artists in the set. See also Bell (G0388).

G0404   Chevalier, Jean, and Gheerbrant, Alain. Dictionnaire des Symboles: Mythes, Rêves, Coutumes, Gestes, Formes, Figures, Couleurs, Nombres. Paris: Robert Laffont, 1969.

With 844 pages this dictionary of symbolism is double the size of Whittick's survey (G0868), and the contents reflect this in their broader coverage. The 1200 entries include explanation of the symbolism, mythological, legendary or religious background and other pertinent facts. Bibliographies are not provided in the articles, but abbreviated references refer one to the general bibliography at the end of the work. See also Seyn (G0455).

G0405   Cirlot, Juan Eduardo. A Dictionary of Symbols. Trans. by Jack Sage. 2nd ed. London: Routledge and Kegan Paul, 1971; New York: Philosophical Library, 1972.

First published as Diccionario de Simbolos Tradicionales, this edition is an updating of the original in which only the bibliography (pp. 387-399) has been thoroughly revised. The arrangement of descriptive entries is alphabetical and includes references to monochrome plates. The definitions are clear and often detailed. See also Appleton (G0385) and Vries (G0464).

G0406   Daniel, Howard. Encyclopedia of Themes and Subjects in Painting: Mythological, Biblical, Historical, Literary, Allegorical and Topical. New York: H.N. Abrams, 1971.

The bulk of this work comprises a dictionary of the most common subjects found in European painting from the early Renaissance to the mid-nineteenth century, and most of the entries are illustrated by monochrome reproductions of painting. The period covered is broader than Bernen (G0291). See also Seyn (G0455).

G0407   Davidson, James Robert. A Dictionary of Protestant Church Music. Metuchen, N.J.: Scarecrow Press, 1975.

Intended in part to replace Stubbings (G0457), this dictionary includes both definitions and longer articles on topics related to church music in the Protestant tradition. Basic sources are listed in the entries, which are lucid and reasonably detailed for basic reference inquiries. There are indexes of names and of titles. This work is intended to be the first phase of a full scale dictionary of church music by Davidson.

G0408   Davies, John Gordon, ed. A Dictionary of Liturgy and Worship. New York: Macmillan Company; London: SCM Press, 1972.

With signed articles by liturgical experts of various traditions and some bibliographical references, this reasonably detailed dictionary seeks to provide sound background information on all aspects of Christian worship both for students and for those involved in its practice. Although concentrating on data relevant to the Christian tradition, some attention is also given to other major world religions. The articles, some quite full, are clear and objective, offering both historical explanations and practical descriptions of terms, concepts and practices. There are numerous cross references and some illustrations but no index. This is an excellent ecumenical dictionary for students at various levels. Davies has been reprinted as The Westminster Dictionary of Worship (Philadelphia, Pa.: Westminster Press, 1979). See also Brinkhoff (G0398) and Jung (G0428).

G0409   Davies, John Gordon. A Select Liturgical Lexicon. Ecumenical Studies in Worship, no. 14. London: Lutterworth Press, 1965; Richmond, Va.: John Knox Press, 1966.

Much less detailed than Davies' later dictionary (G0408), this is a useful work for those requiring basic definitions of key liturgical terms. The entries are concise and brief, providing some information on the origin, use and evolution of terms in various liturgical traditions. See also Hoffmann (G0421).

G0410   Diamond, Wilfrid Joseph. Dictionary of Liturgical Latin. Milwaukee, Wisc.: Bruce Publishing Company, 1961.

More than 1000 words of the Latin liturgy are defined very briefly and clearly in English. For students of liturgical texts this is an excellent tool, as most standard Latin dictionaries are restricted to classical usage. However, Diamond should be limited to the use for which it was prepared as there are more adequate dictionaries for ecclesiastical Latin generally and for medieval Latin. For a guide to the pronunciation of liturgical Latin see De Angelis (G0558). See also Blaise (G0392).

G0411   Dictionnaire du Symbolisme. Par les Religieuses Bénédictines de la Rue Monsieur, Paris. Abbaye de Saint-André, Belgium: L'Artisan Liturgique, 1934.

See also Urech (G0462).

G0412   Drake, Maurice, and Drake, Wilfred. Saints and Their Emblems. Philadelphia, Pa.: J.B. Lippincott; London: T.W. Laurie, 1916. Reprint. Detroit, Mich.: Gale Research Company, 1971.

This useful reference volume includes three main parts: a dictionary of saints, a dictionary of emblems, and a collection of appendixes on patriarchs and prophets, sibyls, patron saints of various callings. Of most use are the notes on emblems and the appendixes. The dictionary of saints deals with some 5000 individuals, listing their rank, feast day, locality, symbols, names of artists and bibliography. See also Husenbeth (G0424).

G0413   Eckel, Frederick L. A Concise Dictionary of Ecclesiastical Terms.

Boston, Mass.: Whittemore Associates, 1960.

This Anglican compilation provides basic definitions of terms supported by illustrative drawings. It is a very slight work which is of some use to those unfamiliar with the vocabulary of liturgical churches in matters of architecture, vestments, vessels and furnishings. See also Lee (G0432).

G0414   Enciclopedia dell'Arte Antica, Classica e Orientale. 7 vols. Rome: Istituto della Enciclopedia Italiana, 1958-1966.

This encyclopedia treats the art history and iconography of the countries of classical antiquity (in Asia, Northern Africa and Europe) from prehistory to about 500 A.D. Articles are signed, bibliographies are provided, and the work is handsomely illustrated. This is a useful reference work for those with knowledge of Italian and is particularly valuable for students of early Christian art and iconography. See also Bénézit (G0359) and Encyclopedia of World Art (G0416).

G0415   Enciclopedia della Musica. 4 vols. Milan: Ricordi, 1963-1964.

Containing more than 15,000 entries prepared by 220 Italian and foreign contributors, this encyclopedia exhibits a clear continental, particularly Italian, slant; this may provide a useful corrective to the larger French and German works. From the standpoint of church music there are useful data on Roman Catholic and medieval aspects of the field. Biographies, concepts, movements and compositions are all treated adequately, and valuable bibliographical data are included. See also Honegger (G0422) and Michel (G0438).

G0416   Encyclopedia of World Art. 15 vols. New York: McGraw-Hill Book Company, 1959-1968.

This encyclopedia covers architecture, sculpture, painting and other artistic objects from all countries and all periods. Articles are signed by the specialist contributors and include extensive bibliographies. It was published simultaneously in Italian (Enciclopedia Universale dell'Arte. Florence: Sansoni, 1958-1967), and articles were translated from various original languages for the English edition. This edition includes more cross references than does the Italian edition, a more extensive article on art of the Americas, and some 300 separate short biographies which provide ready access to information about persons treated in longer monographic articles. This is generally regarded as the most comprehensive work of its kind and contains much information of value on ecclesiological topics and on religious art. The index volume contains approximately 20,000 entries for personal names, geographical names, titles of works of art and a wide range of subjects. See also Bénézit (G0389) and Enciclopedia dell'Arte (G0414).

G0417   Fischer, Albert Friedrich Wilhelm. Kirchenliederlexikon: Hymnologisch-Literarische Nachweisungen über ca. 4500 der Wichtigsten und Verbreitesten Kirchenlieder Aller Zeiten in Alphabetischer Folge nebst einer Ubersicht der Liederdichter. 2 vols. in 1. Gotha: F.A. Perthes, 1878-1879.   Reprint. 2 vols. in 1. Hildesheim: Georg Olms, 1967.

This work includes a Supplement (Gotha: F.A. Perthes, 1886). See also Julian (G0427) and Kornmüller (G0431).

G0418   Gaunt, William. Everyman's Dictionary of Pictorial Art. 2 vols. New York: E.P. Dutton Company; London: J.M. Dent, 1962.

This work attempts to cover painters and periods, forms and techniques of pictorial art in all parts of the world from the earliest times to the present. It includes biographical sketches of some 1200 artists, descriptions of the main periods and schools of art and of some famous paintings, and definitions of terms. Lists of British and American artists are provided in volume 2. Descriptions are concise and there are many illustrations. For a similar single volume treatment see Myers (G0441).

G0419 Harford, George, and Stevenson, Morley, eds. The Prayer Book Dictionary. Rev. ed. London: Sir Isaac Pitman and Sons, 1925.

This work attempts to provide for the Anglican Book of Common Prayer a dictionary comparable to similar surveys devoted to the Bible, covering origins, history, use and teaching. Data are admirably full and accurate, and controversial issues are treated very objectively. Articles are signed, and there is a list of contributors as well as an appendix of contents in Prayer Book order. See also Tatlock (G0458).

G0420   Harper's Encyclopedia of Art; Architecture, Sculpture, Painting, Decorative Arts, Based on the Work of Louis Hourticq.... Trans. under the supervision of Tancred Borenius. Rev. under the supervision of J. Leroy Davidson and Philippa Gerry, with the assistance of the staff of the Index of Twentieth Century Artists, College Art Association, New York City. 2 vols. New York: Harper and Brothers, 1937.

Reprinted as New Standard Encyclopedia of Art (2 vols. in 1. New York: Garden City Publishing Company, 1939), this work is based on Hourticq's Bibliothèque Omnium: Encyclopédie des Beaux Arts; Architecture, Sculpture, Peinture, Arts Decoratifs (2 vols. Paris: Hachette, 1925). It contains definitions of terms, brief bibliographies and biographies. The content is more secular than in many of the similar compilations, and this detracts from its value as an ecclesiastical reference work on the arts. See also Bell (G0388) and Myers (G0442).

G0421   Hoffmann, Alexius. Liturgical Dictionary. Popular Liturgical Library Series III, no. 1. Collegeville, Minn.: Liturgical Press, 1928.

See also Davies (G0409).

G0422 Honegger, Marc, ed. Dictionnaire de la Musique. 4 vols. Paris: Bordas, 1970-1976.

Each volume of this encyclopedic dictionary covers a specific range of material (men and their work in the first two volumes; musical forms, techniques and developments in the remaining volumes). The biographical volumes contain approximately 5500 articles by more than 150 specialists; coverage extends to composers, theorists, musicologists, instrument makers, publishers and similar professions. Bibliographies are provided for many of the entries. The volume on theory covers all aspects of the subject with fairly technical but clearly written definitions. For students of ecclesiastical music the biographies are particularly helpful. For a similar French compilation see Michel (G0438).

G0423 Hughes, Anselm. <u>Liturgical Terms for Music Students: A Dictionary</u>. Boston, Mass.: McLaughlin and Reilly Company, 1940. Reprint. St. Clair Shores, Mich.: Scholarly Press, 1972.

This dictionary contains concise definitions of musical terms used in the Latin rite together with appended tables outlining the traditional structure of the mass and office. See also Carroll (G0402).

G0424 Husenbeth, Frederick Charles. <u>Emblems of Saints by Which They Are Distinguished in Works of Art</u>. 3rd ed. Ed. by Augustus Jessopp. Norwich: A.H. Goose and Company for the Norfolk and Norwich Archaeological Society, 1882.

Like Drake and Drake (G0412), this volume lists the rank, feast day, dates, locality and emblems of some 1500 saints. It is a useful guide to artistic representations of saints but lacks the broad coverage found in Drake.

G0425 Jacobs, Arthur. <u>The New Penguin Dictionary of Music</u>. 4th ed. Harmondsworth: Penguin Books, 1977.

This thoroughly revised edition of a standard work which first appeared in 1958 is a very useful dictionary for basic information on composers, musical compositions, terminology, instruments and movements in the history of music. Definitions are clear, concise and factual, and there are many cross references. This is an excellent guide for various levels of inquiry and is particularly suited to users without extensive musical background. See also Blom (G0390) and Thompson (G0460).

G0426 Jahn, Johannes, ed. <u>Wörterbuch der Kunst</u>. In Verbindung mit Robert Heidenreich und Wilhelm von Jenny verfasst von Johannes Jahn. 3. Aufl. Kröners Taschenausgabe, Bd. 165. Stuttgart: A. Kröner, 1950.

First published in 1940, this dictionary contains entries for both terms and biographies. There are some brief bibliographies and more than 200 illustrations. For readers of German this is an acceptable art dictionary. See also Alscher (G0382).

G0427 Julian, John, ed. <u>A Dictionary of Hymnology, Setting Forth the Origin and History of Christian Hymns of All Ages and Nations</u>. Rev. ed. With new supplement. London: John Murray, 1907. Reprint. 2 vols. New York: Dover Publications, 1957.

First published in 1892, the revised edition includes typographical corrections and a 131 page supplement containing later information. Julian consists of a dictionary, a cross reference index to first lines in various languages, an index of authors and translators, an appendix of additions and corrections to articles in the main dictionary sequence, a new supplement and indexes to the appendixes and supplement. While covering Christian hymns of all countries and periods, Julian places emphasis on the English speaking world. The articles cover hymnology, hymn writers and individual hymns; important subjects are treated in some detail, and there are numerous bibliographies. This is the standard reference work on hymnology for English language users and is being revised for the Hymn Society by L.H. Bunn. See also Fischer (G0417) and Porte (G0451).

G0428   Jung, Wolfgang. Liturgisches Wörterbuch. Edition Merseburger, 1132. Berlin: Verlag Merseburger, 1964.

Written from a German Protestant viewpoint and aimed particularly at that tradition, this dictionary seeks to define and explain a broad range of terms related to liturgy. Ranging in coverage from such words as "ordination" and "confirmation" to such specific festivals as "All Souls' Day", and including a number of specifically liturgical terms ("maranatha", "salutation"), Jung provides nontechnical information of value in a pastoral context. The treatment is somewhat discursive and lacks the sharpness of detail provided by Davies (G0408), but this work is of use to those interested in German liturgical views of the 1960s. For a German work on Roman Catholic liturgy see Berger (G0390).

G0429   Kirschbaum, Engelbert, ed. Lexikon der Christlichen Ikonographie. In Zusammenarbeit mit Günter Bandmann et al. 8 vols. Rome: Herder, 1968-1976.

Similar to other Roman Catholic works on Christian iconography, particularly Aurenhammer (G0386), this extremely detailed compilation provides signed articles, bibliographies and numerous illustrations on the full range of Christian iconography and symbolism. The first four volumes cover Allgemeine Ikonographie in alphabetical sequence with an addendum in volume 4. The remaining volumes cover Ikonographie der Heiligen, again in alphabetical sequence. The entries are impressively detailed, providing for readers of German an indispensible source of information. See also Künstle (G0840), Réau (G0850) and Schiller (G0857).

G0430   Konus, William J. Dictionary of the New Latin Psalter of Pope Pius XII. Westminster, Md.: Newman Press, 1959.

This brief dictionary provides definitions of words and proper names used in the Psalms, including references to their use. Proper names are cited in their Latin and Hebrew spellings in order to acquaint the reader with differences in the RSV and Douay versions of the Bible. This is a useful handbook for seminarians, priests and students. See also Britt (G0399).

G0431   Kornmüller, Utto. Lexikon der Kirchlichen Tonkunst. 2. Aufl. 2 vols. in 1. Regensburg: A. Coppenrath, 1891-1895.

This combined work consists of a dictionary of terms used in Roman Catholic church music together with a subject index in volume 1. The second volume contains a biographical dictionary of church musicians, both Catholic and non-Catholic. See also Porte (G0451) and Fischer (G0417); Weissenbäck (G0465) is less detailed but treats a wider range of material.

G0432   Lee, Frederick George. A Glossary of Liturgical and Ecclesiastical Terms. London: Bernard Quaritch, 1877. Reprint. Detroit, Mich.: Tower Books, 1971.

This work provides information on meanings and applications of about 6000 liturgical terms and other words bearing on the study of ritual. Both Latin and Eastern terms are included. There are many illustrations, and a bibliography is included. The glossary is intended for the general reader as well as for the specialist. See also Eckel (G0413).

G0433 Lercaro, Giacomo. A Small Liturgical Dictionary. Ed. by John Bertram O'Connell. Trans. by J.F. Harwood-Tregear. Collegeville, Minn.: Liturgical Press; London: Burns and Oates, 1959.

> Designed to assist those involved in the liturgical movement, this translation of the second Italian edition of Piccolo Dizionario Liturgico gives clear and accurate definitions of technical terms. Arrangement is alphabetical, and there are adequate cross references but no indexes or bibliographies. The dictionary itself is preceded by three sections on sacred liturgy, the mass and plan of the mass. See also Podhradsky (G0450).

G0434 Lesage, Robert, ed.-in-chief. Dictionnaire Pratique de Liturgie Romaine. [Paris]: Bonne Presse, [1952].

> See also Aigrain (G0381).

G0435   Leuchtmann, Horst, ed.-in-chief. Terminorum Musicae Index Septem Linguis Redactus/Polyglot Dictionary of Musical Terms: English, German, French, Italian, Spanish, Hungarian, Russian. Budapest: Akademiai Kiado, 1978.

> This multilingual dictionary lists words in a single alphabetical sequence, with equivalents provided in each of the other languages. The key word is presented in the language from which the term originated or in German; cross references are provided from terms in the other languages to the key word. This is a most useful compendium for those using foreign language musical works and requiring quick translations. A valuable appendix provides equivalents in all seven languages for terms of musical notation and for a large range of instruments. See also Smith (G0456) and Vannes (G0463).

G0436 Leuchtmann, Horst, ed. Wörterbuch Musik: Englisch-Deutsch, Deutsch-Englisch/Dictionary of Terms in Music: English-German, German-English. 2. Aufl. Munich: Verlag Dokumentation, 1977.

> First published in 1964, this dictionary of equivalent terms in English and German covers practical and theoretical music terms quite thoroughly, and attention is also paid to music psychology and sociology, areas not often treated in such dictionaries. For students of sacred music using German language materials this can be a helpful glossary for translating key terms into English. See also Smith (G0456).

G0437   Mayer, Ralph. A Dictionary of Art Terms and Techniques. New York: Thomas Y. Crowell Publishers, 1969.

> This collection of terms concentrates on those words encountered in the study and practice of the visual arts and in their literature. It includes descriptions of periods, schools and styles but excludes architectural terms and biographies. Basic definitions are presented in clear and concise language with some indication of the historical background of words and usage. This is a useful general dictionary for less advanced students. See also Murray and Murray (G0440).

G0438   Michel, François, ed.-in-chief. Encyclopédie de la Musique. En collaboration avec François Lesure et Vladimir Fédorov et un comité de rédaction composé de Nadia Boulanger et al. 3 vols. Paris: Fasqualle, 1958-1961.

The encyclopedia itself is preceded by more than 200 pages of general essays on music and a chronological table covering 999-1951 A.D. The entries include both brief biographies, definitions and longer articles on theory, significant events, movements and similar topics. However, Michel has been criticized for its uneven treatment and is less acceptable than Honegger (G0422) for this reason.

G0439 Mollett, John William. An Illustrated Dictionary of Art and Archaeology, Including Terms Used in Architecture, Jewelry, Heraldry, Costume, Music, Ornament, Weaving, Furniture, Pottery, Ecclesiastical Ritual. New York: American Archives of World Art, 1966.

First published in 1883 as An Illustrated Dictionary of Words Used in Art and Archaeology, this work contains some 700 engravings and provides helpful definitions of a wide range of terms. Most useful from a liturgical viewpoint are the terms from architecture, costume and ritual. Clearly dated, Mollett is a sound guide for standard definitions of terms where an historical framework is required. See also Adeline (G0380).

G0440 Murray, Peter, and Murray, Linda. A Dictionary of Art and Artists. London: Thames and Hudson, 1965; New York: Praeger Publishers, 1966.

Published in an earlier version with the same title by Penguin Books, this 464 page edition contains three main sections: dictionary of art and artists (1389 entries), major techniques in color (1250 monochrome and color plates arranged chronologically), classified alphabetical bibliographies (nearly 4000 entries, some of which are annotated). There are biographical entries for more than 1000 artists and definitions of a wide range of technical terms, processes and movements. For theological and liturgical needs the biographical and bibliographical notes are the most useful parts of Murray. See also Osborne (G0446).

G0441 Myers, Bernard Samuel, ed. Encyclopedia of Painting: Painters and Painting of the World from Prehistoric Times to the Present Day. 3rd ed. New York: Crown Publishers, 1970.

First published in 1955, this encyclopedia of more than 3000 entries treats artists, movements, styles, techniques and terms from ancient times to the present and includes many illustrations. The arrangement of entries is alphabetical, except in the case of the Orient, where material is organized by countries and periods. This is a suitable encyclopedic dictionary for standard queries of a fairly general nature. For a similar two volume treatment see Gaunt (G0418).

G0442 Myers, Bernard Samuel, ed. McGraw-Hill Dictionary of Art. Assistant ed.: Shirley D. Myers. 5 vols. New York: McGraw-Hill Book Company, 1969.

This detailed encyclopedic work contains more than 15,000 long articles on the lives and careers of artists, artistic styles, periods, buildings and art terms. Bibliographies are included in the articles, and the lack of an index is made less of a problem by the use of numerous cross references. Special attention is paid to Eastern art and to descriptions of important artistic sights in major cities. This is a useful alternative to the Encyclopedia of World Art (G0416) and contains information of relevance to religious or ecclesiastical art. See also Bell (G0388) and Harper's Encyclopedia of Art (G0420).

G0443   Nitschke, Horst. Wörterbuch des Gottesdienstlichen Lebens, Liturgie, Christliche Kunst, Kirchenmusik. Evangelische Enzyklopädie, Bd. 10. Gütersloh: Gütersloher Verlagshaus, 1966.

See also Ortique (G0445).

G0444   Nulman, Mary. Concise Encyclopedia of Jewish Music. New York: McGraw-Hill Book Company, 1975.

This dictionary contains 500 entries on all aspects of Jewish music, including biographies of composers and discussion of their works. The text is clearly written and concise, and is accompanied by 150 illustrations.

G0445   Ortigue, Joseph Louis d'. Dictionnaire Liturgique, Historique et Théoretique de Plainchant et de Musique d'Eglise au Moyen Age et dans les Temps Modernes. Paris: J.-P. Migne, 1853. Reprint. Da Capo Press Music Reprint Series. New York: Da Capo Press, 1971.

See also Nitschke (G0443).

G0446   Osborne, Harald, ed. The Oxford Companion to Art. Oxford: Clarendon Press, 1970.

Designed as a nonspecialist introduction to the fine arts, this dictionary is arranged alphabetically and provides information ranging from brief entries of several lines to short articles on, for example, biography, history and a few technical matters such as perspective and graphic processes. There are cross references, a selective bibliography of over 3000 titles for the general reader, and bibliographical references appended to individual articles for those who require more specialized information. The articles were prepared by specialists. Some illustrations and figures are included.   See also Gaunt (G0418), Murray and Murray (G0440) and Myers (G0441).

G0447   Peusner, Nikolaus; Fleming, John; and Honour, Hugh. A Dictionary of Architecture. Rev. ed. London: Allen Lane, 1975.

First published in 1966 and edited in a second edition by John Fleming and others (The Penguin Dictionary of Architecture, Harmondsworth: Penguin Books, 1972), this standard dictionary of architectural terms includes about 2800 entries on all periods and regions. The definitions are clear and concise and provide some biographical data on leading architects. For students unfamiliar with the field this is an extremely useful dictionary. See also Briggs (G0397) and Saylor (G0454).

G0448   Pfeiffer, Harold A. The Catholic Picture Dictionary. New York: Duell, Sloan and Pearce, 1948.

This 156 page guide contains illustrations of church furnishings, vestments, ceremonies and related subjects as well as identifications of some major works of religious art. Pfeiffer is most useful for its treatment of traditional Roman Catholic liturgical vesture and furniture.

G0449   Picerno, Vincent J. Dictionary of Musical Terms. Studies in Music, no. 42. Brooklyn, N.Y.: Haskell House, 1976.

Geared to the requirements of students and general readers without specialist knowledge, Picerno treats terms from all forms of music in clear language. The definitions are brief but reasonably thorough for basic reference needs, and an annotated bibliography is provided for further information (pp. 407-453). See also Ammer (G0383).

G0450 Podhradsky, Gerhard. New Dictionary of the Liturgy. Trans. by Ronald Walls and Michael Barry. Ed. by Lancelot Sheppard. Staten Island, N.Y.: Alba House; London: Geoffrey Chapman, 1967.

This translation of Lexikon der Liturgie (Innsbruck: Tyrolia Verlag, 1962) provides brief and succinct articles on the Roman Catholic liturgy in light of Vatican II changes. Included are useful notes on the historical and theological background of terms, as well as illustrations and a general bibliography. Podhradsky should be consulted by those interested in liturgical developments within the Roman Catholic tradition, and is a valuable bridge between traditional liturgical guides and those compiled to reflect recent changes. A second edition of the German work appeared in 1967. See also Lercaro (G0433).

G0451   Porte, Jacques, ed.-in-chief. Encyclopédie des Musiques Sacrées. 3 vols. Paris: Editions Lagergerie, 1968-1970.

Volume 1 treats the Far East, the Mediterranean, Africa and America; the remaining volumes discuss Christian traditions from their beginnings to Vatican II. In the volumes devoted to Christian music treatment of the subject is generally by country. Porte is extremely well documented and contains a wealth of information with some bias towards a French Roman Catholic viewpoint. In some places the discussion is quite uneven, and there is no index (a detailed table of contents provides some assistance). A fourth "volume" consists of eight recordings providing samples of sacred music. For Protestant church music see Davidson (G0407); for Roman Catholic church music see Kornmüller (G0431) and Weissenbäck (G0465).

G0452   Russo-Alesi, Anthony Ignatius. Martyrology Pronouncing Dictionary; It Contains the Pronunciation of Over 5000 Names of Martyrs, Confessors, Virgins, Emperors, Cities and Places Occurring in the Roman Martyrology with a Daily Calendar and a List of the Patron Saints. New York: Edward O'Toole Company, 1939.

The subtitle fails to add that authorities for pronunciations are cited and that the many appendixes include one which arranges the American martyrology on a state-by-state basis. The pronunciations are clear but sometimes too Americanized for other users.

G0453 Sadie, Stanley, ed. The New Grove Dictionary of Music and Musicians. 20 vols. London: Macmillan and Company, 1981.

For many years the standard English language music encyclopedia, the new edition contains 22,500 entries and more than 4500 illustrations treating the entire field from 1450 to the present. Coverage includes musical history, practice, theory, terms, biographies, songs and operas. Arranged alphabetically with numerous cross references, the lucid and detailed articles by experts are signed and contain bibliographies. This latest edition is largely rewritten and includes numerous new articles, making it the most complete and up-to-date encyclopedia in its field.

For inquiries of both a general and a scholarly nature this is an indispensible reference tool. See also Blume (G0394).

G0454   Saylor, Henry Hodgman. Dictionary of Architecture. New York: John Wiley and Sons, 1952.

This dictionary of architectural terms indicates pronunciation and gives brief definitions. It represents an American viewpoint. See also Peusner (G0447) and Briggs (G0397).

G0455   Seyn, Eugène de. Dictionnaire des Attributs, Allégories, Emblèmes et Symboles. Turnhout: Brepols, 1948.

Published under the pseudonym of "Eugène Droulers", this alphabetically arranged dictionary includes the names of people, attributes, allegorical figures, symbols and related information. Definitions vary greatly in length but are clear and adequate. There are many illustrations, which are indexed; a bibliography of sources is also provided. See also Bernen (G0291) and Daniel (G0406) for English language counterparts; see also Chevalier and Gheerbrant (G0404).

G0456   Smith, William James. A Dictionary of Musical Terms in Four Languages. London: Hutchinson, 1961.

With entries under the English form, this glossary provides comparable terms in French, Italian and German. There are no language indexes. Entries are arranged systematically in twelve sections, including instruments, choral music, conducting, form, etc. Phonetic pronunciation is provided for the terms in all four languages. While Smith ignores certain important areas, this can be a useful aid for students using foreign language works on music. See also Leuchtmann (G0435).

G0457   Stubbings, George Wilfred. A Dictionary of Church Music. London: Epworth Press, 1949; New York: Philosophical Library, 1950.

Replaced in part by Davidson (G0407), this dictionary covers Anglican, Nonconformist and Roman Catholic music and musical practice. It provides information on forms of church music, parts of church services which require musical treatment and methods of performance.

G0458   Tatlock, Richard. A Prayer Book Dictionary: An Explanation, with Examples, of Obsolete, Unusual and Ambiguous Words Commonly Used in the "Book of Common Prayer" of 1662. London: A.R. Mowbray and Company, 1960.

See also Harford and Stevenson (G0419).

G0459   Thieme, Ulrich, and Becker, Felix. Allgemeines Lexicon der Bildenden Künstler von der Antike bis zur Gegenwart. 37 vols. Leipzig: E.A. Seemann, 1907-1950. Reprint. Zeickau: F. Ullmann, 1963-1964.

Containing between 40,000 and 50,000 entries, this work is the most comprehensive dictionary in existence of painters; it also includes engravers and some architects and sculptors. Bibliographies appended to articles are a particularly notable feature, as they include an extensive collection of monographs and articles. The entries are long, comprehensive and detailed, providing an excellent source of information on artists of all periods for those able to read German. See also Alscher (G0382) and Encyclopedia of World Art (G0416).

G0460   Thompson, Oscar, ed.-in-chief. The International Cyclopedia of Music and Musicians. 10th ed. Ed. by Bruce Bohle. New York: Dodd Mead; London: J.M. Dent, 1975.

First published in 1939 as The Cyclopedia of Music and Musicians, this is the largest and most comprehensive single volume dictionary of music in English. Coverage extends to individuals, concepts, types of music, history, criticism and related fields. Many articles are lengthy and detailed, including bibliographical notes and cross references. For thorough information on a wide range of topics this remains a key reference work, particularly useful for its biographical coverage which includes a calendar of each composer's life and a classified list of his works after each article. See also Apel (G0384) and Jacobs (G0425).

G0461   Thomson, Ronald William. Who's Who of Hymn Writers. London: Epworth Press, 1967.

This guide contains concise biographical sketches of 277 British European and American hymn writers.

G0462   Urech, Edouard. Dictionnaire des Symboles Chrétiens. Neuchâtel: Delachaux et Niestlé, 1972.

See also Dictionnaire du Symbolisme (G0411).

G0463   Vannes, René. Essai de Terminologie Musicale: Dictionnaire Universel Comprenant Plus de 15,000 Termes de Musique en Italien, Espagnol, Portugais, Français, Anglais, Allemand, Latin et Grec, Disposés en un Alphabet Unique. Thann: Société d'Editions Alsatia, 1925.

This useful glossary arranges terms in a single alphabetical sequence according to the original language of words. Brief definitions and equivalents in the other languages are provided for each term, making Vannes a useful glossary for those using foreign language works. See also Leuchtmann (G0435).

G0464   Vries, Ad de. Dictionary of Symbols and Imagery. 2nd ed. Amsterdam: North-Holland Publishing Company, 1976.

With emphasis on literary, mythological, religious and proverbial use, this dictionary covers allegories, metaphors, signs and images in an attempt to supply associations which have been evoked in the past. The definitions are succinct and indicative rather than exhaustive, and examples are drawn from a wide range of sources with religious significance. De Vries covers some material not included in Sills (G0859) and similar guides limited to the Christian framework. See also Appleton (G0385) and Cirlot (G0405).

G0465   Weissenbäck, Andreas. Sacra Musica: Lexikon in der Katholischen Kirchenmusik. Klosterneuburg-bei-Wien: Verlag der Augustinusdruckerei, 1937.

This dictionary of Roman Catholic music includes both brief biographical sketches and definitions of technical terms in a single alphabetical sequence. Music organizations and publishers are also covered. The articles are briefer than those in Kornmüller (G0431) but cover a wider range of subjects and include bibliographies.

G0466   Wessel, Klaus, ed. Reallexikon zur Byzantinischen Kunst. Unter Mitwirkung von Marcell Restle. Vol. 1- . Stuttgart: Anton Hiersemann, 1963- .

Projected in five volumes, this encyclopedic work of some 600 lengthy articles covers all countries of the Eastern Roman Empire, including Constantinople, Armenia, Georgia, Bulgaria and Serbia. There is an index of names and concepts for the entire work in the final volume. Unfortunately, the excessive length of most articles detracts from their value for rapid reference purposes, but the material thus presented is extremely detailed beneath the analytical gloss. For a bibliography of Byzantine art see Allen (G0249).

LITURGY AND WORSHIP: HANDBOOKS

G0467   Alexander, Charles. The Church's Year. London: Oxford University Press, 1950.

Intended to provide information, especially to young people, about the festivals and saints commemorated by the Church of England, this book is arranged chronologicaly by festival or saint's day, beginning with Advent. A detailed table of contents and an index of persons and festivals make use of the work easy. Emphasis is given to British saints. See also Gwynne (G0597).

G0468   Allen, Horace T. A Handbook for the Lectionary. Philadelphia, Pa.: Geneva Press, 1980.

Based on the Reformed tradition, this compendium provides several biblical readings for each Sunday of the year in a triennial cycle. Brief notations are provided to help identify the nature of each passage, and Allen also adds a collect, a Psalm, hymn and anthem suggestions for each Sunday. Although primarily aimed at Protestant churches outside the liturgical tradition, some of the suggestions are useful for those within the latter group as well.

G0469   Allmen, Jean Jacques von. Worship, Its Theology and Practice. New York: Oxford University Press, 1965.

This stimulating work begins with the broad outlines of a theology of worship, written from a pastoral viewpoint for the nonspecialist. The second part deals with problems of celebration of the liturgy: elements of worship, participants, day and place of celebration and structure of worship. Written by a conservative Reformed Church theologian, this is a thorough and original study. Only a short bibliography is provided, and there is no index, although there is a full table of contents. See also Segler (G0742).

G0470   Altar Manual, Compiled from Approved Sources. Rev. ed. New York:

P.J. Kenedy, 1953.

This 32 page work provides a collection of Roman Catholic altar prayers. See also the following entry (G0471).

G0471   Altar Prayers (Enchiridion Precum): The Most Frequently Used Public Prayers and Devotions, Both Those Prescribed for Liturgical Services and Those in General Use As Well As Others Suitable for Various Occasions throughout the Ecclesiastical Year. Rev. in accordance with the Enchiridion Indulgentiarum, 1950 ed. (The Raccolta). New York: Benziger Brothers, 1962.

See also the preceding entry (G0470) and Catholic Church (G0515).

G0472   American Lutheran Church. Commission on Worship and Church Art. The Minister's Manual of the American Lutheran Church. Columbus, Ohio: Lutheran Book Concern, 1940.

See also Lutheran Church in America (G0648).

G0473   Atkinson, Clifford W. Study Guide for the Daily Office, Proposed Book of Common Prayer. Wilton, Conn.: Morehouse-Barlow Company, 1977.

This study guide for the Proposed Book of Common Prayer (G0574) of the Episcopal Church is intended for laymen and parish study groups. The major part of the work reproduces the relevant Proposed Book sections but omits compline and the evening order. The scholarly gloss is minimal and rudimentary, making this a far less satisfactory tool than Miller's complementary work (G0667).

G0474   Auld, William Muir. Christmas Traditions. New York: Macmillan, 1931. Reprint. Detroit, Mich.: Gale Research Company, 1968.

This survey of the origins, antecedents, changes and developments of Christmas traditions through history includes aspects such as paganism, carols and colors. An analytical table of contents is provided, and footnotes are included. See also Crippen (G0545), Dawson (G0556) and Hendricks and Vogel (G0603).

G0475   Babin, David E. Introduction to the Liturgy of the Lord's Supper. New York: Morehouse-Barlow Company, 1968.

See also Brilioth (G0492).

G0476   Bailey, James Martin, and Bailey, Betty Jane. Worship with Youth. Philadelphia, Pa.: Christian Education Press, 1962.

The first part of this work contains fourteen short chapters on aspects of worship with young people such as planning, atmosphere, music, the Bible, audiovisuals and the church year. These are designed to facilitate understanding of the nature of worship and ways in which effective worship services can be developed. The second part contains resources for use in worship, arranged according to the elements of the service or according to subject matter. This is a useful book, based on the authors' own experience with youth. See also Bays and Oakberg (G0479) and Couch (G0544).

G0477   Batiffol, Pierre. History of the Roman Breviary. Trans. by Atwell

M.Y. Bayley from the 3rd French ed. With a new chapter on the decree of Pius X. London: Longmans, Green and Company, 1912.

This translation of Histoire du Bréviaire Romain (3e éd. Paris: A. Picard, 1911) is a reasonably detailed and scholarly account of the development of the breviary to 1911. It provides a sound overview of the topic and is a useful reference volume with its bibliographical notes, appendixes and index. See also Catholic Church (G0518) and Parsch (G0703).

G0478   Baumstark, Anton. Comparative Liturgy. Rev. by Bernard Botte. Eng. ed. by F.L. Cross. Westminster, Md.: Newman Press; London: A.R. Mowbray, 1958.

Originally issued as a series of lectures on the history of the liturgy from a comparative point of view, this work has become a handbook of the history of the liturgy. It is well documented and an extensive bibliographical appendix covers original texts, translations of liturgical books and the Eastern and Western rites of the church. The English edition is a translation of Liturgie Comparée: Principes et Méthodes pour l'Etude Historique des Liturgies Chrétiennes (3e éd. Rev. by Bernard Botte. Collection Irenikon. Chevetogne: Editions de Chevetogne, 1953). See also Garrett (G0588) and Thompson (G0770).

G0479   Bays, Alice Anderson, and Oakberg, Elizabeth Jones. Worship Programs for Juniors. New York: Abingdon Press, 1960.

This collection of services is suggested as a basis for leading boys and girls in worship. A brief section containing suggestions for teachers and leaders is followed by six series of services, some drawing on the work of people such as Albert Schweitzer. Notes, sources for hymns, a selected bibliography and an index of stories and subjects complete the volume. See also Bailey (G0476) and Couch (G0544).

G0480   Benoît, Jean Daniel. Initiation à la Liturgie de l'Eglise Réformée de France. Paris: Editions Berger-Levrault, 1956.

See also Eglise Réformée de France (G0565).

G0481   Benoît, Jean Daniel. Liturgical Renewal: Studies in Catholic and Protestant Developments on the Continent. Trans. by Edwin Hudson. Studies in Ministry and Worship. London: SCM Press, 1958.

This collection represents a significant entry of French Protestant liturgiology into English studies. After an initial section on the sacrament of the eucharist, the two main sections examine recent developments in the French-speaking Reformed Churches and in the Roman Catholic Church, providing valuable comparative material. The brief work does not include an index. See also Sheppard (G0752) and White (G0796).

G0482   Bernard, Charles André. La Prière Chrétienne: Etude Théologique. Essais pour Notre Temps. Section de Théologie, no. 3. Paris: Desclée de Brouwer, 1967.

See also Ferré (G0578).

G0483   Bjerring, Nicholas, ed. The Offices of the Oriental Church, with an Historical Introduction. New York: A.D.F. Randolph and Company, [c.1884]. Reprint. New York: AMS Press, [1969].

See also Littledale (G0643).

G0484   Blunt, John Henry, ed. The Annotated Book of Common Prayer; Being an Historical, Ritual and Theological Commentary on the Devotional System of the Church of England; with an Introductory Notice on the American Book of Common Prayer by the Reverend Frederick Gibson. Rev. ed. New York: E.P. Dutton and Company, 1884.   Reprint. New York: E.P. Dutton and Company, 1903.

This very thorough handbook consists of introductions, commentaries and texts for all services in The Book of Common Prayer. The introductions and notes cover all aspects of the various acts of worship and provide excellent historical, theological and liturgical summaries for students of Anglican worship. A helpful index and glossary conclude the collection. While some of the contributions are now rather dated, they continue to provide sound information in summary form. See also Church of England (G0528), Episcopal Church (G0571) and Waddams (G0782).

G0485   The Book of Easter. New York: Macmillan Company, 1910. Reprint. Detroit, Mich.: Singing Tree Press, 1971.

Covering Good Friday, Easter and Ascension, this collection of useful sources includes poems, stories, hymns, essays and similar material, together with reproductions of paintings. There are also historical accounts and descriptions of customs and legends connected with people and events of the paschal season. This is a valuable compendium which contains many useful ideas for Eastertide worship. See also Wallis (G0785).

G0486   Bouyer, Marie Dominique. Table Prayer. Trans. and adapted by Anselm Jaskolka. New York: Herder and Herder, 1967.

This work contains more than 150 short prayers for various feasts and liturgical seasons, beginning with Advent. It is based on Le Livre de la Table (Paris: Les Editions du Cerf, 1966). A guide to using the book and the table of contents provide adequate information in the absence of an index. This provides a useful Roman Catholic collection of prayers for the particular purpose treated.

G0487   Bowman, Clarice Margurette. Resources for Worship. New York: Association Press, 1961.

See also McElroy (G0652), Wallis (G0788) and Weems (G0791).

G0488   Boyer, Thomas. More Parish Liturgies: Experiments and Resources in Sunday Worship. New York: Paulist Press, 1973.

Based on the experiences of a community of young people, this volume contains material for the Sundays and festivals of the church year, beginning with Advent. A list of selected sources (5pp.) and an index of themes, festivals and special occasions are included. The order of celebration is set out at the beginning of the resource book. See also Bailey (G0476).

G0489   Boyer, Thomas. Parish Liturgies: Experiments and Resources in Sunday Worship. New York: Paulist Press, 1973.

See also Colquhoun (G0541).

G0490   Bradshaw, Paul F. The Anglican Ordinal: Its History and Development from the Reformation to the Present Day. Alcuin Club Collections, no. 53. London: SPCK, 1971.

This work describes the various rites used and proposed for use in the Anglican communion, as well as reasons for and sources of changes made and objections raised to changes. It is liturgical rather than doctrinal. Historical analyses of Puritans and the Ordinal and of Roman Catholics and the Ordinal, discussion of Thomas Cranmer's influence on and understanding of the Ordinal, and of Ordinals and rites of unification in reunion schemes are included. A bibliography and index are provided. See also Church of England (G0530, G0532).

G0491   Brightman, F.E. The English Rite: Being a Synopsis of the Sources and Revisions of the Book of Common Prayer. 2 vols. London: Rivingtons, 1915. Reprint. Ann Arbor, Mich.: University Microfilms, 1966.

See Episcopal Church (G0571); see also Chappell (G0903), Cuming (G0547), Frere (G0585) and Waddams (G0782).

G0492   Brilioth, Yngve Torgny. Eucharistic Faith and Practice: Evangelical and Catholic. Trans. by A.G. Hebert. New York: Macmillan Company; London: SPCK, 1930. Reprint. London: SPCK, 1965.

This revised and shortened translation of the Swedish original published in 1926 provides a comprehensive picture of the diverse types of eucharistic belief and practice. Starting with the NT, ideas are traced down through the early Fathers and to modern times. Separate chapters are devoted to the Lutheran and Reformed traditions, the Anglican and Swedish churches. Indexes of names and subjects are provided. See also Babin (G0475) and Lietzmann (G0642).

G0493   Broderick, Robert Carlton. The Catholic Layman's Book of Etiquette. St. Paul, Minn.: Catechetical Guild Educational Society, [1957].

Despite its unfortunate title, this 240 page introduction provides useful (but dated) information on liturgical practices, customs, social and legal matters of the Roman Catholic Church in America. See also Fenner (G0577).

G0494   Burgess, Stephen W., and Righter, James D. Celebrations for Today: Acts of Worship in Modern English Language. Nashville, Tenn.: Abingdon Press, 1977.

See also Cairns (G0500) and Randolph (G0719).

G0495   Cabrol, Fernand. The Books of the Latin Liturgy. Trans. by a Benedictine of Stanbrook Abbey. Catholic Library of Religious Knowledge, vol. 22. St. Louis, Mo.: B. Herder Book Company; London: Sands and Company, 1932.

This classic work provides a thorough treatment of the history and contents of the official Roman Catholic books used in the Latin rite together with some coverage of various extra-liturgical books. Each chapter contains a bibliography in addition to the general bibliography. This is an excellent guide for scholars and students of worship and its theological aspects. See also Catholic Church (G0503-G0523).

G0496   Cabrol, Fernand. Introduction aux Etudes Liturgiques. 2e éd. Paris: Bloud et Compagnie, 1907.

See also Jones (G0621), Mistrorigo (G0668) and Srawley (G0764).

G0497   Cabrol, Fernand, comp. Liturgical Prayer Book: Mass, Vespers, Ritual, and Principal Catholic Devotions. New York: P.J. Kenedy and Sons, 1925(?).

See also the following entry (G0498) and Nevins (G0679).

G0498   Cabrol, Fernand. Liturgical Prayer, Its History and Spirit. Trans. by a Benedictine of Stanbrook Abbey. Westminster, Md.: Newman Press, 1950.

This translation of Le Livre de la Prière Antique (3e ed. Paris: H. Oudin, 1903) offers a study of Roman Catholic prayer in its different aspects, from forms of prayer used in antiquity through various prayers of Christians (the creeds, etc.) to sanctification prayers and occasional prayers. The work is designed to enable the reader to understand the books containing the liturgy and to take an intelligent interest in the ceremonies of the church. An index is provided. This is a somewhat dated Roman Catholic approach to the subject. See also Martimort (G0659).

G0499   Cabrol, Fernand. The Year's Liturgy: The Sundays, Feriae and Feasts of the Liturgical Year. 2 vols. London: Burns, Oates and Washbourne, 1938-1940.

See also Guéranger (G0595) and Gwynne (G0597).

G0500   Cairns, David, et al., comps. Worship Now: A Collection of Services and Prayers for Public Worship. Edinburgh: St. Andrews Press, 1972. Reprint. Edinburgh: St. Andrews Press, 1976.

This 222 page collection presents contemporary material for worship in the Protestant tradition. It contains eleven suggestions for morning services, eighteen for sacraments and ordinances, eight new forms of worship, seventeen outlines for events in the Christian year and occasional services and a final anthology of twenty-one prayers and introductory sentences. See also Burgess (G0494) and Randolph (G0719).

G0501   Catherine Frederic. The Handbook of Catholic Practices. New York: Hawthorn Books, 1964.

See also Lang (G0634) and Müller (G0671).

G0502   Catholic Church. The Book of Catholic Worship. Washington, D.C.: Liturgical Conference, 1966.

Prepared by an editorial board including pastors, liturgists, musicians and Scripture scholars, this handbook covers masses of the temporal and sanctoral cycles, the hymnal, the psalter, the sacraments and parish services and prayers. There is a general index, as well as indexes of hymns and antiphons and of psalms and canticles. The hymnal includes selections from a number of Protestant and Catholic collections, as well as several previously unpublished hymns and antiphons. See also Müller (G0671) and Stehle (G0765).

G0503 Catholic Church. Breviarium Romanum, ex Decreto Sacrosancti Concilii Tridentini, Restitutum S. Pii V Pontificis Maximi, Jussu Editum, Aliorumque Pontificum Cura, Recognitum Pii Papae X, Auctoritate Reformatum cum Nova Psalterii Versione Pii Papae XII, Jussu Edita. 4 vols. Paris: Desclée, 1950.

Issued in unnumbered volumes covering the four seasons, this is the standard Latin breviary of the Roman rite and should be regarded as the authoritative reference work in studies of the Roman breviary. See also the English translation, The Roman Breviary (G0518).

G0504 Catholic Church. Collectio Rituum, pro Diocesibus Civitatum Foederatarum Americae Septentrionalis. Ritual approved by the National Conference of Bishops of the United States of America. Prepared under the guidance of Walter J. Schmitz. Milwaukee, Wisc.: Bruce Publishing Company, 1964.

Less complete than the full set edited by Weller (G0793), this collection does contain some of the newer rites together with an official English language text. An index is included.

G0505 Catholic Church. English-Latin Roman Missal for the United States of America. New York: Benziger Brothers, 1966.

This translation of Missale Romanum, ex Decreto Sacrosancti Concilii Tridentini Restitutum (New York: Benziger Brother, 1963) contains the text of the mass exactly as it existed from the Council of Trent to Vatican II together with an English translation. As a bilingual edition this is a valuable reference tool for students of the Roman liturgy who are not conversant with Latin. See also Catholic Church (G0520) and Griffith (G0593).

G0506 Catholic Church. The English-Latin Sacramentary for the United States of America: The Prayers of the Celebrant of Mass Together with the Ordinary of the Mass. New York: Catholic Book Publishing Company, 1966.

See also Catholic Church (G0512).

G0507 Catholic Church. Lectionary for Mass for Sundays of Year A, Arranged for Readers: English Translation Approved by the National Conference of Catholic Bishops and Confirmed by the Apostolic See. New York: Pueblo Publishing Company, 1974.

This and the following two entries (G0508, G0509) contain the epistles and gospels read at mass in a three year cycle in the revised Roman Catholic liturgy. Also included are Psalms used between the readings. For related liturgical prayers see The Sacramentary (G0523); see also Sloyan (G0758).

G0508 Catholic Church. Lectionary for Mass for Sundays of Year B, Arranged for Readers: English Translation Approved by the National Conference of Catholic Bishops and Confirmed by the Apostolic See. New York: Pueblo

Publishing Company, 1972.

See also the preceding and following entries (G0507, G0509) and Sloyan (G0758).

G0509 Catholic Church. Lectionary for Mass for Sundays of Year C, Arranged for Readers: English Translation Approved by the National Conference of Catholic Bishops and Confirmed by the Apostolic See. New York: Pueblo Publishing Company, 1973.

See also the preceding entries (G0507, G0508) and Sloyan (G0758).

G0510   Catholic Church. Liturgy of the Hours: Approved by the Episcopal Conferences of the Antilles, Bangladesh, Burma, Canada, of the Pacific (CEPAC), Ghana, India, New Zealand, Pakistan, Papua New Guinea and the Solomons, The Philippines, Rhodesia, South Africa, Sri Lanka, Tanzania, Uganda and the United States of America for Use in Their Dioceses and Confirmed by the Apostolic See; with Proper for the United States. English translation prepared by the International Committee on English in the Liturgy. 4 vols. New York: Catholic Book Publishing Company, 1975-1976.

Also published as The Prayer of Christians, this English translation of the office is based on reforms decreed by Vatican II and is published by papal authority. It is an authoritative version based on the Vatican Typical Edition and should be used whenever the definitive English text of the office is required. See also Mossi (G0670) and O'Shea (G0700).

G0511   Catholic Church. Martyrologium Romanum Gregorii Papae XIII Jussu Editum, Urbani VIII et Clementis X Auctoritatae Recognitum, Ac Deinde Anno MDCCXLIX Benedicti XIV Opera ac Studio Emendatum et Actum. Quarta Post Typicam Editio Iuxta Primam a Typica Editionem Anno MDCCCC-XXII a Benedicto XV Adprobatam. Rome: Typis Polyglotti Vaticanis, 1956.

This official version of the Roman Catholic martyrology for use in the liturgy is also an excellent reference volume, containing more than 200 pages of indexing by name, place, category and other forms. For an English translation see O'Connell (G0698); see also Delehaye (G0560).

G0512   Catholic Church. Ordo for the Celebration of the Divine Office and the Mass in the Dioceses of the United States. Vol. 1- . Quincy, Ill.: Sunday Missal Service, 1977- .

Covering both national and diocesan services, this detailed collection provides names and ranks of observances, liturgical colors, special prayers and information on special types of services. For both pastoral and general reference purposes this is a most valuable guide to current American Catholic liturgical practice. See also the Roman Calendar (G0519) and Catholic Church (G0506).

G0513   Catholic Church. Pontificale Romanum. Editio typica emendata. 3 vols. Vatican City: Typis Polyglottis Vaticanis, 1962-1963.

This is a typical edition of the complete pontifical with the texts of ceremonies together with directions for their performance. Each volume is thoroughly indexed, providing easy access to information for students of Roman Catholic worship. See also Collectio Rituum (G0504) and The

Roman Ritual (G0793). For an encyclopedic commentary see Puniet (G0714).

G0514   Catholic Church. The Prayer of the Church: Interim Version of the New Roman Breviary. 5 vols. and 5 supplements. London: Geoffrey Chapman, 1970.

Prepared as an alternative to The Roman Breviary (G0518) until a definitive translation of the editio typica is ready and approved, this interim version is based on material prepared by the Congregation for Divine Worship for the New Roman Breviary. It reflects the post-Vatican II desire for reform. The main sections are: frequently used psalms, prayers and canticles; weekly prayer; night prayer; readings; common offices. Suggestions for hymns are included, and there are indexes of psalms and of canticles. See also The Hours of the Divine Office (G0608).

G0515   Catholic Church. The Raccolta; or, a Manual of Indulgences, Prayers and Devotions Enriched with Indulgences in Favor of All the Faithful in Church or Certain Groups of Persons, and Now Opportunely Revised, Edited and in Part Newly Translated into English from the 1950 Official Edition, "Enchiridion Indulgentiarum: Preces et Pia Opera" Issued by the Sacred Penitentiary Apostolic. Trans. and ed. by Joseph P. Christopher, Charles E. Spence and John F. Rowan by authorization of the Holy See. New York: Benziger Brothers, 1952.

Containing texts in both English and Latin together with a detailed index, this translation of Enchiridion Indulgentiarum (Vatican City: Typis Polyglottis Vaticanis, 1950) is a useful source book for prayers approved for use in the Roman Catholic Church. See also Nevins (G0679).

G0516   Catholic Church. The Rites of the Catholic Church, As Revised by Decree of the Second Vatican Ecumenical Council and Published by Authority of Pope Paul VI. English trans. prepared by the International Committee on English in the Liturgy. New York: Pueblo Publishing Company, c. 1978.

This compendium contains the revised rites for ceremonies performed by priests in the Roman Catholic Church with emphasis not on prayers and blessings but on ceremonies associated with the sacraments. The items have been selected from the Rituale Romanum (G0517) and Pontificale Romanum (G0513). See also the Roman Pontifical (G0521).

G0517   Catholic Church. Rituale Romanum Pauli V Pontificis Maximi Iussu Editum, Aliorumque Pontificum Cura Recognitum, atque Auctoritate Pii Papae XI ad Normam Codicis Iuris Canonici Accommodatum. Editio Iuxta Typicam Vaticanam. New York: Benziger Brothers, 1944.

This complete Latin text is now of largely scholarly value. For an English translation see Weller (G0793); for selections see Griffith (G0593).

G0518   Catholic Church. The Roman Breviary Restored by the Sacred Council of Trent; Published by Order of S. Pius V, Supreme Pontiff; and Carefully Revised by Other Popes; Reformed by Order of Pope Pius X. An English version compiled by the Benedictine Nuns of the Abbey of Our Lady of Consolation at Stanbrook in Worcestershire. Rev. and ed. by Charles Francis Brown. 4 vols. London: Burns, Oates and Washbourne, 1936-1937.

See also The Hours of the Divine Office (G0608) and Nelson (G0678);

for a history of the breviary see Batiffol (G0477).

G0519   Catholic Church. Roman Calendar: Text and Commentary. Trans. by the International Committee on English in the Liturgy. Washington, D.C.: United States Catholic Conference, 1975.

This translation of the Calendarium Romanum is a revision of the tradition-al liturgical year and lists all feasts in the calendar. Appendixes list saints in the new calendar and those which have been dropped together with reasons for this. The work is thoroughly indexed. See also Catholic Church (G0512).

G0520   Catholic Church. The Roman Missal in Latin and English for Every Day in the Year, in Conformity with the Latest Decrees. 9th ed. Tours: A. Mame and Sons, 1936.

See also Catholic Church (G050), Griffith (G0593) and Schuster (G0739).

G0521   Catholic Church. Roman Pontifical Revised by Decree of the Second Vatican Ecumenical Council and Published by Authority of Pope Paul VI. Vol. 1- . Washington, D.C.: International Committee on English in the Liturgy, 1978- .

Focusing on ceremonies performed by bishops in the Roman Catholic Church, this collection of revised rites covers confirmation, holy orders, religious vows and monastic vows. See also The Rites of the Catholic Church (G0516).

G0522 [no entry]

G0523   Catholic Church. The Sacramentary: Approved for Use in the Dioceses of the United States of America by the National Conference of Catholic Bishops and Confirmed by the Apostolic See. New York: Catholic Book Publish-ing Company, 1974.

Based on the translation prepared by the International Committee on English in the Liturgy, The Sacramentary contains both liturgical prayers and common parts of the mass as revised for use in the American Catholic Church. See also the Lectionary cycle (G0507-G0509) and Mossi (G0669).

G0524   Christensen, James L. The Complete Funeral Manual. Westwood, N.J.: Fleming H. Revell Company, 1967.

See also the following entry (G0520), Hutton (G0614), Leach (G0638), Lockyer (G0647), Poovey (G0711), Rest (G0723) and Wallis (G0784).

G0525   Christensen, James L. Funeral Services. Westwood, N.J.: Fleming H. Revell Company, 1959.

This compendium contains a complete series of funeral services appropriate for those Protestant traditions which do not have a standard service. It is more detailed than Leach (G0638), which contains only brief sugges-tions for services. See also the preceding entry (G0524), Hutton (G0614), Lockyer (G0647), Poovey (G0711), Rest (G0723) and Wallis (G0784).

G0526   Christensen, James L. The Minister's Marriage Handbook. Westwood,

N.J.: Fleming H. Revell Company, 1966.

> This guide to marriage procedures in the Protestant tradition deals with music, etiquette, ceremonies and related topics. It includes suggestions for ceremonies appropriate to various situations. See also Hutton (G0615), Leach (G0637) and Palmer (G0701).

G0527   Christensen, James L. The Minister's Service Handbook. Westwood, N.J.: Fleming H. Revell Company, 1960.

> This anthology of materials for a variety of different services is organized in ten sections including the offering, Communion, marriage, and materials for special occasions. There is a detailed table of contents and notes at the end of the book. Scriptural quotations are from the RSV. See also Hutton (G0616), Reese (G0721) and Segler (G0741).

G0528   Church of England. The Book of Common Prayer and Administration of the Sacraments and Other Rites and Ceremonies of the Church According to the Use of the Church of England; Together with the Psalter or Psalms of David, Pointed As They Are to Be Sung or Said in Churches; and the Form and Manner of Making, Ordaining and Consecrating of Bishops, Priests and Deacons. Oxford: Oxford University Press, 1913.

> See also Bickersteth (G0884) and Waddams (G0782) for companion works; for commentaries/handbooks see Blunt (G0484) and Frere (G0585).

G0529   Church of England. Liturgical Commission. Alternative Services, Second Series (Revised). London: SPCK, 1970.

> See also Church of England (G0528, G0532).

G0530   Church of England. Liturgical Commission. A Commentary on Holy Communion, Series 3. London: SPCK, 1971.

> See also Bradshaw (G0490) and Church of England (G0532).

G0531   Church of England. Liturgical Commission. Modern Liturgical Texts. London: SPCK, 1968.

> This work provides new texts of the Lord's Prayer, Gloria in Excelsis, the Creed, Te Deum and the Gospel Canticles. Useful critical comments are included. A group of canticles with music for congregational singing is also provided. The concluding sections contain further suggested services of baptism and confirmation and a modernized version of the Series 2 Holy Communion Service. This is a useful study for those concerned with liturgical renewal. See also Church of England (G0529, G0530) and Episcopal Church (G0572).

G0532   Church of England. Liturgical Commission. An Order of Holy Communion. Alternative Services, Series 3. With tables of Psalms and lessons. London: Cambridge University Press; London: Oxford University Press, 1973.

> Following the same order of service as that provided in Series 2, this alternative form of eucharistic worship uses various modern versions of the Bible and quite contemporary language in general. A particularly valuable feature is the set of notes at the beginning, as these provide

suggestions for the saying of the service. Also helpful are the tables of Psalms and lessons. While obviously meant for the Church of England, this 54 page version of an important revision of the Anglican liturgy is a useful reference work for anyone interested in liturgical reform. See also Bradshaw (G0490), Church of England (G0530) and Episcopal Church (G0575).

G0533   Church of Scotland. Ordinal and Service Book for Use in Courts of the Church. 3rd ed. London: Oxford University Press, 1962.

G0534   Church of Scotland. Committee of Public Worship and Aids to Devotion. Book of Common Order. Edinburgh: Saint Andrew Press, 1979.

See also the companion prayer book (G0535).

G0535   Church of Scotland. Committee on Public Worship and Aids to Devotion. Prayers for Sunday Services. Edinburgh: Saint Andrew Press, 1980.

This companion to the Book of Common Order (G0534) contains sixteen full sets of prayers for non-communion Sundays plus prayers for different seasons of the church year. The prayers range from those in traditional language to those in the contemporary idiom. This useful 136 page collection is a suitable compendium for most Protestant denominations.

G0536   Church of South India. The Book of Common Worship As Authorised by the Synod, 1962. London: Oxford University Press, 1963.

This ecumenical service book created by a group of denominations in India contains an order for the Holy Eucharist, the Propers, orders for morning and evening worship, baptism, confirmation and other services. Daily Bible readings are suggested; most of the biblical quotations are from the RSV.

G0537   Church of the Brethren. Ministry and Home Mission Commission. Book of Worship. Elgin, Ill.: Brethren Press, 1964.

G0538   Church Ushers Association of New York. Principles of Church Ushering: A Compilation Prepared from Notes by Members of the Church Ushers Association of New York. 4th ed. New York: Church Ushers Association of New York, 1963.

This 44 page work sets out the main considerations relevant to the church usher's work: individual duties, administration, special problems. An index is provided. This is a practical work on this specific topic. See also Elford (G0567), Garrett (G0589) and Lang (G0635).

G0539   Clarke, William Kemp Lowther, ed. Liturgy and Worship: A Companion to the Prayer Books of the Anglican Communion. New York: Macmillan Company, 1932.

Available in numerous reprints, this work is based mainly on the 1662 Prayer Book with subsequent editions referred to by dates when they came into use. The three parts contain a historical introduction, discussion of the Prayer Book services, and additional matter in the form of twelve essays on such subjects as the lesser hours, the Prayer Book as literature, and modern prayers. Additional notes and an index complete the volume.

Anglican problems are studied against the broader background of worship in general. See also Church of England (G0528) and Frere (G0585).

G0540   Coffin, Henry Sloane. The Public Worship of God: A Sourcebook. Philadelphia, Pa.: Westminster Press, 1946.

Focusing on the Reformed tradition, this guide deals with the need for, the nature of and the art of conducting public worship. See also McElroy (G0652) and Wallis (G0788).

G0541   Colquhoun, Frank, comp. and ed. Parish Prayers. London: Hodder and Stoughton, 1967.

This 445 page compilation is an extensive collection of both traditional and modern prayers in the Anglican tradition. Almost 1800 prayers are presented in six main groups, for the church's year, devotional and supplementary prayers, and so on. Indexes of sources and of subjects are included. This is a worthwhile collection for private devotion and public prayer. See also Boyer (G0489) and Shands (G0745).

G0542   Communauté de Taizé. The Taizé Office. London: Faith Press, 1966.

The Taizé Office is the fruit of an experience in community prayer, rooted in the ecumenical tradition. It does not claim to be an official liturgy, and draws on many biblical and liturgical sources. This publication contains introductory material, followed by the office, beginning with the season of Advent. At the end of the volume are indexes to psalms, readings, collects of the week and to the distribution of the psalms, as well as eighteen biblical canticles.

G0543   Congregational Union of England and Wales. A Book of Services and Prayers. London: Independent Press, 1959.

G0544   Couch, Helen F., and Barefield, Sam S., eds. Worship Sourcebook for Youth. New York: Abingdon Press, 1962.

See also Bailey and Bailey (G0476) and Bays and Oakberg (G0479).

G0545   Crippen, Thomas George. Christmas and Christmas Lore. London: Blackie and Son, 1923. Reprint. Detroit, Mich.: Gale Research Company, 1971.

This collection of customs and traditions concerning Christmas is drawn from seventeenth and eighteenth century chapbooks and pamphlets and from a wide range of other sources. The fifty-six chapters deal with such topics as origins, evergreens, hymns, carols, plays and Epiphany. The work is wide ranging and selective rather than exhaustive, and there are useful annotations in each chapter. This remains a valuable reference and resource book for practical ideas. See also Auld (G0474), Dawson (G0556) and Hendricks and Vogel (G0603).

G0546   Croegaert, August Jan Maria Josef. The Mass: A Liturgical Commentary. 2 vols. Westminster, Md.: Newman Press, 1958-1959.

See also Parsch (G0705).

G0547   Cuming, G.J. A History of Anglican Liturgy. New York: St. Martin's

Press; London: Macmillan Company, 1969.

This work concentrates on the history of the Prayer Book to the mid-1960s, providing a wealth of detail on its evolution. Liturgical books of Anglican churches abroad and other compositions related to the Prayer Book are also covered. While providing a valuable coverage of this aspect of Anglicanism this work should be supplemented for reference purposes by Brightman (G0491); see also Chappell (G0903) and Harrison (G0599).

G0548 Currie, David M. Come Let Us Worship God: A Handbook of Prayers for Leaders of Worship. Philadelphia, Pa.: Westminster Press, 1977.

See also Geffen (G0590), Noyes (G0684), Rest (G0724) and Senn (G0744).

G0549   Dabovich, Sebastian. The Holy Orthodox Church; or, The Ritual, Services and Sacraments of the Eastern Apostolic (Greek-Russian) Church. Wilkesbarre, Pa.: n.p., 1898.

This 85 page handbook provides an excellent guide to Orthodox worship, covering in twenty-two chapters aspects such as the sacraments, the hours, fasts of the church, and Holy Communion. See also Heliopoulos (G0602) and Sokolov (G0760).

G0550 Dalmais, Irenée Henri. Eastern Liturgies. Trans. by Donald Attwater. The Twentieth Century Encyclopedia of Catholicism, vol. 112. Section 10: The Worship of the Church. New York: Hawthorn Books, 1960.

This translation from the French provides an introduction to Eastern liturgies of worship, showing the place of each of the liturgical traditions of the Christian East. A table of Eastern liturgies today is followed by analysis of the various Eastern churches (Monophysite, Nestorian, etc.) and liturgical families (Antiochene Anaphora, Syrian, Alexandrian, etc.), and of the particular rites. A select bibliography is provided. There is no index, but the table of contents is quite detailed. See also Day (G0557), King (G0628) and Raes (G0717).

G0551 Dalmais, Irenée Henri. Introduction to the Liturgy. Trans. by Roger Capel. Baltimore, Md.: Helicon Press; London: Geoffrey Chapman, 1961.

See also Cabrol (G0496) and Day (G0557).

G0552 Danielou, Jean. Bible et Liturgie: La Théologie Biblique des Sacraments et des Fêtes d'après les Pères de l'Eglise. Lex Orandi, 11. Paris: Editions du Cerf, 1951.

Intended to assist parish clergy in expounding scriptural types, this work in fact concentrates on the types of baptism, confirmation and the eucharist employed in the four surviving catecheses of the fourth-fifth century period. In this sense it is a useful anthology of the patristic period, although it does not contain any rigorous criticism of the way in which each author handles the biblical types.

G0553 Danjat, Jean. Prayer. Trans. by Martin Murphy. The Twentieth Century Encyclopedia of Catholicism, vol. 37. Section 4: The Means of Redemption. New York: Hawthorn Books, 1964.

See also Guéranger (G0595) and Martimort (G0659).

G0554   Davies, Horton, and Slifer, Morris, comps. Prayers and Other Resources for Public Worship. Nashville, Tenn.: Abingdon Press, 1976.

See also Sandlin (G0733), Uehling (G0772) and Williamson (G0797).

G0555   Davis, Charles. Liturgy and Doctrine: The Doctrinal Basis of the Liturgical Movement. London: Sheed and Ward, 1960.

This 123 page work describes the movement toward self-renewal in Roman Catholicism in terms of the liturgy and of interest in biblical theology. It is mainly suitable for readers with knowledge of the Roman Catholic tradition since it assumes knowledge of the theology of the Roman Mass and of the mysticism of Roman Catholic piety. See also Vagaggini (G0776) and Verheul (G0779).

G0556   Dawson, William Francis. Christmas: Its Origins and Associations, Together with Its Historical Events and Festive Celebrations during Nineteen Centuries. London: E. Stock, 1902. Reprint. Detroit, Mich.: Gale Research Company, 1968.

Arranged more or less in chronological order, this wide ranging survey outlines Christmas origins, rituals, customs and beliefs. Although the focus is on British traditions, there is a chapter on Christmas celebrations in various countries. Although somewhat dated, much of Dawson retains its value, particularly when describing nineteenth century developments and customs. The work is very well written in an interesting narrative fashion which, however, detracts from its usefulness as a reference volume. See also Auld (G0474), Crippen (G0545) and Hendricks and Vogel (G0603).

G0557   Day, Peter D., comp. Eastern Christian Liturgies: The Armenian, Coptic, Ethiopian and Syrian Rites; Eucharistic Rites with Introductory Notes and Rubrical Instructions. Shannon: Irish University Press, 1972.

This work contains the various Eastern Christian rites in English translation. See also Dalmais (G0550), King (G0628), Liesel (G0641) and Raes (G0717).

G0558   De Angelis, Michael. The Correct Pronunciation of Latin According to Roman Usage. With phonetic arrangement of the texts of the ordinary of the mass, requiem mass, responses at mass, benediction hymns and hymns in honor of the Blessed Virgin Mary. Ed. by Nicola A. Montani. Philadelphia, Pa.: St. Gregory Guild, 1937.

This valuable pronunciation guide, while treating texts no longer used in the Roman Catholic Church, is of special relevance to church music and contains much of the traditional choral repertoire in Latin. In other respects it is a sound guide for those who wish to pronounce liturgical Latin correctly. For a dictionary of liturgical Latin see Diamond (G0410).

G0559   Dearmer, Percy. The Parson's Handbook: Practical Directions for Parsons and Others According to the Anglican Use, As Set Forth in the Book of Common Prayer, on the Basis of the Twelfth Edition. Rev. and rewritten by Cyril E. Pocknee. 13th ed. London: Oxford University Press, 1965.

This considerably abbreviated version of Dearmer's handbook has been revised in the light of recent liturgical scholarship. It contains much useful advice, although it has been criticized for some inconsistencies in approach. See also Lamburn (G0631).

G0560   Delehaye, Hippolytus, et al., eds. Martyrologium Romanum: Ad Formam Editionis Typicano Scholiis Historicis Instructum. In Acta Sanctorum, 68. Propylaeum ad Acta Sanctorum Decembris. Brussels: Société des Bollandists, 1940.

This critical edition of Roman Catholic martyrology is based on scholarly methods devised by the Bollandists and serves as a standard reference work in its field. For the basic text see Catholic Church (G0511) and O'Connell (G0688).

G0561   Demaray, Donald E. Alive to God through Prayer: A Manual on the Practices of Prayer. Grand Rapids, Mich.: Baker Book House, 1965.

See also Geffen (G0590).

G0562   Dix, Gregory. The Shape of the Liturgy. [2nd ed.] London: Dacre Press, 1945. Reprint. London: Dacre Press, 1954.

This lengthy (more than 750pp.) examination of the structure of actions and prayers which form the eucharist includes a wealth of historical material. Seventeen chapters, with many subdivisions, examine the topic from a broad perspective, with one focusing more specifically on the Anglican liturgy. A detailed table of contents and an index are included. See also Jones (G0621) and Miller (G0666).

G0563   Douglas, George William. The American Book of Days: A Compendium of Information about Holidays, Festivals, Notable Anniversaries and Christian and Jewish Holy Days, with Notes on Other American Anniversaries Worthy of Remembrance. Rev. by Helen Douglas Compton. New York: H.W. Wilson Company, 1952.

First published in 1937, this 697 page guide is arranged chronologically and provides interesting notes and historical outlines of notable celebrations associated with each day of the year. The index is particularly useful for locating specific types of holidays and feasts. Appendixes include rhymes of the days and seasons, signs of the zodiac, and a list of holidays in the United States. See also Spicer (G0762) and Weiser (G0792).

G0564   Dunkle, William F., Jr., and Quillian, Joseph D., Jr. Companion to "The Book of Worship". Ed. for the Commission on Worship of the United Methodist Church. Nashville, Tenn.: Abingdon Press, 1970.

This 207 page volume is intended for use with The Book of Worship (G0664) adopted by the Methodist Church in 1964. It is also designed to provide background knowledge on worship for Christians of other denominations. It offers practical suggestions based on historical traditions and theological insights. See also Voigt (G0781).

G0565   Eglise Réformée de France. Liturgie. Paris: Editions Berger-Levrault, 1963.

See also Benoît (G0480).

G0566   Eisenhofer, Ludwig, and Lechner, Joseph. The Liturgy of the Roman Rite. Trans. by A.J. Peeler and E.F. Peeler. Ed. by H.E. Winstone. New York: Herder and Herder, 1961.

This translation of Liturgik des Römischen Ritus (6. Aufl. Freiburg im Breisgau: Herder, 1953) is an excellent guide to the Roman liturgy. It deals in depth with prayers, language, actions, setting, equipment and ceremonies, providing detailed information not found in other works of this type. There is also much bibliographical data of value for further study. Although arranged in chapters designed for reading and study rather than reference work, the admirably full coverage gives Eisenhofer a key place among reference volumes on the Roman Catholic liturgy. See also Fortescue and O'Connell (G0582), King (G0630) and Wuest (G0798).

G0567   Elford, Homer J.R. A Guide to Church Ushering. New York: Abingdon Press, 1961.

This brief work is designed to provide practical suggestions to church ushers. Twelve chapters cover aspects such as general preparation, the offering, ushering at Holy Communion, funerals and weddings. A checklist for the head usher is included. There is no index. See also Church Ushers Association of New York (G0538), Garrett (G0589) and Lang (G0635).

G0568   Elford, Homer J.R. A Layman's Guide to Protestant Worship. New York: Abingdon Press, 1963.

See also Schroeder (G0738).

G0569   The English Catholic Prayer Book. London: Faith Press, 19--?

This work is widely regarded as the standard hymnal for Anglo-Catholic worship, as opposed to the more widely representative content of Hymns Ancient and Modern (G0943). For another Anglo-Catholic hymnal see The English Hymnal (G0919).

G0570 [no entry]

G0571   Episcopal Church. Book of Common Prayer and Administration of the Sacraments and Other Rites and Ceremonies of the Church, According to the Use of the Protestant Episcopal Church in the United States of America, Together with the Psalter or Psalms of David. New York: Oxford University Press, 1944.

Available in many different editions since 1944, this contains the approved 1928 revision and is paged according to the standard prayer book adopted in 1934. It includes the additional material of 1943 in the prefatory section. All later trial services and other revisions are based on The Book of Common Prayer, which, with minor variations in different provinces, is the standard Anglican liturgical compendium. See Shepherd (G0748) for a useful commentary, Pepper (G0708) and Johnson (G0619) for indexes, and Simcox (G0755) for a handbook on word meanings.

G0572   Episcopal Church. Liturgical Commission. The Book of Offices: Services for Certain Occasions Not Provided in the Book of Common Prayer. 3rd ed.

New York: Church Pension Fund, 1960.

See also Church of England (G0531).

G0573   Episcopal Church. Liturgical Commission. The Daily Office Revised. Prepared by the Standing Liturgical Commission as part of the program of prayer book revision authorized by the General Conventions of 1967 and 1970. Prayer Book Studies, no. 27. New York: Church Hymnal Corporation, 1973.

See also Episcopal Church (G0574).

G0574   Episcopal Church. Liturgical Commission. The Draft Proposed Book of Common Prayer and Administration of the Sacraments According to the Use of the Protestant Episcopal Church in the United States of America, Otherwise Known as the Episcopal Church, Together with the Psalter or Psalms of David; Presented to the General Convention of 1976 by the Standing Liturgical Commission in Compliance with the Directions of the General Convention of 1973. New York: Church Hymnal Corporation, 1976.

See also Atkinson (G0473), Episcopal Church (G0573) and Miller (G0667).

G0575   Episcopal Church. Liturgical Commission. Services for Trial Use. Authorized Alternatives to Prayer Book Services. New York: Church Hymnal Corporation, 1971.

This work includes the texts of Prayer Book Studies, nos. 18-24. See also Church of England (G0532).

G0576   Fattinger, Rudolf. Liturgisch-Praktische Requisitenkunde, für den Seelsorgsklerus, für Theologen, Architekten, Künstler, Kunst- und Paramenten- werkstätten. In Lexikaler Form. Freiburg im Breisgau: Herder, 1955.

See also Sullivan (G0768, G0769).

G0577   Fenner, Kay Toy. American Catholic Etiquette. Westminster, Md.: Newman Press, 1961.

This 402 page handbook for the laity covers both religious and social aspects of participation in weddings, funerals and other ceremonies. Also treated are forms of address, duties of parishoners, behavior at mass, Catholic home life. Much of the advice now seems very dated, but Fenner can be used as a basic reference volume on various liturgical matters. An index is provided. See also Broderick (G0493).

G0578   Ferré, Nels Frederick Solomon. A Theology for Christian Prayer. Nashville, Tenn.: Tidings, 1963.

See also Bernard (G0482).

G0579   Finck, Theodore K. Lutheran Worship. 2nd ed. Philadelphia, Pa.: Muhlen- berg Press, 1960.

First published in 1936 under the title Worship, this brief volume examines aspects of Lutheran worship such as form and freedom, congregational singing and public prayer. A list of relevant literature is included, but ther is no index. See also Reed (G0720) and Streng (G0766).

G0580 Finn, Edward E. These Are the Rites: A Brief History of the Eastern Rites of Christianity. Collegeville, Minn.: Liturgical Press, c.1979.

Published in a 1961 edition as A Brief History of the Eastern Rites, this volume provides an account under headings such as "diversity amid unity", "heterodoxy and orthodoxy", "separation and union". It is intended mainly for an American readership. See also Liesel (G0640).

G0581 Flannery, Austin; Ryan, Vincent; Maher, Michael; and Keating, Denis. Saints in Season: A Companion to the Lectionary. Dublin: Dominican Publications, 1976.

Following the Roman Catholic lectionary (G0507-G0509) day-by-day through the year, this useful guide provides highlights from the life and work of each saint, a brief comment on the official reading or an appropriate choice and a comment on the gospel reading or related topic. There are supplementary chapters on the communion of saints, distribution of saints, documentation and instructions from councils, the Holy See and other sources. See also Frere (G0584).

G0582 Fortescue, Adrian, and O'Connell, John Bertram. The Ceremonies of the Roman Rite Described. 12th ed. Westminster, Md.: Newman Press; London: Burns, Oates and Washbourne, 1962.

Regarded as the standard authority for many years, this work contains detailed information on vestments, church furnishings and furniture, equipment and ceremonies. There is a full index for reference purposes. In coverage and scope Fortescue is similar to Eisenhofer (G0566), although both are now thought to be somewhat dated. See also O'Connell and Schmitz (G0689) and Wuest (G0798).

G0583 France, Dorothy D. Special Days of the Church Year. St. Louis, Mo.: Bethany Press, 1969.

See also Martin (G0660) and Wallis (G0787).

G0584 Frere, Walter Howard. Black Letter Saints' Days: A Companion to "Collects, Epistles and Gospels for the Lesser Feasts According to the Calendar Set Out in 1928". London: SPCK, 1961.

See also Flannery (G0581).

G0585 Frere, Walter Howard. A New History of the "Book of Common Prayer", with a Rationale of Its Offices, on the Basis of the Former Work by Francis Procter. London: Macmillan and Company, 1902. Reprint. New York: Regis Press; London: Macmillan and Company, 1958.

Reprinted many times, this classic treatment is in two parts. The first provides a general literary history of The Book of Common Prayer (G0528), with eight chapters on topics such as the Elizabethan prayer book and the prayer book in the reign of Charles II. The second part examines sources and rationale of the offices in nine chapters on morning and evening prayer, the litany, etc. There are many additional notes and various documents are included at the end of the first part. A bibliography is provided. See also Brightman (G0491), Clarke (G0539) and Waddams (G0491).

G0586   Frere, Walter Howard. The Principles of Religious Ceremonial. New ed. Milwaukee, Wisc.: Morehouse Publishing Company; London: A.R. Mowbray and Company, 1928.

This work outlines a historical conspectus of the growth of ceremonial and examines analytically the principles of religious ceremonial. Aimed at the educated layman, it covers such aspects as interpretive ceremonial, symbolical ceremonial, and authority in matters of ceremonial. Notes are included at the end of the volume, and an index is provided. See also Maxwell (G0662).

G0587   Gamber, Klaus. Codices Liturgici Latini Antiquiores. 2. Aufl. 2 vols. Spicilegii Friburgensis Subsidia, Bd. 1. Freiburg: Universitätsverlag, 1968.

G0588   Garrett, Thomas Samuel. Christian Worship: An Introductory Outline. 2nd ed. London: Oxford University Press, 1963.

This introductory work includes discussion of the meaning of worship, the legacy of Israel, Christian initiation, the celebration of the Eucharist, ordination, and the development of the "divine office" and the church year. It provides a useful description of liturgical development and a comparison of traditions, and covers contemporary liturgical developments, especially in the younger churches. A brief bibliography and an index are provided. Although originally intended as a textbook for Indian theological students and based on the author's life in the Church of South India, the book has a wider appeal as an introductory treatment of its subject. See also Baumstark (G0478).

G0589   Garrett, Willis Otis. Church Ushers Manual: A Handbook for Church Ushers and All Others Who Would Promote the Spirit of Fellowship in the House of God. New York: Fleming H. Revell Company, 1924.

See also Church Ushers Association of New York (G0538), Elford (G0567), Lang (G0635) and Parrott (G0702).

G0590   Geffen, Roger, comp. The Handbook of Public Prayer. New York: Macmillan Company, 1963.

This handbook is designed to help the minister to prepare services. The collection consists of prayers and scriptural sentences, which are classified in the order typical of a Protestant worship service. A brief (4pp.) bibliography precedes the detailed table of contents. The collection includes a large proportion of prayers from the Bible or with specifically biblical reference. See also Currie (G0548) and Davies (G0554).

G0591   Gilligan, Michael. How to Prepare Mass: A Practical Handbook for the Parish Liturgical Commission. 3rd ed. Oak Park, Ill.: American Catholic Press, 1972.

This useful guide for Roman Catholic parishes discusses how to organize and train a full liturgical team, the resource materials available and where to acquire necessary equipment. There is a bibliography for further study and a comprehensive index. Gilligan is particularly useful in parishes seeking new forms of worship and in those without experience in organizing the mass. See also Maertens and Fisque (G0658).

G0592   Graff, P. Geschichte der Auflösung der Alten Gottesdienstlichen Formen in der Evangelischen Kirche Deutschlands. 2 vols. Göttingen: Vandenhoeck und Ruprecht, 1937-1939.

> For readers of German this work provides a useful history of German Lutheran liturgy and ritual. For a service book see Vereinigte Evangelisch-Lutherische Kirche Deutschlands (G0778); see also Müller and Blankenburg (G0672).

G0593   Griffith, Paul, comp. The Sacristy Manual, Containing the Portions of the Roman Missal Most Frequently Used in Parish Church Functions. New York: P.J. Kenedy, 1947.

> Griffith contains parts of the Rituale Romanum (G0517) most often used in parish churches until recent years. The text is in Latin, English, French and German. This is useful for basic liturgical inquiries; advanced requirements are met by the full version. See also Catholic Church (G0505, G0520).

G0594   Grisbrooke, William Jardine. Anglican Liturgies of the Seventeenth and Eighteenth Centuries. Alcuin Club Collections, no. 40. London: SPCK, 1958.

> Based on a recognition that modern liturgical scholarship is particularly indebted to the rites and liturgical theology of Anglicanism, Grisbrooke sets out to describe and reproduce a number of key rites from this tradition. These include the Scottish liturgies of 1637 and 1764; Nonjurors' liturgies of 1718 and 1734; liturgies of Taylor, Stephens, Whiston and Henley, Rattray. The first part of the volume contains substantial commentaries on these rites, dealing with their history, antecedents, innovations and theology. The second part reproduces each liturgy in full. Bibliographical notes and an index conclude the work, which is a valuable reference collection for students of liturgiology.

G0595   Guéranger, Prosper. The Liturgical Year. Trans. by Laurence Shepherd and the Monks of Stanbrook Abbey. 15 vols. Worcester: Stanbrook Abbey, 1897-1910. Reprint. 15 vols. London: Burns, Oates and Washbourne, 1921-1936. Reprint. 15 vols. Westminster, Md.: Newman Press, 1949-1952.

> Reprinted on various occasions and with several volumes in more than one edition, this classic guide to the liturgical year is arranged according to the seasons of the church calendar (Advent, Christmas, Septuagesima, Lent, Passiontide and Holy Week, Paschal time, time after Pentecost). Each volume or series of volumes includes introductory chapters on special aspects of the particular season, followed by propers for each day of the calendar in Latin and English. This is a most detailed and comprehensive guide which should be consulted by all who require the text of propers for a given day of the year in the traditional liturgical calendar. For narrower treatments see Gwynne (G0597) and Harper (G0598).

G0596   Guptill, Nathanael M. Contemporary Pastoral Prayers for the Christian Year. Philadelphia, Pa.: Christian Education Press, 1960.

> This book suggests a method of preparation and delivery and a set of

prayers for every Sunday of the year. In addition to those for days of
the church year, there are prayers for special days of each season (May
Day, Mothers' Day, Thanksgiving Day, etc.). An index is provided. See
also Micklem (G0665) and Rest (G0724).

G0597   Gwynne, Walker. The Christian Year: Its Purpose and Its History.
New York: Longman, Green and Company, 1915.   Reprint. Detroit, Mich.:
Gale Research Company, 1972.

Reprinted many times, this volume covers the growth of the Christian
year, including adaptations from older rituals, its attendant festivals
and rituals. Each chapter includes a section on liturgical colors. There
is a full list of contents, and appendixes and an index are included. See
also Alexander (G0467), Cabrol (G0499) and Guéranger (G0595).

G0598   Harper, Howard V. Days and Customs of All Faiths. New York: Fleet
Publishing Corporation, 1957.

This 399 page compilation contains a wide range of information on the
calendar in two sections. The first part is arranged chronologically by
months and days, while the second part deals with customs attached
to various types of days (weddings, holidays, festivals, etc.). Coverage
is ecumenical, and the book is written in a popular style. See also Alexander (G0467) and Spicer (G0762).

G0599   Harrison, Douglas Ernest William. Common Prayer in the Church
of England. London: SPCK, 1969.

This is a revision of the 1946 publication, The Book of Common Prayer.
See also Brightman (G0491) and Cuming (G0547).

G0600   Hatch, Verena Ursenbach. Worship in the Church of Jesus Christ
of Latter-Day Saints. [Provo, Utah: M.E. Hatch, 1968].

G0601   Heim, B. Ihr Sollt Mein Volk Sein: Liturgische Entwürfe für Jeden
Sonn- und Feiertag des Kirchenjahrs. Dienst am Wort, Bd. 18. Stuttgart:
Klotz, 1967.

See also Guéranger (G0595).

G0602   Heliopoulos, Demetrius. The Morning Sacrifice: A Brief Explanation
of the Divine Liturgy of the Eastern Orthodox Church. [Pittsburgh, Pa.:
n.p., 1955, c. 1954].

See also Oakley (G0685) and Sokolov (G0760).

G0603   Hendricks, William Cornelius, and Vogel, Cora. Handbook of Christmas
Programs. Grand Rapids, Mich.: Baker Book House, 1978.

This handbook presents a wide range of programs suitable for various
circumstances. It includes instructions on planning, preparation, staging
and related matters. The full length programs are outlined very clearly
and include guidelines for easy staging. See also Auld (G0474), Crippen
(G0545) and Dawson (G0556).

G0604   [no entry]

G0605 Hiscox, Edward Thurston. The Star Book for Ministers. Rev.ed. Philadelphia, Pa.: Judson Press, 1906. Reprint. Valley Forge, Pa.: Judson Press, 1968.

Containing forms and suggestions for services suited particularly to Baptist needs, this handbook is intended as a comprehensive manual for the minister. It contains suggestions for weddings, funerals, etc., scripture suggestions for various services, an episcopal burial service, forms of marriage service, etc., as well as tables of secular facts and figures, assistance in the pronunciation of Bible proper names, and so on. Part of its interest is now historical. See also Reese (G0721).

G0606   Hone, William. The Every-Day Book; or, Everlasting Calendar of Popular Amusements, Sports, Pastimes, Ceremonies, Manners, Customs and Events, Incident to Each of the Three Hundred and Sixty-Five Days in Past and Present Times; Forming a Complete History of the Year, Months and Seasons and a Perpetual Key to the Almanack; Including Accounts of the Weather, Rules for Health and Conduct, Remarkable and Important Anecdotes, Facts and Notices in Chronology, Antiquities, Topography, Biography, Natural History, Art, Science and General Literature Derived from the Most Authentic Sources and Valuable Original Communications, with Poetical Elucidations, for Daily Use and Diversion. 2 vols. London: W. Tegg, 1866. Reprint. 2 vols. Detroit, Mich.: Gale Research Company, 1967.

This work was first published as a weekly in 1825-1826 and subsequently issued as a multi-volume publication on various occasions.

G0607 Hoon, Paul Waitman. The Integrity of Worship: Ecumenical and Pastoral Studies in Liturgical Theology. Nashville, Tenn.: Abingdon Press, 1971.

This balanced theology of worship from a Protestant viewpoint is arranged as a series of essays on theological, psychological and cultural aspects of worship. It is ecumenical and pastoral in character, as its subtitle indicates. It provides a particularly useful approach for Protestant clergy and theologians. See also Segler (G0742).

G0608   The Hours of the Divine Office in English and Latin: A Bilingual Edition of the Roman Breviary Text, Together with Introductory Notes and Rubrics in English Only. 3 vols. Collegeville, Minn.: Liturgical Press, 1963-1964.

See also Catholic Church (G0514, G0518) and Nelson (G0678).

G0609 Hovda, Robert W. There Are Different Ministries. Washington, D.C.: Liturgical Conference, 1975.

This work offers practical guidance to clergy, parish liturgy committees and planning groups, those entrusted with various offices of liturgical ministry and those training such persons. Separate sections deal with assistant ministers, ministers of Holy Communion, ushers and other ministers, with training models and with the rite of institution of ministers. A resource list is included. See also Murch (G0674).

G0610   Hovda, Robert W., and Huck, Gabe. There's No Place Like People: Planning Small Group Liturgies. Planned by the Liturgical Conference, Washington, D.C. 2nd ed. Chicago, Ill.: Argus Communications, 1971.

See also Lloyd (G0646).

G0611   Huggett, Milton, ed. A Concordance to the American Book of Common Prayer. New York: Church Hymnal Corporation, 1970.

Based on the 1928 revision, this exhaustive work produced by computer reflects word usage from 1549 to the present. Undoubtedly the most detailed work of its kind, Huggett is an indispensible guide for students of the Anglican liturgical tradition, although geared specifically to the Episcopal Church's usage. See Episcopal Church (G0571); see also Pepper (G0708) and Simcox (G0755).

G0612   Hunter, Leslie Stannard, ed. A Diocesan Service Book: Services and Prayers for Various Occasions. London: Oxford University Press, 1965.

See also Davies and Slifer (G0554), Geffen (G0590) and Rodenmayer (G0730).

G0613   Hutton, Samuel Ward. Dedication Services. Minister's Handbook Series. Grand Rapids, Mich.: Baker Book House, 1964.

See also Leach (G0639) and McCandless (G0650).

G0614   Hutton, Samuel Ward. Minister's Funeral Manual. Grand Rapids, Mich.: Baker Book House, 1968.

See also Christensen (G0524, G0525), Leach (G0638), Lockyer (G0647), Poovey (G0711), Rest (G0723) and Wallis (G0784).

G0615   Hutton, Samuel Ward. Minister's Marriage Manual. Grand Rapids, Mich.: Baker Book House, 1968.

This guide to preparation for and performance of weddings in the Protestant tradition provides useful suggestions and ideas for various settings. Also included are ceremonies of Baptist, Anglican, Lutheran, Methodist, Presbyterian and Jewish traditions. See also Christensen (G0526), Leach (G0637) and Palmer (G0701).

G0616   Hutton, Samuel Ward. Minister's Service Manual. Grand Rapids, Mich.: Baker Book House, 1965.

First published as A Service Manual for Ministers of Non-Liturgical Churches, this helpful manual contains orders of service for different types of functions. See also Christensen (G0527), Reese (G0721) and Segler (G0741).

G0617   Jagger, Peter J. Christian Initiation, 1552-1969; Rites of Baptism and Confirmation since the Reformation Period. Alcuin Club Collections, no. 52. London: SPCK, 1970.

This 323 page work presents a valuable comparative survey of the liturgical aspects of baptism and confirmation. Although compiled from within the Anglican Church, it contains much of a more catholic interest. The three main parts cover twelve common forms, revisions of the Anglican communion (thirty-seven rites of baptism and communion), and fifteen non-Anglican revisions. Four appendixes cover the Iglesia Filipina Independiente rites 1961, the Church of South India rites 1962, the Church of the Province of East Africa and the East African Church Union. This provides a comprehensive set of texts in chronological order within each section, as well as brief historical notes. For a collection of documents on baptism see Whitaker (G0795).

G0618   Johnson, Alvin D. The Work of the Usher. Valley Forge, Pa.: Judson Press, 1966.

See also Lang (G0635) and Parrott (G0702).

G0619   Johnson, Frederick. A Brief Topical Index of the Book of Common Prayer. [Morristown, N.J.]: n.p., 1968.

See Episcopal Church (G0571); see also Pepper (G0708).

G0620   Johnson, Kenneth M. Church Ushers: Embodiment of the Gospel. New York: Pilgrim Press, c. 1982.

This practical handbook provides a history and theology relevant to church ushers, as well as giving useful advice on how to carry out the ushers' functions and providing a plan for overall organization. As a guide to effective training of church ushers this is a brief and valuable handbook. See also Church Ushers Association of New York (G0538) and Garrett (G0589).

G0621   Jones, Cheslyn; Wainwright, Geoffrey; and Yarnold, Edward, eds. The Study of Liturgy. London: SPCK, 1978.

Intended to replace Liturgy and Worship, this new guide differs in being ecumenical rather than specifically Anglican in content. At the same time it is less complete than its classic predecessor and concentrates on initiation, the eucharist, the divine office and the rites of ordination. There are also peripheral essays on such subjects as music, architecture and ceremonial. There are excellent photographs and drawings, bibliographies and an index. The editors recommend Davies' Dictionary of Liturgy and Worship (G0408) as a companion to their work, which is an excellent and up-to-date text of significant reference value, particularly for Anglicans. See also Dix (G0562) and Rietschel (G0727).

G0622   Jungmann, Josef Andreas. The Mass of the Roman Rite: Its Origins and Development (Missarum Sollemnia). Trans. by Francis A. Brunner. 2 vols. New York: Benziger Brothers, 1951-1955.

This important work for students of all aspects of liturgics covers the history of the mass from its beginnings to the twentieth century, the nature and forms of mass, the ceremonies and rituals. Half of every page is devoted to detailed notes which are a valuable source of information; these are indexed together with the text. In addition, bibliographical references appear throughout the work. This is a significant reference work for students of liturgical history. The 1959 abridged version lacks the detailed notes and so serves as a textbook rather than a reference volume. See also Lietzmann (G0642) and Righetti (G0728).

G0623   Jungmann, Josef Andreas. The Place of Christ in Liturgical Prayer. 2nd ed. Trans. by A. Peeler. Staten Island, N.Y.: Alba House, 1965.

G0624   Kaczynski, Reiner, comp. Enchiridion Documentorum Instaurationis Liturgicae. Vol. 1- . Turin: Marietti, 1976- .

Devoted to the liturgy and ritual of Roman Catholicism, this collection contains texts of various documents which are otherwise scattered throughout the literature. The initial volume covers 1963-1973 and presents relevant texts in numbered paragraphs together with a detailed index. Bibliographical references cover both official texts and secondary sources. Kaczynski is a useful collection for those interested in current Roman Catholic liturgical matters. See also Notitiae (G0683).

G0625   Kakoulides, Chrysostomos Nikolaou. Orthodox Liturgical Dress: An Historical Treatment. Brookline, Mass.: Holy Cross Orthodox Press, 1981.

See also Sokolov (G0760).

G0626   Keifer, Ralph A., gen. ed. The Catholic Liturgy Book: The People's Complete Service Book. Baltimore, Md.: Helicon, 1975.

See also Catholic Church (G0502, G0510) and Megivern (G0663).

G0627   King, Archdale Arthur. Notes on the Catholic Liturgies. London: Longmans, Green and Company, 1930.

This wide survey covers, among others, the Roman rite, Lyon rite, rite of Brage, Ambrosian rite, Mozarabic rite, Byzantine rite and Armenian rite. Each chapter is devoted to a specific rite or derivation and includes a bibliography. There is an index. King, while dated, provides an excellent introductory survey for those unfamiliar with the various liturgies. See also Thompson (G0770).

G0628   King, Archdale Arthur. The Rites of Eastern Christendom. 2 vols. Rome: Catholic Book Agency, 1947-1948.

This important work presents in considerable detail the history and a description of the development of Eastern liturgies. The major liturgical texts of each of the Uniate and separated churches of the East are covered, and both volumes contain bibliographies and indexes. King is one of the few English language works dealing with Eastern Catholics and presents data in a dense but understandable manner; it is a valuable reference tool on its subject. See also Dalmais (G0550), Day (G0557), Raes (G0717) and Solovey (G0761).

G0629   King, Archdale Arthur. Rites of Western Christendom. 4 vols. Milwaukee, Wisc.: Bruce Publishing Company; London: Longmans, Green and Company, 1955-1959.

These detailed volumes are similar in format to King's compendium on Eastern Christianity (G0628) and cover every important rite which has existed in the West. Included are data on historical background, descriptions of ceremonies, excerpts from liturgical texts, pictures of major churches and monasteries. Each volume is devoted to a specific category: liturgies of religious orders, liturgies of the Roman Catholic Church, liturgies of primatial sees, liturgies of the past. In every case King provides substantial details on historical developments, rubrics, ceremonial, vestments, architecture, liturgical books and bibliography. Every volume is well indexed, and overall this series provides excellent reference material for historical and comparative liturgical studies. See also Thompson (G0770).

G0630 King, James W. The Liturgy and the Laity. Westminster, Md.: Newman Press, 1963.

Starting from the discussions on changes in the liturgy of Vatican II, this Roman Catholic treatment of the liturgy examines aspects such as liturgy and history, liturgy and theology, the liturgical movement, the liturgy and the home, the school and sacred art. An index is provided. See also Eisenhofer and Lechner (G0566).

G0631 Lamburn, Edward Cyril Russell. Anglican Services: A Book Concerning Ritual and Ceremonial in the Anglican Communion. 2nd ed. London: W. Knott, 1963.

In twelve chapters this work treats such topics as robes and vestments, the mass, the divine office, the Christian year, the offices of the dead, the ordinal, reservation of the blessed sacrament. A glossary of liturgical terms and an index are provided. Lamburn is important for those concerned with the rubrics and with ceremonial, especially from an Anglo-Catholic viewpoint. See also Dearmer (G0559).

G0632 Lamburn, Edward Cyril Russell.Behind Rite and Ceremony: An Historical Survey of Their Development in the English Church. London: W. Knott, 1961.

See also Frere (G0586) and Maxwell (G0662).

G0633 Lamburn, Edward Cyril Russell, ed. Ritual Notes: A Comprehensive Guide to the Rites and Ceremonies of the Book of Common Prayer of the English Church Interpreted in Accordance with the Latest Revisions of the Western Use. 11th ed. London: W. Knott, 1964.

See also Church of England (G0528).

G0634 Lang, Jovian. Guide for the Priest during Parish Services: Answers to the Question, What Do I Do That Is Different to Carry Out the Liturgical Renewal, When Offering Holy Mass, Administering the Sacraments and Conducting a Bible Service? Chicago, Ill.: Franciscan Herald Press, [1965].

See also Catherine Frederic (G0501).

G0635 Lang, Paul H.D. Church Ushering. St. Louis, Mo.: Concordia Publishing House, 1957.

See also Church Ushers Association of New York (G0538), Elford (G0567), Garrett (G0589) and Parrott (G0702).

G0636 Lang, Paul H.D. The Service Explained for Use in Church Bulletins. St. Louis, Mo.: Concordia Seminary Print Shop, 1969.

G0637 Leach, William Herman. The Cokesbury Marriage Manual. Rev. and enlarged ed. New York: Abingdon Press, 1959.

Following various types of wedding services acceptable in the Methodist Church, this manual provides a summary of American state laws on marriage and divorce and a bibliography for further study. Although most of the ancillary material is now too dated to be of use, the collection of services remains valuable both for comparative study and for practical suggestions. See also Christensen (G0526), Hutton (G0615) and Palmer (G0701).

G0638   Leach, William Herman. The Improved Funeral Manual. New York: Fleming H. Revell Company, 1946. Reprint. Grand Rapids, Mich.: Baker Book House, 1956.

Like Christensen (G0524, G0525), Hutton (G0614) and Lockyer (G0647) this compendium contains useful suggestions for services in the non-liturgical Protestant tradition. See also Poovey (G0711), Rest (G0723) and Wallis (G0784).

G0639   Leach, William Herman, ed. The Minister's Handbook of Dedications. New York: Abingdon Press, 1961.

Consisting of services and litanies of dedication taken from issues of Church Management, this collection of thirty-five complete forms of dedication is suitable for Protestant churches without prescribed liturgical services. Some of the suggestions are also suitable for incorporation into established forms of dedication. See also Hutton (G0613) and McCandless (G0650).

G0640   Liesel, Nikolaus. The Eastern Catholic Liturgies: A Study in Words and Pictures. Westminster, Md.: Newman Press, 1960.

This collection of annotated photographs of the celebration of the Eastern liturgies provides a visual record of the eucharistic liturgy of twelve Eastern rites including the Coptic, Syrian, Maronite, Greek, Russian, Chaldean and Armenian. The photographs were all taken in Italy, thus some of the churches were not furnished according to the relevant rite, and there are no pictures of typical congregations. An introductory chapter provides brief information on the Eastern Patriarchates and on the organization of Eastern Catholic churches, as well as statistics on the latter (for 1951 and 1960). See also Finn (G0580).

G0641   Liesel, Nikolaus. The Eucharistic Liturgies of the Eastern Churches. Trans. by David Heimann. Collegeville, Minn.: Liturgical Press, 1963.

See also Day (G0557) and King (G0628).

G0642   Lietzmann, Hans. Mass and Lord's Supper: A Study in the History of the Liturgy. Trans. by Dorothea H.G. Reeve. Introduction and further enquiry by Robert Douglas Richardson, Leiden: E.J. Brill, 1979.

This volume incorporates, as the first of two parts, a translation of Messe und Herrenmahl: Eine Studie zur Geschichte der Liturgie. It sets out to analyze the influence of the various liturgies upon one another, comparing the authoritative branches of Eastern and Western liturgies. Part 1 examines the Mass and Lord's Supper; part 2 comprises Richardson's inquiry into eucharistic origins, with special reference to NT problems. Appendixes include translations of liturgical texts used by Lietzmann, works of general reference, and a general index. See also Jungmann (G0622), Brilioth (G0492) and Righetti (G0728).

G0643   Littledale, Richard Frederick. Offices from the Service-Books of the Holy Eastern Church: With Translation, Notes and Glossary. London: Williams and Norgate, 1863. Reprint. New York: AMS Press, 1970.

See also Bjerring (G0483).

G0644   Liturgiegeschichtliche Quellen und Forschungen. Bd. 1- . Münster: Ascherdorff, 1918- .

Published under various titles since its inception, this series produced by the liturgically important Maria Laach Abbey is a major collection of ancient and later liturgical texts together with detailed scholarly studies. The series is important not only for research in Roman Catholic worship but also for comparative liturgical investigations. Approximately sixty individual titles have appeared to date. See also Liturgy (G0645), Oppenheim (G0691) and Quasten (G0715).

G0645   Liturgy. Vol. 1- . Washington, D.C.: Liturgical Conference, 1955- ; bimonthly.

Prepared under the National Conference of Catholic Bishops, this serial is designed to keep clergy and others abreast of changes and developments in the liturgy, to communicate official and semi-official information to members of the Conference and liturgical commissions and generally to provide an updating service on liturgical matters of significance to Roman Catholics. It is an invaluable reference and resource guide but lacks the apparatus to give it retrospective reference usefulness. See also Liturgiegeschichtliche Quellen und Forschungen (G0644).

G0646   Lloyd, Trevor. Informal Liturgy: An Examination of the Possibilities of Non-Sacramental Worship. Grove Booklet on Ministry and Worship, no. 6. Bramcote, Nottinghamshire: Grove Books, 1972.

See also Hovda and Huck (G0610).

G0647   Lockyer, Herbert. The Funeral Source Book. Grand Rapids, Mich.: Zondervan Publishing Company, 1967.

This collection of materials has a clear pastoral value. See also Christensen (G0524, G0525), Hutton (G0614), Leach (G0638), Poovey (G0711), Rest (G0723) and Wallis (G0784).

G0648   Lutheran Church in America. Service Book and Hymnal of the Lutheran Church in America. Authorized by the churches cooperating in The Commission on the Liturgy and The Commission on the Hymnal. Philadelphia, Pa.: Lutheran Church in America, 1958.

Prepared as a cooperative venture of several North American Lutheran bodies, this detailed service book is available in both music and text editions, the latter including all liturgical services used by the Lutheran Church in America. The first part of both editions contains the various services and prayers used in Lutheran worship, and these exhibit clear links with standard Anglican worship. Preceding the services are useful sections on the development of the Service Book, on the music of the liturgy and on the calendar; the services conclude with a valuable guide to the rubrics. The hymns constitute the second main part of the work, and the entire volume is thoroughly indexed. As a book of worship, this publication is unsurpassed in the Protestant tradition for its thoroughness and ease of use. As a reference volume, the Service Book and Hymnal includes valuable introductory matter and excellent indexes, making it an excellent source of information for students of Protestant liturgical worship and hymnody. See also American Lutheran Church (G0472), Dahle (G0911) and Vereinigte Evangelisch-Lutherische Kirche Deutschlands (G0778).

G0649   McCabe, Joseph E. Service Book for Ministers. New York: McGraw-Hill Book Company, 1961.

See also McNeil (G0656) and Segler (G0741).

G0650   McCandless, Oleta R. Twenty-Four Planned Services for Installations, Dedications and Devotions. Grand Rapids, Mich.: Baker Book House, 1968.

See also Hutton (G0613) and Leach (G0639).

G0651   McCloud, Henry J. Clerical Dress and Insignia of the Roman Catholic Church. Milwaukee, Wisc.: Bruce Publishing Company, 1948.

With the exception of vestments worn at mass, this detailed work describes all items of clerical dress, explaining when they are worn and by whom, their colors, meaning and history.   A selection of church documents, a bibliography and an index are included. See also Nainfa (G0677) and Pocknee (G0710).

G0652   McElroy, Paul Simpson, comp. and ed. A Sourcebook for Christian Worship. Cleveland, Ohio: World Publishing Company, 1968.

See also Osborn (G0699) and Wallis (G0788).

G0653   Macleod, Donald. Presbyterian Worship: Its Meaning and Method. New rev. ed. Atlanta, Ga.: John Knox Press, 1981.

Although aimed primarily at Presbyterians, this work offers an in-depth look at Christian worship as a whole. Principles common to all denominations are discussed, and the theological significance of meaningful worship is demonstrated on a very broad level. Sunday worship in the Protestant tradition, sacraments, weddings and funerals are covered. A bibliography and an index complete the work, which is suitable both as a textbook and reference manual for students and clergy. For a minister's handbook see Vincent (G0780).,

G0654   McManus, Frederick Richard. Handbook for the New Rubrics. Baltimore, Md.: Helicon Press, 1961.

See also Schmitz (G0737).

G0655   McManus, Frederick Richard. Sacramental Liturgy. New York: Herder and Herder, 1967.

This book contains a commentary on Chapters 1-3 of the Constitution on the Sacred Liturgy, which appeared as part of the documents of Vatican II, and on the executory Instruction issued a year after the Constitution.

It sets out to clarify the background of the text, and the pastoral hopes and prospects which it proposes. There is no direct attempt to discuss the doctrine of the conciliar document. This is a useful Roman Catholic contribution on post-Vatican II liturgical matters. The text of the Constitution is provided in an appendix. See also Schuster (G0739).

G0656   McNeil, Jesse Jai. Minister's Service Book for Pulpit and Parish. Grand Rapids, Mich.: William B. Eerdmans Publishing Coompany, 1961.

This ecumenical manual covers a wide variety of services. See also McCabe (G0649) and Segler (G0741).

G0657   McPhee, Norma. Programs for the Church Year. Valley Forge, Pa.: Judson Press, 1971.

See also Gwynne (G0597).

G0658   Maertens, Thierry, and Fisque, J. Guide for the Christian Assembly: A Background Book of the Mass Day by Day; A Book from St. Andrew's Abbey. Vol. 1- . London: Darton, Longman and Todd, 1967- .

This is a comprehensive guide to the Sunday liturgy and twelve other major days from the Roman Catholic Abbey of St. Andrew at Bruges. A concise exegesis of the epistle and gospel for each Sunday, a historical analysis of other liturgical texts of the day, a statement of theme for the day and pointers to doctrine are provided. This post-Vatican II work is of wider interest than to a purely Roman Catholic audience. It tends to suffer somewhat from overuse of Latinized jargon where more secular English would have been clearer. See also Gilligan (G0591).

G0659   Martimort, Aimé Georges, et al. The Church at Prayer: Introduction to the Liturgy. Trans. by Robert Fisher et al. Ed. by Austin Flannery and Vincent Ryan. Vol. 1- . New York: Desclée Company, 1968- .

This translation of L'Eglise en Prière: Introduction à la Liturgie (3e éd. Paris: Desclée, 1965) is a comprehensive survey by a number of European scholars and authorities on Roman Catholic worship. The four main sections treat fundamentals of the liturgy, the mass and eucharistic devotion, other sacraments and sacramentals, the liturgical seasons and the office. This is a sound and detailed reference guide to the form and shape of the liturgy. See also Cabrol (G0498), Guéranger (G0595), Nocent (G0681) and Parsch (G0705).

G0660   Martin, David E. Worship Services for Special Days: Forty-Four Complete Services of Worship for Eighteen Great Days of the Church. Anderson, Ind.: Warner Press, 1963.

See also France (G0583) and Wallis (G0787).

G0661   Martin, William Benjamin James. Acts of Worship. New York: Abingdon Press, 1960.

This collection of prayers, creeds and litanies is intended to assist in providing a sense of participation in worship. There are six sections: calls to worship and prayers of invocation; affirmations of faith and creedal statements (including responsive declarations of faith); meditations on biblical themes (e.g., the Ten Commandments, the spirit of truth, newness of life); pastoral prayers based on the words of Jesus; litanies (thanksgiving, confession, intercession, etc.); offertory prayers. An index of scripture is provided. See also Wallis (G0661) and White (G0796).

G0662   Maxwell, William Delbert. An Outline of Christian Worship, Its Development and Forms. London: Oxford University Press, 1936. Reprint. London: Oxford University Press, 1949.

This work provides an outline of Christian worship and the forms it has taken from earliest times. A large proportion of the work is devoted to worship of the Reformed churches, particularly their early liturgies. A bibliography (pp. 183-194) and an index are included. Although somewhat dated, this contains much useful information. See also Frere (G0586).

G0663   Megivern, James J., comp. Worship and Liturgy. Official Catholic Teachings, vol. 6. Wilmington, N.C.: Consortium Books, 1978.

This collection of documents on Roman Catholic worship contains papal, conciliar and other materials in numerical sequence. In addition to this selection of texts there is an introductory essay and a subject index. This is a usefully wide ranging collection of source materials for those interested in official Catholic texts. See also Keifer (G0626) and Liturgy (G0645).

G0664   Methodist Church. General Conference. Commission on Worship. The Book of Worship for Church and Home, with Orders of Worship, Services for the Administration of Sacraments and Aids to Worship According to the Usages of the Methodist Church. Nashville, Tenn.: Methodist Publishing House, 1965.

This widely used collection consists of four main parts: The general services of the Methodist Church, prayers and other aids to worship arranged according to the liturgical year, acts of praise, occasional offices of the Methodist Church. In addition to serving a a source book for Methodists, it also functions as a useful collection for other traditions. There are indexes of first lines, biblical references and subjects. For a companion work see Dunkle and Quillian (G0564); see also Voigt (G0781).

G0665   Micklem, Caryl, ed. Contemporary Prayers for Public Worship. Grand Rapids, Mich.: William B. Eerdmans Publishing Company; London: SCM Press, 1967.

Originally intended for the Congregational Church, the material in this book comprises a collection of prayers in modern language for corporate worship. The prayers are new and old, and scriptural allusions are from both the NEB and the RSV. Contents include material for general use, forms for the sacraments and ordinances, and prayers for the Christian year, including paraphrases of the Lord's Prayer. See also Guptill (G0596).

G0666   Miller, John H. Fundamentals of the Liturgy. Notre Dame, Ind.: Fides Publishers Association, 1959.

See also Dix (G0562) and Jones (G0621).

G0667   Miller, Ronald H. Study Guide for the Holy Eucharist, Proposed Book of Common Prayer. Wilton, Conn.: Morehouse-Barlow, 1977.

This study guide for the Proposed Book of Common Prayer (G0574) of the Episcopal Church is intended for laymen and parish study groups. The bulk of the work reproduces the relevant sections of the Proposed Book, which is clearly laid out and includes a useful analysis of the rationale behind the changes. The background study is brief but scholarly and provides a good source of information for beginners. It is not a thorough reference work and, like Atkinson's complementary study (G0473), should be used primarily from the parochial standpoint rather than as a scholarly tool. See also Shands (G0746).

G0668   Mistrorigo, Antonio. La Liturgia. Glossari di Lingua Contemporanea, vol. 9. Rome: A. Armando, 1968.

See also Cabrol (G0496).

G0669   Mossi, John P., ed. Bread Blessed and Broken: Eucharistic Prayers and Fraction Rites. New York: Paulist Press, 1974.

See also Catholic Church (G0523).

G0670   Mossi, John P., ed. Modern Liturgy Handbook: A Study and Planning Guide for Worship. New York: Paulist Press, 1976.

This post-Vatican II approach to planning and adapting the liturgy provides a collection of articles on the structural theory of worship and practical techniques of effective communication. Chapters on specific aspects of the liturgy cover preparation, music, drama, etc. The final chapter treats worship at church and home. The contributors are from academic and pastoral backgrounds, and the handbook is intended for priests, students, liturgy committees and others concerned with liturgical planning. See also O'Shea (G0700).

G0671   Müller, Johann Baptist. Handbook of Ceremonies for Priests and Seminarians. 18th English ed. Rev. and ed. by Adam C. Ellis. St. Louis, Mo.: Herder, 1958.

See also Catholic Church (G0502), Webber (G0790) and Whatton (G0794).

G0672   Müller, Karl Ferdinand, and Blankenburg, Walter, eds. Leiturgia: Handbuch des Evangelischen Gottesdienstes. 5 vols. Kassel: Johannes Stauda Verlag, 1954-1970.

This guide to the German Lutheran liturgy is extremely detailed, containing specialist articles by various German scholars and pastors. The five volumes cover Geschichte und Lehre des evangelischen Gottesdienstes, Gestalt und Formen des evangelischen Gottesdienstes (Hauptgottesdienst, Predigtgottesdienst und tägliche Gottesdienst), Musik des evangelischen Gottesdienstes, Taufgottesdienst. The third volume contains cumulative indexes of biblical passages, personal names and subjects in the first three volumes; each of the remaining volumes is indexed separately. In every case the treatment of topics is thorough, well documented and fully explanatory. Theological, historical and practical aspects of the liturgy are all dealt with adequately, and most articles include bibliographies. With the thorough indexes and numerous subdivisions within articles this work is a valuable reference guide for all students interested in Protestant worship. See also Graff (G0592).

G0673   Mullen, William B. Concordance of the Prayer Book Psalter. Gresham, Oreg.: St. Paul's Press, 1969.

See also Pepper (G0708).

G0674   Murch, James Deforest. Christian Minister's Manual. Cincinnati, Ohio: Standard Publishing Company, 1937.

This work covers every facet of Protestant services in the nonliturgical tradition from ordinations to dedications. See also Hovda (G0609) and Robertson (G0729).

G0675   Murphy, Denis G. The Sacristan's Manual. Westminster, Md.: Newman Press, 1950.

See also O'Brien (G0686).

G0676   Muss-Arnolt, William. The Book of Common Prayer among the Nations of the World: A History of Translations of the Prayer Book of the Church of England and of the Protestant Episcopal Church of America; A Study, Based Mainly on the Collection of Josiah Henry Benton. New York: E.S. Gorham; London: SPCK, 1914.

See Church of England (G0528) and Episcopal Church (G0571).

G0677   Nainfa, John Abel Felix Prosper. Costume of Prelates of the Catholic Church According to Roman Etiquette. Baltimore, Md.: John Murphy Company, 1909.

This guide provides a scholarly description of the clothing of bishops, archbishops, cardinals, patriarchs and monsignori. Heraldry is also covered, and a bibliography and index are provided. See also McCloud (G0651) and Pocknee (G0710).

G0678   Nelson, Joseph A., ed. Roman Breviary in English, Restored by the Sacred Council of Trent; Published by Order of the Supreme Pontiff St. Pius V and Carefully Revised by Other Popes. Reformed by Order of Pope Pius X According to the Vatican Typical Edition, with New Psalter of Pope Pius XII Compiled from Approved Sources. 4 vols. New York: Benziger Brothers, 1950-1951.

This translation of Breviarum Romanum (G0503) is a standard text of value to those interested in comparing English language liturgies with the traditional Roman rite. See also Catholic Church (G0518) and The Hours of the Divine Office (G0608); for a history see Batiffol (G0477).

G0679   Nevins, Albert J. General Intercessions: The Prayer of the Faithful. Rev. and enlarged ed. of Prayers of the Faithful for Every Occasion Covering the Seasonal Cycle, Sanctoral and Special Feasts, Pastoral Masses and Other Occasions. Huntington, Ind.: Our Sunday Visitor, 1978.

Dealing with an important aspect of laicization of the Roman Catholic liturgy, this compendium contains a wide range of prayers useful for the reformed liturgy or for suggesting forms to be followed in composing liturgical prayers. See also Cabrol (G0497) and Catholic Church (G0515).

G0680 Nichols, James Hastings. <u>Corporate Worship in the Reformed Tradition</u>. Philadelphia, Pa.: Westminster Press, 1968.

This survey of the history of Reformed Church worship traces the development of the Reformed liturgies and changes resulting from Puritanism, evangelicalism, rationalism and romanticism. Due account is taken of the various political, psychological and sociological factors which have contributed to shaping this liturgical tradition. Notes and person and subject indexes are included. See also Elford (G0568) and Schroeder (G0738).

G0681   Nocent, Adrian. <u>The Liturgical Year</u>. 4 vols. Collegeville, Minn.: Liturgical Press, 1977.

The first English language commentary on post-Vatican II liturgy, each volume of Nocent treats the liturgies for each Sunday. It gives biblical and liturgical reflections on the season, the structure and themes of the season together with an historical perspective and brief readings for the three seasons. For Roman Catholic clergy this is an indispensible guide. The best commentaries for pre-Vatican II liturgies are Martimort (G0659) and Parsch (G0704); see also Guéranger (G0595).

G0682   Norris, Herbert. <u>Church Vestments: Their Origin and Development</u>. London: J.M. Dent, 1949; New York: E.P. Dutton, 1950.

This expansion of the first volume of <u>Costume and Fashion</u> (3 vols. London: Dent, 1927-1938) is well illustrated with plates and line drawings. It covers the history of ecclesiastical vestments up to the fifteenth century, clearly showing the development of traditional liturgical vestments. Although dated in view of recent changes, Norris remains the most adequate guide in its field. An index and a bibliography are provided. See also Pocknee (G0710).

G0683 <u>Notitiae: Commentarii ad Nuntia et Studia de Re Liturgica</u>. Vol. 1- . Vatican City: Libreria Editrice Vaticana, 1965- ; monthly.

This official Roman Catholic publication reproduces liturgical texts, documents dealing with the liturgy and allied topics. It also includes articles on liturgical topics but is primarily of use for those seeking current liturgical documentation. See also Kaczynski (G0624).

G0684 Noyes, Morgan Phelps, comp. and ed. <u>Prayers for Services: A Manual for Leaders of Worship</u>. New York: Charles Scribner's Sons, 1934. Reprint. New York: Charles Scribner's Sons, 1951.

This book contains a collection of prayers in relatively straightforward English, organized in two parts. The first contains prayers corresponding to the order followed in many churches (the call to worship, the prayer of invocation, the prayer of confession, and so on); the second contains prayers for special occasions (the funeral service, the marriage service, etc.). References to sources are provided after the prayers, and there are a list of sources, indexes of first lines, of authors and anthologies and a concise topical index at the end of the work. See also Currie (G0548),

Rest (G0724) and Senn (G0744).

G0685   Oakley, Austin. The Orthodox Liturgy. Alcuin Club ed. Studies in Eucharistic Faith and Practice. New York: Morehouse-Gorham; London: A.R. Mowbray and Company, [1958].

See also Dabovich (G0549) and Sokolov (G0760).

G0686   O'Brien, William Alexis. In Sacristy and Sanctuary: A Guide for the Sacristan with Detailed Instructions Accompanied by Directive Schedules and Diagrams Showing How and What to Get Ready for the Proper Carrying Out of Liturgical Functions Generally, According to the Roman Ceremonial. New ed. with directions for the new Holy Week liturgy. New York: Benzinger Brothers, 1958.

See also Murphy (G0675).

G0687   O'Connell, John Bertram. The Celebration of Mass: A Study of the Rubrics of the Roman Missal. 4th ed. 3 vols. Milwaukee, Wisc.: Bruce Publishing Company, 1964.

This study of the rubrics of the Roman missal seeks to provide a detailed and accurate explanation and interpretation, taking into account the rubrics of other liturgical books, canon law, decisions of the Congregation of Sacred Rites, custom and usage. Volume 1 covers general rubrics of the missal together with votive, parochial, conventual and requiem masses. Volume 2 deals with the rite of the celebration of low mass, while the third volume treats high and sung mass. At the end of each volume is a glossary of liturgical terms, bibliography and index. For background information, explanatory notes and practical assistance O'Connell is a valuable guide to pre-Vatican II liturgical practice. See also Roguet (G0731).

G0688   O'Connell, John Bertram, ed. The Roman Martyrology; in Which Are To Be Found the Eulogies of the Saints and Blessed Approved by the Sacred Congregation of Rites Up to 1961. An English trans. from the 4th ed. after the typical ed. (1956) approved by Pope Benedict XV (1922). Westminster, Md.: Newman Press; London: Burns and Oates, 1962.

This English translation of the standard Vatican text (G0511) includes a thorough index. See also Delehaye (G0560).

G0689   O'Connell, Laurence John, and Schmitz, Walter J. The Book of Ceremonies. Rev. ed. Milwaukee, Wisc.: Bruce Publishing Company, 1956.

This work is not as complete as Fortescue and O'Connell (G0582) but it includes an adequate index. See also Wuest (G0798).

G0690   Oglesby, Stuart Roscoe. Prayers for All Occasions: A Book of Short Prayers for Everyday Life. Richmond, Va.: John Knox Press, 1940. Reprint. Grand Rapids, Mich.: Baker Book House, 1960.

Prepared by a Presbyterian pastor for use in the weekly church bulletin, these prayers are written in a clear, simple style. There are prayers for everyday, for special days, for special occasions, for special needs, for children, and graces. The title indicates the theme of each prayer which is accompanied by a scriptural quotation. See also Rodenmayer (G0730).

G0691   Oppenheim, Philippus. Institutiones Systematico-Historicae in Sacrum Liturgiam. Editio altera. 9 vols. Turin: Marietti, 1944-1946.

This extensive work is intended to present a full history of Roman Catholic ecclesiastical law in the field of liturgy and to prove that the pope is the supreme legislator in liturgical matters. Each volume is extremely detailed and thorough, presenting the background, texts and meanings of various liturgical decisions made by the papacy. Each volume is indexed by subject, and there is a general index of names in volume 4. While Oppenheim clearly lacks the objectivity preferred in historical surveys, this is an essential reference work for students of liturgical law and history. See also Liturgiegeschichtliche Quellen und Forschungen (G0644).

G0692   Orthodox Eastern Church. The Divine Liturgy of St. John Chrysostom. The Greek Text with a Reading in English. 3rd ed. London: Faith Press, 1948; Brookline, Mass.: Greek Orthodox Theological Institute Press, 1950.

See also Shereghy (G0753).

G0693   Orthodox Eastern Church. The Ferial Menaion; or, The Book of Services for the Twelve Great Festivals and the New Year's day. Trans. from a Slavonian edition of the last century printed identically with the latest issues in Moscow and published as now by the Most Holy Governing Synod of Russia. Trans. by Nicolas Orloff. London: J. Davy and Sons, 1900.

See also the following entries (G0694, G0695) and Upson (G0774).

G0694   Orthodox Eastern Church. The Festal Menaion. Trans. by Mother Mary and Kallistos Ware. The Service Books of the Orthodox Church. London: Faber and Faber, 1969.

Intended for English speaking Orthodox and for Christians of other churches who wish to understand Orthodoxy, this is an unabridged translation of the original Greek texts in a version intended for public liturgical use. The book provides outline plans of the divine offices and the eucharist and how they vary, details of Orthodox service books, a glossary of technical terms and notes on the feasts and their themes, as well as the translation of nine of the twelve great feasts of the Orthodox liturgical year. The texts include many of the vital themes of Orthodox theology. The translation uses the English of the Authorized Version of the Bible. An introduction on "The Worshipping Church" examines Orthodox approaches to liturgical and private prayer and how the two are related. See also Orthodox Eastern Church (G0693, G0695) and Upson (G0774).

G0695   Orthodox Eastern Church. The General Menaion; or, The Book of Services Common to the Festivals of Our Lord Jesus Christ, of the Holy Virgin and of the Different Orders of Saints. Trans. from the Slavonian 16th ed. of 1862 by Nicolas Orloff. Printed in Moscow and published by the Most Holy Governing Synod of Russia. London: J. Davy and Sons, 1899.

See also the preceding entries (G0693, G0694) and Upson (G0774).

G0696   Orthodox Eastern Church. Liturgy and Catechism of the Eastern

Orthodox Church in Albanian and English. Trans. by Fan Stylian Noli. Boston, Mass.: Albanian Orthodox Church in America, 1955.

See also Oakley (G0685).

G0697   Orthodox Eastern Church. The Orthodox Liturgy; Being the Divine Liturgy of S. John Chrysostom and S. Basil the Great According to the Use of the Church of Russia, Together with the Manner of Setting Forth the Holy Gifts for the Liturgy and Devotions before and after Partaking of the Holy Cup. London: SPCK for the Fellowship of SS. Alban and Sergius, 1939. Reprint. London: SPCK for the Fellowship of SS. Alban and Sergius, 1954.

This standard English translation of the Russian Orthodox liturgy has a useful preface on the ceremonies of the liturgy. This is followed by the office of preparation for Holy Communion, the ordering of the liturgy, the liturgy itself and the office of thanksgiving. A glossary of liturgical terms completes the work, which is a useful compendium for those interested in Orthodox worship. See also Orthodox Eastern Church (G0692) and Patrinacos (G0706).

G0698   Orthodox Eastern Church. Service Book of the Holy Orthodox-Catholic Apostolic Church. 3rd ed. Comp. and trans. by Isabel Florence Hapgood. Brooklyn, N.Y.: Syrian Antiochian Orthodox Archdiocese of New York and All North America, 1956.

Compiled and arranged from the Old Church-Slavonic service books of the Russian Orthodox Church, this work is collated with the comparable service books of the Greek Orthodox Church, thereby forming a useful reference volume for students interested in comparing various Orthodox liturgies. See also Littledale (G0643).

G0699   Osborn, George Edwin. Christian Worship: A Service Book. 2nd ed. St. Louis, Mo.: Christian Board of Publication, 1958.

See also Coffin (G0540) and McElroy (G0652).

G0700   O'Shea, William J. The Worship of the Church: A Companion to Liturgical Studies. Westminster, Md.: Newman Press, 1957.

This volume is intended as a supplement to the texts of the liturgy for students and teachers. Eighteen chapters examine such aspects as the purpose of the liturgy, liturgical music, the altar and its adornment, the liturgical year, the sacraments. A bibliography (pp. 618-628) and an index are provided in this work which will be of particular interest to Roman Catholic readers. See also Mossi (G0670).

G0701   Palmer, Gordon. A Manual of Church Services; with a Summary of State Laws Governing Marriage. New York: Fleming H. Revell Company, 1950.

See also Christensen (G0526), Hutton (G0615) and Leach (G0637).

G0702   Parrott, Leslie. The Usher's Manual: A Spiritual and Practical Guidebook. Grand Rapids, Mich.: Zondervan Publishing House, 1970.

See also Church Ushers Association of New York (G0538), Elford (G0567), Garrett (G0589) and Lang (G0635).

G0703   Parsch, Pius. The Breviary Explained. Trans. by William Nayden and
Carl Hoegerl. St. Louis, Mo.: Herder, 1952.

Primarily a guide to understanding the office with some historical notes
and occasional commentary, Parsch covers in three sections fundamental
notions and history, the elements constituting each hour and seasonal
changes. The work is now somewhat dated and even when first published
was criticized for not taking cognizance of current reforms. See also
Battifol (G0477) and Catholic Church (G0518).

G0704   Parsch, Pius. The Church's Year of Grace. Trans. by Daniel Francis
Coogan, Jr. and Rudolf Kraus. 5 vols. Collegeville, Minn.: Liturgical Press,
1953-1958.

This important and highly regarded guide to the Roman Catholic daily
liturgy explains the meaning and history of each feast in terms of the
mass and office of the day. Meditations and the biographies of saints
are also included. Each volume is arranged in two sections: proper of
the seasons, proper of the saints. This is a widely used guide to the meaning of the liturgy equal in its authoritative treatment to works by Guéranger (G0595), Martimort (G0659) or Nocent (G0681).

G0705   Parsch, Pius. The Liturgy of the Mass. Trans. by Frederic C. Eckhoff.
St. Louis, Mo.: Herder, 1950.

In twenty-five chapters this study examines the various parts of the
mass and includes discussion of historical development and of preparation
for mass. An index is included. This provides an example of pre-Vatican II
liturgical study. Ssee also Croegaert (G0546) and Peil (G0707).

G0706   Patrinacos, Nicon D., ed. The Orthodox Liturgy: The Greek Text
with a Completely New Translation Followed by Notes on the Text, the
Sunday Gospel and Apostolic Readings, Together with Tracing the Development of the Orthodox Liturgy from the Second Century to This Day. [Garwood,
N.J.: Graphic Arts Press, 1974].

See also Orthodox Eastern Church (G0692-G0698).

G0707   Peil, Rudolf. A Handbook of the Liturgy. Trans. by H.E. Winstone.
New York: Herder and Herder, 1960.

See also Parsch (G0705).

G0708   Pepper, George Wharton. An Analytical Index to the Book of Common
Prayer; and a Brief Account of Its Evolution. Together with a Revision of
Gladstone's Concordance to the Psalter. Philadelphia, Pa.: Winston, 1948.

Based on the 1928 revision and 1943 prefatory additions, this is a thorough
index to the American Episcopal Prayer Book (G0571). It includes a table
showing the principal changes in the Psalter made in the 1928 revision
and a concordance to the Psalter. This is an essential reference work
for liturgical studies in the Anglican tradition in spite of recent experimen-
tation by the Episcopal Church. See also Huggett (G0611), Johnson (G0619)
and Mullen (G0673).

G0709   Pflieger, André. Liturgicae Orationis Concordantia Verbalia. Vol. 1- .

Rome: Herder, 1964 [c.1963]- .

G0710   Pocknee, Cyril Edward. Liturgical Vesture: Its Origin and Development. London: A.R. Mowbray and Company, 1960; Westminster, Md.: Newman
Press, 1961.

Also published as Alcuin Club Tracts, no. 20 (London: A.R. Mowbray
and Company for the Alcuin Club), this work deals in turn with various
items of liturgical vesture (the albe, the chasuble, the cope, the surplice,
etc.), with episcopal insignia and with the altar and its vesture. A select
bibliography is included, and plates and drawings illustrate the subject
matter. See also McCloud (G0651), Nainfa (G0677), Norris (G0682) and
Pugin (G0713).

G0711   Poovey, William Arthur. Planning a Christian Funeral: A Minister's
Guide. Minneapolis, Minn.: Augsburg Publishing House, 1978.

This resource guide for Protestant clergy conducting Christian burial
services discusses practice, goals, use of music, special situations, assistance for mourners and related topics. Guidelines and suggestions for
worship practice are also included. See also Christensen (G0524, G0525),
Hutton (G0614), Leach (G0638), Lockyer (G0647), Rest (G0723) and Wallis
(G0784).

G0712   Puckle, Bertram S. Funeral Customs, Their Origin and Development.
London: T.W. Laurie, 1926. Reprint. Detroit, Mich.: Singing Tree Press, 1968.

This survey examines the ceremonies, prayers, rites and practices used
in burying the dead throughout history. It is a valuable source of information on burial practices for students of both liturgical history and pastoral
practices. Thirty-five illustrations and an index are included.   See also
Wallis (G0784).

G0713 Pugin, Augustus Welby Northmore. Glossary of Ecclesiastical Ornament
and Costume, Compiled from Ancient Authorities and Examples. 3rd ed.
Enlarged and rev. by Bernard Smith. London: Bernard Quaritch, 1868.

See also Pocknee (G0710) and Roulin (G0732).

G0714   Puniet, Pierre de. The Roman Pontifical: A History and Commentary.
Trans. for the Benedictines of Stanbrook Abbey by Mildred Vernon Harcourt.
Vol. 1- . London: Longmans, Green and Company, 1932- .

This translation of Le Pontifical Romain: Histoire et Commentaire is
a scholarly history of the origins of the pontifical and includes theological
commentary on the ceremonies and prayers. For a complete edition of
the pontifical see Catholic Church (G0513); for the revised version see
Catholic Church (G0521).

G0715   Quasten, Johannes, comp. Monumenta Eucharistica et Liturgica Vetustissima Collegit. 7 vols. Bonn: Petri Hanstein, 1935-1937.

This excellent collection of source materials from patristic texts deals
with the eucharist and other sacraments, providing brief introductions
to the texts, biographies of the writers and full references to the complete
printed versions for further study. Extremely detailed notes include cross

references and indicate similar passages in other early writings. Each volume is thoroughly indexed. This is a sound reference collection for students of liturgical history and theology. See also Liturgiegeschichtliche Quellen und Forschungen (G0644).

G0716   Radó, Polikarp. Enchiridion Liturgicum: Complectens Theologiae Sacramentalis et Dogmata et Leges, Iuxta Novum Codicem Rubricarum. 2 vols. Rome: Herder, 1961.

The Latin text of this work discusses the Roman liturgy in general, including special sections on the mass, the office, prayers, devotions and each of the sacraments. Each section is followed by a detailed bibliography, which is indexed in volume 2. There is also a general index to this traditionalist treatment of the liturgy and its meaning. See also Croegaert (G0546).

G0717   Raes, Alphonse. Introductio in Liturgiam Orientalem. Rome: Pontificio Institutum Studiorum Orientalium, 1947.

• This work contains more bibliographical material than King (G0628) and also covers both uniate and separated churches with emphasis on the Byzantine group. A useful index is provided for quick reference. See also Dalmais (G0550) and Day (G0557); a complementary work on Western liturgy is provided by Schmidt (G0736).

G0718   Rahner, Hugo. A Theology of Proclamation. Trans. by Richard Dimmler et al. Adapted by Joseph Halpin. New York: Herder and Herder, 1968.

This volume contains valuable reflection on the dogmatic foundation of the priestly ministry. It investigates the gap between the concepts and theses of theology and the immediate work of the pastor, and attempts to show how the latter can deal with the theology of proclamation. This translation and adaptation is based on Rahner's Eine Theologie der Verkundigung (2. Aufl. Freiburg im Breisgau: Herder, 1939), which is a classic German interpretation of the theology of preaching containing stimulating insights for readers at all levels.

G0719   Randolph, David James. God's Party: A Guide to New Forms of Worship. Nashville, Tenn.: Abingdon Press, 1975.

Focusing on the parish church and local congregation, this work analyzes contemporary worship and offers guidelines, considering new liturgical forms as expressions of living theology. Data were collected primarily from United States parish churches. The final chapter offers a pattern by which a local church may assess its worship, become aware of resources and exercise options toward more meaningful worship. A bibliography and notes are included. See also Burgess (G0494) and Cairns (G0500).

G0720   Reed, Luther Dotterer. The Lutheran Liturgy: A Study of the Common Liturgy of the Lutheran Church in America. Rev. ed. Philadelphia, Pa.: Muhlenberg Press, [1959?].

This 824 page study contains a wealth of carefully organized material of interest to teachers in Lutheran seminaries and to those such as choir masters and organists who are technically interested in the liturgy. In addition to treatment of the Lutheran liturgy in America it provides background on the history of worship and the liturgy in Europe. See also Finck (G0579) and Streng (G0766).

G0721   Reese, J. Irving. A Service Manual for Ministers. Des Plaines, Ill.: Regular Baptist Press, 1966.

See also Christensen (G0527), Hiscox (G0605), McCabe (G0649) and Segler (G0741).

G0722   Reinertsen, Peter Amos. Acolytes and Altar Guilds: A Chancel Ministry. Rock Island, Ill.: Augustana Press, 1960.

Written by a Lutheran layman as a source of information to pastors and laymen, this book is intended to assist in developing informed lay participation in Christian worship. The first part discusses worship, liturgical form, furnishings and the language of symbolism. The second focuses on serving the congregation at worship: the altar guilds and preparation for worship; acolytes in worship (the various sections of the service are treated). Notes, references, appendixes and an index complete the volume. Much useful information, which can be used according to the particular congregation's needs, is provided in the manual.

G0723   Rest, Friedrich. Funeral Handbook. Valley Forge, Pa.: Judson Press, c. 1982.

See also Christensen (G0524, G0525), Hutton (G0614), Leach (G0638), Lockyer (G0647), Poovey (G0711) and Wallis (G0784).

G0724   Rest, Friedrich. Worship Services for Church Groups. Philadelphia, Pa.: Christian Education Press, 1962.

See also Currie (G0548) and Guptill (G0596).

G0725   Revell, Peter, comp. Fifteenth Century English Prayers and Meditations: A Descriptive List of Manuscripts in the British Library. Garland Reference Library of the Humanities, vol. 19. New York: Garland Publishing Company, 1975.

Arranged by subject, this compilation provides detailed bibliographical entries for an important range of manuscripts. Revell is indexed by author, initia and manuscript number.

G0726   Richardson, Lovella Stoll. Handbook for the Church Office. Cincinnati, Ohio: Standard Publishing Company, 1972.

G0727   Rietschel, Georg. Lehrbuch der Liturgik. 2. Aufl. von Paul Graff. 2 vols. Göttingen: Vandenhoeck und Ruprecht, 1951-1952.

This textbook on liturgy and worship in the Protestant tradition seeks to cover all aspects of the topic, including development of the Christian cult, architecture, music, forms of worship, art, meaning in worship. The text is detailed and scholarly, covering both Roman Catholic and Protestant liturgies; the treatment of each aspect of the topic is extremely thorough and includes very full notes and references to other writings. Rietschel is an excellent historical survey for advanced students with knowledge of German. See also Fattinger (G0576) and Jones (G0621).

G0728   Righetti, Mario. Manuale di Storia Liturgica. 3. ed. 4 vols. Milan: Editrice Ancora, 1959-1966.

Long considered a standard work on the history of the Roman Catholic liturgy, this revised and amplified edition of Righetti takes into considera- tion Vatican II decrees and other important factors in liturgical renewal. There are numerous bibliographies for further study, and the index greatly adds to the reference value of this important Italian language work. In its coverage of the liturgical year, the mass and other sacraments Righetti is a valuable source of data for various levels of inquiry. See also Jungmann (G0622) and Lietzmann (G0642).

G0729   Robertson, James Douglas. Minister's Worship Handbook. Grand Rapids, Mich.: Baker Book House, 1974.

See also McCabe (G0649) and Murch (G0674).

G0730   Rodenmayer, Robert N., ed. The Pastor's Prayerbook, Selected and Arranged for Various Occasions. New York: Oxford University Press, 1960.

Intended for the use of pastors, this work contains a range of prayers from those taken from ancient sources to those written for this publication. The prayers are arranged under headings such as "Blessings", "Sickness", "Missions", "Thanksgiving", and cover public and private occasions. A list of sources, notes and indexes of subjects and authors are included. See also Colquhoun (G0541), Hunter (G0612) and Oglesby (G0690).

G0731   Roguet, A.M. The New Mass: A Clear and Simple Explanation of the Mass As Restored and Renewed in Accord with the Decrees of Vatican Council II. Trans. by Water van de Putte. New York: Catholic Book Publishing Company, 1970.

This is a practical guide to the new mass, its rites and signs. Although intended primarily for Catholic clergy and laity, Roguet is also useful for showing non-Roman Catholics key ideas and attitudes underlying the revision. See also Seasholtz (G0740) for documentary material on liturgical revisions of the twentieth century; see also O'Connell (G0687).

G0732   Roulin, Eugène Augustin. Vestments and Vesture: A Manual of Litur- gical Art. Trans. by Justin McCann. St. Louis, Mo.: Herder; London: Sands and Company, 1931. Reprint. Westminster, Md.: Newman Press, 1950.

This practical guide to the selection of modern vestments is geared primar- ily to the requirements of Roman Catholic usage but is suitable for other liturgical traditions as well. It is not intended as an historical or artistic treatment but rather as a practical handbook. An index is provided. For a more historical guide see Pocknee (G0710); see also McCloud (G0651) and Nainfa (G0677).

G0733   Sandlin, John Lewis. A Prayer for Every Meeting. Westwood, N.J.: Fleming H. Revell Company, 1964.

See also Davies and Slifer (G0554), Uehling (G0772) and Williamson (G0797).

G0734   Schmemann, Alexander. Introduction to Liturgical Theology. Trans. by Ashleigh E. Moorhouse. Library of Orthodox Theology, no. 4. Portland,

Maine: American Orthodox Press; London: Faith Press, 1966.

This work on the liturgical theology of the Orthodox tradition focuses particularly on the Typicon or Ordo, the set of rules by which the Orthodox Church orders its liturgical life. This historical development of the liturgy is treated in three main periods: from the origins of the liturgy to the Constantinian peace; from Constantine to the ninth century; from the ninth century onwards. This is a useful study for more advanced theological students.

G0735 Schmemann, Alexander. Sacraments and Orthodoxy. New York: Herder and Herder, 1965.

Originally prepared as a study guide for a student conference, this 142 page version is intended for the general reader. It is written by a notable Orthodox participant in the ecumenical dialogue, and offers insights into Orthodox theology especially for those concerned with unity. It is brief and lacks scholarly apparatus so is more suitable as an introduction and starting point than as offering a more scholarly approach. See also Dabovich (G0549) and Heliopoulos (G0602).

G0736 Schmidt, Herman. Introductio in Liturgiam Occidentalem. Rome: Herder, 1960.

This general guide to the Roman Catholic liturgy covers its origins, documentary sources, liturgical revival, the sacraments and devotions, the calendar, sacred art and music. Despite some omissions and sketchy treatment in places, Schmidt has been well received as a valuable pastorally oriented approach to the liturgy. It contains significant bibliographical material and an index. For a complementary work on Eastern liturgies see Raes (G0717); see also King (G0627, G0629).

G0737 Schmitz, Walter J. Follow the Rubrics. Ed. by Eugene J. Weitzel. Washington, D.C: Catholic University of America Press, 1964.

See also McManus (G0654).

G0738 Schroeder, Frederick W. Worship in the Reformed Tradition. Philadelphia, Pa.: United Church Press, 1966.

This work, written within the free church tradition, stresses the role of theology in determining worship. It has been criticized for inadequate documentation and failure to discuss recent liturgical movements. See also Elford (G0568) and Nichols (G0680).

G0739 Schuster, Idelfonso. The Sacramentary (Liber Sacramentorum): Historical and Liturgical Notes on the Roman Missal. Trans. by Arthur Levelis-Marke. 5 vols. London: Burns, Oates and Washbourne, 1924-1930.

This detailed study of the Roman missal covers theology, spirituality, history and archeology as they relate to the missal. Arrangement is by the liturgical calendar, which facilitates rapid reference; but there is neither an index nor a bibliography. The translation is clear, although some of the comments have become very dated as a result of changing attitudes to the missal since Vatican II. See also Catholic Church (G0520) and McManus (G0655).

G0740   Seasholtz, R. Kevin, ed. The New Liturgy: A Documentation, 1903-1965. New York: Herder and Herder, 1966.

This collection of papal and other church documents deals with liturgical reforms from the Motu Proprio of Pius X on sacred music to the Liturgical Constitution of Vatican II. An index is provided. For students of liturgical history and of Roman Catholic institutional thinking on the subject this is an important collection. See also Roguet (G0731).

G0741   Segler, Franklin M. The Broadman Minister's Manual. Nashville, Tenn.: Broadman Press, 1968.

Also entitled A Minister's Manual, this guide contains considerable material of value to Protestant clergy from nonliturgical traditions but who are involved in conducting and planning various types of services and worship programs. See also Christensen (G0527), Hutton (G0616), McNeil (G0656) and Reese (G0721).

G0742   Segler, Franklin M. Christian Worship: Its Theology and Practice. Nashville, Tenn.: Broadman Press, 1967.

This study of public worship in the Protestant tradition covers the meaning of worship, means of expression, planning and conducting services. It draws on other authors to a large extent, but also offers interesting insights on the material presented. See also Allmen (G0469) and Hoon (G0607).

G0743   Seidel, Uwe, and Zils, Diethard, eds. Aktion Gottesdienst. 2 vols. Wuppertal: Jugenddienst-Verlag; Düsseldorf: Verlag Hans Altenberg, 1970.

Volume 1 covers evangelische und katholische Gottesdienstmodelle, okumenische Gottesdienste, Gebete, Meditationen, Bekentnisse. Volume 2 covers Kirchenjahr evangelische und katholische Gottesdienstmodelle, Texte, Denkanstösse, Flugblätter, Tagesmessen.

G0744   Senn, Frank C. The Pastor As Worship Leader: A Manual for Corporate Worship. Minneapolis, Minn.: Augsburg Publishing House, 1977.

See also Currie (G0548), Geffen (G0590) and Noyes (G0684).

G0745   Shands, Alfred Rives. The Liturgical Movement and the Local Church. Rev. ed. New York: Morehouse-Barlow Company, 1965.

This small paperback is a revised and enlarged edition of a volume published by SCM Press in 1959. Written by an Episcopalian, it is concerned not only with the form of worship but also with issues such as participation and reintegration. It includes rather radical proposals and views on patterns of worship. See also Colquhoun (G0541).

G0746   Shands, Alfred Rives, and Evans, H. Barry. How and Why: An Introduction to the Three New Trial Eucharists and the Daily Office of the Episcopal Church. New York: Seabury Press, 1971.

Aimed at Episcopalians using Services for Trial Use: Authorized Alternatives to Prayer Book Services (the "green book"), this study guide seeks to familiarize parishioners with the design concept of the new services. It includes an introduction to the new liturgical principles followed by discussion of the three trial eucharistic liturgies and daily offices. A collection of resources for creating liturgy concludes the handbook which is a sound starting point for students of Anglican worship and of modern liturgies in general. See also Miller (G0667).

G0747   Shann, G.V. Euchology: A Manual of Prayers of the Holy Orthodox Church Done into English. Kidderminster: n.p., 1981.   Reprint. New York: AMS Press, 1969.

This collection contains a brief synopsis of the prayers used in daily worship of the Orthodox Church. It is arranged according to the various services (vespers, compline, matins, hours, etc.) and presents the prayers in standard English translations. Ssee also Vaporis (G0777).

G0748   Shepherd, Massey Hamilton, Jr. The Oxford American Prayer Book Commentary. New York: Oxford University Press, 1950.

This is a facsimile reproduction of the 1944 Oxford edition of the Book of Common Prayer and contains commentary on facing pages. Prepared by a noted liturgical scholar, the commentary is thorough, informative and judicious, making this an indispensible work for studies in the Anglican liturgy. See also Episcopal Church (G0571).

G0749   Shepherd, Massey Hamilton, Jr. The Worship of the Church. The Church's Teaching, vol. 4. Greenwich, Conn.: Seabury Press, 1952.

This work is concerned with the interpretation of the public, corporate worship of the church, particularly the form of worship embodied in the liturgy of the Episcopal Church. References are to the American Book of Common Prayer. The first part examines the principles of Christian worship; the second deals with particular parts of the liturgy. A comprehensive bibliography (pp. 213-236) and an index are provided. See also Simcox (G0754).

G0750   Sheppard, Lancelot Capel. How to Use the New Breviary. London: Darton, Longman and Todd, 1961.

See also Catholic Church (G0514).

G0751   Sheppard, Lancelot Capel. The Liturgical Books. New York: Hawthorn Books, 1962.

This work treats the history and development of each of the principal liturgical books of the Roman rite, providing detailed information on the history of the rites contained in each. Successive chapters cover the Roman missal, breviary, martyrology, pontifical and ritual. The concluding chapter discusses liturgical reform of the twentieth century. A select bibliography is included. For the works discussed see Catholic Church (G0503, G0505, G0506, G0511, G0513, G0517, G0518, G0520, G0521).

G0752   Sheppard, Lancelot Capel, ed. The People Worship: A History of the Liturgical Movement. New York: Hawthorn Books, 1967.

This Roman Catholic work includes material by the Sacerdotal Communities of St. Severin of Paris and St. Joseph of Nice. Written in the light of Vatican II reforms, it provides a short history of the liturgical movement in various countries, a discussion of the fundamental ideas of the liturgical revival, analysis of advances regarding the liturgy and the divine office, pastoral practice, etc., and, finally, four basic documents of the liturgical renewal. A select bibliography, (pp. 265-268), an index and notes on the contributors are included. See also Benoît (G0481) and White (G0796).

G0753   Shereghy, Basil. The Liturgy of St. John Chrysostom, Ruthenian Form: Historical Background, Introduction and Commentary. Collegeville,   Minn.: Liturgical Press, 1961.

See also Orthodox Eastern Church (G0692).

G0754   Simcox, Carroll Eugene. Understanding the Sacraments. New York: Morehouse-Gorham, 1956.

Written within an Anglican framework, this brief work examines the basic sacramental principle, then the NT foundation of each of the sacraments. Liturgical technicalities of baptism, confirmation, holy matrimony, holy orders, etc. are dealt with only secondarily. There is no index. See also Shepherd (G0749).

G0755   Simcox, Carroll Eugene. The Words of Our Worship: A Study in Prayer Book Meanings. New York: Morehouse-Gorham, 1955.

This book takes from the Book of Common Prayer seventy-six familiar words or phrases, expounding each either in the form of a simple explanation or definition or a more lengthy treatment. Each word or phrase is listed in the table of contents, which is presented in sections (morning prayer, evening prayer, holy communion, etc.). Page references are to the American Book of Common Prayer (G0571). See also Johnson (G0619) and Huggett (G0611).

G0756   Skoglund, John E. A Manual of Worship. Valley Forge, Pa.: Judson Press, 1968.

This collection of worship materials for the free church tradition provides a useful resource, with liturgical materials for regular and special services and classified prayers, affirmations of faith, assurances of pardon, etc. An introductory essay discusses eight principles that should mark Christian worship. The materials have been carefully selected and edited.   See also the following entry (G0757) and White (G0796).

G0757   Skoglund, John E. Worship in the Free Churches. Valley Forge, Pa.: Judson Press, 1965.

This introduction to the concept of liturgical renewal, produced primarily for the free churches, draws on established authorities in the field and is well presented. It includes a useful digest of Protestant liturgical thinking. See also Coffin (G0540) and White (G0796).

G0758   Sloyan, Gerard Stephen. Commentary on the New Lectionary. New York: Paulist Press, c.1975.

These comments on the Bible readings for the three year cycle of the Roman lectionary inaugurated in November 1969 are intended to help clergy and others who promote weekly worship. Knowledge of the liturgy is assumed; the comments are mainly of an exegetical nature. After a table of Sundays, feasts and seasons, 1975-1980, arrangement is by year, and within each by season, beginning with the first Sunday of Advent. Feasts of Jesus, Mary and the saints are listed at the end, and an index is provided. For the lectionary see Catholic Church (G0507-G0509).

G0759   Smart, Ninian. The Concept of Worship. New York: St. Martin's Press; London: Macmillan and Company, 1972.

See also Spielmann (G0759) and Underhill (G0773).

G0760   Sokolov, Dimitrii Pavlovich. A Manual of the Orthodox Church's Divine Services. Trans. from the Russian. New York: Wynkoop, Hallenbeck, Cranford Company, 1899.

This 166 page manual explains all aspects of the traditional Orthodox liturgy, including sacraments, feasts, fasts, cycle of services and vestments. See also Heliopoulos (G0602), Oakley (G0685) and Schmemann (G0735).

G0761   Solovey, Melitius Michael. Eastern Liturgical Theology: General Introduction. Weston, Ontario: Ukranian Catholic Religion and Culture Society of Etobicoke (Toronto) and Ukranian Catholic Youth of Canada, 1970.

See also King (G0628).

G0762   Spicer, Dorothy Gladys. The Book of Festivals. New York: The Woman's Press, 1937. Reprint. Detroit, Mich.: Gale Research Company, 1969.

The first part of this compendium discusses the major festivals of thirty-nine nationalities, both Eastern and Western. The second part tells the story of seven calendars, including Christian, Jewish and Moslem. An appendix presents a glossary of religious and festival terminology in common use. See also Gwynne (G0597) and Walsh (G0789).

G0763   Spielmann, Richard M. History of Christian Worship. New York: Seabury Press, 1966.

Written to provide historical perspective for those concerned with the origins of acts and principles of Christian worship in an age of liturgical renewal, this popular and nontechnical volume sketches Christian liturgical development from NT times to the present. It does not attempt to cover more technical aspects of various traditional liturgical forms. It does, however, go into some detail on The Book of Common Prayer. See also Smart (G0759) and Underhill (G0773).

G0764   Srawley, James Herbert. The Early History of the Liturgy. The Cambridge Handbooks of Liturgical Study. Cambridge: Cambridge University Press, 1947.

Intended to provide beginners with a study of the main factors in the history of the development of the early liturgy, this work covers roughly the first four centuries. It includes discussion of developments in Alexandria and Egypt, Palestine and Syria, Africa and Italy, and liturgical development in East and West. A bibliography and an index are provided. See also Jones (G0621).

G0765 Stehle, Aurelius. Manual of Episcopal Ceremonies; Based on the "Caere-moniale Episcoporum", Decrees of the Sacred Congregation of Rites and Approved Authors. 5th ed. Rev. by Emmeran A. Rettger. 2 vols. Latrobe, Pa.: Archabbey Press, 1961.

This liturgical reference work contains detailed instructions and some texts for episcopal ceremonies in the Roman Catholic Church. An index is included to facilitate usage. An abbreviated version based on the fourth edition is available as Ordinary Episcopal Ceremonies: A Section of the "Manual of Episcopal Ceremonies". Rev. and rearranged to include episcopal ceremonies used frequently in cathedral, abbatial and parish churches by Emmeran A. Rettger (Latrobe, Pa.: Archabbey Press, 1959). See also Catholic Church (G0502).

G0766   Streng, William D. Toward Meaning in Worship: An Introduction to Lutheran Liturgy. Minneapolis, Minn.: Augsburg Publishing House, 1964.

Written primarily for laymen, this work attempts to facilitate intelligent and devotional use of the Lutheran liturgy, and to assist the cause of ecumenicity. Chapters on aspects of the liturgy's history or importance and on particular elements (invocation, confession, etc.) are followed by prayers, references to appropriate collects and hymns. A glossary of liturgical terms and full table of contents are provided; there is no index. See also Finck (G0579) and Reed (G0720).

G0767 Suffling, Ernest Richard. Church Festival Decorations; Being Full Directions for Garnishing Churches for Christmas, Easter, Whitsuntide and Harvest, and Notes on Other Feasts or Festivals. 2nd ed. London: L. Upcott Gill; New York: Charles Scribner's Sons, 1967. Reprint. Detroit, Mich.: Gale Research Company, 1974.

This substantial volume covers every aspect of decorations for the church and includes a brief history of church festival ornamentation. Suffling is geared to practical needs, presenting information on wreath materials, lettering, adhesives and related topics. Specific suggestions for decorations are provided in chapters on the major festivals of the church year, and the volume is well illustrated. See also Gwynne (G0597).

G0768   Sullivan, John Francis. The Externals of the Catholic Church: A Hand-book of Catholic Usage. Rev. by John C. O'Leary. 2nd ed. New York: P.J. Kenedy, [c.1959].

Designed for the layman, this 403 page handbook provides clear and suc-cinct explanations of church government, religious orders, the apostolate, sacraments, the mass, liturgical books and seasons, the Bible and devo-tions. Although lacking a bibliography, Sullivan is suitable for the beginner who wishes to have traditional views on most aspects of Roman Cathol-icism. See also the following entry (G0769) and Fattinger (G0576).

G0769   Sullivan, John Francis. The Visible Church, Her Government, Ceremon-ies, Sacramentals, Festivals and Devotions: A Compendium of the "Externals of the Catholic Church". 6th ed. New York: P.J. Kenedy and Sons, 1922.

This illustrated textbook for Catholic schools in catechism format is dated but retains value as a source of basic information on worship and related topics of pre-Vatican II Catholicism. See also the preceding entry (G0768).

G0770   Thompson, Bard, ed. Liturgies of the Western Church. Cleveland, Ohio: Meridian Books, 1961.

This survey for beginning students provides a reasonably detailed analysis of some principal liturgies from Justin Martyr to the Sunday worship of North American Methodism. Each text is supplied with an introduction designed to elucidate the liturgy and the tradition in which it stands. Bibliographies are appended to each chapter, and a general bibliography is provided. See also Baumstark (G0478) and King (G0627, G0629).

G0771   [no entry]

G0772   Uehling, Carl T. Prayers for Public Worship. Philadelphia, Pa.: Fortress Press, 1972.

This collection contains prayers in contemporary language for use in different forms of worship and to be read either by the minister or by others or an entire congregation. The table of contents indicates the occasion for which the prayer is intended (days of the church year, prayers for particular occasions, intercessions for particular people or events, etc.). There is no index. Various typefaces are used to indicate where modifications to the prayers might be made, or where sections might be read by different persons. See also Davies and Slifer (G0554), Sandlin (G0733) and Williamson (G0792).

G0773   Underhill, Evelyn. Worship. New York: Harper and Brothers, 1937.

This classic study from an Anglo-Catholic viewpoint of the nature and principles of worship includes discussion of the chief forms in which worship is expressed in Christendom. The first part studies the fundamental characteristics of Christian worship. Descriptive and historical studies in the second part (Jewish worship, Catholic worship - Eastern and Western, worship in the Reformed churches, the Anglican tradition, etc.) illustrate the principles as embodied in the chief types of cultus. Bibliographical footnotes are included, and although there is no index the full, descriptive table of contents facilitates use. See also Smart (G0759) and Spielmann (G0763).

G0774   Upson, Stephen H.R. A Brief Synopsis of the Orthodox Christian Year. 2nd ed. Brooklyn, N.Y.: Syrian Antiochian Archdiocese of New York and All North America, [c.1953].

This 112 page introduction to the Orthodox ecclesiastical year lists and explains the feast and saints' days on a month-by-month basis. See also Orthodox Eastern Church (G0693-G0695).

G0775   Urlin, Ethel Lucy Hargreave. Festivals, Holy Days and Saints' Days: A Study in Origins and Survivals in Church Ceremonies and Secular Customs. London: Simpkin, Marshall, Hamilton, Kent and Company, 1915. Reprint. Ann Arbor, Mich.: Gryphon Books; London: Simpkin, Marshall, Hamilton, Kent and Company, 1971.

Focusing particularly on England, Urlin considers religious ceremonies of the early twentieth century and traces their connection to rites and customs of the pre-Christian era, the Middle Ages and other periods. Materials on ceremonies, festivals, customs and similar topics are arranged according to the calendar. See also Walsh (G0789) and Weiser (G0792).

G0776   Vagaggini, Cipriano. Theological Dimensions of the Liturgy: A General Treatise on the Theology of the Liturgy. Trans. by Leonard J. Doyle and W.A. Jurgens. Collegeville, Minn.: Liturgical Press, 1976.

This lengthy and detailed exposition covers the nature of liturgy in the Roman Catholic Church, liturgy and the Bible, liturgy and theology, liturgy and life. Throughout the work emphasis is placed on spiritual values inherent in worship. The English translation takes Vatican II decisions into account, making the analysis suitably up-to-date. There is an analytical index and a name index to this excellent Catholic sourcebook on the theology of worship. See also Davis (G0555) and Verheul (G0779).

G0777   Vaporis, Nomikos Michael. Orthodox Prayer Book. Brookline, Mass.: Holy Cross Orthodox Press, c.1977.

See also Shann (G0747).

G0778   Vereinigte Evangelisch-Lutherische Kirche Deutschlands, ed. Agende für Evangelisch-Lutherische Kirchen und Gemeinden. 4 vols. and 2 supplements. Berlin: Lutherisches Verlagshaus, 1960-1969.

Available in various editions for each volume, this collection of German Lutheran ceremonies covers Hauptgottesdienst (4th ed., 1969); Gebetsgottesdienste (1st ed., 1960); Amtshandlungen (2nd ed., 1963); Ordinations-, Einsegungs-, Einführungs- und Einwehrungshandlungen (2nd ed., 1966); Handreichung für den seelsorgerlichen Dienst (1st supplement, 3rd ed., 1967); Kindergottesdienst (2nd supplement, 1st ed., 1964). See also Lutheran Church in America (G0648) and Müller and Blankenburg (G0672).

G0779   Verheul, A. Introduction to the Liturgy: Towards a Theology of Worship. Trans. by Margaret Clarke. Collegeville, Minn.: Liturgical Press; London: Burns and Oates, 1968.

This work is intended to foster understanding of the liturgy in the Roman Catholic Church in the light of Vatican II. It is based on lectures given to theological students, and is written for the nonspecialist. The first part is concerned with the theology of the liturgy; the second considers contemporary problems of liturgical piety. An index of persons and biblical references is included. See also Davis (G0555) and Vagaggini (G0776).

G0780   Vincent, Marvin Richardson. The Minister's Handbook, Containing Forms for Baptism, Marriage, Burial, the Lord's Supper, Church Service and the Ordination of Elders, with Classified Sections of Scripture for the Sick Room and Collects for Various Occasions. Rev. and enlarged ed. New York: Lentilhon and Company, 1900.

This manual sets out the forms listed in its title, particularly for the use of Presbyterian ministers. Those for the ordination of elders and deacons are based on the Presbyterian directory; two forms are provided for the celebration of marriage. The table of contents provides adequate access in the absence of an index. See also Macleod (G0653).

G0781   Voigt, Edwin Edgar. Methodist Worship in the Church Universal. Nashville, Tenn.: Graded Press, 1965.

See also Dunkle and Quillian (G0564) and Methodist Church (G0664).

G0782   Waddams, Herbert. Companion to the "Book of Common Prayer". London: A.R. Mowbray and Company, 1966.

Designed to help people explore and use the Prayer Book effectively, this work reviews briefly the history of the Book of Common Prayer, and provides commentary on the service of Holy Communion, sections on daily prayers, the Psalms, belief, marriage, health and sickness, etc. Tables of contents, side-by-side, for the English (1662), American and Canadian Books of Common Prayer are included. While the Companion has been criticized for some omissions, such as discussion of differences in the central part of the Holy Communion service, it is nonetheless a helpful guide for Anglicans. See Church of England (G0528) and Episcopal Church (G0571); see also Brightman (G0491) and Frere (G0585).

G0783   Wallis, Charles Langworthy, ed. A Complete Sourcebook for the Lord's Supper. Grand Rapids, Mich.: Baker Book House, 1978.

Similar to The Table of the Lord (G0786), this work includes eight complete services, forty communion prayers, 168 meditations, 107 suggestions for music and much additional material on the eucharist. There are complete indexes of texts, poems, days and seasons, subjects, authors and sources. The devotional and homiletical contributions are drawn from such individuals as Justin Martyr, Bunyan, Jeremias, Gore and Wesley.

G0784   Wallis, Charles Langworthy, ed. The Funeral Encyclopedia, a Source Book. New York: Harper and Brothers, 1953. Reprint. Grand Rapids, Mich.: Baker Book House, 1973.

This well indexed compendium contains typical funeral services for various situations in traditions without a set form of worship, funeral sermons, prayers, an anthology of poetry and a section on professional conduct. Scriptural quotations are from the AV. A list of sources is included. See also Christensen (G0524, G0525), Hutton (G0614), Leach (G0638), Lockyer (G0647), Poovey (G0711) and Rest (G0723).

G0785   Wallis, Charles Langworthy, ed. Lenten-Easter Sourcebook. New York: Abingdon Press, 1961. Reprint. Grand Rapids, Mich.: Baker Book House, 1978.

This worship and preaching guide to the Easter season for clergy and lay leaders is arranged in a series of chapters which cover Lent and Holy Week chronologically. The work is thoroughly indexed (contributors and sources, poetry, subjects). See also The Book of Easter (G0485).

G0786   Wallis, Charles Langworthy, ed. The Table of the Lord: A Communion Encyclopedia. New York: Harper and Brothers, 1958.

This 228 page compilation includes eucharistic liturgies, prayers and sermons suitable for Protestant churches. It includes critical, theological and interpretive matter, but selections were made primarily in terms of usefulness in preaching and worship. Four sections of communion services, prayers, preaching and poetry material are followed by indexes of texts, of poetry, of days and seasons, of authors and sources and of subjects. See also Wallis' Complete Sourcebook (G0783).

G0787   Wallis, Charles Langworthy, ed. Worship Resources for Special Days. Grand Rapids, Mich.: Baker Book House, 1976.

See also France (G0583) and Martin (G0660).

G0788   Wallis, Charles Langworthy, ed. Worship Resources for the Church Year. New York: Harper and Brothers, 1954.

This 483 page compilation is an extensive and wide ranging collection of worship and homiletical materials for the special days and occasions generally included in the evangelical Protestant calendar. The book is divided according to four major emphases: the Christian heritage, mission, home, nation. Categories of material include calls to worship, litanies and responsive prayers, prayers for pulpit use and group worship, topics, texts and homiletic suggestions. Scriptural matter is from the AV in almost all cases. The volume is thoroughly indexed (authors and sources, texts, poetry, special days and occasions, topics). See also Bowman (G0487), Coffin (G0540) and Skoglund (G0756, G0757).

G0789   Walsh, William Shepard, comp. Curiosities of Popular Customs and of Rites, Ceremonies, Observances and Miscellaneous Antiquities. Philadelphia, Pa.: J.B. Lippincott Company; London: Gibbings and Company, 1898. Reprint. Philadelphia, Pa.: J.B. Lippincott COmpany, 1925.

Focusing particularly on the religious scene, Walsh presents an interesting compilation on holidays, rites, and associated ceremonies. The work covers strange and unusual observances not found in other sources and is particularly useful for tracing the development and history of customs regarded as noteworthy in the nineteenth century. The arrangement of material is alphabetical, and there are some cross references. The lack of an index is something of a drawback. See also Urlin (G0775) and Weiser (G0792).

G0790   Webber, Frederick Roth. Practical Studies in the Liturgy, Indicating the Manner in Which Holy Communion, Matins,   Vespers and the Various Other Services May Be Conducted. Erie, Pa.: Ashby, 1936.

See also Müller (G0671).

G0791   Weems, Ann. Reaching for Rainbows: Resources for Creative Worship. Philadelphia, Pa.: Westminster Press, 1980.

See also Bowman (G0487), Coffin (G0540) and White (G0796).

G0792   Weiser, Francis Xavier. Handbook of Christian Feasts and Customs: The Year of the Lord in Liturgy and Folklore. New York: Harcourt, Brace and World, 1958.

Containing three earlier works, this valuable compendium is a detailed introduction to the feasts, customs and holy days of the church as found in folklore and custom. Although containing no bibliographies as such, the chapters are well documented; an index and a dictionary of terms are also provided. Combining sound scholarship with a highly readable narrative, this is an excellent handbook for general readers and beginning students rather than for advanced researchers. See also Urlin (G0775) and Walsh (G0789).

G0793   Weller, Philip Thomas, trans. and ed. The Roman Ritual in Latin and English, with Rubrics and Plainchant Notation. 3 vols. Milwaukee, Wisc.: Bruce Publishing Company, 1946-1952.

This standard edition contains the complete Roman Catholic ceremonies as used by the church in the United States. Both Latin and English texts of the Rituale Romanum (G0517) are provided. The three volumes deal with sacraments and processions; burial, exorcism, reserved blessings, etc.; blessings. Each volume is thoroughly indexed. Now dated because of its limitation to pre-Vatican II ceremonies, Weller is a valuable guide to liturgical practices of the past. See also Collectio Rituum (G0504) and Pontificale Romanum (G0513).

G0794   Whatton, G.A.C., ed. The Priest's Companion: A Manual of Instructions and Prayers for Priests and Religious. London: W. Knott, 1960.

See also Müller (G0671).

G0795   Whitaker, Edward Charles. Documents of the Baptismal Liturgy. 2nd ed.   Alcuin Club Collections, no. 42. London: SPCK, 1970.

This collection comprises English translations of the main documents on baptism from the first century to medieval times, originating in both East and West.   A brief glossary of technical terms is supplied. This edition contains an introductory essay which argues the absence of a confirmation rite from early Syrian usage, and there are enlarged sections on Tertullian, St. John Chrysostom and St. Cyprian. For a handbook on baptism see Jagger (G0617).

G0796   White, James F. New Forms of Worship. Nashville, Tenn.: Abingdon Press, 1971.

This 222 page introduction to worship and preaching provides a useful rationale for new forms of worship and a reasonable analysis of older forms. It is addressed to clergy and lay members of worship committees. Three norms for Christian worship are discussed: pastoral, theological, historical. Forms of worship are considered in terms of the environment of worship, physical movement, sounds and sights, the sacraments as sign-activities, preaching and the words of worship. This is a practical work, informed with historical and theological insight and with pastoral concern. It is useful for clergy and laymen concerned with liturgical renewal. See also Benoît (G0481), Cairns (G0500) and Sheppard (G0752).

G0797   Williamson, Robert L. Effective Public Prayer. Nashville, Tenn.: Broadman Press, 1960.

This study of the place and function of public prayer in worship and of the manner in which it should be prepared and prayed is intended as an aid to ministers. Such aspects as the function, content and language of pastoral prayer are considered in separate chapters. The style is straightforward. A bibliography and notes are included. See also Davies and Slifer (G0554), Sandlin (G0733) and Uehling (G0772).

G0798   Wuest, Joseph. Matters Liturgical: The Collectio Rerum Liturgicarum. Trans. by Thomas W. Mullaney. Re-arranged and enlarged by William T. Barry. 10th ed. New York: F. Pustet Company, 1959.

This guide does not contain complete instructions for ceremonies in the Roman Catholic tradition but rather provides answers to specific problems encountered in worship. A useful index is provided for quick reference. See also Fortescue and O'Connell (G0582) and O'Connell and Schmitz (G0689).

G0799   Zeidler, Clemens H. Altar Prayers for the Church Year. Minneapolis, Minn.: Augsburg Publishing House, 1962.

Intended primarily for use by pastors of liturgical churches, this volume contains a series of alternate altar prayers for all the Sundays and chief festivals of the church year. It offers prayers related in theme, biblical forms of thought and content to the propers appointed for that day. The table of contents lists the day for which each prayer is offered, providing adequate guidance to the collection in the absence of an index. For Roman Catholic altar prayers see Altar Prayers (G0471).

ART AND ARCHITECTURE: HANDBOOKS

G0800 Anson, Peter Frederick. The Building of Churches. The New Library of Catholic Knowledge, vol. 10. New York: Hawthorn Books, 1964.

See also Gordon (G0823).

G0801   Baker, John, and Lammer, Alfred. English Stained Glass. New York: H.N. Abrams; London: Thames and Hudson, 1960.

Containing text by Baker and illustrations by Lammer, this interesting work is arranged in sections: English stained glass in general, twelfth and thirteenth centuries, fourteenth century, fifteenth century, sixteenth century. There are lengthy and detailed captions accompanying the 103 monochrome and thirty-four color illustrations. There is a brief bibliography and an index of illustrations.

G0802   Bartoli, Luciano. Manuale di Arte Sacra. Turin: Marietti, 1965.

See also Conlay and Anson (G0813).

G0803   Bittel, Kurt, et al., eds. Propylaen Kunstgeschichte. Vol. 1- . Berlin: Propylaen Verlag, 1966- .

Projected in eighteen volumes, this valuable and detailed survey contains several volumes of value for students of ecclesiastical art; there are three particularly useful volumes on the Middle Ages. Each title includes numerous illustrations, detailed notes, a bibliography, chronology and index. Bittel is a well produced set which contains essential information and admirably thorough reference aids. See also Henze (G0830).

G0804   Bles, Arthur de. How to Distinguish the Saints in Art by Their Costumes, Symbols and Attributes. New York: Art Culture Publications, 1925. Reprint. Detroit, Mich.: Gale Research Company, 1975.

The first section of Bles contains twelve chapters on symbolism in general and for different groups (Virgin Mary, monastic orders, etc.) and explanations of pictures which show symbols. The second part consists of a series of useful appendixes: alphabetical table of martyrdoms, table of saints classified by habitual costume, table of saints classified by categories, alphabetical list of symbols and attributes together with the names of those who bear them, a chronological list of bishops of Rome and popes, list of illustrations and a general index. See also Drake (G0412), Post (G0849) and Waters (G0865).

G0805   Bond, Francis. An Introduction to English Church Architecture from the Eleventh to the Sixteenth Century. 2 vols. London: Oxford University Press, 1913.

This expansion of Gothic Architecture in England (London: B.T. Batsford, 1912) is a detailed survey which provides data on both churches and cathedrals. There are 1400 illustrations and many ground plans, and the text treats individual buildings very fully. There is a glossary in English and French, an index locorum and an index rerum. Footnote references and bibliographies accompany sections and chapters. Bond is an indispensible and thorough guide to English ecclesiastical architecture for the period.

G0806   Bottomley, Frank. The Church Explorer's Guide to Symbols and Their Meaning. London: Kaye and Ward, 1978.

The alphabetically arranged entries in this 176 page handbook deal with the symbolism of decoration, furniture and fabric in churches. Emphasis is placed on historical and doctrinal aspects of these elements, particularly as exemplified in a British setting. While lacking a broad scholarly view of the field, this is a useful dictionary handbook for beginners and interested laymen. Ssee also Thompson (G0863).

G0807   Bouyer, Louis. Liturgy and Architecture. Notre Dame, Ill.: University of Notre Dame Press, 1967.

This monograph examines the arrangement of church interiors in relation to the conduct of worship. Much of it is a historical survey, beginning with arrangements in a synagogue at the time of the early church. Focuses for the liturgy within the church are discussed and illustrated with diagrams. See also Debuyst (G0815) and Hammond (G0826).

G0808   Bradner, John. Symbols of Church Seasons and Days. Wilton, Conn.: Morehouse-Barlow Company, 1977.

See also Child (G0810).

G0809   Burgess, Frederick Bevan. English Churchyard Memorials. London: Lutterworth Press, 1963.

An interesting survey of a neglected but important topic, Burgess covers the origin and development of churchyards and cemeteries, an historical analysis of types of monuments from 2500 B.C. to 1900 A.D., techniques associated with their development (training, quarries, transport, wages and prices). Most interesting from an architectural viewpoint are the first two sections. There are detailed chapter notes and indexes of stone carvers, place names and subjects. A brief glossary (pp. 299-302) adds to the reference value of Burgess. See also Crossley (G0814) and Esdaile (G0819).

G0810   Child, Heather, and Colles, Dorothy. <u>Christian Symbols, Ancient and Modern: A Handbook for Students</u>. London: Bell, 1971; New York: Charles Scribner's Sons, 1972.

This 270 page compilation is concerned with visual Christian symbols as used in the church and includes both descriptive text and illustrations (drawings and photographs). Individual chapters deal with, among other topics, the cross, the trinity, images of Christ, the Virgin Mary, the nativity of Christ, the Holy Spirit, the eucharist, angels, good and evil. The work is admirably complete and includes a detailed index. See also Bradner (G0808) and Ferguson (G0820).

G0811   Christ-Janer, Albert, and Foley, Mary Mix. <u>Modern Church Architecture: A Guide to the Form and Spirit of 20th Century Religious Buildings</u>. New York: McGraw-Hill Book Company, Dodge Book Department, 1962.

This is a collection of articles on forty Christian churches, monasteries and seminaries, grouped under three main headings: contemporary Catholic, contemporary Protestant, monasteries and seminaries. They explain how modern structure and form developed, the working philosophies of the architects and major schools of modern design, and attempt to interpret something of the spirit of the various faiths for the architect. The work is well illustrated and an index is provided. This is a valuable source for the pastor, church building committees and interested laymen. See also Gieselmann (G0822).

G0812   Christie, Yves, <u>et al</u>. <u>Art of the Christian World A.D. 200-1500: A Handbook of Styles and Forms</u>. New York: Rizzoli, 1982.

This reference volume contains basic introductory essays on early Christian, Byzantine, Romanesque and Gothic styles in art. These are followed by 1700 chronologically arranged line drawings of painting, sculpture, architecture and decorative arts of each period. The lack of an index greatly hampers use of the work, which otherwise provides a useful survey and overview of Christian art. See also Bourguet (G0818), Graber (G0825) and Michel (G0846).

G0813   Conlay, Iris, and Anson, Peter Frederick. <u>The Art of the Church</u>. The New Library of Catholic Knowledge, vol. 11. New York: Hawthorn Books; London: Burns and Oates, [1964].

See also Bartoli (G0802).

G0814   Crossley, Frederick Herbert. <u>English Church Monuments, A.D. 1500-1550</u>. London: B.T. Batsford, 1933.

This study deals adequately with monuments as a branch of sculpture in the medieval period, and it is well illustrated. Reference use is hampered by the lack of a bibliography and an index. See also Esdaile (G0819) for a continuation and Burgess (G0809) for a more technical study.

G0815   Debuyst, Frederic. <u>Modern Architecture and Christian Celebration</u>. Ecumenical Studies in Worship, no. 18. London: Lutterworth Press, 1968.

Based on the annual lectures delivered at the Institute for the Study of Worship and Religious Architecture, University of Birmingham in 1966, this Roman Catholic work deals briefly with aspects such as the idea of celebration, the genesis of the modern church, the post-conciliar church and images past and present. An index of persons and places is provided. It is a valuable contribution on the problem of church building. See also Bouyer (G0807) and Hammond (G0826).

G0816   Delderfield, Eric R. A Guide to Church Furniture. Newton Abbot: David and Charles, 1966; New York: Taplinger Publishing Company, 1967.

See also Gordon (G0823) and Lesage (G0842).

G0817   Didron, Adolf Napoleon. Christian Iconography: The History of Christian Art in the Middle Ages. Trans. by E.J. Millington. 2 vols. New York: Frederick Ungar Publishing Company, 1965.

This standard reference work on medieval Christian art presents very detailed information and in depth studies of the full range of figures, concepts and symbols of the church in the Middle Ages as depicted in artistic representations. It contains useful bibliographical references and a full index. See also Künstle (G0840).

G0818   Du Bourguet, Pierre. Early Christian Painting. Trans. by Simon Watson Taylor. New York: Viking Press; London: Weidenfeld and Nicolson, 1966.

This monograph deals with early Christian painting up to and even past the fourth century A.D., representing a transitional period between Roman and Byzantine painting. The importance of painting in this period, the subjects represented, the origin of the choice of subjects, the artistic interest of the painting, and social evidence are discussed. A bibliography is included, as well as lists of illustrations and of the color plates, which add to the value of this small volume. See also Christie (G0812), Grabar (G0825) and Michel (G0846).

G0819   Esdaile, Katharine Ada. English Church Monuments, 1510 to 1840. New York: Oxford University Press; London: B.T. Batsford, 1946.

This continuation of Crossley (G0814) is a well illustrated guide to church monuments in England to the mid-nineteenth century. The text is informative and descriptive, providing sound insights for those interested in monumental sculpture. See also Burgess (G0809).

G0820   Ferguson, George Wells. Signs and Symbols in Christian Art. With Illustrations from Paintings of the Renaissance. 2nd ed. New York: Oxford University Press; London: Zwemmer, 1955.

First published in 1954, Ferguson is intended as a quick reference manual and basic reference guide for students. The 346 pages are arranged in fourteen sections and employ simple language to describe signs and symbols. The explanations are accompanied by numerous drawings and reproductions of paintings to help illustrate the use of symbols. There is a general index. See also Child (G0810) and Webber (G0866).

G0821   Frere-Cook, Gervis. Art and Architecture of Christianity. Cleveland, Ohio: Press of Case Western Reserve University, 1972.

See also White (G0867). For a French language series on art and architecture in European churches see Dictionnaire des Eglises de France, Belgique, Luxembourg, Suisse (Histoire Générale des Eglises de France, Belgique, Luxembourg, Suisse, vol. 2- . Paris: R. Laffont, 1966-).

G0822   Gieselmann, Reinhard. Contemporary Church Architecture. London: Thames and Hudson, 1972.

See also Christ-Janer and Foley (G0811).

G0823   Gordon, Esmé. A Handbook on the Principles of Church Building: Furnishing, Equipment and Decoration. Edinburgh: Church of Soctland, Advisory Committee on Artistic Questions, 1963.

See also Anson (G0800) and Hoefler (G0832).

G0824   Grabar, André. Christian Iconography: A Study of Its Origins. Trans. by Terry Grabar. Princeton, N.J.: Princeton University Press, 1968; London: Routledge and Kegan Paul, 1969.

This brief work examines the sources of inspiration of Christian iconography, particularly links between Christian and Roman art. Christian portraits and representations of biblical narratives, images representing theological ideas, dogmas represented by juxtaposed images, etc. are considered in turn. Particularly valuable for its plates, this volume provides insights for the church historian and the theologian on early Christian art and the context in which it arose. For the medieval period see Didron (G0817).

G0825   Grabar, André. Early Christian Art; from the Rise of Christianity to the Death of Theodosius. Trans. by Stuart Gilbert and James Emmons. The Arts of Mankind, vol. 9. New York: Odyssey Press, 1968.

This study of Christian art to the close of the fourth century provides background material on chronology, society, forms and aesthetic, etc. Two main sections examine painting and sculpture up to the fourth century and art in the fourth century, including tomb paintings, mosaics, churches and basilicas. A chronological table, glossary-index, bibliography, list of illustrations, plan and map are included at the end of the volume. See also Christie (G0812), Du Bourguet (G0818) and Michel (G0846).

G0826   Hammond, Peter. Liturgy and Architecture. London: Barrie and Rockliff, 1960; New York: Columbia University Press, 1961.

This work contains discussion of the modern church, new trends in church planning on the Continent 1923-1940, church planning in England 1928-1940, post-war developments in church planning in Western Europe and America, liturgy and architecture in the church in England since 1945, etc. The importance of liturgical and theological renewal in relation to church architecture is emphasized. Fifty-three plates and a selective annotated bibliography of books and periodicals in English and other languages add to the value of the study, which, although primarily concerned with the Church of England, is of wider interest. See also Bouyer (G0807) and Debuyst (G0815).

G0827   Harvey, John Hooper. The English Cathedral. 2nd ed. London: B.T. Batsford, 1956.

First published in 1950, Harvey contains six chapters dealing with English cathedrals in general, Norman, Early English, Decorated, Perpendicular and Renaissance cathedrals. Each chapter includes historical and descriptive notes on cathedrals of the period together with plans. A glossary, list of sources and an analytic index complete the work, which is a detailed guide to its subject. See also Thompson (G0862).

G0828   Hay, George. The Architecture of Scottish Post-Reformation Churches, 1560-1843. London: Oxford University Press, 1957.

This survey of some 350 pages covers architectural development in the first part, features and fittings in the second part, an inventory and index of churches by counties in the appendix. There is also a brief glossary of architectural and ecclesiastical terms and a select bibliography. The work is well illustrated and usefully complements the earlier coverage provided by MacGibbon (G0844).

G0829   Henry, Hugh Thomas. Catholic Customs and Symbols: Varied Forms and Figures of Catholic Usage, Ceremony and Practice Briefly Explained. New York: Benziger Brothers, 1925.

This 322 page guide contains basic explanations of Catholic symbolism, church architecture and furnishings, vestments, liturgical colors, seasons and ceremonies, various customs. A bibliography, glossary and index are included. Although prepared long before the era of liturgical renewal, Henry is a sound guide and reference work on traditional liturgical matters. See also Hirn (G0831) and Lesage (G0842).

G0830   Henze, Anton. Das Kunsthandwerk im Dienste der Kirche. Der Christ in der Welt: Eine Enzyklopädie. 15. Reihe: Die Christliche Kunst, 8. Band. Aschaffenburg: P. Pattloch, 1963.

See also Bittel (G0803).

G0831   Hirn, Yrjö. The Sacred Shrine: A Study of the Poetry and Art of the Catholic Church. London: Macmillan and Company, 1912.

This 574 page compilation contains a wide range of artistic, literary and liturgical information on the mass, altar, sanctuary, host, remonstrance, tabernacle, Mary and relics. Useful bibliographies accompany the highly personal but interesting text. This is a useful reference volume for those seeking new views on elements of Roman Catholic worship. See also Henry (G0829).

G0832   Hoefler, Richard Carl. Designed for Worship: A Study of the Furniture, Vessels, Linens, Paraments and Vestments of Worship. Columbia, S.C.: State Printing Company, 1963.

This brief work summarizes what liturgical scholars have said regarding furniture, vessels, etc. used in Christian worship. It examines the history, styles, size and other aspects of the altar, furnishing the altar, the paraments, church linens, sacramental vessels, church furniture, vestments and general items. The full table of contents lists individual items (alb, chasuble, surplice, etc.). Illustrations accompany the straightforward text. See also Delderfield (G0816), Ireland (G0833) and Rietschel (G0851).

G0833   Ireland, Marion P. Textile Art in the Church: Vestments, Paraments and Hangings in Contemporary Worship, Art and Architecture. Nashville, Tenn.: Abingdon Press, 1971.

Intended to stimulate an interest in the use of new creative textiles for the expression of the life of the church, this work is ecumenical in approach. It includes excellent color photographs, an extensive bibliography and a helpful glossary. It has been criticized for neglecting problems relating to art and the church, such as the usefulness of kneeling in contemporary worship. See also Hoefler (G0832).

G0834   Jameson, Anna Brownell. The History of Our Lord As Exemplified in Works of Art: With That of His Types, St. John the Baptist and Other Persons of the Old and New Testament. Completed by Lady Elizabeth Eastlake. New ed. 2 vols. London: Longmans, Green and Company, 1890. Reprint. Detroit, Mich.: Gale Research Company, 1976.

First published in 1864 and available in various editions and imprints, these volumes were intended as companions to the author's other works on Christian art (G0835-G0837). Arrangement is chronological, beginning with an examination of Christian art on the fall of Lucifer and creation of the world, followed by OT types and prophets, history of the Innocents and of John the Baptist, the life and passion of Christ, etc. Each volume contains a detailed table of contents and list of the many illustrations. There are indexes of subjects, artists and locations.

G0835   Jameson, Anna Brownell. Legends of the Madonna As Represented in the Fine Arts, Forming the Third Series of "Sacred and Legendary Art". 7th ed. London: Longmans, Green and Company, 1885. Reprint of 1890 ed. Detroit, Mich.: Gale Research Company, 1972.

Available in many editions from several publishers, this useful compendium covers the history of devotion to Mary, relevant symbols and attributes, various representations in art. An index is provided. See also Rohault de Fleury (G0856).

G0836   Jameson, Anna Brownell. Legends of the Monastic Orders As Represented in the Fine Arts, Forming the Second Series of "Sacred and Legendary Art". Corrected and enlarged ed. Boston, Mass.: Houghton Mifflin, 1911. Reprint. New York: AMS Press, 1976.

Available in numerous impressions, this companion volume to Sacred and Legendary Art (G0837) examines religious paintings done for various monastic communities from artistic and aesthetic viewpoints, with some reference to points of faith and similar topics. Arrangement is by order, including Benedictines, Augustinians, Jesuits and the mendicant orders, and individuals are treated within these groupings. Although there is no index, the detailed table of contents provides easy access. There is also a reprint of the 1866 edition (Boston, Mass.: Ticknor and Fields) published in 1978 by AMS Press.

G0837   Jameson, Anna Brownell. Sacred and Legendary Art; Containing Legends of Angels and Archangels, the Evangelists, the Apostles, the Doctors of the Church and St. Mary Magdalene As Represented in Fine Art. 2 vols. London: Longmans, Green and Company, 1905. Reprint of 1896 ed. St. Clair Shores, Mich.: Scholarly Press, 1972.

First published in 1848, this compendium deals with biblical personalities, angels, patron and other saints, martyrs, early bishops, hermits and doctors of the church. Each item includes a brief explanation plus references to relevant works of art. Each volume contains a lengthy table of contents, and many illustrations are provided. Indexes cover subjects plus names of artists, galleries and churches. This is one of the more substantial works in its field and remains a valuable reference source. See also the preceding entries (G0834-G0836).

G0838   Janson, Horst Woldemar, and Janson, Dora Jane. History of Art: A Survey of the Major Visual Arts from the Dawn of History to the Present Day. 2nd ed. Englewood Cliffs, N.J.: Prentice Hall; New York: H.N. Abrams, 1977.

This revision of a standard textbook includes an enlargement of the pre-historic and modern sections in particular, and the bibliography (pp. 751-755) has been updated. Otherwise it is little changed, remaining one of the best summaries of Western painting, sculpture and architecture. As a reference work, Janson provides basic factual data in a wide range of subjects and is well indexed. See also Lützeler (G0843) and Pevsner (G0847).

G0839   Krautheimer, Richard. Early Christian and Byzantine Architecture. Baltimore, Md.: Penguin Books, 1965.

This specialized study examines architecture from the beginnings of Christian building to the fifth century and from early Byzantine building to the late Byzantine period. Notes, a glossary, a selected bibliography, plates and an index are provided. The table of contents makes it easy to find discussion of the architecture of a particular time in a particular country.

G0840   Künstle, Karl. Ikonographie der Christlichen Kunst. 2 vols. Freiburg im Breisgau: Herder, 1926-1978.

The first volume discusses in some detail the history of symbolism in Christian art through the medieval period, animal and other symbolism from nature, representations of subjects from the Bible. The second, volume, entitled Ikonographie der Heiligen, is a dictionary of saints which includes brief biographical data, indication of saints' emblems, how depicted in art and bibliographical references to printed descriptions of these representations. This is an extremely thorough work which for the saints is more detailed than Bles (G0804) or Drake (G0412). For a newer German work on iconography see Aurenhammer (G0386), which is less adequate for information on saints. See also Kirschbaum (B0429), Réau (G0850) and Schiller (G0857).

G0841   Leask, Harold Graham. Irish Churches and Monastic Buildings. 3 vols. Dundalk: Dundalgan Press, 1955-1960.

This well illustrated and detailed survey of Irish ecclesiastical architecture covers the early period and Romanesque in volume 1, Gothic to 1400 A.D. in volume 2 and medieval Gothic and latest phases in the final volume. Many ground plans are provided, and there are numerous chapter references. For students of Irish church buildings this is an important study which analyzes the subject in some detail.

G0842   Lesage, Robert. Vestments and Church Furniture. Trans. by Fergus Murphy. The Twentieth Century Encyclopedia of Catholicism, vol. 114. Section 10: The Worship of the Church. New York: Hawthorn Books, 1960.

This Roman Catholic work is in two main parts: the altar and its furniture; vestments. The first deals in turn with the altar, crucifix, sacred vessels, lighting, liturgical books, the thurible, the font, vessels for holy oils and church bells. The second contains nine chapters on the various vestments and insignia. The full table of contents lists individual items under the main chapter headings. A select bibliography is provided. See also Henry (G0829).

G0843   Lützeler, Heinrich. Weltgeschichte der Kunst. Die Grosse Bertelsmann Lexikon. Bibliothek, Bd. 6. Gütersloh: Bertelsmann, 1959.

This balanced history of world art is arranged in six parts, Europe being treated in the final section. There are 320 pages of plates and illustrations accompanying the text, which gives a brief but sound overview of the field for those unfamiliar with art history. Religious art is treated adequately. There is a bibliography (pp. 789-815) and a detailed index of names and places (pp. 818-830). See also Janson (G0838) and Pevsner (G0847).

G0844 MacGibbon, David, and Ross, Thomas. The Ecclesiastical Architecture of Scotland from the Earliest Christian Times to the Seventeenth Century. 3 vols. Edinburgh: D. Douglas, 1896-1897.

This survey covers the earlier period in considerable detail and provides much valuable information on medieval ecclesiastical architecture fo r those already familiar with basic principles and developments. See also Hay (G0828).

G0845   Mâle, Emile. L'Art Religieux de la Fin du XVIe Siècle du XVIIe Siècle et du XVIIIe Siècle: Etude sur l'Iconographie après le Concile de Trente: Italie, France, Espagne, Flandres. 2e éd. Paris: A. Colin, 1951.

First published in 1932 as L'Art Religieux après le Concile de Trente, this authoritative work by a noted scholar of religious iconography covers Catholic Europe from the mid-sixteenth to the eighteenth century. There are more than 250 plates, and an index of works of art cited is also included (pp. 513-526). See also Pigler (G0848).

G0846   Michel, André. Histoire de l'Art Depuis les Premiers Temps Chrétiens Jusqu'à Nos Jours. 8 vols. in 17. Paris: A. Colin, 1905-1929.

Largely concerned with Western Europe, this important history contains valuable data for both beginners and advanced students. Of particular value from a Christian standpoint are the volumes on early Christian art, Gothic art and the Renaissance. Each volume contains individual sections by well known scholars which survey the development of particular themes and periods. There are many illustrations and valuable sectional bibliographies. See also Christie (G0812), Du Bourguet (G0818) and Grabar (G0825).

G0847   Pevsner, Nikolaus, ed. Pelican History of Art. Vol. 1- . Baltimore, Md.: Penguin Books, 1953- .

This massive series, intended to be complete in fifty volumes, covers world art and architecture of all periods. Each volume, which focuses on a region or country for a given period, is written by a specialist in the field and contains numerous plates and substantial bibliographies. Valuable studies from an ecclesiastical viewpoint are those by Frankl on Gothic architecture, by Beckwith on early Christian and Byzantine art, by Lasko on ars sacra from 800 to 1200. All of the volumes are detailed in coverage and form excellent reference guides. See also Janson (G0838) and Lützeler (G0843).

G0848   Pigler, A. Barockthemen: Eine Auswahl von Verzeichnis zur Ikonographie des 17. und 18. Jahrhunderts. 2 vols. Budapest: Verlag der Ungarischen Akademie der Wissenschaften, 1956.

This thorough guide to themes in Baroque art covers religious themes in the first volume and Greek and Roman themes in the second. The religious themes encompass OT and NT, saints, legends and history and other religious topics in some detail. A name and subject index to the entire set concludes the second volume. See also Mâle (G0845).

G0849   Post, Willard Ellwood. Saints, Signs and Symbols. 2nd ed. New York: Morehouse-Barlow Company, 1974; London: SPCK, 1975 [1974].

This basic guide to the 200 most popular saints in Anglican and other traditions provides monochrome illustrations of the symbols most commonly associated with them. Both personal attributes and theological concepts are treated. It also includes symbols associated with baptism and the other sacraments. Although not a scholarly compendium, Post has some usefulness for those engaged in liturgical art at the practical level. See also Bles (G0804), Husenbeth (G0424) and Waters (G0865).

G0850   Réau, Louis. Iconographie de l'Art Chrétien. 3 vols. in 6. Paris: Presses Universitaires de France, 1955-1959.

This standard French language work classifies iconographic themes, indicates their variations and evolution and lists principal works of art in which they are represented. Coverage includes medieval Western and Byzantine art, which is more limited than some of the German works of similar scope, particularly those by Aurenhammer (G0386) and Kirschbaum (G0429). Bibliographies and many illustrations are included. The work is divided into three main parts: general introduction (volume 1); biblical iconography of the OT and of the NT (volume 2); iconography of the saints (volume 3 in three parts). See also Didron (G0817) and Künstle (G0840).

G0851   Rietschel, Christian. Paraments und Geräte des Evangelischen Gottesdienstes. Handbücherei für Gemeindarbeit, Heft 43. Gütersloh: Gütersloher Verlagshaus G. Mohn, 1968.

This German Lutheran study is designed to give practical advice to the pastor and parish. It discusses the basis for Christian art and decoration in the church, then the type, materials, form and size of liturgical vestments and paraments, and eucharistic and baptismal vestments. Practical suggestions on cleaning, preservation and so on are included. For the German reader this contains much useful material. See also Hoefler (G0832).

G0852   Roeder, Helen. Saints and Their Attributes; with a Guide to Localities and Patronage. London: Longmans, Green and Company, 1955.

This 391 page guide deals with the emblems, pictorial representations and statuary of saints. The arrangement is alphabetical by subject, with subdivisions according to saints' names. For each saint the date of death and religious order are provided. There are indexes of saints, patronage and localities; a brief bibliography is also provided. See also Drake (G0412), Husenbeth (G0424) and Post (G0849).

G0853   Rohault de Fleury, Charles. Archéologie Chrétienne. Les Saints de la Messe et Leurs Monuments; Etudes Continuée par Son Fils. 10 vols. Paris: Libraries-Imprimeries Réunies, 1893-1900.

In ten substantial volumes Rohault de Fleury provides both plates and commentary on the forty saints traditionally named in the Roman Catholic mass. The treatment includes detailed descriptions of the major churches and shrines dedicated to these saints, and a bibliography is provided for each church. The volumes are well indexed, and form an indispensible guide for students of ecclesiastical architecture. See also Waters (G0865).

G0854   Rohault de Fleury, Charles. L'Evangile: Etudes Iconographiques et Archéologiques. 2 vols. Tours: A. Mame et Fils, 1874.

Concentrating on ancient churches and works of art, this detailed volume describes symbols which depict the person and life of Christ. It is well indexed and provides very thorough coverage of European art and architecture on this subject. See also Schiller (G0857).

G0855   Rohault de Fleury, Charles. La Messe: Etudes Archéologiques sur Ses Monuments; Continuée par Son Fils. 8 vols. Paris: V.A. Morel, 1883-1889.

Replete with bibliographies, illustrations and indexes in each volume, this masterful survey of the mass concentrates on the iconography of the liturgy. It covers such items as altars, vessels, vestments and church furnishings, providing very complete coverage of ancient European artifacts.

G0856   Rohault de Fleury, Charles. La Sainte Vierge: Etudes Archéologiques et Iconographiques. 2 vols. Paris: Poussielgue Frères, 1878.

This is a useful guide to representations of Mary, her life and devotion in art and archeology. Full indexes and bibliographical notes are provided in each volume. See also Jameson (G0835).

G0857   Schiller, Gertrud. Ikonographie der Christlichen Kunst. Vol. 1- . Gütersloh: Gütersloher Verlagshaus G. Mohn, 1966- .

The contents of this multi-volume work are arranged topically to cover the life of Christ (including incarnation, passion, resurrection) in the first three volumes and ecclesia, Mary, the last judgment and the OT in the two final volumes. The text, which is separate from the illustrations, deals more or less chronologically and in some detail with the iconography of a given subject. References to biblical sources are provided together with a discussion of thematic treatments in art, and bibliographical footnotes refer to specialized studies. See also Kirschbaum (G0429), Réau (G0850) and Aurenhammer (G0386) for works of similar scope and content.

Schiller has the advantage of also appearing in English translation as Iconography of Christian Art (Trans. by Janet Seligman, Vol. 1- . Greenwich, Conn.: New York Graphic Society; London: Lund Humphries, 1971-). See also Künstle (G0840).

G0858   Seasholtz, R. Kevin. The House of God: Sacred Art and Church Architecture. New York: Herder and Herder, 1963.

See also Debuyst (G0815).

G0859   Sill, Gertrude Grace. A Handbook of Symbols in Christian Art. New York: Macmillan Company, 1975.

This handbook contains fifty-two entries arranged alphabetically and includes a selected bibliography and a subject index. The intention of the work is to acquaint users with the basic images in Christian art. Although intended in its arrangement as a reference volume, it is necessary to consult the index for the full range of data on a given subject. Many illustrations, listed at the end of the book, are included. See also Child (G0810) and Webber (G0866).

G0860   Simpson, Frederick Moore. History of Architectural Development. New ed. 5 vols. London: Longmans, Green and Company, 1954- .

First published as a three volume set in 1905-1911, Simpson is a standard work widely regarded as a sound scholarly treatment of architectural history. Each volume treats a specific period (ancient and classical, early Christian and Byzantine, Gothic, Renaissance, modern). Bibliographies, footnote references, plates, drawings and ground plans make the work a valuable reference tool for those seeking information on the development of ecclesiastical architecture.

G0861   Sovik, E.A. Architecture for Worship. Minneapolis, Minn.: Augsburg Publishing House, 1973.

This work aims to indicate an alternative path for church architecture in the 1970s, proposing that structures should not necessarily be built with what is thought of as ecclesiastical character. Five chapters examine the heritage of history, the return to the "non-church", suggestions for renewal of church buildings, etc. Illustrations accompany the text. This is an innovatory approach for those concerned with this aspect of worship. See also Seasholtz (G0858) and White (G0867).

G0862   Thompson, Alexander Hamilton. Cathedral Churches of England. New York: Macmillan Company; London: SPCK, 1925.

See also Harvey (G0827).

G0863   Thompson, David Walter. Symbols of the Church. Needham Heights, Mass.: Whittemore Associates, 1973.

Including drawings and an index in its 64 pages, this Anglican guide for the layman indicates the major symbols associated with seasons, festivals, principal saints and key concepts of the church. It is a useful compendium for artists and others involved in visual displays related to the liturgical calendar or in preparing church furnishings. See also Bottomley (G0806).

G0864   Warham Guild. Handbook: Historical and Descriptive Notes on "Orna-
ments of the Church and the Ministers Thereof". 2nd ed. London: A.R. Mowbray and Company, 1963.

See also Hoefler (G0832) and Rietschel (G0851).

G0865   Waters, Clara Erskine Clement. A Handbook of Christian Symbols
and Stories of the Saints As Illustrated in Art. Boston, Mass.: Ticknow and
Company, 1886. Reprint. Detroit, Mich.: Gale Research Company, 1971.

This standard handbook of artistic representations of the saints throughout
history is a good reference volume for basic inquiries. It is adequately
indexed. See also Bles (G0804), Drake (G0412) and Post (G0849).

G0866   Webber, Frederick Roth. Church Symbolism: An Explanation of the
More Important Symbols of the Old and New Testament, the Primitive, the
Mediaeval and the Modern Church. 2nd ed. Cleveland, Ohio: J.H. Jansen,
1938. Reprint. Detroit, Mich.: Gale Research Company, 1971.

This compilation includes a helpful glossary of more important symbols
(pp. 357-388) and a bibliography (pp. 389-394). The main part of the work
is arranged by topic (e.g., Trinity, Holy Spirit, Virgin Mary, sacraments,
saints) and provides numerous drawings and plates to illustrate the various
symbols. An index of items is also provided. See also Child (G0810) and
Ferguson (G0820).

G0867   White, James F. Protestant Worship and Church Architecture: Theological and Historical Considerations. New York: Oxford University Press, 1964.

This work is both an important contribution to the history of Protestant
church architecture in America and it explores effectively the historical
and theological considerations essential to building for Protestant worship.
A very good bibliography with separate lists for various traditions is
appended. Diagrams are included, although there are no illustrations
which would have added to the value of a work on this subject. For a
Roman Catholic approach see Debuyst (G0815); see also Frere-Cook (G0821).

G0868   Whittick, Arnold. Symbols, Signs and Their Meanings. Newton, Mass.:
Branford; London: L. Hill, 1960.

This survey of general symbolism is divided into four main parts: introduction to the field; symbolism in its precise and applied forms and its practical uses; encyclopedic dictionary dealing with traditional and familiar
symbols, their origins, meaning and history; instinctive, creative and
imaginative symbolism. Mainly Western in focus, Whittick is most useful
for its dictionary section, which includes some symbolism of a religious
nature. See also Chevalier and Gheerbrant (G0404) and Sill (G0859).

G0869   Whone, Herbert. Church, Monastery, Cathedral: A Guide to the Symbolism of the Christian Tradition. Short Hills, N.J.: Ridley Enslow Publishers,
c.1977.

See also Ferguson (G0820).

MUSIC: HANDBOOKS

G0870 Abraham, Gerald. The Concise Oxford History of Music. Oxford: Oxford University Press, 1980.

This work provides carefully researched information in a concise and informative manner. The excellent table of contents facilitates use of the history. See also Westrup (G1022).

G0871   Adler, Guido, ed. Handbuch der Musikgeschichte. Unter Mitwirkung von Fachgenossen. 2. Aufl. 2 vols. Berlin-Wilmersdorf: H. Keller, 1930.

First published in 1924, this handbook provides a chronological treatment of music up to 1880; volume 1 treats the field to 1750, and volume 2 covers the remaining years.   Each section is by a recognized authority in the field and includes substantial bibliographical data. There is a detailed index to both volumes at the end of the work (pp. 1258-1294). For readers of German this is a useful general history which provides adequate data for straightforward reference needs. See also Abraham (G0870) and Westrup (G1022).

G0872   Aigrain, René. Religious Music. Trans. by Charles Mulcahy. To which is added a further section by the translator on English and Irish religious music. London: Sands and Company, 1931.

This 292 page survey is a translation of La Musique Religieuse (Paris: Bloud et Gay, 1929). See also Huot-Pleuroux (G0941).

G0873   Albrecht, Christoph. Einführung in die Hymnologie. Göttingen: Vandenhoeck und Ruprecht, 1973.

For an English language work on the subject see Routley (G0991).

G0874   Alford, Delton L. Music in the Pentecostal Church. Cleveland, Tenn.: Pathway Press, 1967.

G0875   American Hymns, Old and New. 2 vols. New York: Columbia University Press, 1980.

This collection contains more than 600 hymns representing a fairly broad range of ethnic and denominational traditions. Sixty of the hymns were commissioned for this work. The second volume contains notes on the literary and scriptural sources of each hymn, analyzes the words and musical settings, and provides biographies of composers and authors. See also Episcopal Church (G0920) and Metcalf (G0959).

G0876   Anderson, Margaret Swainson. A Guide to Effective Hymn Playing: Practical Suggestions Concerning the Interpretation of Hymns, Including Registrations for Electronic Instruments. Minneapolis, Minn.: Augsburg Publishing House, 1964.

See also Auld (G0879).

G0877   Apel, Willi. Gregorian Chant. Bloomington, Ind.: Indiana University Press; London: Burns and Oates, 1958.

This history and analysis of Gregorian chant covers structure and development of the liturgy, the texts, notation, tonality and psalmody of the chant, and a stylistic analysis. Ambrosian and Old Roman chants are included. There are frequent bibliographical notes, and an index is provided. For an index of Gregorian chant see Bryden and Hughes (G0269).

G0878   Appleby, David P. History of Church Music. Chicago, Ill.: Moody Press, 1965.

See also Weinmann (G1019) and Wilson (G1025).

G0879   Auld, Wilda Jackson. A Handbook for the Church Pianist. Ed. by Lyle Prescott. Kansas City, Mo.: Lillenas Publishing Company, 1964.

See also Anderson (G0876).

G0880   Bailey, Albert Edward. The Gospel in Hymns: Backgrounds and Interpretations. New York: Charles Scribner's Sons, 1950.

This provides historical background on 313 hymns found in one or more of ten main English language Protestant hymnals published between 1918 and 1941. A bibliography and an index are provided. See also Routley (G0989).

G0881   [no entry]

G0882   Baümher, Wilhelm. Das Katholische Deutsche Kirchenlied in Seinen Singweisen von den Früchsten Zeiten bis Gegen des 17. Jahrhunderts. Hildesheim: Georg Olms, 1962.

For German Protestant church music see Zahn (G1026).

G0883   Bauman, William A. The Ministry of Music: A Guide for the Practicing Church Musician. Washington, D.C.: Liturgical Conference, 1975.

This work is intended particularly for two audiences: those individuals concerned about worship and the ministry of music in a professional sense, and for use in a series of workshop sessions for church musicians. A full and balanced picture of the ministry of music in the church is offered in the nine chapters which cover, for example, competence in performance, in repertoire and in planning worship, and sound liturgical and pastoral judgment. See also Lawrence (G0947), National Liturgical Conference (G0966) and Walter (G1018).

G0884   Bickersteth, Edward Henry. The Hymnal Companion to the Book of Common Prayer with Accompanying Tunes. 3rd ed. London: Church Book Room Press, 1954.

See Church of England (G0528) for The Book of Common Prayer.

G0885   Blume, Clemens. Thesauri Hymnologici Hymnarium. Die Hymnen des "Thesaurus Hymnologicus" H.A. Daniels und Anderer Hymnar-Ausgaben. 2 vols. Analecta Hymnica Medii Aevi, vols. 51-52. Leipzig: O.R. Reisland,

1908-1909. Reprint. 2 vols. New York: Johnson Reprint Corporation, 1962.

See also the following entry (G0886).

G0886   Blume, Clemens. Thesauri Hymnologici Prosarium. 2 vols. in 3. Analecta Hymnica Medii Aevi, vols. 53-55. Leipzig: O.R. Reisland, 1911-1912. Reprint. 2 vols. in 3. New York: Johnson Reprint Corporation, 1961.

See also the preceding entry (G0885).

G0887   Blume, Friedrich. Protestant Church Music: A History. In collaboration with Ludwig Finscher et al. New York: W.W. Norton Company, 1974; London: Victor Gollancz, 1975.

This translation of Geschichte der Evangelischen Kirchenmusik (2. Aufl. Kassel: Barenreiter Verlag, 1965) includes three additional chapters prepared specifically for the English language edition. The nine chapters cover the period from the Reformation to the present day, discussing developments in individual countries. There is an extensive bibliography (pp. 733-800) which includes monographs and periodical articles. The index (pp. 805-831) is adequate for reference purposes. See also Borlisch (G0889) and Etherington (G0922).

G0888   Bogolepov, Aleksandr Aleksandrovich. Orthodox Hymns of Christmas, Holy Week and Easter. New York: Russian Orthodox Theological Fund, [1965].

See also Neale (G0967).

G0889   Borlisch, Hans. Kleine Geschichte der Evangelischen Kirchenmusik. Berlin: Merseburger, 1961.

See also Valentin (G1017).

G0890   Bowen, C.A., gen. ed. The Cokesbury Worship Hymnal. New York: Abingdon-Cokesbury Press, 1938.

Prepared for the Methodist Church by its General Board of Christian Education, this compilation begins with brief outlines of the orders of worship in this tradition and then presents a broad selection of hymns and music for various occasions and seasons. Also included is the communion service as used in the Methodist Church. Bowen is particularly useful as a guide to Protestant hymns, as it includes both standard and traditional ones together with newer ones of the early twentieth century. See also Methodist Church (G0960-G0962).

G0891   Bowers, John Dykes, and Wicks, Allan, comps. A Repertory of English Cathedral Anthems. London: Church Music Society, 1965.

See also Frere (G0925) and Frost (G0926).

G0892   Breck, Flora Elizabeth. Choir Ideas for Choir Members, Directors, Preachers and Congregations. Boston, Mass.: W.A. Wilde, 1952.

See also Nordin (G0969) and Wienandt (G1024).

G0893   Britt, Matthew, ed. The Hymns of the Breviary and Missal. Rev.

ed. with latest hymns. New York: Benziger Brothers, 1955.

This compilation is a collection of verse translations of 176 Latin hymns together with the Latin text, literal translations and notes on authorship and liturgical use. Arrangement is by place in the office, and there are Latin and English indexes. See also Catholic Church (G0899) and Connelly (G0910).

G0894   Brooke, Charles William Alfred, comp. Companion to "Hymns Ancient and Modern" (Old Edition). London: Sir Isaac Pitman and Sons, 1914.

See Hymns Ancient and Modern (G0943); see also Dearmer (G0912) and Frere (G0925).

G0895   Brown, F. Eugene; Hosch, Jon A.; and Skrobak, Dave F. The Singing Church: A Practical Approach to Individual and Congregational Singing. Ed. by Irma Lee Batey. [Nashville, Tenn.]: I.L. Batey, [1968].

See also Churchill (G0908) and Gelineau (G0930).

G0896   Brownlie, John, trans. Hymns of the Holy Eastern Church, Translated from the Service Books, with Introductory Chapters on the History, Doctrine and Worship of the Church. Paisley: A. Gardner, 1902.

See also Neale (G0967) and Wellesz (G1021).

G0897   Brownlie, John, trans. Hymns of the Russian Church; Being Translations, Centos and Suggestions from the Greek Office Books, with an Introduction. London: Oxford University Press, 1920.

See also Gardner (G0928).

G0898   Campbell, Sidney S. Music in the Church: A Handbook of Church Music. The Student's Music Library. London: S. Dobson, 1951.

See also Appleby (G0878), Foote (G0924) and Sims (G1000).

G0899   Catholic Church. The Breviary and Missal Hymns. Trans. by John Fitzpatrick. London: Sands and Company, 1931.

See also Britt (G0893) and Connelly (G0910).

G0900   Catholic Church. The Westminster Hymnal. New and rev. ed. Authorised by the Hierarchy of England and Wales for use in all churches and oratories. London: Burns, Oates and Washbourne, 1948.

See also Connelly (G0910).

G0901   Catholic Church. Congregatio Sacrorum Rituum. Sacred Music and Liturgy: The Instruction of the Sacred Congregation of Rites Concerning Sacred Music and Sacred Liturgy in Accordance with the Encyclical Letters of Pope Pius XII, "Musicae Sacrae Disciplina" and "Mediator Dei". Trans. with a commentary by John Bertram O'Connell. Westminster, Md.: Newman Press, 1959.

See also Hayburn (G0938) and Mytych (G0964).

G0902   Cavarnos, Constantine. Byzantine Sacred Music: The Traditional Music of the Orthodox Church, Its Nature, Purpose and Execution. Belmont, Mass.: Institute for Byzantine and Modern Greek Studies, 1956.

See also Savas (G0995), Tillyard (G1016) and Wellesz (G1020).

G0903   Chappell, Paul. Music and Worship in the Anglican Church, 597-1967. Studies in Christian Worship, no. 10. London: Faith Press, 1968.

See also Brightman (G0491), Cuming (G0547) and Long (G0950).

G0904   Christian Science Publishing Society. Concordance to Christian Science Hymnal and Hymnal Notes. Boston, Mass.: Christian Science Publishing Company, 1967.

G0905   The Church Hymnary. Rev. ed. Authorized for Use in public worship by the Church of Scotland, the United Free Church of Scotland, the Presbyterian Church in Ireland, the Presbyterian Church of England, the Presbyterian Church of Wales, the Presbyterian Church of New Zealand [and] the Presbyterian Church of South Africa. With music. London: Oxford University Press, 1927.

G0906   Church Music Handbook, 1982-1983. Princeton, N.J.: Pilgrim Press, 1982.

See also Kirchenmusikalisches Jahrbuch (G0945).

G0907   Church of England. Anglican Hymn Book. London: Church Book Room Press, c.1965.

This comprehensive collection of 663 hymns contains both traditional and new hymns (largely of a more conservative kind). A thematic metrical index of tunes is provided, and with each tune is an acknowledgment of composer and arranger. Other indexes are also provided, e.g., a list of scriptural references. Carefully edited and compiled by a committee of twelve, the collection has nonetheless been criticized for a failure to meet the needs of contemporary society. See also Frere (G0925); for more modern hymns see Saward (G0996).

G0908   Churchill, John. Congregational Singing: The Congregation's Part in Public Worship. Croydon: Royal School of Church Music, 1966.

See also Brown (G0895) and Sydnor (G1007).

G0909   Congregational Union of England and Wales. The New Congregational Hymn Book: Psalms and Hymns for Divine Worship. London: Hodder and Stoughton, 1855(?).

G0910   Connelly, Joseph, ed. Hymns of the Roman Liturgy. Westminster, Md.: Newman Press, 1957.

This collection presents prose translations in English of 154 Latin hymns. Included are annotations on authorship, source, liturgical use and other relevant information. Author and first line indexes increase the reference value of this work. See also Britt (G0893) and Catholic Church (G0899, G0900). For a handbook on Roman Catholic hymnals used in America between 1871 and 1964 see J. Vincent Higginson, Handbook for American Catholic Hymnals (New York: Hymn Society of America, 1976).

G0911   Dahle, John. Library of Christian Hymns. Trans. by M. Casper Johnshoy. 2 vols. Minneapolis, Minn.: Augsburg Publishing House, 1924-1928. Reprint. 2 vols. New York: AMS Press, 1975.

These volumes cover the history of hymns used by the Lutheran churches of America, following the order of hymns in The Lutheran Hymnary. Biographical sketches of hymn writers are provided. See also Lutheran Church in America (G0648).

G0912   Dearmer, Percy, comp. "Songs of Praise" Discussed: A Handbook to the Best Known Hymns and to Others Recently Introduced. With notes on the music by A. Jacob. London: Oxford University Press, 1933. Reprint. London: Oxford University Press, 1952.

See also Brooke (G0894), Frere (G0925) and Frost (G0927).

G0913   Dickinson, Edward. Music in the History of the Western Church, with an Introduction on Religious Music among Primitive and Ancient Peoples. New York: Charles Scribner's Sons, 1902. Reprint. New York: Greenwood Press, 1969.

See also Grout (G0934) and Sydnor (G1008).

G0914   Doane, William Howard. ed. The Baptist Hymnal for Use in the Church and Home. Philadelphia, Pa.: American Baptist Publication Society, 1883.

This hymnal sets out to provide a useful selection of hymns with a large choice of popular as well as newer and more elaborate melodies. Arrangement is under headings such as God, Christ, the Holy Spirit, the church, temperance, time and eternity. Eleven indexes provide ready access. See also Green (G0933) and Reynolds (G0980, G0981).

G0915   Douglas, Charles Winfred. Church Music in History and Practice: Studies in the Praise of God. Rev. with additional material by Leonard Webster Ellinwood. New York: Charles Scribner's Sons, 1962.

This work treats the text of the liturgical services and words of the hymns together with the music which has grown up with them. Treatment is broadly chronological, with subsections in each chapter on particular aspects of church music of the period. A bibliography (pp. 275-284) and two indexes (subjects and music, books, texts) are provided; a list of relevant recordings illustrative of various periods and types of music is also included. The work is intended primarily for clergy, seminarians and organists. See also Dickinson (G0913) and Sydnor (G1008).

G0916   Dreves, Guido Maria, and Blume, Clemens, eds. Analecta Hymnica Medii Aevi. 55 vols. Leipzig: O.R. Reisland, 1886-1922. Reprint. Johnson Reprint Corporation, 1961.

This monumental collection provides texts of hymns as well as detailed historical and bibliographical notes. For an index see Mearns (G0321).

G0917   Dunstan, Alan. These Are the Hymns, with Some Examples of Orders for Special Services. London: SPCK, 1973.

See also Lovelace (G0951).

G0918   Ellinwood, Leonard Webster. Religious Music in America. Princeton, N.J.: Princeton University Press, 1961.

See also Metcalf (G0959) and Stevenson (G1006).

G0919   The English Hymnal Service Book. London: Oxford University Press, 1962.

Based on The English Hymnal with Tunes (Oxford: Oxford University Press, 1966) and geared especially to the needs of congregational singing, this collection contains 298 hymns from the parent work plus a supplement of thirty-seven hymns and carols. The canticles, Psalms, versicles and responses for Matins and Evensong are simply pointed and provided in familiar settings for ease of chanting. There is also a separate, full music edition suitable for choirs and clergy. Although less comprehensive than many other hymnals, this is a useful collection for those who need advice on popular, simply arranged congregational music. See also Episcopal Church (G0920).

G0920   Episcopal Church. "The Hymnal 1940" Companion. 3rd ed. New York: Church Pension Fund, [1956].

The introduction to this useful denominational guide includes a brief history of hymnology, a chronological list of texts and tunes and a short historical sketch of The Hymnal. Following this, part 1 contains historical essays on texts and tunes, while part 2 contains biographies of authors, translators, composers and arrangers. There are six indexes to this work, which has considerable reference value. See also The English Hymnal (G0919).

G0921   Episcopal Church. Diocese of Minnesota. Department of Music. The Episcopal Choirmaster's Handbook. Sauk Center, Minn.: Diocese of Minnesota, Department of Music, n.d.

See also Rowlands (G0994).

G0922   Etherington, Charles L. Protestant Worship Music: Its History and Practice. New York: Holt, Rinehart and Winston, 1962.

This work, by an American nonliturgical Protestant who is a practising church musician, provides a relatively complete history of Protestant church music. It is written in nontechnical language; for those who require further details, lists of composers, works and/or collections which illustrate the musical style of the period under discussion are included at the end of relevant sections. This provides a survey of use to church musicians and parish clergy. See also Blume (G0887) and Steere (G1005).

G0923   Fellerer, Karl Gustav. The History of Catholic Church Music. Trans. by Francis A. Brunner. Baltimore, Md.: Helicon Press, 1961.

See also Hume (G0940) and Nemmers (G0968).

G0924   Foote, Henry Wilder. Music in the Life of the Church; Manual. The Covenant Life Curriculum. Richmond, Va.: CLC Press, 1968.

See also Campbell (G0898), Douglas (G0915) and Sims (G1000).

G0925   Frere, Water Howard. Hymns Ancient and Modern for Use in the Services of the Church, with Accompanying Tunes. Historical Edition, with Notes on the Origin of Both Hymns and Tunes and a General Historical Intro- duction, Illustrated by Facsimiles and Portraits. London: W. Clowes and Sons for the Proprietors of Hymns Ancient and Modern, 1909.

See also Dearmer (G0912) and Frost (G0927).

G0926   Frost, Maurice, ed. English and Scottish Psalm and Hymn Tunes. New York: Oxford University Press; London: SPCK, 1953.

This analysis first treats "Old Version" psalters and describes their contents in some detail (pp. 1-52). It then presents tunes, partly in score, associated with these psalters between 1556 and 1677. For an index to the tunes treated see Rogers (G0353).

G0927   Frost, Maurice, ed. Historical Companion to "Hymns Ancient and Modern". London: W. Clowes for the Proprietors of Hymns Ancient and Modern, 1962.

This radical revision of Frere (G0925) provides notes on the words and tunes of 636 hymns in the revised edition of Hymns Ancient and Modern. Biographical sketches of hymn writers, translators and composers, indexes of first lines and tunes, a metrical index and list of sources are also provided to make this a very useful reference tool. See also Dearmer (G0912).

G0928   Gardner, Johann von. Russian Church Singing. Trans. by Vladimir Morosan. Vol. 1- . Crestwood N.Y.: St. Vladimir's Seminary Press, 1980- .

This is a translation of System und Wesen des Russischen Kirchengesanges. See also Brownlie (G0897).

G0929   Gealy, Fred Daniel. Companion to the Hymnal: A Handbook to the 1964 Methodist Hymnal. Nashville, Tenn.: Abingdon Press, 1970.

Containing tunes by Austin C. Lovelace and biographies by Carlton R. Young, this annotated guide to the Methodist hymnal presents material in title sequence and includes an index of individuals treated biographically in the work. See Methodist Church (G0962); see also Lightwood (G0949) and McCutchan (G0955).

G0930   Gelineau, Joseph. Voices and Instruments in Christian Worship: Prin- ciples, Laws, Applications. Trans. by Clifford Howell. Collegeville, Minn.: Liturgical Press, 1964.

This translation of Chant et Musique dans la Culte Chrétien: Principes, Lois et Applications (Paris: Editions Fleurus, 1962) examines the role of singing in Christian worship, the coordination of music with ritual action and the function of music in this context. It deals with the Roman rite as it existed at the time of writing. The book does not aim to be a practical textbook on sacred music; rather it is an examination of relations between music and Christian worship. An index and list of selected readings are included. See also Brown (G0895), Churchill (G0908) and Wienandt (G1024).

G0931   Le Gradual Romain. Ed. critique par les moines de Solesmes. Vol. 1- . Solesmes: Abbaye Saint-Pierre, 1957- .

The Roman Gradual, an outgrowth of the Missal containing all the chants used at mass for every day of the year, is a new critical edition designed to supersede the Vatican work of 1907. In addition to containing all the relevant chants it also includes useful historical and bibliographical information. This is an excellent compendium not only for Roman Catholic use but also for those interested in the history of traditional sacred music.

G0932   A Grammar of Plainsong. By a Benedictine of Stanbrook Abbey. Liverpool: Rushworth and Dreaper, 1934.

This general introduction for singers covers pronunciation of Latin, notation, tonality, rhythm, accompaniment and other relevant aspects of plainsong. The history of chant is also explained, and there is an index. This is a suitable introduction for practical rather than scholarly requirements.

G0933   Green, Samuel Gosnell, comp. The Baptist Church Hymnal. Rev. ed. London: Psalms and Hymns Trust, 1933.

This work was first published in 1900 as a two volume collection of hymns, chants and anthems with music. See also Doane (G0914) and Martin (G0957).

G0934   Grout, Donald Jay. A History of Western Music. Rev. ed. New York: W.W. Norton Company, 1973.

This standard text for students of music surveys the entire field in clear and nontechnical language. A glossary, extensive bibliography (pp. 738-775), music chronology and numerous illustrations add substantially to the value of Grout. There is a title, subject and name index. For those seeking to understand the place of sacred music in the overall spectrum of Western musical history, this is a very worthwhile reference work. See also Abraham (G0870) and Dickinson (G0913).

G0935   Haeussler, Armin. The Story of Our Hymns: The Handbook of the Hymnal of the Evangelical and Reformed   Church. St. Louis, Mo.: Eden Publishing House, 1952.

Essentially a companion to the 561 hymns in this denominational compilation, Haeussler usefully discusses the background and meaning of each hymn in the main text. Introductory articles discuss hymns in general and provide interesting insights into their development and use. Seven indexes make this work easily consulted for reference purposes. Overall it is a sound guide for many traditions, containing very helpful notes on hymns found in a wide range of hymnals.

G0936   Haserodt, E.V. Concordance to "The Lutheran Hymnal". St. Louis, Mo.: Concordia Publishing House, 1956.

This word index to The Lutheran Hymnal aims to facilitate the selection of appropriate hymns for use in the service. All major words are listed in alphabetical order; references to hymns in which they occur are in numerical order. Thus one can locate a suitable hymn by referring to a key word in the concordance. See also Lutheran Church in America (G0648).

G0937   Hatchett, Marion J. Music for the Church Year: A Handbook for Clergymen, Organists and Choir Directors. New York: Seabury Press, 1964.

This handbook is designed to assist clergy, organists and choir directors in the proper planning and selection of service music. Discussion is based on The Hymnal (1940) of the Episcopal Church and on the Episcopal calendar. The introduction discusses choice of and teaching of hymns, suitable organ music, etc. The two main sections cover music for the church year and music for special occasions. A list of publishers and an index of themes are included. See also Heaton (G0939) and Lawrence (G0947).

G0938   Hayburn, Robert F. Digest of Regulations and Rubrics of Catholic Church Music. Rev. ed. Boston, Mass.: McLaughlin and Reilly Company, 1961.

See also Catholic Church (G0901) and Mytych (G0964).

G0939   Heaton, Charles Huddleston. A Guidebook to Worship Services 'of Sacred Music. St. Louis, Mo.: Bethany Press, 1962.

This handbook deals with matters related to the planning of special services, including advance preparation, promotional efforts, administrative details, finding adequate financial backing. In addition sample services are presented from well known and smaller choral groups. Services include those for Christmas, hymn festivals, Easter season services and services centering on a particular theme. Names and addresses of major music publishing companies and a bibliography are useful features. See also Hatchett (G0937).

G0940   Hume, Paul. Catholic Church Music. New York: Dodd, Mead and Company, 1956.

This 259 page text contains ten chapters on such aspects of Roman Catholic church music as the role of the choir director, music for weddings, the church organist. There are also six appendixes which include relevant papal documents, a suggested reading list and a listing of sacred music on records. An index is provided. See also Fellerer (G0923) and Nemmers (G0968).

G0941   Huot-Pleuroux, Paul. Histoire de la Musique Religieuse des Origines à Nos Jours. Paris: Presses Universitaires de France, 1957.

See also Aigrain (G0872).

G0942   Hustad, Donald P. Jubilate! Church Music in the Evangelical Tradition. Carol Stream, Ill.: Hope Publishing Company, c.1981.

Addressed primarily to nonliturgical, pietist groups, this work develops a philosophy for contemporary American church musicians. Church music is approached as a functional art which must be judged by how well it serves God and the church in a particular cultural context. See also Etherington (G0922), Steere (G1005) and Terry (G1012).

G0943   Hymns Ancient and Modern. Rev. ed. London: William Clowes and Sons for the Proprietors of Hymns Ancient and Modern, 1950.

First published in the 1860s as Hymns Ancient and Modern for Use in the Services of the Church with Accompanying Tunes, this standard Anglican hymnal contains more than 600 hymns from all denominational circles. Probably one of the most popular English language hymnals, it is a useful reference work because of the way in which it has absorbed standard hymns from so many traditions. There is a table of hymns suited to various festivals and themes, as well as an index listing first words, authors, tune names and composers. See also Brooke (G0894) and The English Hymnal (G0919) for other Anglican compilations. A complete revision of the work was due for release in 1983; this should provide an interesting alternative to Saward (G0996). See Frere (G0925) for the earlier version.

G0944   Keith, Edmond D. Christian Hymnody. Nashville, Tenn.: Convention Press, 1956.

See also Northcott (G0970), Reynolds (G0982) and Routley (G0988-G0991).

G0945   Kirchenmusikalisches Jahrbuch. Vol. 1- . Regensburg: F. Pustet Verlag, 1876- ; annual.

This yearbook was originally entitled Caecilien-Kalender from 1876 to 1885. See also Church Music Handbook (G0906).

G0946   Krieg, Franz. Katholische Kirchenmusik, Geist and Praxis. Mit geschichtlichen Beiträgen von Ernst Tittel. Teuffen: A. Niggli und W. Verkauf, [1954].

See also Lenacher and Fellerer (G0948).

G0947   Lawrence, Joy E. A Musician's Guide to Church Music. Philadelphia, Pa.: Pilgrim Press, 1981.

This work examines the role of music in worship, and music's relationship to liturgical and nonliturgical services. Aspects such as planning and selecting music, conducting senior and junior choirs and the purchase and maintenance of an organ are discussed. This provides comprehensive coverage useful to the novice as well as the experienced church musician, to the pastor or music committee. See also Bauman (G0883), Hatchett (G0937) and Heaton (G0939).

G0948   Lemacher, Heinrich, and Fellerer, Karl Gustav, eds. Handbuch der Katholischen Kirchenmusik. Essen: Fredbeul und Koenen, 1949.

See also Krieg (G0946).

G0949   Lightwood, James Thomas. The Music of the Methodist Hymn-Book; Being the Story of Each Tune with Biographical Notices of the Composers. [New ed.] Ed. and rev. by Francis B. Westbrook. London: Epworth Press, 1957.

See also Methodist Church (G0960, G0961).

G0950   Long, Kenneth R. The Music of the English Church. New York: St.
Martin's Press, [1972, c.1971]; London: Hodder and Stoughton, 1972.

Intended as a handy reference book for organists, choirmasters, students
and all who are interested in English church music, this substantial volume
treats the history of English church music from the sixteenth century
to the present. It includes a wealth of material, including studies of
many individuals, a classified bibliography (pp. 441-451), an index to
music examples and a general index. See also Chappell (G0903).

G0951   Lovelace, Austin C. Hymn Festivals. Papers of the Hymn Society
of America, no. 31. New York: Hymn Society of America, 1979.

This work deals with the history, purpose and function, types of services,
planning and resources relevant to hymn festivals. See also Dunstan (G0917).

G0952   Lovelace, Austin C. The Organist and Hymn Playing. A Basic Music
Book, no. 110. New York: Abingdon Press, 1962.

Intended specifically for the organist, this brief book discusses technical
aspects such as articulation and touch, hymn forms and tempos, in the
context of the organist's role in leading the congregation in worship.
A bibliography (pp. 66-68) and an index are provided. See also Walter
(G1018).

G0953   Lovelace, Austin C., and Rice, William C. Music and Worship in
the Church. New York: Abingdon Press, 1960.

Intended for the general reader as well as the church music specialist,
this handbook examines the role of the minister, the organist, adult,
children's or youth choirs, the soloist, the congregation and others in
relation to music and worship in the church. Music in Christian education
is also considered. A glossary, bibliography (pp. 207-216) and an index
are provided. See also Foote (G0924), Rhys (G0983) and Thayer (G1013).

G0954   McCutchan, Robert Guy. Hymn Tune Names: Their Sources and Significance. Nashville, Tenn.: Abingdon Press, 1957.

This publication lists alphabetically the names of hymn tunes, indicating
melody and time, and giving the origin and history of the name. A melodic
index and an index of first words of lines of hymns are provided. See
also Routley (G0989).

G0955   McCutchan, Robert Guy. Our Hymnody: A Manual of "The Methodist
Hymnal". With an index of scriptural texts by Fitzgerald Sale Parker. 2nd ed.
New York: Abingdon Press, 1942.

This manual provides information about each hymn and tune in The Methodist Hymnal (G0962), and about the chants, responses and other aids
to worship contained in it. The source and first publication of hymns
and tunes, changes in the texts of the hymns and in the melodies and
harmonization are discussed. A calendar of the hymnal is included. The
manual does not attempt to provide directions for the singing of the
hymns. A brief chapter on the antecedents of The Methodist Hymnal,

a bibliography and nine indexes are provided. See also Gealy (G0929).

G0956   Mahrenholz, Christhard, and Sohngen, Oskar, eds. Handbuch zum Evangelischen Kirchengesangbuch. Vol. 1- . Göttingen: Vandenhoeck und Ruprecht, 1970- .

This guide to German Protestant hymns has been published in parts. See also Zahn (G1026).

G0957   Martin, Hugh, ed. A Companion to the Baptist Church Hymnal. London: Psalms and Hymns Trust, [1953].

See also Green (G0933) and Reynolds (G0980, G0981).

G0958   Mennonite Church. Joint Hymnal Committee. The Mennonite Hymnal. Newton, Kans.: Faith and Life Press; Scottdale, Pa.: Herald Press, 1969.

G0959   Metcalf, Frank Johnson. American Writers and Compilers of Sacred Music. New York: Abingdon Press, 1925. Reprint. New York: Russell and Russell, 1967.

In 366 pages Metcalf provides narrative entries on American sacred tune composers from the beginning of the eighteenth to the end of the nine-teenth century. Arrangement is chronological by the individual's date of birth, and almost 100 composers are included. There are twenty-two illustrations, and an index is provided. See also Ellinwood (G0918) and Stevenson (G1006).

G0960   Methodist Church. Hymns and Songs: A Supplement to "The Methodist Hymn-Book". London: Methodist Publishing House, 1969.

This supplement to the main work (G0961) includes a number of hymns which have become popular in the mid-twentieth century. Although obvious-ly aimed at the Methodist tradition, it does encompass hymns which are very broad in their appeal. Unfortunately, the contents of this supple-ment have not been treated in the excellent index (G0324) to the parent work. See also Lightwood (G0949).

G0961   Methodist Church. The Methodist Hymn-Book with Tunes. London: Methodist Conference Office, 1933. Reprint. London: Methodist Conference Office, 1954.

Including revised text and biographical details in the 1954 reprint and also available in an edition without music, this is the standard hymnal for British Methodists. Many of the hymns are very well known, but there are also interesting examples of lesser known works by the Wesleys and others in this tradition. One should also consult both the supplementary Hymns and Songs (G0960) and the very useful Subject, Textual and Lineal Indexes (G0324). The latter in particular is a valuable reference tool, since it provides a variety of detailed approaches to hymns used in many traditions. See also Lightwood (G0949).

G0962   Methodist Church. Methodist Hymnal: Official Hymnal of the Methodist Church. Nashville, Tenn.: Methodist Publishing House, c.1966.

See also Gealy (G0929), McCutchan (G0955) and Methodist Church (G0960,

G0961).

G0963   Moffatt, James. Handbook to the "Church Hymnary". London: Oxford University Press, 1927.

As the handbook to the Church Hymnary (revised edition), this guide contains notes on words and music of the hymns; biographical and historical notes on authors, composers and sources; a calendar of the hymnary; five indexes. See also Patrick (G0972) for a supplement.

G0964   Mytych, Joseph F. Digest of Church Laws on Sacred Music. Toledo, Ohio: Gregorian Institute of America, 1959.

This Roman Catholic guide describes and explains approximately 200 church laws under twenty-two subject headings. In each case reference is made to main documents and canons, and the work includes an index. See also Catholic Church (G0901) and Hayburn (G0938).

G0965   Nason, Elias. The Congregational Hymn Book for the Service of the Sanctuary. Boston, Mass.: J.P. Jewett and Company, 1857.

See also Parry (G0971) and The Pilgrim Hymnal (G0976).

G0966   National Liturgical Conference. A Manual for Church Musicians. Washington, D.C.: National Liturgical Conference, 1964.

See also Bauman (G0883), Lawrence (G0947) and Walter (G1018).

G0967   Neale, John Mason, trans. Hymns of the Eastern Church, with Notes and an Introduction. London: J.T. Hayes, 1862.

Also available in later editions (5th ed. London: J.T. Hayes, 1888), this early study in English of Eastern hymnody covers the period from the fifth to the eleventh century. It includes indexes of first lines and of measures, an introduction, and a note on epochs of Greek ecclesiastical poetry. See also Brownlie (G0896) and Wellesz (G1021).

G0968   Nemmers, Erwin Esser. Twenty Centuries of Catholic Church Music. Milwaukee, Wisc.: Bruce Publishing Company, 1949.

This brief history provides useful definitions of terms and individuals, short accounts of movements and events and a bibliography. Each chapter is devoted to a specific period and includes lists of books and music. American church music is well represented, and the work contains an index. See also Fellerer (G0923) and Hume (G0940).

G0969   Nordin, Dayton W. How to Organize and Direct the Church Choir. West Nyack, N.Y.: Parker Publishing Company, 1973.

See also Breck (G0892).

G0970   Northcott, William Cecil. Hymns in Christian Worship: The Use of Hymns in the Life of the Church. Ecumenical Studies in Worship, no. 13. Richmond, Va.: John Knox Press; London: Lutterworth Press, 1964.

This brief work examines the nature and function of Christian hymns, the hymn in history and in liturgy, and hymns in the life of the church. Indexes of hymns and of psalm and hymn books are provided. There is no bibliography, but footnote references are given. See also Keith (G0944), Reynolds (G0982) and Routley (G0988-G0991).

G0971   Parry, Kenneth Lloyd, ed. Companion to "Congregational Praise". With notes on the music by Erik Routley. London: Independent Press, 1953.

This companion to Congregational Praise contains notes on hymns and authors and on tunes and composers. In addition a general introduction examines the history of hymns, there are notes on children's hymns and on hymn-books of the Congregational Church, and eight special articles on such topics as names of hymn tunes, music of the chants, and Bach chorales. A chronological list of sources cited in the musical notes constitutes a bibliography of the most important psalm and hymn books from 1524 to 1951. See also Nason (G0965) and The Pilgrim Hymnal (G0976).

G0972   Patrick, Millar, ed. Handbook to the "Church Hymnary": Supplement. London: Oxford University Press, 1935.

See Moffatt (G0963) for the main work.

G0973   Patrick, Millar. The Story of the Church's Song . Rev. for American Use by James Rawlings Sydnor. Richmond, Va.: John Knox Press, 1962.

Originally designed as a summary account of the development of Christian hymnody, as illustrated by the contents of the revised Church Hymnary, this revised edition is based on three American hymnals. The twenty-four chapters cover the period from biblical times to the twentieth century. An appendix treats American hymnody from 1927 to 1961. The bibliography of the first edition (pp. 193-194) has been updated for the American edition (pp. 195-198). Two indexes are provided. This work gives a helpful introduction to the subject. See also Douglas (G0915) and Sydnor (G1008).

G0974   [no entry]

G0975   Phillips, Charles Henry. The Singing Church: An Outline History of the Music Sung by Choir and People. New ed. Prepared by Arthur Hutchings. London: Faber and Faber, 1968.

This work, published in the first edition in 1945, provides a summary of English ecclesiastical music used in Anglican churches in the 1930s. It is a readable survey, but also interesting as a historical document itself, presenting a high Anglican viewpoint regarding music in worship. The new edition contains only slight changes, including updated bibliographies, clearer plates, larger type and omission of the glossary of musical terms. See also Bowers and Wicks (G0891) and H. Everett Titcomb, Anglican Ways: A Manual on Liturgical Music for Episcopal Choirmasters ([New York: H.W. Gray Company], 1954).

G0976   The Pilgrim Hymnal. Rev. ed. Boston, Mass.: Pilgrim Press, 1935.

Including a Congregational order of worship, prayers and related worship resources at the end, this is a substantial hymnal. For a guide see Ronander and Porter (G0986); see also Nason (G0965) and Parry (G0971).

G0977 Proske, Karl, ed. Musica Divina; sive, Thesaurus Consentuum Selectiss Imorum Omni Cultui Divino Totius Anni Juxta Ritum Sanctae Ecclesiae Cathol- icae Inserventium: Ab Excellentissimus Superioris Aevi Musicis Muneris Har- monicis Compositoram. Quos e Codicibus Originalibus Tam Editis Quam Ineditis Accuratissime in Partitionem Redactos ad Instaurandam Polyphoniam Vere Ecclesiasticam Publice Offert Carolus Proske. 8 vols. Ratisbonae: Friedrich Pustet, 1853-1878(?).

See also Robertson (G0985).

G0978   Quinn, Eugene F., comp. A Hymnal Concordance. Louisville, Ky.: Personalized Printing, 1966.

G0979   Ratliff, Foster. The New Baptist Song Book 1971: A Collection of Good Hymns, Songs and Ballads. Lookout, Ky.: n.p., 1971.

See also Thomas (G1014).

G0980   Reynolds, William Jensen. Companion to "Baptist Hymnal" (1975 Edition). Nashville, Tenn.: Broadman Press, 1976.

Like the earlier work by Reynolds (G0981), this guide presents background information on the texts, tunes, authors, composers and historical milieu of hymns in the Baptist Hymnal. The first section is arranged alphabet- ically by hymn text, and the tunes are discussed under the related texts. Authors and composers are listed alphabetically in the second section. See also Doane (G0914).

G0981   Reynolds, William Jensen. Hymns of Our Faith: A Handbook for the "Baptist Hymnal". Nashville, Tenn.: Broadman Press, 1964.

This detailed discussion of the 554 hymns in the Baptist Hymnal presents data on the authors, the background to each piece of music, their historical milieu and tunes. The later work by Reynolds (G0980) is keyed to the 1975 edition of the hymnal and adds data on hymns not found in the earlier edition. See also Doane (G0914) and Martin (G0957).

G0982   Reynolds, William Jensen. A Survey of Christian Hymnody. New York: Holt, Rinehart and Winston, 1963.

See also Keith (G0944), Northcott (G0970) and Routley (G0988-G0991).

G0983   Rhys, Stephen, and Palmer, King. ABC of Church Music. Boston, Mass.: Crescendo Publishing Company; London: Hodder and Stoughton, 1967.

This handbook includes much practical and also more technical information. Chapters cover topics such as prose set to music, the organ, the organist, human relationships and official bodies. A very useful bibliography and a list of publishers of music and relevant books are included. Hymn books used by various denominations are discussed: the work is not only for Anglicans. See also Lovelace (G0953) and Thayer (G1013).

G0984   Rice, William Carroll. A Concise History of Church Music. New York: Abingdon Press, 1964.

This concise reference work compresses much information into a small space. It concentrates on British and American composers, devoting less space to other European hymns. A marginal index is included. This work should be supplemented by more detailed material on historical aspects. See also Appleby (G0878) and Wilson (G1025).

G0985   Robertson, Alec. Christian Music. Twentieth Century Encyclopedia of Catholicism, vol. 125. Section 12: Catholicism and the Arts. New York: Hawthorn Books, 1961.

Concerned primarily with music composed for the liturgy of the Roman Catholic Church, this work deals with pre-Christian sacred music; pre-Gregorian, Gregorian and other Christian chant; English church music to the sixteenth century; and similar topics through to the twentieth century. A select bibliography and reasonably detailed table of contents are provided. The work is intended for a Roman Catholic readership. See also Proske (G0977).

G0986   Ronander, Albert C., and Porter, Ethel K. Guide to "The Pilgrim Hymnal". Philadelphia, Pa.: United Church Press, 1966.

See The Pilgrim Hymnal (G0976); see also Nason (G0965) and Parry (G0971).

G0987   Routley, Erik. Church Music and Theology. Studies in Ministry and Worship. London: SCM Press, 1959; Philadelphia, Pa.: Muhlenberg Press, 1960. Reprint. Philadelphia, Pa.: Fortress Press, 1965.

This work attempts to blend the insights of theology and church music into a compatible relationship, offering interpretations from the minister's viewpoint. It is critical of certain forms of contemporary music used in worship. See also Söhngen (G1004).

G0988   Routley, Erik. An English-Speaking Hymnal Guide. Collegeville, Minn.: Liturgical Press, 1979.

Based on the holdings of approximately thirty collections in North America and Britain, this guide lists 888 of the most popular hymns in English and indicates with symbols the collections in which each is found. For each hymn the compiler supplies notes on the metrical form, rhyme, historical data on origins, biographical details on composer and similar details. The main listing is arranged alphabetically by first lines of 832 native English hymns; this is followed by a list of fifty-six hymns of foreign origin in multiple English translations. There are several introductory essays on English hymns, which are especially helpful for the beginner. A chronological index of hymnodists is also included. See also Bailey (G0880).

G0989   Routley, Erik. Hymn Tunes: An Historical Outline. Royal School of Church Music Study Notes, no. 5. Croydon: Royal School of Church Music, [196-].

This 16 page pamphlet provides a very brief account. See also McCutchan (G0954).

G0990   Routley, Erik. Hymns Today and Tomorrow. New York: Abingdon Press, 1964; London: Darton, Longman and Todd, 1966.

This provocative work investigates the words, images and literary style of hymns, seeking to establish a principle of intelligent criticism by which to evaluate hymnody. A chapter on the choice of hymns contains useful practical suggestions and descriptions of hymn usage in various liturgical traditions. The work is helpful in illuminating the relationship between theology and music. See also Routley's other works on this subject (G0988, G0989, G0991).

G0991   Routley, Erik. A Panorama of Christian Hymnody. Collegeville, Minn.: Liturgical Press, 1979.

In this stimulating survey Routley divides hymnody into twenty-seven historical sections and introduces each with a brief essay on the period, place or author. A final section comprises hymns from modern foreign sources. The texts of 593 hymns are provided together with major variants and (in the case of translations) the original versions. There is a table of sources based primarily on those used for the same author's English-Speaking Hymnal Guide (G0988) and a biographical appendix. Author and first line indexes complete the work. See also Keith (G0944), Northcott (G0970) and Reynolds (G0982).

G0992   Routley, Erik. Twentieth Century Church Music. Studies in Church Music. New York: Oxford University Press, 1964.

Aiming to stimulate interest in contemporary church music, to suggest future research and to assess some of the social implications of developments in church music, this volume provides stimulating material for the minister and church musician. It tends to concentrate on British church music, and is written from a Protestant viewpoint. See also Saward (G0996).

G0993   Routley, Erik. Words, Music and the Church. Nashville, Tenn.: Abingdon Press, 1968; London: Herbert Jenkins, 1969.

This work considers the significance of words and music in the contemporary life of the church. It contains useful material for both musicians and clergymen, written by a Fellow of the Royal School of Church Music and British Congregationalist pastor. One difficulty for the American reader is that many of the illustrations are from British liturgical practice; a further criticism that has been made is that Routley gives rather weak treatment to the eucharist.

G0994   Rowlands, Leo. Guide Book for Catholic Church Choirmasters. Enlarged ed. Boston, Mass.: McLaughlin and Reilly Company, 1962.

See also Episcopal Church (G0921).

G0995   Savas, Savas I. Byzantine Music in Theory and in Practice. Trans. by Nicholas Dufault. Boston, Mass.: [Hercules Press], 1965.

See also Tillyard (G1016) and Wellesz (G1020).

G0996 Saward, Michael, and Wilson, David, eds. Hymns for Today's Church. Music and words ed. London: Hodder and Stoughton, 1982.

Intended basically as an accompaniment to the Church of England's Alternative Service Book and as a replacement for Hymns Ancient and Modern (G0943), this 114 page hymnal contains 592 hymns plus thirty songs. Of the hymns 360 are traditional, 100 are from newer collections and 140 are completely new. Although the music in the first two categories is little changed, the words in all hymns have been completely modernized to reflect current English usage. The thirty songs in a separate section are suitable primarily for family worship. While Saward has received a mixed reception because of its revision of the language in traditional hymns, it is an excellent resource volume for those interested in modern hymnody, as well as a suitable hymnal in parishes using modern liturgies. See also Routley (G0992).

G0997   Seipt, Allen Anders. Schwenkfelder Hymnology and the Sources of the First Schwenkfelder Hymn-Book Printed in America. Americana Germanica: Monographs Devoted to the Study of the Literary, Linguistic and Other Cultural Relations of Germany and America, no. 7. Philadelphia, Pa.: American Germanica Press, 1909. Reprint. New York: AMS Press, 1971.

Originally a thesis presented to the University of Pennsylvania, this detailed study of the music of a small denomination contains valuable data on the history of America hymnology. Individuals, historical developments and ideas in Schwenkfelder music are dealt with very thoroughly, and there is a useful bibliography (pp. 17-36).

G0998   Siebel, Katherine. Sacred Songs: A Guide to Repertory. New York: W.W. Gray Company, 1966.

See also Slenk (G1002).

G0999   Sims, Walter Hines, comp. and ed. Baptist Hymnal. Nashville, Tenn.: Convention Press, 1956.

See also Doane (G0914) and Reynolds (G0980, G0981).

G1000 Sims, Walter Hines. Church Music Manual. Nashville, Tenn.: Convention Press, 1957.

See also Campbell (G0898), Foote (G0924) and Rhys (G0983).

G1001   Sims, Walter Hines, and Downey, Charles H. Church Music Administration. Nashville, Tenn.: Convention Press, 1969.

See also Sydnor (G1009).

G1002   Slenk, Howard J. A Well Appointed Church Music. Grand Rapids, Mich.: William B. Eerdmans Publishing Company, 1960.

This compilation contains fifty-eight lists of choral and organ music for Protestant worship services. The theme for each list, which in itself is intended to provide all that is necessary for an individual service, is based on a section of the Heidelberg Catechism. Hymns are those found in the Psalter Hymnal (Grand Rapids, Mich.: Christian Reformed Church, Publication Committee, 1959). In addition to hymns each service includes organ prelude, offertory and postlude, as well as three anthems chosen for ease of performance. This provides constructive ideas for clergy and musicians in churches with an independent worship program.

See also Siebel (G0998).

G1003   Society of St. Gregory of America. The White List: With a Selection of Papal Documents and Other Information Pertaining to Catholic Church Music. Ed. 1- . Glen Rock, N.J.: Society of St. Gregory of America, 1928- ; irregular, with supplements.

This irregularly issued series contains the texts of selected papal and other documents from the fourteenth century to the present together with an approved list of hymns, mass settings and organ works. A partial blacklist is also included. For each item the author, title, publisher and a note on degree of difficulty of performance are indicated. There is a classified bibliography as well, making this a valuable bibliographical listing for both parish music needs and scholarly research.

G1004   Söhngen, Oskar. Theologie der Musik. Kassel: Johannes Stauda Verlag, 1967.

This is a most interesting survey of the theology of music which in 358 pages treats the topic under five main headings: die Stellung des Neuen Testament und der Reformatoren zur Musik, Erscheinungsweisen und Bedeutungsgestalten der Musik, Theologische Voraussetzungen der Kirchenmusik, Grundsätzliche Uberlegungen zum geschichtlichen Verhältnis von Musik und Theologie, Versuch einer trinitarischen Begründung der Musik. The work is completed by an index of names and subjects. While some of Söhngen's views are open to question, this must be regarded as a significant contribution to the field for those requiring both basic data and extended discussion of the theological aspects of music in the church. See also Routley (G0987).

G1005   Steere, Dwight. Music in Protestant Worship. Richmond, Va.: John Knox Press, 1960.

Written primarily for ministers by a church musician, and concerned particularly with nonliturgical churches, this practical handbook provides information on various aspects of church music: the choir, the organ, the role of the minister and of the choirmaster and organist, the processional and recessional, organ music, the solo, and so on. It fills many gaps which might be neglected in seminary training on this aspect of worship. A bibliography (pp. 243-245), notes and an index are included. See also Etherington (G0922) and Stevenson (G1006).

G1006   Stevenson, Robert Murrell. Protestant Church Music in America: A Short Survey of Men and Movements from 1564 to the Present. New York: W.W. Norton and Company, 1966.

This admirable introductory history is a useful reference work although it covers earlier developments more thoroughly than those in recent periods. It refers to recent research, and many quite detailed and critical footnotes are included.   Reprints of key documents and examples of music illustrate the work. See also Ellinwood (G0918), Metcalf (G0959) and Steere (G1005).

G1007   Sydnor, James Rawlings. The Hymn and Congregational Singing. Richmond, Va.: John Knox Press, 1960.

This 192 page study analyzes the factors which contribute to effective congregational singing and briefly treats the history of hymns and gospel songs together with their influence on American hymnody. A useful bibliography is provided, but there is no index. This is a practical and non-technical work of some interest to church musicians (although it is rather elementary) but perhaps more suitable for the minister or the lay leader of worship concerned with this subject. See also Brown (G0895) and Churchill (G0908).

G1008   Sydnor, James Rawlings. Music in the Life of the Church: Manual. The Covenant Life Curriculum. Richmond, Va.: CLC Press, 1968.

See also Dickinson (G0913) and Patrick (G0973).

G1009   Sydnor, James Rawlings. Planning for Church Music. New York: Abingdon Press, 1961.

This work states the functions of music in the life of a local congregation; describes the leadership needed to provide an adequate program of music; and discusses in detail the selection of the physical equipment needed. A bibliography, a list of agencies and an index add to the value of this handbook for those concerned with planning an effective program of church music. See also Sims (G1001).

G1010   Szoverffy, Josef. Die Annalen der Lateinischen Hymnendichtung: Ein Handbuch. 2 vols. Berlin: E. Schmidt, 1964-1965.

This guide to the study of Latin hymnology from its beginnings to the end of the Middle Ages surveys both the history and poetry of Latin hymns. Material is arranged in groups by either author or period; there are numerous bibliographies, tables, lists and an index. See also Blume (G0885, G0886).

G1011   Temperley, Nicholas. The Music of the English Parish Church. 2 vols. Cambridge: Cambridge University Press, 1979.

Volume 1 deals with the development, history and forms of English parish music; it includes a bibliography (pp. 359-415) and a detailed index. Volume 2 is an anthology of the music discussed in the first volume. This is a thorough, scholarly and up-to-date survey of Anglican church music for reference and liturgical purposes.

G1012   Terry, Lindsay. How to Build an Evangelistic Church Music Program. Nashville, Tenn.: T. Nelson, 1974.

See also Hustad (G0942) and Whittlesey (G1023).

G1013   Thayer, Lynn W. The Church Music Handbook. Grand Rapids, Mich.: Zondervan Publishing House, 1978.

First published as The Church Music Handbook: A Handbook of Practical Procedures and Suggestions (Grand Rapids, Mich.: Zondervan Publishing House, 1971), this handbook emphasizes the role of the adult choir in the church's music program and offers many suggestions for successful organization in this area. See also Lovelace (G0953).

G1014   Thomas, E.D., comp. A Choice Selection of Hymns and Spiritual Songs for the Use of the Baptist Church and All Lovers of Songs. Wayne, W.Va.: Arrowood Brothers, [1970?].

See also Ratliff (G0979).

G1015   Thomas, Nancy White. A Guide to Hymn Study. New York: Hymn Society of America, 1964.

This 14 page essay is reprinted from The Hymn 15 (July 1964).

G1016   Tillyard, Henry Julius Wetenhall. Byzantine Music and Hymnography. London: Faith Press, 1923. Reprint. New York: AMS Press, 1976.

See also Savas (G0998) and Wellesz (G1020).

G1017   Valentin, Erich, comp. Die Evangelischen Kirchenmusik: Handbuch für Studium und Praxis. Hrsg. von Erich Valentin und Friedrich Hofmann. Regensburg: Bosse, [1967?].

See also Borlisch (G0889).

G1018   Walter, Samuel. Basic Principles of Service Playing. New York: Abingdon Press, 1963.

This brief work sets out useful information for the church organist. Ten chapters discuss hymn playing, organ solos, music for specific occasions, improvisation, organ registration, etc. Lists of recommended books (pp.81-83) and of organ music (pp.84-93), as well as an index are included. See also Bauman (G0883), Lovelace (G0952) and National Liturgical Conference (G0966).

G1019   Weinmann, Karl. History of Church Music. New York: F. Pustet, 1910. Reprint. Westport, Conn.: Greenwood Press, 1970.

See also Appleby (G0878) and Wilson (G1025).

G1020   Wellesz, Egon. A History of Byzantine Music and Hymnography. 2nd ed. Oxford: Clarendon Press, 1961.

This comprehensive volume provides authoritative information not only on the Byzantine liturgy but also on Greek classical music, gnosticism, the Christological and Iconoclastic controversies, etc. The material on music and hymnography is meticulously detailed, well documented (the second edition includes extended footnotes) and finely produced. See also Cavarnos (G0902), Savas (G0998) and Tillyard (G1016).

G1021   Wellesz, Egon. Die Hymnen der Ostkirche. Basilienses de Musica Orationes, H.1. Basel: Bärenreiter Verlag, 1962.

See also Brownlie (G0896) and Neale (G0967).

G1022   Westrup, Jack Allan, ed.-in-chief. New Oxford History of Music. Vol. 1- . London: Oxford University Press, 1954- .

With Dom Anselm Hughes on the editorial board and with contributions from many noted ecclesiastical musicologists, this detailed history of ultimately ten volumes on specific eras is the most valuable survey of its kind. In each volume information on church music is provided in full where relevant, and there are extensive notes for further reference. Each volume is well indexed, and the text (particularly in the volumes edited by Fortune and Hughes) is clear and lucid. As a reference history this work is indispensible. See also Abraham (G0870) and Adler (G0871).

G1023   Whittlesey, Federal Lee. A Comprehensive Program of Church Music. Philadelphia, Pa.: Westminster Press, 1957.

This book seeks to give practical help in problems one may encounter in organizing, training and using a multiple choir system. It stresses the religious educational values of church choirs and the spiritual side of the ministry of music. There are two main parts: choirs; music and worship. Each has subdivisions indicated in the table of contents. There are notes but no index. See also Hatchett (G0937) and Terry (G1012).

G1024   Wienandt, Elwyn Arthur. Choral Music of the Church. New York: Free Press, [1965].

Designed as a text for courses concerned with the literature and history of church music, this volume concentrates on three principal liturgical streams: Roman Catholic, Anglican, Lutheran. It examines changes in organization, forms, functions and styles of church music, developments spanning more than ten centuries. A bibliography (pp.462-474) and an index are provided in this substantial source of information. See also Gelineau (G0930); for a narrower approach see Phillips (G0975).

G1025   Wilson, John F. An Introduction to Church Music. Chicago, Ill.: Moody Press, 1965.

See also Rice (G0984) and Weinmann (G1019).

G1026   Zahn, Johannes. Die Melodien der Deutschen Evangelischen Kirchen-lieder, aus den Quellen Geschöpft und Mitgeteilt. 6 vols. Gütersloh: C. Bertelsmann, 1889-1893. Reprint. 6 vols. Hildesheim: Georg Olms Verlagsbuchhandlung, 1963.

This substantial handbook provides a line-by-line analysis of German Protestant church music, including both words and melodies. Notes indicate the historical derivations and developments in brief, thereby providing music historians with much useful information. See also Mahrenholz and Sohngen (G0956).

Homiletics

HOMILETICS: BIBLIOGRAPHIES

G1027   Cleary, James W., and Haberman, Frederick W., comps. and eds. Rhetoric and Public Address: A Bibliography, 1947-1961. With the assistance of Ned A. Shearer. Madison, Wisc.: University of Wisconsin Press, 1964.

This valuable collection is based on annual bibliographies in the Quarterly Journal of Speech between 1947 and 1951 and in Speech Monographs between 1952 and 1961. Theses entries have been reviewed, corrected, deleted where necessary and supplemented with an additional 1500 items. The result is a thorough and detailed alphabetical list of 8035 items with an adequate subject index. There is a list of practitioners and theorists and an index of reviewers. Cleary is continued by "Bibliography of Rhetoric and Public Address" in Communication Monographs, which is the successor to Speech Monographs.

G1028   Knower, Franklin Howard. Bibliography of Communications Dissertations in American Schools of Theology. n.p.: n.p., 1961?

G1029   Moll, Otto E. Sprichwörterbibliographie. Frankfurt am Main: Klostermann, 1957-1958.

This extensive bibliography of more than 9000 items is arranged by language and then by period or locality. It includes all European languages plus those of Africa, Asia and the Pacific; precedence is given to proverbs familiar in the West. There is an author index but no subject index. See also Stephens (G1030).

G1030   Stephens, Thomas Arthur. Proverb Literature: A Bibliography of Works Relating to Proverbs. Ed. by Wilfred Bonser. Folk-lore Society Publications, no. 89. London: W. Glaischer, 1930.

This collection is an annotated bibliography of more than 4000 works on the proverbs of all nations. It includes collections of special subjects and particular localities and serves as a detailed bibliographic guide to more esoteric fields of some value in homiletical illustration. See also Moll (G1029).

G1031   Toohey, William, and Thompson, William D., eds. Recent Homiletical Thought: A Bibliography, 1933-1965. Nashville, Tenn.: Abingdon Press, 1967.

Compiled from Protestant and Roman Catholic resources, this topical listing treats various aspects of preaching and homiletical theory. More than 2000 books, articles and theses are listed; an indication of Catholic or Protestant authorship is given when known for the 446 books included in the bibliography. Therre are brief annotations for most items, and the author index and appendix of key periodicals add to the reference value of this compilation. While the coverage of books is perhaps too selective, the scope of periodical articles is wide ranging and quite representative. Given the interest in homiletics vis-à-vis new forms of preaching and liturgical renewal in recent years, an updated edition is greatly needed.

HOMILETICS: DICTIONARIES

G1032   Herrera Oria, Angel, ed. The Preacher's Encyclopedia. English version trans. and ed. by David Greenstock. 4 vols. Westminster, Md.: Newman Press, 1964-1965.

This valuable work covers the Roman Catholic liturgies for each Sunday, discussing the assigned texts and providing general comments of a liturgical, exegetical and moral nature. Reference is made to writings of the fathers, theologians and spiritual writers and to papal texts. There are suggested sermon schemes based on the epistel and gospel for each Sunday. Each volume is devoted to a particular liturgical season and includes an adequate index.

G1033   Nicoll, William Robertson, and Stoddart, Jane T. The Expositor's Dictionary of Texts,   Containing Outlines, Expositions and Illustrations of Bible Texts, with Full References to the Best Homiletic Literature. With the cooperation of James Moffatt. New York: George H. Doran Company; London: Hodder and Stoughton, [1911]. Reprint. 2 vols. Grand Rapids, Mich.: William B. Eerdmans Publishing Company, 1953.

In this collection a chapter is devoted to each book of the Bible. The texts provide comments on the book under consideration, brief analysis of main themes, quotations of biblical texts as illustrations, etc. References to relevant literature are given after subsections. Although dated, this is a valuable reference work for the preacher. See also Moffatt (G1142).

G1034   Spurgeon, Charles Haddon. Spurgeon's Expository Encyclopedia: Sermons by Charles H. Spurgeon, Classified and Arranged for Ready Reference. 15 vols. Grand Rapids, Mich.: Baker Book House, 1951.

HOMILETICS: HANDBOOKS

G1035   Abbey, Merrill R. Communication in Pulpit and Parish. Philadelphia, Pa.: Westminster Press, 1973.

This study examines the homiletic task in the light of recent developments in the field of communication. It includes a survey of past as well as current approaches. Although strong on modern communication theory, Abbey has been criticized for neglecting the theological dimension of preaching, and for omitting any bibliographical guidance for further research. See also Brack (G1048, G1049), Kirkpatrick (G1077) and Kraemer (G1080).

G1036   Abbey, Merrill R. Preaching to the Contemporary Mind. New York: Abingdon Press, 1963.

Containing suggestions for relating the gospel message to the modern human situation, this work describes major issues facing society, common attitudes and moods, and emphasizes the need for preaching to be relevant. At the end of each chapter are bibliographical suggestions for further study and practical helps for the preacher, such as steps in developing a sermon plan. The book poses a number of serious issues, although some of the solutions it suggests are rather superficial. See also Baillargeon (G1042) and Baumann (G1046).

G1037   Achtemeier, Elizabeth Rice. The Old Testament and the Proclamation of the Gospel. Philadelphia, Pa.: Westminster Press, 1973.

This 224 page study includes concise treatment of the theological traditions of the OT and NT and the relation of the two, and provides suggestions for sermon preparation. Sermons delivered by the author are included in the last section. There are many footnotes in this work, which provides a theological perspective for preaching. See also Barth (G1044) and Macpherson (G1089).

G0138   Adamer, Peter. Predigtkunde: Ein Handbuch für die Praxis. Mainz: Matthias-Grunewald-Verlag, 1953.

G1039   Allmen, Jean Jacques von. Preaching and Congregation. Trans. by B.L. Nichols. Ecumenical Studies in Worship, no. 10. Richmond, Va.: John Knox Press, 1962.

Also published by Lutterworth Press in London, this classic little study seeks to present preaching within the context of worship and to analyze its place and role in this situation. Five chapters deal with preaching and the sermon from various aspects and with preaching as the Reformed Church's contribution to the ecumenical movement. An index is provided. See also Howe (G1071).

G1040   Babin, David E. Week in, Week out: A New Look at Liturgical Preaching. New York: Seabury Press, 1976.

This work stresses the communication aspect of preaching, emphasizing listening and hearing. It derives from a strong Anglican and liturgical background and is designed particularly for the clergyman. Step-by-step methods for preparing the weekly sermon are included. The approach is traditional and unprovocative. See also Bass (G1045) and Fuller (G1069).

G1041   Baillargeon, Anatole O., ed. Handbook for Special Preaching. New York: Herder and Herder, 1965.

G1042   Baillargeon, Anatole O., ed. New Media, New Forms: Contemporary Forms of Preaching. Chicago, Ill.: Franciscan Herald Press, 1968.

See also Abbey (G1036).

G1043   Barth, Karl. Homiletik: Wesen und Vorbereitung der Predigt. Zurich: EVZ-Verlag, 1966.

This is a revised edition, approved by Barth, of official records taken at a homiletic seminar conducted by him at the University of Bonn in 1932-1933 under the title "Exercises in the Preparation of Sermons". The introduction emphasizes that theology is essentially preparation for preaching. Three sections then deal with the nature of preaching, systematically expound criteria for preaching, and discuss actual sermon preparation. Three outlines of sermons effectively illustrate how one should preach. This is a useful little book for the minister.   See also Davis (G1059).

G1044   Barth, Karl. The Preaching of the Gospel. Trans. by B.E. Hooke. Philadelphia, Pa.: Westminster Press, 1963.

See also Achtemeier (G1037).

G1045   Bass, George M. The Renewal of Liturgical Preaching. Minneapolis, Minn.: Augsburg Publishing House, 1967.

The thesis of this book is that the sermon should have the same setting and basic themes regardless of the emphases of various seasons of the church year. The liturgical sermon is seen as a necessity in view of the focus of the liturgy. A system for adequate sermon preparation and effective preaching is proposed, and suggestions made for varying preaching in accordance with seasonal thrusts of the church year while maintaining the substance of preaching. This is an interesting considera- tion of the relation of liturgy and preaching. See also Babin (G1040) and Fuller (G1069).

G1046   Baumann, J. Daniel. An Introduction to Contemporary Preaching. Grand Rapids, Mich.: Baker Book House, 1972.

See also Abbey (G1036).

G1047   Bohren, Rudolf. Predigtlehre. Einfuhrung in die Evangelische Theologie, Bd. 4. Munich: Chr. Kaiser Verlag, 1971.

Including indexes of names, topics and biblical citations, this substantial volume of more than 500 pages is an encyclopedic review of homiletical theory. The five parts and thirty-two subsections cover approaches to preaching, the source of the sermon, forms of preaching, the preacher, the hearer. Relying heavily on the work of Karl Barth and his circle, Bohren presents a highly detailed analysis of preaching replete with numerous examples with particular emphasis on the Protestant tradition. This superb volume is an important text and reference work for students with a working knowledge of German. See also Barth (G1043).

G1048   Brack, Harold Arthur. Effective Oral Interpretation for Religious Leaders. Englewood Cliffs, N.J.: Prentice-Hall, 1964.

See also Abbey (G1035), Brack (G1049), Kirkpatrick (G1077) and Kraemer (G1080).

G1049   Brack, Harold Arthur, and Hance, Kenneth G. Public Speaking and Discussion for Religious Leaders. Englewood Cliffs, N.J.: Prentice-Hall, 1961.

This volume is designed for preachers, clergymen, directors of religious education, laymen and others in the service of the church. It is not directed at any particular denomination or at organizations of a specific size. It sets out to provide a practical analysis of public speaking and discussion situations and of problems encountered by religious leaders and to help the reader in public speaking. There are two main parts: the first contains nine chapters on public speaking (speaking from notes, clarifying explanations, strengthening one's argument, etc.); the second deals with discussion and conference situations in eight chapters on matters such as subjects for discussion, leadership of and participation in discussion or conference, presiding at meetings, etc. An index is provided. This is a useful, practical reference or textbook for individual use or for preaching classes. See also Abbey (G1035), Brack (G1048), Kirkpatrick (G1077) and Kraemer (G1080).

G1050   Breit, Herbert, and Westermann, Claus, eds. Calwer Predigthilfen. Vol. 1- . Stuttgart: Calwer Verlag, 1962- .

This work is based on the Ordnung der Predigttexte of the German Lutheran Church. See also Eichholz and Falkenroth (G1064), Konrad (G1079) and Voigt and Doerne (G1116).

G1051   Brilioth, Yngve T. A Brief History of Preaching. Trans. by Karl E. Mattson. The Preacher's Paperback Library. Philadelphia, Pa.: Fortress Press, 1965.

This translation of Predikans Historia presents a concise history of preaching from the NT to the twentieth century, focusing primarily on Lutheran interests. The book reveals the author's knowledge of vast ranges of literature, but treatment of such a broad field is bound to be uneven and there are some gaps. Three primary elements in preaching are stressed: liturgical, exegetical and prophetic. Relative emphases on form or content are also traced. An annotated bibliography and an index of names are provided, as well as an appendix on the history of preaching in Sweden. For a more detailed approach see Dargan (G1058) and Turnbull (G1112).

G1052   Broadus, John A. On the Preparation and Delivery of Sermons. 4th ed. Revised by Vernon L. Stanfield. New York: Harper and Row, 1979.

This classic textbook covers all aspects of preaching and is regarded as an essential guide to homiletics. Thirty-six chapters cover classification, style, preparation and delivery. In this edition some dated material has been deleted and more contemporary material added, the contents have been rearranged and attention has been called to a broad range of homiletical literature. See also Davis (G1059) and Sangster (G1103).

G1053   Brooks, George. 201 Sermon Outlines. Minister's Handbook Series. Grand Rapids, Mich.: Baker Book House, 1966.

See also Moore (G1092) and White (G1120).

G1054   Brown, Henry Clifton, Jr.; Clinard, H. Gordon; and Northcott, Jesse J. Steps to the Sermon: A Plan for Sermon Preparation. Nashville, Tenn.: Broadman Press, 1963.

See also Broadus (G1052) and Sangster (G1103).

G1055   Browne, Robert Eric Charles. The Ministry of the Word. Studies in Ministry and Worship. London: SCM Press, 1958.

See also Farmer (G1066).

G1056   Chambers, Robert, ed. The Book of Days: A Miscellany of Popular Antiquities in Connection with the Calendar, Including Anecdote, Biography and History, Curiosities of Literature and Oddities of Human Life and Character. 2 vols. Philadelphia, Pa.: J.B. Lippincott Company; London: W. and R. Chambers, 1862-1864. Reprint. 2 vols. Detroit, Mich.: Gale Research Company, 1967.

This order work is a compendium of interesting but not always accurate details on the history and features of holy days, fasts, feasts, phenomena connected with the seasons and notable events of the calendar. Chambers remains a good source of homiletical suggestions, although not intended for this purpose; it should be used in conjunction with Hone (G0606). See also Deems (G1060).

G1057   Church Pulpit Year Book: A Complete Set of Expository Sermon Outlines for the Sundays of the Year, Also for Saints' Days and Special Occasions. Vol. 1- . London: Chansitor Publications, 1903- ; annual.

See also Fichtner (G1068) and Lockyer (G1084).

G1058   Dargan, Edwin Charles. The History of Preaching. 2 vols. New York: A.C. Armstrong and Son; London: Hodder and Stoughton, 1905-1912. Reprint. 2 vols. Grand Rapids, Mich.: Baker Book House, 1968-1970.

This survey, although very dated in some respects, remains one of the most authoritative works in its field. Historically it is quite accurate, but in matters of interpretation some of Dargan's views have been disproved by subsequent research. Volume 1 covers A.D.70-1572; volume 2 covers 1572-1900. The work is brought relatively up-to-date by Turnbull (G1112), which in effect forms a third volume. See also Fant (G1065).

G1059   Davis, Henry Grady. Design for Preaching. Philadelphia, Pa.: Muhlenberg Press, 1958.

This examination of the relationship between form and content in sermon design has long been a standard text for students new to the field of homiletics. It proposes various forms which a sermon might take, types of continuity, the modes of the sermon, and processes in interpretation. Examples of sermons are given as illustrations and analyzed step-by-step. The book is rich in theological and professional insights. See also Broadus (G1052), Brown (G1054) and Sangster (G1103).

G1060   Deems, Edward Mark, comp. Holy-Days and Holidays: A Treasury of Historical Material, Sermons in Full and in Brief, Suggestive Thoughts and Poetry Relating to Holy Days and Holidays. New York: Funk and Wagnalls, 1902. Reprint. Detroit, Mich.: Gale Research Company, 1968.

See also Chambers (G1056) and Lockyer (G1084).

G1061   Demaray, Donald E. An Introduction to Homiletics. Grand Rapids, Mich.: Baker Book House, 1974.

See also White (G1119).

G1062   Devine, George. If I Were to Preach. 3 vols. New York: Alba House, 1974-1976.

This presentation of liturgical homiletic aids for series A, B, and C of the Roman Catholic ordinal is similar to Fichtner (G1068).

G1063   Dreher, Bruno. Biblisch Predigen: Ein Homiletisches Werkbuch. Werkhefte zur Bibelarbeit, Bd. 7. Stuttgart: Verlag Katholisches Bibelwerk, 1968.

See also Miller (G1091) and Perry (G1095).

G1064   Eichholz, Georg, and Falkenroth, Arnold, eds. Hören und Fragen: Meditationen in Neuer Folge. Eine Predigthilfe. Vol. 1- . Wuppertal: E. Müller, 1967- .

Planned in six volumes, this work is based on texts prescribed by the Lutheran confession. See also Breit and Westermann (G1050) and Voigt and Doerne (G1116).

G1065   Fant, Clyde E., Jr., and Pinson, William M., Jr., comps. Twenty Centuries of Great Preaching: An Encyclopedia of Preaching. 13 vols. Waco, Tex.: Word Books, 1971.

Including selective bibliographies and illustrations, this multivolume compilation contains sermons from all traditions throughout the history of Christianity. It is the most extensive work of its kind and as a collection of materials forms an excellent source of primarily documentation for historical and homiletical study. See also Dargan (G1058), Proclamation Aids (G1096) and Steimle (G1108).

G1066   Farmer, Herbert Henry. The Servant of the Word. New York: Charles Scribner's Sons; London: Nisbet and Company, 1942. Reprint. The Preacher's Paperback Library. Philadelphia, Pa.: Fortress Press, 1964.

This brief work, designed especially for ministers and those training for the ministry but also for those who listen to sermons, looks clearly at the reasons for preaching and presents the author's theological understanding of the nature of preaching. It contains five chapters on topics such as the need for concreteness, and preaching as personal encounter. An index is provided. See also Keir (G1074).

G1067   Fendt, Leonhard. Homiletik. 2. Aufl. Neu bearb. von Bernhard Klaus. De Gruyter Lehrbuch. Berlin: Walter de Gruyter and Company, 1970.

See also Barth (G1043).

G1068   Fichtner, Joseph. Proclaim His Word: Homiletic Themes for Sundays and Holy Days. Vol. 1- . New York: Alba House, 1973- .

This work is similar to Devine (G1062) in covering the three Roman Catholic cycles of lessons.   See also Church Pulpit Year Book (G1057) and Lockyer (G1084).

G1069   Fuller, Reginald Horace. What Is Liturgical Preaching? 2nd ed. Studies in Ministry and Worship. London: SCM Press, 1960.

This discussion of liturgical preaching provides a more detailed examination than a journal article would but is nonetheless brief (60pp.) and concise. It includes chapters on the aim of liturgical preaching, on sermons without liturgy and vice versa and on liturgical preaching in relation to the Epistles, Gospels and the OT. The concluding chapter contains practical and evangelistic considerations. Indexes of biblical references and of names and subjects are provided. See also Babin (G1040) and Bass (G1045).

G1070   Grasso, Domenico. Proclaiming God's Message: A Study in the Theology of Preaching. Liturgical Studies, vol. 8. Notre Dame, Ind.: University of Notre Dame Press, 1965.

This Roman Catholic study of the theology of preaching emphasizes the ecumenical nature of proclamation. It is a scholarly work dealing with aspects such as the nature of revelation and its relation to preaching, preaching and liturgy, the role of the minister. See also Rust (G1102) and Wingren (G1121).

G1071   Howe, Reuel L. Partners in Preaching: Clergy and Laity in Dialogue. New York: Seabury Press, 1967.

This brief (127pp.) study outlines various ways in which the congregation may become involved with the preacher in proclamation in the context of scepticism about and dissatisfaction with modern preaching. The book includes suggestions on study groups, instruction of laymen on how to listen to a sermon, and provision of feedback on preaching. An appendix contains analysis of a taped discussion of a sermon by church members. See also Allmen (G1039).

G1072   Jackson, Edgar Newman. A Psychology for Preaching. Great Neck, N.Y.: Channel Press, 1961.

This work attempts to bring the insights of modern psychology into the service of preaching, demonstrating, for example, that some knowledge of psychology can help in assessing the particular needs of a congregation. It has been criticized on a number of counts, including unsubstantiated attacks on traditional preaching, unwarranted restriction of the role of the preacher, inadequate analysis of the nature of preaching. See also Skinner (G1107) and Welsh (G1118).

G1073   Jones, Ilion Tingnal. Principles and Practice of Preaching. New York: Abingdon Press, 1957. Reprint. Nashville, Tenn.: Abingdon Press, 1974.

Suitable especially for beginners, this work sets forth in skeletal form the basic principles of homiletics. It makes no pretence to be more than a beginner's text. Jones adequately outlines major principles and forms in scholarly but simple fashion. A selected bibliography and an index are provided. See also Reu (G1099).

G1074   Keir, Thomas H. The Word in Worship: Preaching and Its Setting in Common Worship. London: Oxford University Press, 1962.

This volume of Warrack Lectures delivered at the Universities of Glasgow and Aberdeen in 1960 deals with the relation of the sermon to public worship from a Scottish reformed point of view. Such aspects as the relation of sermon and liturgy, the nature of the service of Communion, and the language of worship are treated in a solid, biblical and learned manner. See also Farmer (G1066).

G1075   Kemp, Charles F. Pastoral Preaching. St. Louis, Mo.: Bethany Press, 1963.

This study begins with an introduction and three chapters on general principles of pastoral preaching. The remainder is divided into four sections composed of sermons addressed to particular needs of listeners in particular settings: sermons by outstanding leaders of local congregations; sermons for those with special needs (in hospitals, prisons, etc.); sermons for the needs of pastors themselves; sermons from masters of the art of preaching. The unifying theme is the sermon as an instrument of pastoral care. This is a useful handbook for the local pastor. See also the following entry (G1076) and Teikmanis (G1109).

G1076   Kemp, Charles F. The Preaching Pastor. St. Louis, Mo.: Bethany Press, 1966.

Written primarily for the local pastor, this work emphasizes the importance of relevant preaching. The first part focuses on preaching to human needs and as a means of Christian growth. The second deals with eight specific areas such as doubt, guilt, hostility, restlessness. Each need is introduced in a way which underlines its significance, and concrete suggestions are offered as to how the pastor can minister to that need through his preaching. A sermon by one of the great preachers of the past and one from the present are then included. This is both a stimulating work and a useful source of reference for the pastor. See also the preceding entry (G1075), Lloyd-Jones (G1083) and Teikmanis (G1109).

G1077   Kirkpatrick, Robert White. The Creative Delivery of Sermons. New York: Macmillan Company, 1944. Reprint. New York: Macmillan Company, 1954.

As a work which offers specific and practical suggestions for sermon delivery, this is a useful book for the preacher. Eleven chapters cover aspects such as the minister's aim in sermon delivery, application of the natural laws of expression, general and specific preparation and delivery of the sermon, and some results of the creative delivery of sermons. A bibliography is included, as well as several charts and illustrations. See also Abbey (G1035), Brack (G1048, G1049) and Kraemer (G1080).

G1078   Koller, Charles W. Expository Preaching without Notes. Evangelical Pulpit Library. Grand Rapids, Mich.: Baker Book House, 1962.

This book is intended to help the preacher to a sound and effective approach to the craftsmanship of preaching. Chapters on steps in preparing an expository sermon, structural components, etc. introduce the reader to various homiletical techniques, with the emphasis on exposition. An expository sermon is included at the end of the book. The work has been criticized for some inconsistency in its theology of preaching, for a surfeit of not always discriminatingly selected quotations, and for the intricate system of presentation with many divisions and subdivisions. See also Kirkpatrick (G1077), Liske (G1082) and Unger (G1114).

G1079   Konrad, Joachim. Die Evangelische Predigt: Grundsätze und Beispiele Homiletischer Analysen, Vergleiche und Kritiken. 2. Aufl. Sammlung Dieterich, Bd. 226. Bremen: Schünemann, 1966.

This 527 page introductory study of preaching in the German Protestant framework deals less with principles than with historical developments and examples of sermons. The historical treatment (pp. 13-225) spans 500 years with particular attention paid to Luther, Francke, Schleiermacher and similar personalities. The other major section of this work (pp. 227-433) consists of twelve sermons exemplifying various modes and approaches. For the student interested in a case study approach to preaching and with some background in homiletical principles this is a useful survey. Otherwise more basic textbooks should be consulted to provide the necessary framework and definitions of concepts. See also Breit and Westermann (G1050) and Voigt and Doerne (G1116).

G1080   Kraemer, Hendrick. The Communication of the Christian Faith. Philadelphia, Pa.: Westminster Press, 1956; London: Lutterworth Press, 1957.

This elaboration of a theology of communication focuses particularly on reasons behind difficulties in communicating the Christian faith adequately and convincingly. The five chapters were originally delivered in Knox College, Toronto, as the Laidlaw Lectures in 1955. They deal with communication in biblical perspective, historical aspects of communication, psychological, sociological and cultural factors which hinder communication, the breakdown of Christian communication and possibilities of restoring it. The work is compact and contains many sound observations. See also Abbey (G1035), Brack (G1048, G1049) and Kirkpatrick (G1077).

G1081   La Russo, Dominic A. Basic Skills of Oral Communication. Speech Communication Series. Dubuque, Iowa: W.C. Brown Company, 1967.

See also Ross (G1101) and Weaver and Strausbaugh (G1117).

G1082   Liske, Thomas V. Effective Preaching. 2nd ed. New York: Macmillan Company, 1960.

This Roman Catholic work is presented in four main parts dealing with the delivery of the sermon, the voice, sermon preparation, sermon writing. There are additional notes and speech exercises as well as an index at the end of the volume. This is designed as a useful handbook for the priest, giving much practical information and advice. See also Mac-Nutt (G1087), Koller (G1078) and Valentine (G1115).

G1083   Lloyd-Jones, David Martyn. Preaching and Preachers. London: Hodder and Stoughton, 1971.

This 325 page study contains sixteen chapters on aspects such as the primacy of preaching and the character of the message. It reflects long experience and a personal approach to the topic. See also Kemp (G1076) and Mannebach and Mazza (G1090).

G1084   Lockyer, Herbert. All the Holy Days and Holidays; or, Sermons on All National and Religious Memorial Days. Grand Rapids, Mich.: Zondervan Publishing House, 1968.

The contents of this collection of sermons and sermon ideas are limited to American holidays and those religious festivals recognized by Protestants. For some days there is more than one sermon or outline, and a bibliography is included. The suggestions are fairly straightforward and often unimaginative but have some homiletical reference value in a conservative context. See also Church Pulpit Year Book (G1057), Deems (G1060) and Fichtner (G1068).

G1085   Luthi, Walter, and Thurneysen, Eduard. Preaching. Confession. The Lord's Supper. Trans. by Francis J. Brooke III. Richmond, Va.: John Knox Press, 1960.

This volume contains three substantial essays first published in German in 1957. Luthi's on preaching emphasizes preaching as proclamation of the Word, following Barth in approach. Thurneysen deals with confession in the Reformed tradition, distinguishing the Roman Catholic and evangelical views of confession and emphasizing that evangelical confession cannot be interpreted apart from the doctrine of the church. Luthi, in the final essay, studies the traditional aspects of Holy Communion and examines many pastoral problems related to it. This is a collection of interest to ministers and teachers of preaching and liturgics. See also Macleod (G1086).

G1086   Macleod, Donald. Word and Sacrament: A Preface to Preaching and Worship. Englewood Cliffs, N.J.: Prentice-Hall, 1960.

This compact work for ministers and those concerned with worship is presented in four sections. Preaching is considered as communication as well as proclamation in the first. The second contains a historical survey of public worship. The main section is devoted to the theme that preaching finds its significance only in the context of a worship which is theologically oriented, psychologically conditioned and in touch with life. The final section contains four meditations and two sermons, emphasizing the importance of understanding worship from a theological and biblical point of view. This is a useful work written from a Protestant viewpoint. See also Luthi and Thurneysen (G1085).

G1087   MacNutt, Sylvester F. Gauging Sermon Effectiveness. Dubuque, Iowa: Priory Press, 1960.

This book on sermon criticism is designed for priests and homiletics teachers, to help them in criticizing sermon content. It is not concerned with problems of delivery. The first part gives the critical method with a checklist to apply in sermon criticism. The second part explains the points in the checklist in six chapters under headings such as subject matter and development and style. The book, which reflects the Roman Catholic viewpoint, draws on the teachings of the Church, moral theology, rhetoric and the methods of public speaking. Footnotes have been kept to a minimum in what is designed as a practical tool. See also Liske (G1082) and Valentine (G1115).

G1088 Macpherson, Ian. The Art of Illustrating Sermons. New York: Abingdon Press, 1964.

See also Sangster (G1104).

G1089 Macpherson, Ian. Bible Sermon Outlines. Nashville, Tenn.: Abingdon Press, 1966.

See also Achtemeier (G1037) and Perry (G1094).

G1090 Mannebach, Wayne C., and Mazza, Joseph M. Speaking from the Pulpit. Valley Forge, Pa.: Judson Press, 1969.

See also Lloyd-Jones (G1083) and Valentine (G1115).

G1091 Miller, Donald George. The Way to Biblical Preaching. New York: Abingdon Press, 1957.

This clear guide to the preparation and presentation of expository sermons offers stimulus and direction to the preacher. Seven chapters cover such aspects of preaching as approach, theme, balance, development, purpose and atmosphere. Emphasis is placed on the preacher's message as the outgrowth of his continuous study of the scriptures. See also Perry (G1095) and Thompson (G1110).

G1092 Moore, Walter Lane. Outlines for Preaching. Nashville, Tenn.: Broadman Press, 1965.

See also Brooks (G1053) and White (G1120).

G1093 Müller-Schwefe, Hans Rudolf. Homiletik. 3 vols. Hamburg: Furche Verlag, 1961-1973.

Written from a German Protestant viewpoint, this detailed study of preaching is both a complete textbook and excellent reference work for students with a reading knowledge of German. The first volume is essentially an introduction to homiletics, while the second volume (Die Lehre von der Verkündigung: Das Wort und die Wirklichkeit) deals at length with the theology content and means of preaching in a series of scholarly and erudite chapters. The third volume (Die Praxis der Verkündigung: Möglichkeiten Geistlicher Rede in Unserer Zeit) carries the discussion into practical areas of sermon presentation and delivery. A bibliography, name index and index of biblical passages conclude the work, which forms an excellent complement to less detailed works in English. See also Trillhaas (G1111).

G1094   Perry, Lloyd Merle. Biblical Sermon Guide: A Step-by-Step Procedure for the Preparation and Presentation. Grand Rapids, Mich.: Baker Book House, 1970.

See also Macpherson (G1089).

G1095   Perry, Lloyd Merle. A Manual for Biblical Preaching. Grand Rapids, Mich.: Baker Book House, 1965.

See also Miller (G1095) and Thompson (G1110).

G1096   Proclamation Aids for Interpreting the Lessons of the Church Year. 25 vols. Philadelphia, Pa.: Fortress Press, 1974-1976.

Designed to assist clergy in sermon preparation, this series offers exegetical interpretations of the lessons for each Sunday and many festivals of the church year together with homiletical suggestions and insights. It is based on lectionaries adopted recently by Presbyterians, Lutherans, Episcopalians, Roman Catholics and the United Church of Christ in the United States.   Each of the three series in these new lectionaries is covered in outline form in the collection. See also Fant and Pinson (G1065).

G1097   Rahner, Karl, ed. The Renewal of Preaching: Theory and Practice. Concilium: Theology in the Age of Renewal; Pastoral Theology, vol. 33. New York: Paulist Press, 1968.

This volume sets out to deal with present day problems regarding preaching. There are three main parts.   The first contains eight articles by mainly European contributors. These deal with biblical-theological and with dogmatic aspects, with "demythologization" and the sermon, with the mechanics of preaching, with sacramental worship and preaching, with moral sermons, and with the psychological and sociological structures of preaching. There are also articles on the laity and preaching and on preaching on the radio. The second part contains a bibliographical survey which investigates by what means preaching is helped in individual countries and what is being done to solve the difficulties of preaching by means of institutions, congresses and periodicals. Eleven articles deal with individual countries or areas including Europe, Latin America, North America. The final part is concerned with documentation. Reference is made to Concilium, vol. 20 for further bibliographical material on the sermon. See also Randolph (G1098).

G1098   Randolph, David James. The Renewal of Preaching. Philadelphia, Pa.: Fortress Press, 1969.

This book begins with preaching and the new hermeneutic, and questions the idea that preaching is a part of a branch of classical rhetoric. Emphasis is on preaching as an event, not on what a sermon is. The remainder of the book is concerned with "concern", "confirmation", "concretion", "construction". The author is widely acquainted with homiletical and other theological literature, and provides bibliographical references in the footnotes. This Protestant work is useful in emphasizing the dynamic of preaching, but it is not sufficiently detailed to serve as a homiletical textbook. See also Rahner (G1097) and Sittler (G1106).

G1099 Reu, Johann Michael. Homiletics: A Manual of the Theory and Practice of Preaching. Trans. by Albert Steinhauser. Grand Rapids, Mich.: Baker Book House, 1967 [c.1924].

Designed as a handbook for pastors and seminarians, this volume begins with an introduction on the definition of, justification of and division of homiletics. A substantial part of the main text (pp. 37-246) is devoted to the nature and purpose of the sermon, and there are sections on subject matter and its derivation (pp. 247-388) and on structure (pp. 389-526). Practical illustrations are given at the end to illustrate application of the theories in the manual and to show step-by-step the making of a sermon. Indexes are provided. The manual reflects a Lutheran viewpoint. See also Jones (G1073).

G1100 Ritschl, Dietrich. A Theology of Proclamation. Richmond, Va.: John Knox Press, 1960.

The thesis of this work is that it is the content, not the form and technique, of preaching that really matters. Emphasis is on why and what, rather than on how, one preaches. Following Barth, the author analyzes the authority of the Word of God and its relation to preaching; seeks to elucidate the relationship of the office of proclamation to the worship of the congregation; and examines the nature of the sermon, emphasizing expository preaching. See also Barth (G1043, G1044).

G1101   Ross, Raymond Samuel. Speech Communication: Fundamentals and Practice. Englewood Cliffs, N.J.: Prentice-Hall, 1965.

See also La Russo (G1081) and Weaver and Strausbaugh (G1117).

G1102   Rust, Eric Charles. The Word and Words: Towards a Theology of Preaching. Macon, Ga.: Mercer University Press, 1982.

See also Grasso (G1070) and Wingren (G1121).

G1103   Sangster, William Edwin. The Craft of Sermon Construction: A Source Book for Ministers. The Westminster Source Books. Philadelphia, Pa.: Westminster Press, 1951.

This useful handbook on the technique of preaching deals with subject matter, structural types, psychological method, the beginning and conclusion of the sermon, methods of preparation, and mistakes commonly made. This is full of practical help and stimulating advice for the preacher. See also Barth (G1043), Broadus (G1052) and Davis (G1059).

G1104   Sangster, William Edwin. The Craft of Sermon Illustration. The Westminster Source Books. Philadelphia, Pa.: Westminster Press, 1950.

This brief work deals with the place and use of illustration in sermons, types and sources of illustration, quotations, and mistakes commonly made. An index is included. Most of the illustrations given are the author's own, drawn mainly from publications of his occasional addresses. See also Macpherson (G1088).

G1105   Sangster, William Edwin. Power in Preaching. New York: Abingdon Press; London: Epworth Press, 1958.

This book contains the thirty-ninth series of Fondren Lectures delivered at Southern Methodist University, Dallas, Tex. They are presented as seven chapters with brief titles such as "Keep to centralities" and "Make it practical". An index of names is provided. See also the preceding entries (G1103, G1104) and White (G1119).

G1106 Sittler, Joseph. The Ecology of Faith: The New Situation in Preaching. Philadelphia, Pa.: Muhlenberg Press, 1961. Reprint. Philadelphia, Pa.: Fortress Press, 1970.

Based on the Lyman Beecher Lectures on preaching, delivered at Yale Divinity School in 1959, this book contains five chapters on topics such as the role of the imagination in preaching and the search for theological method and its requirement of preaching. There is also an appendix on the shape of the church's response in worship. See also Randolph (G1098).

G1107 Skinner, Craig. The Teaching Ministry of the Pulpit: Its History, Theology, Psychology and Practice for Today. Grand Rapids, Mich.: Baker Book House, 1973.

See also Jackson (G1072), Welsh (G1118) and Wingren (G1121).

G1108 Steimle, Edmund A., ed. The Preacher's Paperback Library. Philadelphia, Pa.: Fortress Press, 1964- .

This continuing series presents some of the significant preaching of both past and present together with important monographs on various aspects of preaching (e.g., Brilioth on the history of this field). See also Fant and Pinson (G1065).

G1109 Teikmanis,   Arthur L. Preaching and Pastoral Care. Successful Pastoral Counselling Series. Englewood Cliffs, N.J.: Prentice-Hall, 1964.

In this relatively brief (144pp.) work preaching is interpreted as a pastoral function. More than half the work is devoted to specific examples of sermons on many pastoral subjects, each sermon condensed but clear in form and outline. The book is valuable in synthesizing theological and psychological insights and offers a stimulus and guide to ministers concerned with the pastoral emphasis in preaching. See also Kemp (G1075, G1076).

G1110 Thompson, William D. Preaching Biblically: Exegesis and Interpretation. Nashville, Tenn.: Abingdon Press, 1981.

Thompson presents a careful analysis of how to transform the principles and techniques of biblical exegesis and interpretation into homiletical form. The author's theory and method are illustrated by a detailed case study and clarified by comments on how to preach from a variety of scriptural literary forms. For Protestant and Catholic preachers hoping to bridge the gap between scholarship and practice this is an enlightening text and reference volume. See also Miller (G1091) and Perry (G1095).

G1111   Trillhaas, Wolfgang. Evangelische Predigtlehre. 5. Aufl. Munich: Chr. Kaiser Verlag, 1964.

This standard German language textbook on preaching is divided into four main parts, treating principles of homiletics, textual material for preaching, formal homiletics and pastoral homiletics. Each of the twenty chapters deals with a distinct topic within this broad framework and presents basic principles in a straightforward but scholarly manner. While some of Trillhaas' views on the structure and pastoral aspects of preaching have been superseded by less formal approaches, much of what he says on the principles and sources remains valid for those within the Protestant tradition. There are indexes of names and biblical passages. See also Müller-Schwefe (G1093) for a newer and more detailed approach to preaching in a similar vein; see als Uhsadel (G1113).

G1112   Turnbull, Ralph G. A History of Preaching: From the Close of the Nineteenth Century to the Middle of the Twentieth Century, and American Preaching during the Seventeenth, Eighteenth and Nineteenth Centuries. Grand Rapids, Mich.: Baker Book House, 1974.

This continuation of Dargan (G1058) explores the course of American preaching and of preaching in Britain and on the Continent. It attempts to follow Dargan in relating preaching to its religious, political and cultural setting in each area. An index makes use of the volume for quick reference relatively easy. A valuable bibliography (38pp.) is provided. While some of the theological judgments offered may be superficial, this work provides a comprehensive historical review of preaching.

G1113   Uhsadel, Walter. Die Gottesdienstliche Predigt: Evangelische Predigtlehre. Praktische Theologie, Bd. 1. Heidelberg: Quelle und Meyer, 1963.

See also Trillhaas (G1111).

G1114   Unger, Merrill Frederick. Principles of Expository Preaching. Grand Rapids, Mich.: Zondervan Publishing House, 1965. Reprint. Grand Rapids, Mich.: Zondervan Publishing House, 1973.

See also Koller (G1078).

G1115   Valentine, Ferdinand. The Art of Preaching: A Practical Guide. London: Burns, Oates and Washbourne, 1951; Westminster, Md.: Newman Press, 1952.

See also Liske (G1082) and White (G1119).

G1116   Voigt, Gottfried, and Doerne, Martin, eds. Homiletische Auslegung der Predigttexte. Vol. 1- . Göttingen: Vandenhoeck und Ruprecht, 1969- .

Planned in six volumes, this collection of sermon outlines is based on liturgical texts approved for the German Lutheran church year. See also Breit and Westermann (G1050), Eichholz and Falkenroth (G1064) and Konrad (G1079).

G1117   Weaver, Carl Harold, and Strausbaugh, Warren L. Fundamentals of Speech Communication. New York: American Book Company, 1964.

See also La Russo (G1081) and Ross (G1101).

G1118   Welsh, Clement. Preaching in a New Key: Studies in the Psychology of Thinking and Listening. Philadelphia, Pa.: United Church Press, 1974.

> This essay began as a series of explorations designed to find out what goes on in the mind of anyone listening to a sermon, and then as a series of lectures delivered in 1971 (the Lester Bradner Lectures at the Episcopal Theological School, Cambridge, Mass.). The book is concerned with the listener rather than the preacher and does not deal with many of the usual topics in works on homiletics. Eight chapters discuss aspects such as models of universes, perception and cognition. There are notes at the end of the volume; there is no index. See also Jackson (G1072) and Skinner (G1107).

G1119   White, Reginald E.O. A Guide to Preaching: A Practical Primer of Homiletics. Grand Rapids, Mich.: William B. Eerdmans Publishing Company, 1973.

> See also Demaray (G1061) and Valentine (G1115).

G1120   White, Reginald E.O. Sermon Suggestions in Outline. Vol. 1- . Grand Rapids, Mich.: William B. Eerdmans Publishing Company, 1965- .

> See also Brooks (G1053) and Moore (G1092).

G1121   Wingren, Gustaf. The Living Word: A Theological Study of Preaching and the Church. Trans. by Victor C. Pogue. Philadelphia, Pa.: Muhlenberg Press, 1960. Reprint. The Preacher's Paperback Library, vol. 5. Philadelphia, Pa.: Fortress Press, 1965.

> This translation from the Swedish edition of 1949 is concerned with the fundamental theological issues involved in preaching rather than with techniques of the preacher's art. It is a significant Lutheran contribution to ecumenical understanding. Sixteen chapters examine themes such as the Bible and preaching, the ministry of reconciliation, and the law and the gospel. Indexes of names and subjects, and of biblical references are provided. Biblical quotations are normally from the RSV. Many footnotes in the original Swedish edition have been omitted. See also Grasso (G1070) and Rust (G1102?.

HOMILETICS: QUOTATIONS AND ILLUSTRATIONS

G1122   Alexander, Patricia, comp. Eerdmans' Book of Christian Poetry. With biographies by Veronica Zundel. Grand Rapids, Mich.: William B. Eerdmans Publishing Company, 1981.

> See also Keble (G1138) and Morrison (G1143).

G1123   Barnhouse, Donald Grey. Let Me Illustrate: Stories, Anecdotes, Illustrations. Westwood, N.J.: Fleming H. Revell Company; London: Pickering and Inglis, 1967.

> See also Hefley (G1134), Prochnow (G1147) and Wallis (G1156).

G1124   Baron, Joseph Louis, ed. A Treasury of Jewish Quotations. New rev. ed. South Brunswick, N.J.: T. Yoseloff, 1965.

This inclusive compilation covering the entire range of Jewish thought and history in all ages and places is arranged alphabetically under a number of key topics. It is estimated that 10,000 of the quotations have never before been published in English, which indicates in part why some critics find the selection too generous. Nevertheless, as an encyclopedic compilation of Jewish quotations, Baron is the most likely source of data in its field. There is an author index, a subject index, a bibliography and a glossary ("Jewish Thought from Biblical Days to Present Times").

G1125   Bartlett, John. A Compact Anthology of Bartlett's Quotations. Comp. and arranged by Theodore B. Backer. Middle Village, N.Y.: Jonathan David Publishers, 1974.

See Bartlett (G1126) for the work from which this adequate condensation is derived.

G1126   Bartlett, John. Familiar Quotations: A Collection of Passages, Phrases and Proverbs Traced to Their Sources in Ancient and Modern Literature. 14th ed., rev. and enlarged.   Ed. by Emily Morison Beck. Boston, Mass.: Little, Brown and Company, 1968.

First published in 1855 and since then the most popular compilation in its field, Bartlett is of significant value for the preacher and public speaker.   Arrangement is chronological by author, and there is an extensive keyword index of more than 117,000 entries. Both the Bible and Book of Common Prayer are sources for many quotations, as are many authors from various fields related to religion. See Backer's condensation (G1125) for a briefer version. Although the fourteenth edition is an extensive revision of earlier editions, some of these (especially the twelfth) include items dropped from the latest compilation and so should not be ignored. See also Smyth (G1151); for a less comprehensive work see Robertson (G1149).

G1127   Benham, William Burney. Benham's Book of Quotations, Proverbs and Household Words. New and rev. ed. With supplement and full indexes. New York: G.P. Putnam's Sons, 1949,

First published in 1907 and revised in 1936, this work of nearly 1300 pages divides the entries into five parts: British and American quotations (pp. 1-440); quotations from the Bible and Book of Common Prayer (pp. 441-465); political phrases, epitaphs and similar sayings (pp. 466-512); foreign quotations (pp. 513-764); proverbs (pp. 765-928). It includes more than 30,000 quotations from around the world on a wide range of topics. The index (pp. 929-1259) is detailed and extensive, and the supplement includes its own index. Benham has been reprinted many times. See also Stevenson (G1153).

G1128   Browne, Benjamin P. Illustrations for Preaching. Nashville, Tenn.: Broadman Press, 1977.

The first section of this work contains practical advice on how to locate illustrations and ways in which they can be most effectively employed. The second part contains a treasury of illustrations arranged under topics of particular value to the preacher. See also Hefley (G1134) and Person (G1146).

G1129   Brussell, Eugene E. Dictionary of Quotable Definitions. Englewood Cliffs, N.J.: Prentice-Hall, 1970.

In this collection dictionary definitions of words are replaced by famous metaphors and aphorisms. The work is arranged alphabetically by subject, and the author (but not the source) of each definition is given. Brussell has some value for the preacher but should not be used in place of the standard dictionaries of quotations such as Smyth (G1151).

G1130   Chapin, John, ed. The Book of Catholic Quotations: Compiled from Approved Sources, Ancient, Medieval and Modern. New York: Farrar, Straus and Cudahy, 1957; London: Calder, 1957.

This comprehensive work contains more than 10,400 quotations arranged alphabetically by subject, accompanied by a detailed analytical index of subjects and an index of sources. Confined primarily to Roman Catholic sources from the English speaking world (but including papal pronouncements and canon law), this is a valuable reference volume which would be improved by a new edition.

G1131   Doan, Eleanor Lloyd, comp. The Speaker's Sourcebook of 4,000 Illustrations,   Quotations, Sayings, Anecdotes, Poems, Attention Getters, Sentence-Sermons. Grand Rapids, Mich.: Zondervan Publishing House, 1960.

This work is arranged alphabetically by subject. See also Hefley (G1134) and Prochnow (G1147).

G1132   Evans, Bergen. Dictionary of Quotations, Collected, Arranged and with Comments. New York: Delacorte Press, 1968.

With more than 2000 pages, this work is a reasonably comprehensive collection which includes many items not found in standard dictionaries of quotations. It uses a topical arrangement similar to Stevenson (G1154) and includes a keyword index with the addition of references to names or terms occurring in the notes. There is also an author index. See also Magill (G1139).

G1133 Granger, Edith. Granger's Index to Poetry. 6th ed., rev. and enlarged, indexing anthologies published through 31 December 1970. Ed. by William James Smith. New York: Columbia University Press, 1973.

First published in 1904, the latest edition of this standard reference work covers 514 anthologies. Access to individual poems is provided by title and first line index, author index and subject index; these direct one to the anthology or anthologies where the particular poem may be found.

G1134 Hefley, James C. A Dictionary of Illustrations: Over 900 Illustrations for Teachers, Speakers and Ministers. Grand Rapids, Mich.: Zondervan Publishing House, 1971.

See also Barnhouse (G1123), Browne (G1128) and Doan (G1131).

G1135 Holdcraft, Paul Ellsworth. Sayings and Sentences for Church Bulletins. Nashville, Tenn.: Abingdon Press, 1967.

G1136   Hoyt, Jehiel Keeler. Hoyt's New Cyclopedia of Practical Quotations Drawn from the Speech and Literature of All Nations, Ancient and Modern, Classic and Popular, in English and Foreign Text. With copious indexes. Rev. and enlarged by Kate Louise Roberts. New York: Funk and Wagnalls, 1922. Reprint. New York: Funk and Wagnalls, 1940.

This comprehensive collection contains 21,000 quotations arranged alphabetically by subject and including exact references to sources. Biblical passages are omitted, but in other respects this is an excellent guide to sayings of writers from earlier generations. There is an excellent index of quoted authors which includes brief biographical data, and there is also a concordance of quotations. See also Jones (G1137).

G1137   Jones, Hugh Percy, ed. Dictionary of Foreign Phrases and Classical Quotations, Comprising 14,000 Idioms, Proverbs, Maxims, Mottoes, Technical Words and Terms, and Press Allusions from the Works of the Great Writers in Latin, French, Italian, Greek, German, Spanish, Portuguese. Alphabetically Arranged, with English Translations and Equivalents. New and rev. ed. New York: Barnes and Noble; Edinburgh: J. Grant, 1963.

This sizeable collection contains over 500 pages of quotations arranged alphabetically in the seven languages listed in the title. The quotation is given in the original language in the left-hand column with English translation opposite in the right-hand column. Where an explanation of a proverb, for example, is required, this follows the literal translation. Authors are named where appropriate. This contains a wealth of proverbs, quotations, etc. A list of authors quoted is provided at the end of the volume. See also Hoyt (G1136).

G1138   Keble, John. The Christian Year: Thoughts in Verse for the Sundays and Holidays throughout the Year. New York: Appleton, 1896. Reprint. Detroit, Mich.: Gale Research Company, 1975.

Containing more than 100 poems by Keble, this collection presents items dealing with all the Sundays and major festivals of the Christian year. The items are arranged seasonally, and there is an index of first lines. For sermon illustrations in a situation where devotional poetry is appropriate, Keble is a good resource volume in the Anglican tradition. See also Alexander (G1122) and Morrison (G1143).

G1139   Magill, Frank Northern, ed. Magill's Quotations in Context. New York: Harper and Row, 1966.

This useful compilation attempts to go beyond standard collections by providing background comments or summaries of the original context of quotations. The 2000 entries are arranged alphabetically, and there are keyword and author indexes.   The source, author, date and type of work are indicated for each quotation. Since the number of entries is limited, Magill is useful primarily as a supplement to larger works. See also the second series (G1140); see also Evans (G1132).

G1140   Magill,   Frank Northern, ed. Magill's Quotations in Context. 2nd Series. Associate ed.: Tench Francis Tilghman. New York: Harper and Row, 1969.

This is not a revision but an extension of the original collection (G1139).

It contains an additional 1500 entries arranged in the same manner and with keyword and author indexes.

G1141   Mead, Frank Spencer, comp. and ed. The Encyclopedia of Religious Quotations.   Westwood, N.J.: Fleming H. Revell Company; London: Peter Davies, 1965.

This comprehensive work contains some 12,000 quotations from non-Christian and Christian (including biblical) sources, both prose and poetry. Entries are arranged under 170 subject headings, and there is an index of topics. The author index does not include biblical authors, and there are some obvious omissions from the work. Otherwise Mead is a thorough, wide ranging and judicious selection which is well indexed for rapid reference. See also Neil (G1144) and Woods (G1158).

G1142   Moffatt, James. The Expositor's Dictionary of Poetical Quotations. London: Hodder and Stoughton, 1914.

For specifically religious poetry see Alexander (G1122), Keble (G1138) and Morrison (G1143).

G1143   Morrison, James Dalton, ed. Masterpieces of Religious Verse. New York: Harper and Brothers, 1948.

In this collection poems are arranged under seven broad topics. The material is suitable for sermon illustrations and for parish newsletters. See also Alexander (G1122) and Keble (G1138).

G1144   Neil, William, comp. Concise Dictionary of Religious Quotations. Grand Rapids, Mich.: William B. Eerdmans Publishing Company, 1974; London: A.R. Mowbray, 1975.

This collection of religious quotations from Christian and non-Christian sources is designed to provide easy access to relevant material for preachers and others.   The generally brief quotations are arranged under alphabetical subject headings and sources are indicated.   Extracts from the Bible (using the NEB version) and from the Book of Common Prayer appear at the beginning of each theme. Useful subject and source indexes, the former including cross references, are provided. This is a concise, selective, easily used collection. See also Mead (G1141).

G1145   Oxford Dictionary of English Proverbs. 3rd ed. Rev. by F.P. Wilson. Oxford: Clarendon Press, 1970.

This companion volume to Smyth (G1151) contains more than 10,000 proverbs alphabetized under significant words. Liberal cross references are included from all other significant words in a given proverb, usually with an easily identified phrase to assist recognition. Dated references are provided to show the earliest uses and sources of each proverb, as well as variant usages. Many items have been incorporated from Morris P. Tilley's A Dictionary of the Proverbs in England in the 16th and 17th Centuries (Ann Arbor, Mich.: University of Michigan Press, 1950). This revision by Wilson, together with Stevenson (G1153), is an indispensible guide to proverbs and their origins for preachers and other speakers.

G1146   Person, Amy L. Illustrations from Literature. Preaching Helps Series, Grand Rapids, Mich.: Baker Book House, 1966.

See also Browne (G1128), Hefley (G1134) and Robertson (G1149), and for a work in the same series Whitman (G1157).

G1147   Prochnow, Herbert Victor. The Speaker's Book of Illustrations. Natick, Mass.: W.A. Wilde Company, 1960.

This collection contains hundreds of epigrams, quotations, anecdotes, humorous stories and similar items of value to public speakers in general. See also Barnhouse (G1123) and Hefley (G1134).

G1148   Proctor, F.B., comp. Treasury of Quotations on Religious Subjects from the Great Writers and Preachers of All Ages. Grand Rapids, Mich.: Kregel Publications, c.1977.

This classified listing contains quotations from 722 authors and preachers on 3000 subjects. The personalities represented include Bunyan, Lightfoot, Pusey, Schaff, Temple and Wesley. See also Neil (G1144) and Simcox (G1150).

G1149   Robertson, James Douglas, ed. Handbook of Preaching Resources from English Literature. New York: Macmillan Company, 1962.

This volume is intended to make easily accessible to pastors and seminary students relevant items from literature. These 657 items are listed under clear headings, alphabetically arranged, with adequate cross references. Sources of quotations are indicated. Indexes of topics and of authors and sources facilitate use of the collection, and related topics are usefully listed alongside main topics as a guide to further reading. This is a handy, easily used handbook to aid in the preparation of sermons or in tracing appropriate quotations or references for other purposes. See also Person (G1146).

G1150   Simcox, Carroll Eugene. A Treasury of Quotations on Christian Themes. New York: Seabury Press, c.1975.

This collection comprises quotations from Christian and non-Christian sources arranged under six sections: God, creation, man, Christ and His Church, life in the Spirit, the end. All biblical quotations are from the AV or KJV unless otherwise indicated. Indexes of sources, of biblical passages and of subjects make access to the collection easy. The author or source of each quotation is given immediately after it. See also Proctor (G1148) and Stevenson (G1152).

G1151   Smyth, Mary Alice, gen. ed. Oxford Dictionary of Quotations. 2nd ed. rev. New York: Oxford University Press, 1953. Reprint. New York: Oxford University Press, 1970.

First published in 1941, this valuable collection of items chosen for their familiarity covers English speaking authors, foreign authors, the Bible, Book of Common Prayer and anonymous works in a single alphabetical sequence. It gives exact references to sources and is indexed by keywords. The second edition omits 250 entries from the first edition but adds another 1300 new items. This is an excellent collection equal to Bartlett (G1126) in its usefulness. See also the Oxford Dictionary of English Proverbs (G1145).

G1152   Stevenson, Burton Egbert, ed. The Home Book of Bible Quotations. New York: Harper and Brothers, 1949.

Based on the KJV and including the Apocrypha, this collection includes 75,000 quotations under more than 1200 subjects.   Each entry includes the exact reference to book, chapter and verse, and there is a full index of authors. The quantity of material, range of subjects, use of cross references and index and accuracy of citations make this the most valuable collection of biblical quotations for homiletical or other purposes. See also Neil (G1144) and Simcox (G1150).

G1153   Stevenson, Burton Egbert, ed. The Home Book of Proverbs, Maxims and Familiar Phrases. New York: Macmillan Press, 1948.

Reprinted as The Macmillan Book of Proverbs, Maxims and Familiar Phrases (New York: Macmillan Press, 1965), this very comprehensive work includes 73,000 expressions from many languages and periods. It attempts to trace items familiar in English language usage back to their origins and to show their derivation. "Proverb" is interpreted in the widest possible sense, which gives Stevenson a wide range of material on which to draw. Entries are arranged by subject, and each item includes dates, an English translation where necessary and the original language version. There is a detailed keyword index. See also Benham (G1127), and the Oxford Dictionary of English Proverbs (G1145).

G1154   Stevenson, Burton Egbert, ed. The Home Book of Quotations, Classical and Modern. 10th ed. rev. New York: Dodd, Mead and Company, 1967.

First published in 1934, this comprehensive guide to more than 50,000 quotations is arranged alphabetically by subject and topic. Each entry usually includes an exact citation. There is an excellent author index, which includes name, identifying phrase, dates, references to all quotations cited. The subject index treats each quotation by its leading words but excludes the words of smaller topics within the broad subjects. With the exception of this indexing peculiarity, Stevenson is a valuable guide to quotations and is often used in conjunction with Smyth (G1151). See also Bartlett (G1126).

G1155   Tripp, Rhoda Thomas, comp. The International Thesaurus of Quotations. New York: Thomas Y. Crowell Company, 1970.

Following an arrangement similar to Stevenson (G1154), this collection lists entries under a number of alphabetically arranged "idea categories". Tripp includes a number of subjects and many quotations not found in Stevenson, making it a useful supplementary volume.

G1156   Wallis, Charles Langworthy, ed. Speakers' Illustrations for Special Days. New York: Abingdon Press, 1956.

See also Barnhouse (G1123); for specifically Christian festivals see Keble (G1138).

G1157   Whitman, Virginia. Illustrations from Nature for Preachers and

Speakers. Preaching Helps Series.   Grand Rapids, Mich.: Baker Book House, 1965.

See also Person (G1146) for a work in the same series.

G1158   Woods, Ralph Louis, comp. and ed. The World Treasury of Religious Quotations: Diverse Beliefs, Convictions, Comments, Dissents and Opinions from Ancient and Modern Sources. New York: Hawthorn Books, 1966.

In more than 1100 pages this compilation contains 10,000 quotations arranged chronologically under 1500 subject headings. Coverage is international, but poetry and the Bible are excluded. Author, title and date of publication are given for each quotation. There is an author index but no keyword index, the latter omission being a serious handicap in using Woods quickly and efficiently. See also Mead (G1141) and Neil (G1144).

Education

G1159   Abrams, Nick, ed. Audio-Visual Resource Guide. 9th ed. New York: Friendship Press, 1972.

Geared specifically to the needs of religious education, this 477 page guide is an essential accompaniment to the planning of educational programs for all age groups. Abrams covers all available materials in religious education, and the evaluations are highly reliable, concise and objective. See also Andover Newton Theological School (G1160) and Dalglish (G1179-G1181).

G1160   Andover Newton Theological School. Audio-Visual Resource Catalog. Newton Center, Mass.: Andover Newton Theological School, 1970.

See also Abrams (G1159) and Dalglish (G1179-G1181).

G1161   Annual Review of Research in Religious Education. Schenectady, N.Y.: Union College, Character Research Project, 1980- ; annual.

This work provides a review of relevant research; a listing of reports (some 130 in the 1980 issue); a set of abstracts (86 in the 1980 issue) of reports in eighteen journals or other publications; three topical listings (including theses in United Kingdom universities in the field of religious education, 1970-1978); and a listing of authors whose work has been abstracted (with addresses where known). See also Kartei (G1191).

G1162   Arnold, Darlene Baden, and Doyle, Kenneth O., Jr. Education/Psychology Journals: A Scholar's Guide. Metuchen, N.J.: Scarecrow Press, 1975.

This compilation lists 122 journals of professional interest to psychologists, educationists, educational psychologists and educators. It is intended to assist such individuals in deciding which journals to read and to which serials professional manuscripts should be submitted. The entries provide usual directory information together with content description, disciplines served, audience, criteria for accepting articles, style requirements for manuscripts. See also Camp and Schwark (G1171), Krepel and DuVall

(G1193) and United Nations Educational, Scientific and Cultural Organization (G1228).

G1163   Audio-Visual Aids: Films, Filmstrips, Transparencies, Wallsheets and Recorded Sound. 5 vols. London: Educational Foundation for Visual Aids, 1971.

This index is divided into eight major subjects and subdivided into smaller topical units; religion is treated in the first part. The entries are annotated fairly and accurately, although the content is clearly British and European in focus. A title index, list of distributors and price list are included. Supplements are published regularly in Visual Education to help keep the main work up-to-date. See also Audiovisual Market Place (G1164), Limbacher (G1194) and Rufsvold and Guss (G1225).

G1164   Audiovisual Market Place. New York: R.R. Bowker Company, 1969- ; annual.

See also Audio-Visual Aids (G1163), Limbacher (G1194) and Rufsvold and Guss (G1225).

G1165   Barbin, René. Bibliographie de Pédagogie Religieuse: Introductions et Commentaires. Montréal: Editions Bellarmin, 1964.

This guide for teachers of religion at all levels covers the Bible, liturgy, anthropology, psychology, missiology, art and catechetics in a series of well annotated bibliographies. Audio-visual items and periodicals are also listed, giving Barbin a rather wide scope. Most items are in French and reflect a Roman Catholic bias, but some English language materials are included.   See also Centre Documentaire Catéchetique (G1173).

G1166   Berry, Dorothea M. A Bibliographic Guide to Educational Research. Metuchen, N.J.: Scarecrow Press, 1975.

This concise guide for students of education is intended mainly to assist them in making adequate use of library collections. It contains an annotated listing of approximately 500 items arranged by type of material: periodicals, research studies, government publications, reference materials and similar categories. There are author, title and subject indexes. See also Humby (G1189) for a British work of similar scope; see also Richmond (G1224).

G1167   British Education Index. Vol. 1- . London: British Library, Bibliographic Services Division, 1954- ; quarterly with annual cumulations.

This indexing service seeks to cover articles in English language journals which are published or distributed in Britain; the 175 titles scanned each year yield approximately 3500 relevant articles, of which about two dozen deal with religious education. Entries are arranged by subject in the main listing, and there is a subject index plus an author index; full citations appear in both the subject listing and in the author index. This guide is quite up-to-date, clearly arranged and adequately indexed; unfortunately, few of the journals treated give much space to religion. Nevertheless, this is a valuable guide for students of education in its broader aspects.   See also Education Index (G1184) and Current Index to

Journals in Education (G1178).

G1168   Broudy, Harry S., et al. Philosophy of Education: An Organization of Topics and Selected Sources. Urbana, Ill.: University of Illinois Press, 1967.

Based on a project which set out to identify and classify the topics and literature in the philosophy of education, this provides information on the project and methodology, then presents material in sections (nature and aims of education, curriculum design and validation, etc.) with subsections (epistemology, ethics, value theory, etc.). An index of topics is provided, and there is a useful supplementary volume by Smith and Broudy (G1226). See also Powell (G1219).

G1169   Bulletin Signalétique: Sciences de l'Education. Vol. 1- . Paris: Centre National de la Recherche Scientifique, 1947- ; quarterly.

Produced under various titles, this guide to francophone education articles now presents some 6000 indicative abstracts and references in each volume. Entries are presented in a classified arrangement of five main headings, and each issue carries indexes of authors, concepts and types of documents. There is also a list of periodicals abstracted in each number, and overall this compilation is well suited to the needs of inquirers. However, coverage of religious education, while not insignificant, is less adequate than one might expect. English language readers need consult this work only for comparative purposes.

G1170   Bureau Protestant de Recherches Catéchetiques. Audiovisuel et Foi: Equipe, Monde et Foi. Vol. 1- . Lyon: Editions du Chalet, 1970- .

See also Dalglish (G1179-G1181).

G1171   Camp, William L., and Schwark, Bryan L. Guide to Periodicals in Education and Its Academic Disciplines. 2nd ed. Metuchen, N.J.: Scarecrow Press, 1975.

First published in 1968 as Guide to Periodicals in Education, this 552 page compilation provides information on 602 periodicals in education and related disciplines issued in the United States.   Data include address, editorial policy, notes on manuscript preparation, subscription information. This is more extensive in coverage than Arnold and Doyle (G1162) and very similar to Krepel and DuVall (G1193); see also United Nations Educational, Scientific and Cultural Organization (G1228).

G1172   Carey, Marie Aimée. A Bibliography for Christian Formation in the Family. Glen Rock, N.J.: Paulist Press, 1964.

This annotated bibliography is aimed in general at family life education in a Christian context. It covers such topics as Christian marriage, liturgy, prayer, sex education, Christian culture and catechetical instruction in 175 pages. There is an author index to assist in retrieving data from the topical sections. Some of the coverage reflects a conservative Roman Catholic viewpoint. See also Wilt (G1231).

G1173 Centre Documentaire Catéchetique. Ou En Est l'Enseignement Religieux? Tournai: Editions Casterman, 1937.

For some years considered the most adequate bibliography of Catholic religious instruction and noted for its fulness of coverage, this international guide covers all aspects of education relevant to Roman Catholic religious pedagogy. It includes an author index and, when used with the supplements (3rd. Louvain, 1942) remains one of the most comprehensive guides in its field. Today it is particularly useful for its references to older works of interest to those tracing the historical development of Christian education. See also Barbin (G1165).

G1174   Columbia University. Teachers College. Library. Dictionary Catalog of the Teachers College Library. 36 vols. Boston, Mass.: G.K. Hall and Company, 1970.

See also Harvard University. Widener Library (G1188) and University of London (G1230).

G1175   Corrigan, John T., ed. Periodicals for Religious Education Resource Centers and Parish Libraries: A Guide to Magazines, Newspapers and Newsletters. Haverford, Pa.: Catholic Library Association, 1976.

Arranged alphabetically by title, this list of 106 religious periodicals for school and church libraries provides full bibliographical citations and descriptive annotations for each item. Corrigan also evaluates periodicals helpful in selecting media for religious education. This is a useful guide to educational serials for Catholic students and general readers.

G1176   Cronin, Lawrence J., comp. Resources for Religious Instruction of Retarded People. Boston, Mass.: Archdiocese of Boston, Office of Religious Education, 1974.

Including materials for retarded students, their parents and teachers, Cronin provides annotated entries for books, articles and suitable audiovisual aids. These entries are arranged by form and subject. This is a particularly helpful bibliography for the teacher.

G1177 Current Contents: Education. Philadelphia, Pa.: Institute for Scientific Information and Encyclopaedia Britannica Educational Corporation, 1961- ; weekly.

Both title and content vary greatly, but since 1968 this compilation has concentrated solely on education in the broadest sense. It is a weekly guide to the contents pages of more than 600 educational journals; entries are classified in four main categories, and there is no alphabetical arrangement within the sections. Most users find the categories too broad, and there is no subject index to overcome this failing. The author index is useful, but without an annual cumulation use of Current Contents is rather difficult. Because of these difficulties and shortcomings, the benefits gained from using this tool are overshadowed by the time taken to scan it. See also Current Index to Journals in Education (G1178).

G1178   Current Index to Journals in Education. Vol. 1- . New York: Macmillan Information, 1967- ; monthly with semi-annual cumulations.

Covering approximately 700 English language journals in education and related fields, this index contains some 20,000 entries annually. In the main entry section each citation includes full bibliographical details plus a brief abstract. The subject index then lists entries by alphabetically arranged headings and again provides bibliographical data but not the abstracts, and a given entry may appear under more than one heading. The author index provides information on author and title together with main entry reference numbers. Finally, the journal content index lists all articles covered in order of the journals and individual issues. This is an exceptionally up-to-date indexing service which provides very comprehensive coverage of education, including religious education. All entries are stored in the ERIC (Educational Resources Information Center) data base and thus are available for on-line searching. See also British Education Index (G1167) and Education Index (G1184).

G1179   Dalglish, William A., ed. Media for Christian Formation: A Guide to Audio-Visual Resources.   Associate eds.: Roger E. Beaubien and Walter R. Laude. Dayton, Ohio: G.A. Pflaum, 1969.

This guide lists and evaluates more than 400 films, filmstrips, posters, records and tapes from Catholic, Protestant and secular sources. Evaluative annotations indicate the denominational focus and age level of each entry. The arrangement is alphabetical by title, and a detailed subject index is included. There is a list of sources (distributors), as well as a directory of religious and secular film and tape libraries. See also the two supplementary volumes (G1180, G1181), Abrams (G1159) and Andover Newton Theological School (G1160).

G1180   Dalglish, William A., ed. Media Three; for Christian Formation: A Guide to Audio-Visual Resources.   Associate eds.: Roger E. Beaubien et al. Dayton, Ohio: G.A. Pflaum/Standard, 1973.

This is a supplement to Media Two (G1181); see also the main volume (G1179).

G1181   Dalglish, William A., ed. Media Two; Media for Christian Formation: A Guide to Audio-Visual Resources. Associate eds.: Roger E. Beaubien and Walter R. Laude. Dayton, Ohio: G.A. Pflaum, 1970.

This supplement to the main volume (G1179) contains 502 pages; see also Media Three (G1180).

G1182   Drouin, Edmond Gabriel. The School Question: A Bibliography on Church-State Relationships in American Education, 1940-1960. Washington, D.C.: Catholic University of America Press, 1963.

Covering books, pamphlets, periodical articles, book reviews, dissertations and court decisions, this bibliography represents all points of view fairly and thoroughly. More than 12,000 items are listed in classified order, and some descriptive annotations are provided. There is an index of authors and titles. See also Little (G1199).

G1183   Education Book List. Vol. 1- . Washington, D.C.: Pi Lambda Theta, 1968- ; annual.

Published annually to cover the preceding year's output, this is a classified list of important or major works on education. It is limited to substantial monographs but covers all aspects of the discipline, serving as a useful means of keeping abreast of recent scholarship in educational fields.

The coverage of Christian education is minimal, but many of the entries in each volume have an indirect bearing on areas relevant to this part of the educational process.   See also Educational Press Association of America (G1186).

G1184   Education Index: A Cumulative Author Subject Index to a Selected List of Educational Periodicals, Proceedings and Yearbooks. Vol. 1- . New York: H.W. Wilson Company, 1929- ; monthly with annual cumulations.

Cumulating monthly throughout the year in addition to the annual cumulations, this standard reference tool indexes approximately 340 periodicals and related publications on all phases of education, including religion, religious education and church schools. Arrangement is alphabetical by subject and topic; the subject headings and subdivisions are very detailed. For each entry the standard bibliographical details are provided, and full details of titles indexed are provided in each issue. Devoted to English language materials, particularly those from North America, this is a useful complement to the British Education Index (G1167). Because it is indexed by subject and author (although the latter was omitted between 1961 and July 1969) and because it is quite current in coverage, Education Index is used very regularly by those interested in up-to-date information on religious education. See also Current Index to Journals in Education (G1178), which is a much more comprehensive but less widely available index.

G1185   Educational Media Council. The Educational Media Index. 14 vols. New York: McGraw-Hill Book Company, 1964.

This comprehensive multivolume directory of nonbook instructional materials treats a specific subject in each volume; the first two are devoted to specific levels of education (through grade six), and the remaining volumes cover topics. Religion is not included as a special subject, but some of the other fields incorporate materials with marginal value in religious instruction. A successor to Education Film Guide, the Index contains a total of 50,000 items in the area of teaching aids and devices. See also Audio-Visual Aids (G1163), which includes religion in its coverage, and the publications of the National Information Center for Educational Media (G1205-G1213).

G1186   Educational Press Association of America. America's Education Press: A Classified List of Educational Publications Issued in the United States and Canada. Vol. 1- . Washington, D.C.: Educational Press Association of America, 1926- ; biennial.

Issued annually to cover the preceding year's publications until it became biennial in 1950, this is an ongoing bibliography of North American publications. See also Education Book List (G1183).

G1187   Hamilton, Malcolm C. Directory of Educational Statistics: A Guide to Sources. Ann Arbor, Mich.: Pierian Press, 1974.

This 71 page guide lists ninety-nine bibliographic sources according to subject treated; these include general areas, public elementary and secondary schools, public school economic and financial matters, private schools, higher education, degrees and enrollment, international education. Although clearly American in focus, there is a section on British education.

The entry for each source includes a brief description of the publication. There are indexes of titles and subjects.

G1188   Harvard University. Widener Library. Education and Education Period- icals. 2 vols. Widener Library Shelflist, vols. 16-17. Cambridge, Mass.: Harvard University Press, 1968.

See also Columbia University. Teachers College. Library (G1174), United Nations Educational, Scientific and Cultural Organization (G1228) and University of London (G1230).

G1189   Humby, Michael. A Guide to the Literature of Education. 3rd ed. Educational Libraries Bulletin, supplement 1. London: University of London, Institute of Education, 1975.

This successor to the second edition by S.K. Kimmance published in 1958 aims to provide selected examples of the various types of publica- tions likely to be found in an education library. The 572 entries are arranged by type, including guides to the literature of education, bibliog- raphies, encyclopedias, dictionaries, directories and yearbooks and biograph- ies. There is an index. See also Berry (G1166) for a similar compilation but with an American focus; see also Richmond (G1224) and Woodbury (G1232).

G1190   Institute of Christian Education at Home and Overseas. A Bibliog- raphy for the Use of Teachers of Religious Knowledge. 5th ed. London: Institute of Christian Education at Home and Overseas, 1959.

See also Panoch (G1214).

G1191   Kartei der Literaturdokumentation für Religionsunterricht und Kirch- liche Bildungsarbeit. Munich: Institut für Katechetik und Homiletik, 1976- .

Covering approximately 170 German language journals, this card index service of materials on catechetics provides details of content of the title listed, of the readership for which it is intended and of the character of the publication (bibliography, etc.). A dictionary of key words is available separately, the Thesaurus Religionspädagogik. Approximately 1600 cards are provided annually. See also Annual Review of Research in Religious Education (G1161) and Räber (G1220).

G1192   Klein, Bernard, ed. Guide to American Educational Directories. 4th ed. New York: B. Klein, 1975.

In each edition of the Guide "directory" is broadly interpreted to include yearbooks, biographical dictionaries, registers, bibliographies, general and special directories and related types of materials. Entries are classif- ied by subject and listed alphabetically by title in each section. The annotations are descriptive and concise, providing clear outlines of the range of directories discussed. See also Woodbury (G1232).

G1193   Krepel, Wayne J., and DuVall, Charles R. Education and Education Related Serials: A Directory. Littleton, Colo.: Libraries Unlimited, 1977.

Similar in content to Camp and Schwark (G1171), this compilation provides information on 501 periodicals and newsletters related to education, teaching and learning. Entries include data on submitting articles for publication, style requirements and standard directory information. A particularly useful appendix lists indexing and abstracting services in education. See also Arnold and Doyle (G1162).

G1194 Limbacher, James L. A Reference Guide to Audiovisual Information. New York: R.R. Bowker, 1972.

This useful reference volume contains an annotated list of approximately 400 books and 100 periodicals which deal with audio-visual information. There is also a glossary of 350 terms, a directory of publishers and a supplementary subject list of titles which are not primarily reference tomes. As a basic bibliography, this is a very useful reference work for those seeking some expertise in audio-visual matters. See also Audio-Visual Aids (G1163), Audiovisual Market Place (G1164) and Rufsvold and Guss (G1225).

G1195 Little, Lawrence Calvin. Abstracts of Selected Doctoral Dissertations on Adult Religious Education. Pittsburgh, Pa.: Department of Religious Education, University of Pittsburgh, 1966.

See also The Resource Guide for Adult Religious Education (G1222).

G1196 Little, Lawrence Calvin. A Bibliography of American Doctoral Dissertations in Religious Education, 1885 to 1959. Pittsburgh, Pa.: University of Pittsburgh, 1962.

See also Parker (G1215).

G1197 Little, Lawrence Calvin. Bibliography of Doctoral Dissertations in Character and Religious Education. Pittsburgh, Pa.: Department of Religious Education, University of Pittsburgh, 1960.

See also Little's other work on this area (G1200).

G1198 Little, Lawrence Calvin. A Bibliography of Doctoral Dissertations on Adults and Adult Education. Rev. ed. Pittsburgh, Pa.: University of Pittsburgh, 1963.

See also Little's other bibliography on this subject (G1201).

G1199 Little, Lawrence Calvin, comp. Religion and Public Education: A Bibliography. 3rd ed. Pittsburgh, Pa.: University of Pittsburgh Book Center, 1968.

The 3200 items in this compilation are grouped by type of document and cover books and pamphlets by individuals or educational agencies, pronouncements and reports by religious bodies and school systems, dissertations and theses, journal articles and selected Supreme Court decisions. Unfortunately there is no detailed subject approach provided, which makes it difficult to extract information on a given topic from more than 200 pages of entries. See also Drouin (G1182).

G1200 Little, Lawrence Calvin. Researches in Personality, Character and Religious Education: A Bibliography of American Doctoral Dissertations, 1885-1959. Pittsburgh, Pa.: University of Pittsburgh Press, 1962.

This list of 6304 dissertations is arranged alphabetically by author; each entry includes title, university and date. There is a detailed subject index which is accurate and complete, making the location of entries quite easy. As a guide to completed dissertations, this is an important bibliography now in need of updating. See also Little's other work on this area (G1197).

G1201   Little, Lawrence Calvin. Toward Understanding Adults and Adult Education: Contributions of 100 Selected Doctoral Dissertations. Pittsburgh, Pa.: Department of Religious Education, University of Pittsburgh, 1963.

See also Little's other bibliography on this subject (G1198).

G1202   Mannheim, Theodore; Dardarian, Gloria L.; and Satterthwaite, Diane A. Sources in Educational Research: A Selected and Annotated Bibliography. Vol. 1- . Detroit, Mich.: Wayne State University Press, 1969.

Intended as an introduction to the research literature in various fields of education, these handbooks concentrate on titles which are most useful for graduate or advanced undergraduate students. The first issue deals with general educational research tools; successive parts deal with particular areas such as social studies education and comparative education. Material is arranged according to type (dictionaries, encyclopedias, etc.). Periodicals are listed alphabetically by title. These are useful guides to the literature. See also Berry (G1166), Humby (G1189), Research Studies in Education (G1221) and Richmond (G1224).

G1203   Miller, Albert Jay. A Selective Bibliography of Existentialism in Education and Related Topics. New York: Exposition Press, 1969.

G1204   Monroe, Will Seymour. Bibliography of Education. New York: D. Appleton, 1897. Reprint. Detroit, Mich.: Gale Research Company, 1968.

See also Richmond (G1224).

G1205   National Information Center for Educational Media. Index to Educational Audio tapes. 4th ed. Los Angeles, Calif.: National Information Center for Educational Media, University of Southern California, 1977.

G1206   National Information Center for Educational Media. Index to Educational Overhead Transparencies. 4th ed. Los Angeles, Calif.: National Information Center for Educational Media, University of Southern California, 1975.

G1207   National Information Center for Educational Media. Index to Educational Records. 4th ed. Los Angeles, Calif.: National Information Center for Educational Media, University of Southern California, 1977.

G1208   National Information Center for Educational Media. Index to Educational Slides. 3rd ed. Los Angeles, Calif.: National Information Center for Educational Media, University of Southern California, 1977.

G1209   National Information Center for Educational Media. Index to Educational Videotapes. 4th ed. Los Angeles, Calif.: National Information Center for Educational Media, University of Southern California, 1977.

G1210   National Information Center for Educational Media. Index to 8mm

Motion Cartridges. 5th ed. Los Angeles, Calif.: National Information Center for Educational Media, University of Southern California, 1977.

G1211   National Information Center for Educational Media. Index to 16mm Educational Films. 5th ed. Los Angeles, Calif.: National Information Center for Educational Media, University of Southern California, 1975.

   Produced in new editions at regular intervals, this index lists several thousand current educational films alphabetically by title; each entry provides data on content, audience level and suggested teaching value. In the second part films are classified under twenty-six subject categories to facilitate the location of relevant items. There is also a directory of producers and distributors for those who wish to acquire a particular film for showing.

G1212   National Information Center for Educational Media. Index to 35mm Educational Filmstrips. 6th ed. Los Angeles, Calif.: National Information Center for Educational Media, University of Southern California, 1977.

G1213   National Information Center for Educational Media. NICEM Update of Nonbook Media. Vol. 1- . Los Angeles, Calif.: National Information Center for Educational Media, University of Southern California, 1973/1974- ; biennial in ten monthly vols.

   Published as an updating service for the Center's fourteen volumes of indexes which appear in alternate years, this series is an indispensible guide for those seeking the most current information on the newest audio-visual releases. See also Educational Media Council (G1185).

G1214   Panoch, James V., and Barr, David L. Religion Goes to School: A Practical Handbook for Teachers. New York: Harper and Row, 1968.

   See also Institute of Christian Education (G1190).

G1215   Parker, Franklin. Catholic Education: A Partial List of 189 American Doctoral Dissertations. Austin, Tex.: n.p., 1961.

   See also Little (G1196).

G1216   Perkins, Ralph. The New Concept Guide to Reference in Education: A Quick Answer to "Where Can I Find It?" Grand Forks, N. Dak.: n.p., 1965.

G1217   Pita, Enrique B. Educación Cristiana: Bibliografía. Buenos Aires: Señales Presentación, 1956.

G1218   Pitts, V. Peter. Concept Development and the Development of the God Concept in the Child: A Bibliography. Schenectady, N.Y.: Character Research Press, 1977.

   This bibliography of conceptual development is useful for those interested in religious education and in child development. The bibliography (pp. 15-51) includes much twentieth century research in religious education. An author and a journal index facilitate use of the work.

G1219   Powell, John Percival, comp. Philosophy of Education: A Select

Bibliography. 2nd ed. Manchester: Manchester University Press, 1968.

> This bibliography is intended for teachers and students of the philosophy of education in universities and colleges of education. A list of periodicals cited precedes the classified bibliography of 707 titles. Section headings include moral education, equality, freedom and authority, and there are sections on educational theories and theorists. An author index is provided. See also Broudy (G1168) and Smith and Broudy (G1226).

G1220   Räber, Ludwig. Bibliographie: Christliche Erziehung und Bildung. Mitarb.: Hans Venetz et al. Lucerne: Arbeitsstelle für Bildungsfragen, 1970.

> See also Kartei (G1191).

G1221   Research Studies in Education: A Subject and Author Index of Doctoral Dissertations, Reports and Field Studies; and a Research Methods Bibliography. Vol. 1- . Bloomington, Ind.: Phi Delta Kappa, 1953- ; annual.

> First published in 1953 to cover 1941-1951, this reasonably up-to-date index covers doctoral dissertations completed or under way in American universities. It is a useful starting point for postgraduate researchers and others interested in tracing major research undertakings. The coverage of reports and field studies is of marginal value, but the research methods bibliography is a reasonable guide to methodological studies. See also Review of Educational Research (G1223) and United States. Office of Education (G1229).

G1222   The Resource Guide for Adult Religious Education. Rev. ed. Kansas City, Mo.: National Catholic Reporter Publishing Company, 1975.

> This 208 page guide lists more than 1000 books, audio-visual materials and pamphlets of value to those engaged in adult catechetics in the Roman Catholic tradition. Full bibliographical details are provided together with brief annotations and ordering information. Entries are arranged by subject, and there are no indexes. This is a very useful work but now requires revision in view of the excellent teaching aids which have been produced in recent years. See also Carey (G1172), Dalglish (G1179-G1181) and Little (G1195).

G1223   Review of Educational Research. Vol. 1- . Washington, D.C.: American Educational Research Association, 1931- ; five per annum.

> Each issue of the Review is devoted to one of eleven major topics, each of which is covered every three years. The issues are divided into chapters which survey research during the period under review, and each number concludes with a comprehensive bibliography. Although selective and primarily North American in focus, this is a valuable source for those requiring some indication of current research activities in a wide range of educational topics. See also Research Studies in Education (G1221) and United States. Office of Education (G1229).

G1224   Richmond, William Kenneth. The Literature of Education: A Critical Bibliography, 1945-1970. London: Methuen and Company, 1972.

> This selective, classified bibliography of 206 pages contains ten topical chapters, each of which includes a background survey of the particular

topic and a detailed bibliography with many annotations. Although there is no index and the contents reflect a British viewpoint, this is a useful starting point for general materials in education. Topics covered include educational theory, philosophy of education, history of education. See also Berry (G1166) and Humby (G1189).

G1225   Rufsvold, Margaret Irene, and Guss, Carolyn. Guides to Educational Media: Films, Filmstrips, Kinescopes, Phonodiscs, Phonotapes, Programmed Instruction Materials, Slides, Transparencies, Videotapes. 3rd ed. Chicago, Ill.: American Library Association, 1971.

First published in 1961 as Guides to Newer Educational Media, this guide contains 153 numbered entries covering media catalogs and lists, specialized periodicals which provide information on nonprint educational media, as well as services of professional organizations. See also Audio-Visual Aids (G1163), Audiovisual Market Place (G1164) and Limbacher (G1194).

G1226   Smith, Christiana M., and Broudy, Harry S. Philosophy of Education: An Organization of Topics and Selected Sources: Supplement 1969. Urbana, Ill.: University of Illinois Press, 1969.

Following the pattern of the main volume by Broudy (G1168), this supplement in 139 pages adds significant material to the basic guide and is an import updating. See also Powell (G1219).

G1227   Sociology of Education Abstracts. Vol. 1- . Liverpool: Department of Adult Education and Extra-Mural Studies, 1965- ; quarterly.

Providing more than 250 indicative and informative abstracts of articles in some fifty journals, this service arranges entries by authors. Each abstract presents data under standard headings (hypotheses, conclusions, etc.) for ease of consultation, and the compilation is indexed annually. Coverage is limited strictly to the sociology of education, particularly in the English speaking world, and the resulting data are of marginal value for Christian education except in the broadest sense.

G1228   United Nations Educational, Scientific and Cultural Organization. Education Periodicals. 2nd ed. International Directories of Education, no. 3. Paris: Unesco, 1963.

This work includes brief data on 5000 current education serials published in 100 countries. Entries include title and subtitle, date founded, frequency of publication, length, language, publisher's address. Part 1 is an international and country listing; part 2 is a classified list of titles. See also Arnold and Doyle (G1162), Camp and Schwark (G1171), Harvard University. Widener Library (G1188) and University of London (G1230).

G1229   United States. Office of Education. Educational Resources Information Center. Research in Education. Vol. 1- . Washington, D.C.: Government Printing Office, 1966- .

This important reference series contains about 10,000 abstracts per annum, which are arranged in nineteen major subject groups. It includes both recently completed and current research undertaken throughout the United States in the full range of educational fields. The extensive

annual index covers authors, subjects and institutions. This ERIC compilation provides excellent and up-to-date data for a wide range of users
interested in current edicational research. See also Review of Educational
Research (G1223) and Research Studies in Education (G1221).

G1230   University of London. Institute of Education. Library. Catalogue
of Periodicals in the Library. London: University of London Library, 1968.

See also Harvard University. Widener Library (G1188) and United Nations
Educational, Scientific and Cultural Organization (G1228).

G1231   Wilt, Matthew Richard, ed. Books for Religious Education: An Annotated Bibliography. Haverford, Pa.: Catholic Library Association, 1976.

Compiled by a number of specialists, this work lists titles for both
children and adults and includes a directory of publishers active in the
field of religious education. See also Carey (G1172).

G1232   Woodbury, Marda. A Guide to Sources of Educational Information.
Washington, D.C.: Information Resources Press, 1976.

This 371 page work is adequately indexed and reasonably comprehensive.
See also Humby (G1189), Klein (G1192) and Richmond (G1224).

G1233   Wychoff, D. Campbell. Bibliography of Christian Education for
Presbyterian College Libraries, 1960; Submitted by the Joint Committee
of Nine for Use in the Program for the Preparation of Certified Church
Educators (Assistants in Christian Education). Philadelphia, Pa.: United
Presbyterian Church in the U.S.A., 1960.

This work and its irregularly issued addenda have appeared under various
titles (Suggested Bibliography in Christian Education for Presbyterian
College Libraries, Suggested Bibliography in Christian Education for
Seminary and College Libraries) and cover 1961-1972.

EDUCATION: DICTIONARIES

G1234   Anderson, Scarvia B.; Ball, Samuel; and Murphy, Richard T. Encyclopedia of Educational Evaluation. San Francisco, Calif.: Jossey-Bass Publishers,
1975.

This work seeks to present major concepts and techniques of educational
evaluation in a single alphabetical sequence. The entries are detailed
but nontechnical, and this is a particularly useful work for the nonspecialist or student new to the field. There are bibliographic references
in many articles, which vary in length from a few lines to substantial
treatment. Anderson is indexed to allow quick access to data.

G1235   Blishen, Edward, ed. Encyclopedia of Education. New York: Philosophical Library, 1970.

Also published as Blond's Encyclopaedia of Education (London: Blond,
1969), this work by 150 contributors contains approximately 2150 entries
which exhibit a British focus. The articles are not particularly scholarly

and are often far too brief for detailed research requirements. There are many cross references, short bibliographies and some biographical sketches. In the fifteen appendixes space is devoted to journals, museums and similar topics. For general reference other works of this type are to be preferred for their more incisive articles. See also Dewey (G1239) and Page (G1252).

G1236   Collins, K.T., et al. Key Words in Education. London: Longman, Green and Company, 1973.

See also Page (G1252).

G1237   Cully, Kendig Brubaker, ed. The Westminster Dictionary of Christian Education. Philadelphia, Pa.: Westminster Press, 1963.

This substantial (812pp.) compilation by some 390 contributors contains concise, signed articles on the biblical, cultic, theological, philosophical, psychological and educational aspects of Christian education. It also includes a bibliography (41pp.) and a table of subject headings with special references to the bibliography. Ecumenically oriented, this is one of very few modern works on the subject and is an excellent reference volume for inquiries at various levels. See also Gable (G1241).

G1238   Deighton, Lee C., et.-in-chief. Encyclopedia of Education. 10 vols. New York: Macmillan Company, 1971.

Containing more than 1000 articles by an equal number of contributors, this encyclopedia emphasizes various aspects of American education, including history, theory, research, philosophy and structure. The articles, often several pages in length, are scholarly but nontechnical and include bibliographies. Closely related articles are often grouped under broad headings to facilitate consultation. The separate index volume includes a directory of contributors, detailed subject index, an alphabetical listing of articles. This is a standard encyclopedia for educators and should be a starting point for more specific inquiries. See also Ebel (G1240).

G1239   Dewey, John. Dictionary of Education. Ed. by Ralph Bubrich Winn. New York: Philosophical Library, 1959.

This comprehensive dictionary of professional terms contains concise and accurate definitions, although many reflect Dewey's personal views more strongly than is necessary. Arrangement is alphabetical by word, and there are numerous cross references. In the back of the work are alphabetical lists of terms and definitions in education for Denmark, Britain, France, Germany and Italy. See also Blishen (G1235) and Good (G1242).

G1240   Ebel, Robert L., ed. Encyclopedia of Educational Research. Project of the American Educational Research Association. Associate ed.: Victor H. Noll. 4th ed. New York: Macmillan Company, 1969.

First published in 1940, this completely revised and rewritten edition is arranged alphabetically by subject and contains 1522 pages of signed articles by specialists. The work is not limited to research but covers all types of contributions to educational knowledge. The detailed, selective bibliographies are especially useful as indicators of additional sources of information. The full index is located on yellow pages in the middle of the volume. This dictionary/encyclopedia is suitable for more advanced inquiries by those with background knowledge of the field. See also Deighton (G1238) and Good (G1242).

G1241   Gable, Lee J., ed. Encyclopedia for Church Group Leaders. New York: Association Press, 1959.

This collection of writings is primarily for volunteer leaders in local church groups, but it provides useful material for ministers, church officials and organizers and students. Chapters by numerous contributors are presented in twenty-two sections under four main headings: basic truths for church group leaders; some basic questions about Christian nurture; ways of working with church groups; administering the education- al program. An index is provided. This is a useful compendium, giving access to a wide range of theoretical and practical material. See also Cully (G1237).

G1242   Good,   Carter Victor, ed. Dictionary of Education. Prepared under the auspices of Phi Delta Kappa. 3rd ed. Assistant ed.: Winifred R. Merkel. New York: McGraw-Hill Book Company, 1973.

First published in 1945, this scholarly dictionary presents terms and words which have particular or special meanings in education. The 33,000 entries in the third edition include 8000 new terms, but French, German and other foreign language terms found in earlier editions are no longer included. Educational terms used in Canada, England and Wales are found in a separate section at the end of the work. This is a standard educational dictionary. See also Dewey (G1239) and Ebel (G1240).

G1243   Hopke, William E., ed.-in-chief. The Encyclopedia of Careers and Vocational Guidance. 3rd ed. 2 vols.   Chicago, Ill.: J.G. Ferguson Publishing Company, 1975.

Intended for secondary school students, parents, teachers and counselors, this useful guide covers career planning in the first volume and careers and occupations in the second. Volume 1 presents general information on choice of vocation and specialist chapters on various occupations and professions. Volume 2 presents more specific information about particular careers and branches of professions. This is a very useful reference work for the audience at which it is aimed.

G1244   Jacques Cattell Press, ed. Leaders in Education. 5th ed. New York: R.R. Bowker Company, 1974.

First published in 1932, this biographical dictionary contains sketches of 17,000 personalities in American education. Coverage includes officers of institutions of higher education, professors of education, directors and staff of educational research institutes, public officials responsible for education, leading figures in public and private schools, officers of educational foundations and major educational associations, authors of important pedagogical books. There is both a subject index and a geographical index to the fifth edition. See also Ohles (G1251).

G1245 Knowles, Asa Smallidge, ed.-in-chief. The International Encyclopedia of Higher Education. 10 vols. San Francisco, Calif.: Jossey-Bass Publishers,

1977.

This international work is alphabetically arranged by broad topics, and there is some grouping of material to avoid duplication of data. The types of entries cover national educational systems, topical essays, fields of study, educational associations, research centers, documentation centers, reports on higher education. Volume 1 lists the contents, contributors, acronyms and glossary; volume 10 includes the indexes, which are essential if efficient use is to be made of this important work.

G1246   Korherr, Edgar Josef, and Hierzenberger, Gottfried, eds. Praktisches Wörterbuch der Religionspädagogik und Katechetik. Unter Mitarbeit von P. Anzenberger et al. Vienna: Herder, 1973.

See also Lentner (G1247).

G1247   Lentner, Leopold, ed. Katechetisches Wörterbuch. Hrsg. in Verbindung mit Hubert Fischer, Franz Bürkli und Gerhard Fischer. Freiburg im Breisgau: Herder, 1961.

This carefully edited work contains long, signed articles on technical terms, biography, organizations, the history of catechetics and the state of religious instruction in different countries. Bibliographies are included, and thorough indexes provide ready access. See also Korherr and Hierzenberger (G1246).

G1248   Lexikon der Pädagogik. 3 vols. Bern: A. Francke, 1950-1952.

This detailed Swiss encyclopedia is divided into two main sections; volumes 1 and 2 contain a systematic arrangement of long, signed articles together with valuable bibliographies, while volume 2 deals exclusively with the history of education and includes a long (pp. 19-496) biographical section with sketches of nearly 1300 educational figures worldwide. In this respect it is more suitable than Deighton (G1238), which is particularly weak on biography. For another German language work see Rombach (G1255).

G1249   McNeill, George S., ed. Sunday School Encyclopedia. Wheaton, Ill.: National Sunday School Association, 1965.

G1250   Monroe, Paul, ed. A Cyclopedia of Education. 5 vols. New York: Macmillan Company, 1911-1913.

Reprinted many times, this now dated compilation retains value for its wide range of historical and biographical articles. The signed entries by specialists are arranged alphabetically and include good bibliographies together with helpful illustrations where necessary. Although American subjects predominate, Monroe covers education in all countries and periods. The analytical index in volume 5 groups articles by larger subjects than those used in the main listing of more than 7000 articles. This is a helpful older work for general inquiries. See also Rivlin (G1254) and Watson (G1257).

G1251   Ohles, John F., ed. Biographical Dictionary of American Educators. 3 vols. Westport, Conn.: Greenwood Press, 1978.

This massive compilation presents biographical information on important figures in American education from the colonial period to 1976. National leaders, state figures and subject specialists are all included. The signed articles, usually a page in length, outline the person's education, employment, professional activities and contributions to the field of education. There is a general index in volume 3, and appendixes list individuals by place of birth, state of service, field of work, year of birth. See also Jacques Cattell Press (G1244).

G1252   Page, G. Terry; Thomas, John Bernard; and Marshall, Alan R. International Dictionary of Education. New York: Nichols Publishing Company; London: Kogan Page, 1977.

This 381 page dictionary lists more than 10,000 terms in education; these cover concepts, expressions, international bodies, national associations, educators and similar material. Appendixes list abbreviations for associations and organizations, as well as American educational societies. For very basic data on the full range of educational terminology but with a strong organizational focus Page is a suitable dictionary. See also Blishen (G1235) and Good (G1242).

G1253   Prentice-Hall Editorial Staff, ed. Teacher's Encyclopedia. Englewood Cliffs, N.J.: Prentice-Hall, 1966.

Intended as a presentation of information on practical learning situations and teaching experiences, this is a useful reference volume for church school teachers at all levels. The chapters by specialists are arranged in seven sections; there are chapter outlines, numerous subtitles and other devices to enhance the usefulness of this compilation. Bibliographies are included for further reference. As a reference work this is more a manual or handbook than dictionary but is of practical value for teaching situations. See also Smith (G1256).

G1254   Rivlin, Harry Nathaniel, ed. Encyclopedia of Education. Associate ed.: Herbert Schüler. New York: Philosophical Library, 1943. Reprint. 2 vols. Port Washington, N.Y.: Kennikat Press, 1969.

Containing initialled articles of medium length on specific topics, this encyclopedic dictionary covers all aspects of education and describes the educational systems in major countries, focusing particularly on the United States. The use of cross references is extensive, and short bibliographies accompany most articles. Rivlin is intended mainly for the layman and serves as a general reference work for students unfamiliar with the field. The explanations are clear and concise, and the emphasis on educational theory and practice usefully supplements the contents of Monroe (G1250); see also Watson (G1257).

G1255   Rombach, Heinrich, ed.-in-chief. Wörterbuch der Pädagogik. [Neue Ausg.] Hrsg. vom Willmann-Institut, München, Wien. 3 vols. Freiburg im Breisgau: Herder, 1977.

Previously entitled Lexikon der Pädagogik and not to be confused with the secular Swiss work of the same title (G1248), this Roman Catholic educational encyclopedia is international in scope and contains short articles on all aspects of education. Individuals, organizations, educational systems, concepts and theories are all treated; bibliographies accompany each article, and the system of cross references is impressive in its thoroughness. The three volumes are arranged as follows: Abendschulen bis genetische Methode, Geographieunterricht bis politische Bildung, politische Okonomie bis zweiter Bildungsweg. As a religious encyclopedia, this work deserves a wider reputation among those engaged in religious education at various levels. With its slight continental bias Rombach is a useful complement to Deighton (G1238).

G1256   Smith, Edward Williams; Krouse, Stanley W., Jr.; and Atkinson, Mark M. The Educator's Encyclopedia. Englewood Cliffs, N.J.: Prentice-Hall, 1961.

See also Prentice-Hall Editorial Staff (G1253).

G1257   Watson, Foster, ed. The Encyclopaedia and Dictionary of Education; a Comprehehsive, Practical and Authoritative Guide on All Matters Connected with Education, Including Educational Principles and Practice,   Various Types of Teaching Institutions and Educational Systems throughout the World. 4 vols. London: Sir I. Pitman and Sons, 1921-1922. Reprint. 4 vols. Detroit, Mich.: Gale Research Company, 1969.

This old but still valuable work on broad educational subjects was initially issued in twenty-nine parts and published in sections as The New Educator's Library. The articles, which vary in legnth, are arranged alphabetically and include short bibliographies in many cases. In content and form it is similar to Monroe (G1250).

EDUCATION: HANDBOOKS

G1258   Alexander, Carter, and Burke, Arvid James. How to Locate Educational Information and Data; an Aid to Quick Utilization of the Literature of Education. 4th ed. New York: Bureau of Publications,   Teachers College, Columbia University, 1958.

This revised edition aims to provide information to facilitate use of literature on education. An introduction on the potential of libraries is followed by two main parts: basic techniques of library utilization; special applications of these techniques. The former contains a wealth of practical suggestions on locating books or periodicals, using indexes, compiling bibliographies, etc. The latter examines particular types of publication and their use. An index is provided. This is a useful, time-saving reference work. See also Burke and Burke (G1275).

G1259   Allen, Dwight W., and Seifman, Eli, eds. The Teacher's Handbook. Glenview, Ill.: Scott, Foresman and   Company, 1971.

This 832 page guide contains contributions by more than eighty authors on educational topics. It is designed specifically for the teacher. The sections contain essays on the teacher (educating teachers, in-service training, teacher organizations, etc.); human growth and development; the instructional process; curriculum and method areas; the school system; the foundations of education; contemporary issues (urban education, minority problems, the disadvantaged child, etc.). Twelve appendixes include a survey of trends in American education, 1960-1970, and a selected list of standardized tests.

G1260   American Association of Bible Colleges. Directory. Wheaton, Ill.: American Association of Bible Colleges, 1948- ; annual.

See also White (G1417).

G1261   American Evangelical Lutheran Church. Board of Parish Education, et al. The Functional Objectives for Christian Education; Prepared in Connection with the Long-Range Program of Lutheran Boards of Parish Education. 2 vols. n.p.: n.p., 1959.

This report is part of American Lutheran efforts to develop a plan to guide the development of parish education. Volume 1 focuses on functional objectives, discussing these in the context of the church, the family, the Sunday school, etc. and in relation to education at various levels, from preschool to adult. A bibliography is included. Volume 2 contains statistical material drawn from a survey of congregations in 1958-1959. There are 167 tables on the Sunday church school, catechetical instruction, leadership and other topics discussed in the first volume. See also Evenson (G1312) and Stump (G1402).

G1262   Arnhem, Carol van, comp. Directory of Centers for Religious Research and Study. Louvain: International Federation of Institutes for Social and Socio-Religious Research, 1968.

Although slightly dated, this geographically arranged guide covers many institutions, schools and libraries still in existence which specialize in religious research. Each entry provides adequate descriptive data on the activities and specific aims of the particular institution. The lack of an index hampers rapid use of this volume, which otherwise is a useful international handbook. See also White (G1417).

G1263   Association of Theological Schools in the United States and Canada. Directory. Vandalia, Ohio: Association of Theological Schools in the United States and Canada, 1918- ; annual.

Intended for use by the general public, this directory lists all institutions holding membership of the Association, providing brief institutional descriptions. Schools are identified according to denominational, interdenominational or nondenominational designations. A geographical listing of schools is also provided. The Directory also lists affiliated organizations with an interest in theological education but not offering educational programs leading to a degree. This is a useful source of brief information on major institutional resources for theological education in North America. See also Council on the Study of Religion (G1298), Revell's Guide to Christian Colleges (G1384) and White (G1417).

G1264   Association of Theological Schools in the United States and Canada. Fact Book on Theological Education. Vandalia, Ohio: Association of Theological Schools in the United States and Canada, 1971- ; annual.

This volume is based on information received from North American schools which are members of the Association (there were 179 in 1970). Twenty-two main tables contain data on enrollments, staffing, finance, staff salaries, etc.; in addition there are almost fifty appendix tables.

This is a useful source of data on theological education in North America. See also the Association's Directory (G1263).

G1265 Barnes, Donald L. Psychological Considerations in Religious Education. Ball State Monograph, no. 5. Muncie, Ind.: Ball State University, 1966.

Based on various studies of American youth, this brief work examines findings regarding modern morality, the impact of religion on the individual and society, problems inherent in the search for a common religious purpose, and psychological factors related to value change. The implications for religious education are discussed and specific programming ideas are put forward. The study is intended for teachers, ministers and other religious educators. See also Jaarsma (G1332).

G1266 Behrmann, Elmer, and Mall, Ann Dolores, eds. Directory of Catholic Special Facilities and Programs in the United States for Handicapped Children and Adults. 5th ed. Washington, D.C.: National Catholic Educational Association, 1971.

First published as Directory of Catholic Facilities for Exceptional Children in the United States, this directory provides statistical data and other basic information on institutions, programs and related training facilities related to education of the handicapped at all levels.

G1267 Best, John W. Research in Education. 2nd ed. Prentice-Hall Series in Educational Measurement, Research and Statistics. Englewood Cliffs, N.J.: Prentice-Hall, 1970.

G1268 Blazier, Kenneth D. Building an Effective Church School: Guide for the Superintendent and Board of Christian Education. Valley Forge, Pa.: Judson Press, 1976.

G1269 Blazier, Kenneth D., and Huber, Evelyn M. Planning Christian Education in Your Church: A Guide for Boards or Committees of Christian Education. Valley Forge, Pa.: Judson Press, 1974.

See also Bower (G1271) and Cober (G1296).

G1270 Bowen, James. A History of Western Education. Vol. 1- . London: Methuen and Company, 1972- .

This is projected as a three volume historical survey of Western education.

G1271 Bower, Robert K. Administering Christian Education: Principles of Administration for Ministers and Christian Leaders. Grand Rapids, Mich.: William B. Eerdmans Publishing Company, 1964.

Including a useful bibliography (pp. 219-223), this 227 page handbook on educational administration treats both theoretical and practical matters. Organization, planning, delegation, leadership, coordination and control are discussed in turn, and examples of applied administrative techniques are given. Useful charts and figures are also included. There is no index, but the detailed table of contents provides adequate access to this practical work. See also Blazier (G1268, G1269).

G1272 Brown, Carolyn C. Developing Christian Education in the Smaller

Church. Nashville, Tenn.: Abingdon Press, [1982].

This 96 page handbook provides practical guidance on achieving important educational tasks in smaller churches. Realistic suggestions for classroom arrangement, opening assemblies, etc. are made. This is a useful manual for those concerned with Christian education programs.

G1273   Brownfield, Rod, comp. Teaching Religion: A Catechist Collection. Dayton, Ohio: Pflaum Publications, 1974.

See also Caster (G1281).

G1274   Burgess, Harold William. An Invitation to Religious Education. Mishawaka, Ind.: Religious Education Press, 1975.

This work develops categories for analysis and evaluation of contemporary educational theory (traditional theological, social-cultural, etc.) and considers writers representative of each approach from the perspectives of aim, content, teacher, student, environment and evaluation. It is a useful work for college or seminary religious education theory courses and for promoting understanding of the relation between theory and practice. See also Cox (G1300) and Rood (G1387).

G1275 Burke, Arvid James, and Burke, Mary A. Documentation in Education. New York: Teachers College Press, Teachers College, Columbia University, 1967.

This introductory textbook on educational research and resources is suitable for individual or classroom use. It contains three sections: fundamentals of information storage and retrieval, locating educational information or data, bibliographic searching in education. For students beginning research in Christian education and with little experience in the broader discipline, this is a useful but slightly dated guide. It should be used for its general content rather than as a guide to Christian education in particular. See also Alexander and Burke (G1258).

G1276 Burns, James Aloysius. The Growth and Development of the Catholic School System in the United States. New York: Benziger Brothers, 1912. Reprint. New York: Arno Press, 1969.

This continuation of Burns' other publication (G1277) focuses on the historical development of Catholic schools in America. The analysis is reasonably detailed and includes a bibliography. Although dated, this classic work remains an important guide for students of Catholic educational growth. See also McCluskey (G1354).

G1277   Burns, James Aloysius. The Principles, Origin and Establishment of the Catholic School System in the United States. New York: Benziger Brothers, 1912. Reprint. New York: Arno Press, 1969.

Although older than A History of Catholic Education (G1278), this work is more detailed and covers the subject more adequately from a reference viewpoint. A bibliography of older titles is included. This is a valuable source of data for students of early Catholic educational development in America. The work was first published in 1908 as The Catholic School System in the United States: Its Principles, Origin and Establishment (New York: Benziger Brothers). For a continuation see Burns' complementary volume (G1276); see also McCluskey (G1354).

G1278   Burns, James Aloysius, and Kohlbrenner, Bernard J. A History of Catholic Education in the United States: A Textbook for Normal Schools and Teachers' Colleges. New York: Benziger Brothers, 1937.

This unified attempt to chronicle the history of American Catholic education in a comprehensive and scholarly fashion is based on the two earlier works by Burns (G1276, G1277). Unfortunately, it is less accurate and more open to criticisms of inadequacy than the preceding volumes. Nevertheless, for those seeking a broad outline of the subject and basic information this is an acceptable reference guide. Bibliographies at the end of each chapter provide valuable guidance to rather scarce literature on this topic. See also McCluskey (G1354).

G1279   Butler, James Donald. Religious Education: The Foundations and Practice of Nurture. New York: Harper and Row, 1962.

This work reflects a Protestant viewpoint, but the author indicates sections which are likely to be of interest to readers of other denominations. A section on the history of nurture covers the period from the early church to the present. Other aspects treated include the functions in nurture of theology and the Bible, psychology and nurture in the church, as well as practical aspects, method, curriculum, administration. A bibliography (pp. 303-314) and an index are provided. See also Wyckoff (G1420.

G1280   Callinicos, Constantine N. The Greek Orthodox Catechism: A Manual of Instruction on Faith, Morals and Worship. New York: Published under the auspices of the Greek Archdiocese of North and South America, 1953.

Published for use by Greek Orthodox youth in catechetical schools in America, this manual contains three parts: dogmatical, ethical, ceremonial. Within each part brief chapters deal with detailed aspects of the subject. There is neither index nor separate bibliography. See also Niholaj (G1369) and Noli (G1370).

G1281   Caster, Marcel van. God's Word Today: Principles, Methods and Examples of Catechesis. New York: Benziger Brothers; London: Geoffrey Chapman, 1966.

See also Brownfield (G1273).

G1282   Caster, Marcel van. The Structure of Catechetics. 2nd augmented ed. Adapted by the author and trans. by Edward J. Dirkswager, Jr., et al. New York: Herder and Herder, 1965.

This Roman Catholic study begins with a brief review of the growth in catechesis since 1900. The main part is concerned both with theological aspects and with practical methods of communicating the word of God. An index is provided. See also Goldbrunner (G1318).

G1283   Catholic Church. Congregatio de Seminariis et Studiorum Universitatibus. Seminaria Ecclesiae Catholicae. Rome: Typis Polyglottis Vaticanis, 1963.

This 1757 page guide to all Catholic diocesan seminaries throughout the world mentions very briefly their history, number of students, curriculum, size of library and number of graduates. It excludes the numerous and often important seminaries maintained by religious orders for their members. There is an index of dioceses and cities. See also Center for Applied Research (G1290).

G1284   Catholic Church. Congregatio pro Clericis. General Catechetical Directory. Washington, D.C.: Publications Office, United States Catholic Conference, 1971.

This translation of Directorium Catechisticum Generale, the official Roman Catholic guide for religious education, explains every topic that should be contained in a catechism or catechetical course. Prepared by the Sacred Congregation for the Clergy, it includes a subject index. See also United States Catholic Conference (G1408).

G1285   Catholic Church. National Conference of Catholic Bishops. Basic Teachings for Catholic Religious Education. Washington, D.C.: Publications Office, United States Catholic Conference, 1973.

See also Dyer (G1308) and Hardon (G1325).

G1286   Catholic Colleges and Universities Directory: A Guide in the Selection of a Catholic College. [Ed. 1-]. Chicago, Ill.: Catholic College Bureau, 1946- ; irregular.

A useful work for guidance counselors, this irregularly published directory lists more than 200 Roman Catholic colleges in America and provides basic information on their programs, facilities and academic requirements. It is well indexed for advisers, covering study programs and career specializations. See also Official Guide to Catholic Educational Institutions (G1371).

G1287   Catholic Education Council for England and Wales. Catholic Education: A Handbook. London: Catholic Education Council for England and Wales, 1960- ; annual?

This directory of Catholic schools and educational groups is a British counterpart of Catholic Schools Guide (G1288). It also contains articles on current topics in Catholic education. See also Directory of Catholic Schools and Colleges (G1305).

G1288   Catholic Schools Bureau. Catholic Schools Guide. New York: Catholic News, 1946- ; annual.

Originally prepared by the Catholic College Bureau as A Guide in the Selection of a Catholic School, this guide to educational and career opportunities for Catholic secondary school graduates covers universities, junior colleges, nursing schools and religious communities for men and women. For each institution the fields of study, costs, admission requirements and related matters are listed. See also Catholic Schools in America (G1289), Official Guide to Catholic Educational Institutions (G1371) and NCEA (G1364).

G1289   Catholic Schools in America. Prepared by the Curriculum Information

Center in cooperation with the National Catholic Educational Association. Vol. 1- . Denver, Colo.: Curriculum Information Center, 1977- ; annual.

First published to cover 1976/76 as a successor to Catholic Schools in the United States, this is a complete reference guide on United States Roman Catholic education. Diocesan and state statistics on elementary and secondary schools are presented, and directory information on enrollment and teachers, on all Roman Catholic schools and diocesan school offices is provided. See also Catholic Schools Bureau (G1288), NCAE (G1364) and Official Guide to Catholic Educational Institutions (G1371).

G1290   Center for Applied Research in the Apostolate. U.S. Catholic Institutions for the Training of Candidates for the Priesthood: A Sourcebook for Seminary Renewal, 1971. Washington, D.C.: Center for Applied Research in the Apostolate, 1971?

See also Catholic Church (G1283).

G1291   Christian Education Handbook: 157 Outlines on Various Phases of the Church's Teaching Program, Organization and Personnel. Cincinnati, Ohio: Standard Publishing Company, 1960.

This compilation contains useful ideas for teachers at all levels. It draws on the work of 143 contributors. Each educational level is treated separately, from the "cradle roll department" to the adult education level. A bibliography is given after each. Details on contributors and an index are included.

G1292   Christian Schools Directory. Grand Rapids, Mich.: Christian Schools International, 1920- ; annual.

See also Church Educational Agencies (G1293).

G1293   Church Educational Agencies. Wheaton, Ill.: Evangelical Teacher Training Association, 1968.

See also Christian Schools Directory (G1292).

G1294   Church Union. A Catechism of Christian Faith and Practice. [Rev. ed.] London: SPCK, 1964.

This is a revision of the 1927 original. See also Oldham (G1372) and Watts (G1413).

G1295   Cober, Kenneth Lorne. The Church's Teaching Ministry. Valley Forge, Pa.: Judson Press, 1974.

Written for those involved in Christian education, this brief work includes both theoretical and practical considerations, and attempts to relate theology and educational theory to effective functional procedures. An interpretation of Christian education is offered, and program structures, administrative and leadership questions are discussed. References for further reading are provided, but there is no index. See also Gilbert (G1317) and Pearce (G1377).

G1296   Cober, Kenneth Lorne. Shaping the Church's Educational Ministry:

A Manual for the Board of Christian Education. Valley Forge, Pa.: Judson Press, 1971.

See also Blazier and Huber (G1269).

G1297   Continuing Education: A Guide to Career Development Programs. Syracuse, N.Y.: Gaylord Professional Publications, 1977.

This 704 page directory covers approximately 2500 institutions and organizations which offer programs in continuing education. The institutions are arranged by states, while organizations are listed alphabetically in a separate section. Information is concise and clearly presented, allowing users to see at a glance what is offered by whom. A guide to career areas forms a subject outline to the programs, and there is an index of institutions and organizations. See also Yearbook of Adult and Continuing Education (G1421).

G1298   Council on the Study of Religion. Directory of Departments and Programs of Religion in North America.   Waterloo, Ontario: Council on the Study of Religion, 1973- ; triennial.

This work has also appeared as Directory of Departments and Programs of Religious Studies in North America. See also Association of Theological Schools (G1263), Revell's Guide to Christian Colleges (G1384) and White (G1417).

G1299 Cox, Alva I. Christian Education in the Church Today. Gen. ed. Henry M. Bullock. Nashville, Tenn.: Graded Press, 1963.

See also Cully (G1303).

G1300   Cox, Edwin. Changing Aims in Religious Education. The Student's Library of Education. New York: Humanities Press; London: Routledge and Kegan Paul, 1966.

This book examines the present situation of religious education, the influence on it of current ideas in theology and educational psychology, reasonable aims for teachers of the subject and appropriate methods. The legal position in the United Kingdom is presented in the first chapter. An analytical table of contents is provided, and there are suggestions for further reading. This briefly covers the area in the United Kingdom in the mid-1960s. See also Cox (G1300).

G1301   Cully, Iris V. Christian Worship and Church Education. Philadelphia, Pa.: Westminster Press, 1967.

After a brief discussion of the history and form of worship, this work focuses on the individual worshipper and his needs at various age levels. Basic elements such as scripture, sermon, prayer and music are treated, as well as aspects such as worship in the church school and congregational worship. The book contains useful material for ministers of education, Bible school teachers and others concerned with worship and education. A substantial bibliography is included.

G1302   Cully, Iris V. Ways to Teach Children. [Rev. ed.] Philadelphia, Pa.: Fortress Press, 1966 [c.1965].

See also Montessori (G1362).

G1303   Cully, Kendig Brubaker. The Teaching Church: An Introduction to Christian Education for Parents and Teachers. Philadelphia, Pa.: United Church Press, 1963.

This brief work for lay persons is designed to help them see their task in local educational situations and in the family as part of the worldwide ministry of the Christian church. It is introductory, but a bibliography contains suggestions for further reading. Written from a Protestant viewpoint, it is presented in a popular style. See also Cox (G1299).

G1304   Directory of Campus Ministry. [Ed. 1-]. Washington, D.C.: United States Catholic Conference, 1970- ; annual.

This compilation lists the Roman Catholic chaplains at all universities and colleges in the United States. Also included are data on the institutions served, their students and chaplaincy programs.

G1305   Directory of Catholic Schools and Colleges. London: Truman and Knightly Educational Trust, 1935- ; annual.

Including Roman Catholic schools of all types in the United Kingdom, this compilation is arranged by type of schools and provides basic information on programs, expenses and related details. See also Catholic Education Council (G1287).

G1306   Directory of Special Programs for Minority Group Members: Career Information Services, Employment Skills Banks, Financial Aid. Garrett Park, Md.: Garrett Park Press, 1974- ; annual.

This useful annual compilation for educators, counselors and students contains information on general employment and educational assistance programs, federal aid programs, women's programs, university and college awards. The focus is entirely American.

G1307   Doan, Eleanor Lloyd, and Blankenbaker, Frances. How to Plan and Conduct a Primary Church, with a Special Section for Kindergarden Leaders. Grand Rapids, Mich.: Zondervan Publishing House, 1961.

This brief work gives practical information on organizing a children's church program, including questions of leadership, finance, the program, use of visual aids, etc. A section on the kindergarten church deals with preschool requirements. Examples of complete worship services are provided, and there is a bibliography of further reference material. This is a concise, practical guide, written from a Protestant viewpoint. See also Washburn and Cook (G1412).

G1308   Dyer, George J., ed. An American Catholic Catechism. New York: Seabury Press, 1975.

This is a straightforward catechism which uses question-and-answer format to deal with the standard areas of catechetical instruction. An adequate index is provided. It is less detailed than Hardon (G1325) and less advanced than A New Catechism (G1368).

G1309   Eastman, Francis W., ed. Guidelines for Evaluating Christian Education in the Local Church. Philadelphia, Pa.: United Church Press, 1973.

This is a brief (46pp.) but useful guide to the evaluation of a parish
educational program.

G1310   Ecumenical Directory of Retreat and Conference Centers. Vol. 1- .
Boston, Mass.: Jarrow Press, 1974- .

This ecumenical guide lists Protestant and Roman Catholic centers
in North America which provide either conference or retreat facilities.
For each center information on facilities, costs, location and similar
data are presented. This is a useful reference work for libraries, educational institutions and parishes.

G1311   Education Yearbook. New York: Macmillan Company, 1972- .

See also The World Yearbook of Education (G1418).

G1312   Evenson, C. Richard, ed. Foundations for Educational Ministry.
Yearbooks in Christian Education, vol. 3. Philadelphia, Pa.: Fortress Press,
1964.

This collection of chapters by sixteen contributors was prepared in
the context of a Lutheran review of the educational ministry of the
church, and contains views on conceptual foundations for future functional programs. Historical, educational, sociological, psychological and
theological aspects of Christian education are examined. There is no
index, but the table of contents provides adequate access. See also
American Evangelical Lutheran Church (G1261).

G1313   Feiner, Johannes, and Vischer, Lukas, eds. The Common Catechism:
A Book of Christian Faith. With the cooperation of Josef Blank et al. New
York: Seabury Press; London: Search Press, 1975.

This 690 page translation of Neues Glaubensbuch: Der Gemeinsame
Christliche Glaube (Freiburg im Breisgau: Herder; Zurich: Theologischer
Verlag, 1973) is an important ecumenical attempt to provide a joint
Protestant-Roman Catholic treatment of the major points of Christian
doctrine in handbook form. The first four parts deal with God, Jesus,
man and faith; the fifth treats questions in dispute between the two
traditions. There is an appendix of agreed statements and a subject
index. This work is very useful as a concise survey of basic similarities
and differences which exist.

G1314   Ferré, Nels Frederick Solomon. A Theology for Christian Education.
Philadelphia, Pa.: Westminster Press, 1967.

This volume begins with discussion of various methodological considerations and the role of psychology, sociology and philosophy in relation
to a theology of education. The second part proposes a theology for
Christian education and examines how it deals with sin, salvation, the
problem of evil, other religions, eschatology. An index is provided.
See also Wyckoff (G1419).

G1315   Gangel, Kenneth O. Leadership for Church Education. Chicago, Ill.:

Moody Press, 1970.

G1316   Getz, Gene A. Audiovisual Media in Christian Education. 2nd ed. Chicago, Ill.: Moody Press, 1972.

This useful text on religious audio-visual education was first published in 1959 as Audio-Visuals in the Church. See also Harrell (G1326, G1327), Jensen and Jensen (G1335), Rumpf (G1389) and Waldrup (G1410, G1411).

G1317   Gilbert, W. Kent. As Christians Teach. Philadelphia, Pa.: Fortress Press, 1964.

This work was first published in the Leadership Education Series (Philadelphia, Pa.: Lutheran Church Press, 1962), which included phonograph records and a teacher's guide. See also Cober (G1295).

G1318   Goldbrunner, Josef, ed. New Catechetical Methods. Trans. by M. Veronica Riedl. Contemporary Catechetics Series. Notre Dame, Ind.: University of Notre Dame Press, 1965.

This Roman Catholic collection of essays, translated from Katechetische Methoden Heute (Munich: Kösel Verlag, 1962), examines changes in religious educational methods, gives examples of specific lessons, and discusses how catechetical method can serve personal encounter. Four contributors wrote the ten essays. The book does not contain an index. See also Caster (G1281, G1282) and Hoger Katechetisch Institut (G1331).

G1319   Goldman, Ronald. Readiness for Religion: A Basis for Developmental Religious Education. London: Routledge and Kegan Paul, 1965; New York: Seabury Press, 1968.

This work outlines a program of religious instruction intended to be consistent with what is known of child development and more in accord with modern educational theory than traditional Bible dominated programs. The first part deals with psychological bases of religious education; the second with content and method. An index is provided. This is a stimulating, clearly presented work for religious educators. See also Montessori (G1362).

G1320   Goldman, Ronald. Religious Thinking from Childhood to Adolescence. London: Routledge and Kegan Paul, 1964.

This descriptive account of how school pupils think about religion and the content of their thoughts as they are taught religion is largely diagnostic and designed to assist teachers, parents and clergy involved in religious education. It includes consideration of concepts of the Bible, of prayer, of the church, etc. The final chapter examines implications of the research findings for religious education. Three appendixes on research methods and a glossary, a bibliography (6pp.) and indexes of subjects and names complete the study. See also Cully (G1302) and Montessori (G1362).

G1321   Hakes, J. Edward, ed. An Introduction to Evangelical Christian Education. Chicago, Ill.: Moody Press, 1964.

See also Kittel (G1338).

G1322   Halbfas, Hubert. Theory of Catechetics: Language and Experience in Religious Education. New York: Herder and Herder, 1971.

This translation of Fundamentalkatechetik (Düsseldorf: Patmos-Verlag, 1968) is in two parts. The first provides a framework, discussing religion, language and teaching; the second considers religious textbooks today and their inadequacies, and makes suggestions regarding the communication of religious knowledge. The work is strong in its presentation of theology and analysis of language, and takes an ecumenical approach to religions. An index is provided.

G1323   Hall, Brian P. Value Clarification as Learning Process: A Guidebook. Consultant authors: Michael J. Kenney and Maury Smith. Educator Formation Books. New York: Paulist Press, c.1973.

This practical handbook, a companion to Hall's sourcebook (G1324), contains exercises, games, group dynamics and texts to help students in the process of decision-making, creativity and celebration. Both conference formats and classroom strategies are provided for training people in value clarification. Photographs and designs accompany the exercises.

G1324   Hall, Brian P. Value Clarification as Learning Process: A Sourcebook. Consultant authors: Michael J. Kenney and Maury Smith. Educator Formation Books. New York: Paulist Press, c.1973.

See also the preceding entry (G1323).

G1325   Hardon, John A. The Catholic Catechism. Garden City, N.Y.: Doubleday and Company, 1975.

This 623 page catechism concentrates on post-Vatican II Roman Catholicism and presents a detailed explication of the faith in this context. The excellent index and frequent references to source materials give Hardon particular reference value. See also Dyer (G1308) and Catholic Church (G1285).

G1326   Harrell, John Grinnell. Basic Media in Education. Winona, Minn.: St. Mary's College Press, 1974.

This contains detailed illustrations of many simple, inexpensive but effective media forms. The techniques suggested are practical for the volunteer church teacher and for professional church staff. The contents include flat pictures, posters, charts and handmade projections. Bibliographies and an index are provided. See also Getz (G1316), Jensen and Jensen (G1335), Rumpf (G1389) and Waldrup (G1410, G1411).

G1327   Harrell, John Grinnell. Teaching Is Communicating: An Audio-Visual Handbook for Church Use. New York: Seabury Press, 1963.

This work is concerned with both theory and practice, and also discusses theological implications of communication. Both teacher and student communication are discussed. There are suggestions for further reading and references to specific audio-visual productions. An index and a section of illustrations are included. See also Getz (G1316), Jensen and Jensen (G1335), Rumpf (G1389) and Waldrup (G1410, G1411).

G1328   Herrup, Steven J. Your Future in Religious Work. New York: Richard Rosen Press, 1980.

This handbook provides guidance for the young person on careers in religious work. It describes parish ministry, teaching of religion in schools and colleges, careers in religious social work, and contains an appendix on institutions with undergraduate and graduate departments offering relevant degree courses. See also Landis (G1343), Rand (G1380) and Sheneman (G1395).

G1329   Hodgson, Charles. The Church Study Group: A Manual for Group Leaders and Members, with Material for a Year's Work for Study Groups. London: A.R. Mowbray and Company, 1966.

See also Robertson (G1386).

G1330   Hofinger, Johannes, and Stone, Theodore, C., eds. Pastoral Catechetics. New York: Herder and Herder, 1964.

This Roman Catholic work examines the catechetical renewal and its pastoral role in the church. It presents a traditional view of faith, and proposes that living faith is the aim of religious education. It contains fifteen chapters by different contributors. The final seven are concerned with the transmission of God's message, including course content, training of lay catechists, etc. Notes on contributors and an index are provided.

G1331 Hoger Katechetisch Institut. Fundamentals and Programs of a New Catechesis. Trans. by Walter van de Putte. Pittsburgh, Pa.: Duquesne University Press, 1966.

See also Goldbrunner (G1318).

G1332   Jaarsma, Cornelius Richard. Human Development, Learning and Teaching: A Christian Approach to Educational Psychology. Grand Rapids, Mich.: William B. Eerdmans Publishing Company, 1961.

See also Barnes (G1265).

G1333   Jackson, Benjamin Franklin, Jr., ed. Communication for Churchmen Series. Vol. 1- . Nashville, Tenn.: Abingdon Press, 1968- .

Four volumes are planned in this series which is intended to provide pragmatic, easily accessible information to churchmen. Volume 1 is in four parts: communication for churchmen; learning and the church; using print as a resource for learning; using audio-visual resources. It is a substantial reference work, combining the concerns for effective ministry with those relating to the psychology of education and awareness of sophisticated educational technology. Volume 2 is to deal with television, radio and film for churchmen; volume 3 with audio-visual facilities and equipment for churchmen; volume 4 with creative communication skills for churchmen (written and oral communication, creation of inexpensive resource materials, tape recordings and slides). The published volume is very readable, contains helpful illustrations, and is itself an example of good print communication.

G1334   Jepp, Elizabeth McMahon. Classroom Creativity: An Idea Book for Religion Reachers. New rev. ed. New York: Seabury Press, 1977.

See also Rusbuldt (G1390).

G1335 Jensen, Mary, and Jensen, Andrew. Audiovisual Idea Book for Church-es. Minneapolis, Minn.: Augsburg Publishing House, 1974.

This practical and concise book contains hundreds of suggestions on how to use audio-visuals more effectively in the congregation. A brief bibliography (2pp.) is included. See also Getz (G1316), Harrell (G1326, G1327), Rumpf (G1389) and Waldrup (G1410, G1411).

G1336 Jewish Education Register and Directory. Ed. 1- . New York: American Association for Jewish Education, 1951- ; irregular.

Last appearing in the third edition of 1965, this guide to North American Jewish education begins with a general section on the various phases of instruction in this tradition. The directory itself covers educational agencies, schools, libraries, museums and similar establishments.

G1337 Joyce, Bruce R., and Weil, Marsha. Models of Teaching. Englewood Cliffs, N.J.: Prentice-Hall, 1972.

This work analyzes fifteen different approaches to teaching and includes bibliographical references. It is a useful tool for the teaching minister as well as the public school educator.

G1338 Kittel, Helmuth. Evangelische Religionspädagogik. De Gruyter Lehr-buch. Berlin: Walter De Gruyter and Company, 1971.

This work includes a useful bibliography (pp. xxi-xxvii) of continental resources. See also Hakes (G1321).

G1339 Knowles, Malcolm Shepherd. The Modern Practice of Adult Education: Andragogy versus Pedagogy. New York: Association Press, 1970.

This is a comprehensive and practical guide to the theory and practice of the art and science of helping adults to learn. Bibliographical refer-ences are included. See also McKenzie (G1356).

G1340 Köhler, Hans. Theologie der Erziehung. Munich: A. Pustet Verlag, 1965.

See also Schilling (G1392).

G1341 Konstant, David. A Syllabus of Religious Instruction for Catholic Primary Schools. Prepared in Committee under the Chairmanship of David Konstant. 2nd ed. London: Burns and Oates, Macmillan and Company, 1967.

G1342 Konstant, David. A Syllabus of Religious Instruction for Catholic Secondary Schools. Prepared in Committee under the Chairmanship of David Konstant. New York: St. Martin's Press; London: Burns and Oates, Macmillan and Company, 1967.

G1343 Landis, Benson Young. Careers of Service in the Church: A Des-cription of Many Interesting and Satisfying Vocations. New York: M. Evans,

1964.

See also Herrup (G1328), Rand (G1380) and Sheneman (G1395).

G1344   Lawler, Ronald David, ed. The Teachings of Christ: A Catholic Catechism for Adults. Huntingdon, Ind.: Our Sunday Visitor, 1976.

This substantial catechism deals clearly and thoroughly with all areas of instruction. It attempts to strike a balance between traditional and more radical views, using biblical, conciliar and other materials to illuminate each teaching. For a catechism more closely related to Vatican II see Hardon (G1325); see also A New Catechism (G1368).

G1345   Lee, James Michael, ed. Catholic Education in the Western World. Notre Dame, Ind.: University of Notre Dame Press, 1967.

This work contains brief histories with bibliographies of Catholic education in France, Germany, Holland, Italy, England and the United States. Details of organization, finances, curricula, religious education, staff and student services are given. The appendix serves as an index to each section. The essays on France and the United States have been particularly praised. See also McCluskey (G1354).

G1346   Lee, James Michael. The Flow of Religious Instruction: A Social-Science Approach. Dayton, Ohio: Pflaum Press/Standard, 1973.

This second title in a projected three volume series on religious education deals specifically with the teaching enterprise in practice, while the proposed third volume intends to focus on the content of religious instruction. This volume is practical in approach, offering effective pedagogical guidelines anchored in sound teaching theory. Indexes of names and of subjects are included. See also The Shape of Religious Instruction (G1348).

G1347   Lee, James Michael. Principles and Methods of Secondary Education. McGraw-Hill Catholic Series in Education. New York: McGraw-Hill Book Company, 1963.

G1348   Lee, James Michael. The Shape of Religious Instruction: A Social-Science Approach. Dayton, Ohio: Pflaum Press, 1971.

The first volume of a projected trilogy on a social science approach to religious education, this work deals with the foundations and rationale of the approach. It argues that religious instruction is a mode of social science rather than a form of theology, and calls for an ecumenical approach, drawing on both Protestant and Catholic contributions in this field. Bibliographical references are given in the notes to each chapter, and there are indexes of names and of subjects. See also the second volume (G1346).

G1349   Lee, James Michael, and Pallone, Nathaniel J. Guidance and Counseling in Schools: Foundations and Processes. McGraw-Hill Catholic Series in Education. New York: McGraw-Hill Book Company, 1966.

G1350   Little, Lawrence Calvin. Foundations for a Philosophy of Christian Education. New York: Abingdon Press, 1962.

This volume is primarily a textbook in the philosophy of Christian education for theological seminaries and departments of religious education,
but the needs of pastors, church officers and the general reader have
also been kept in mind. Psychological and cultural, religious and theological foundations for a philosophy of Christian education are discussed.
A lengthy bibliography (pp. 203-231) and an index are provided. See
also Ferré (G1314) and Schreyer (G1393).

G1351   Lubienska de Lenval, Hélène. How to Teach Religion. Trans. by
Paul Joseph Oligny. Chicago, Ill.: Franciscan Herald Press, 1967.

This Roman Catholic work deals primarily with theological and theoretical
aspects of religious education, paying attention to liturgical tradition
and to fidelity to Catholic tradition. It is brief (98pp.) and there is
no index. See also Reichert (G1381).

G1352   McBride, Alfred. Catechetics: A Theology of Proclamation. Milwaukee,
Wisc.: Bruce Publishing Company, 1966.

See also Little (G1350) and Miller (G1360).

G1353   McCarthy, Thomas Patrick. Guide to the Diocesan Priesthood in
the United States. Washington, D.C.: Catholic University of America Press,
1959.

This 180 page successor to the 1956 edition is intended basically as
a guide for Roman Catholic postulants interested in the diocesan priesthood. It explains in general the requirements and training program and
provides information on the diocese. An index is provided. For those
interested in Roman Catholic theological training this now dated compendium is a reasonable source of background information.

G1354   McCluskey, Neil Gerard, ed. Catholic Education in America: A Documentary History. Classics in Education, no. 21. New York: Columbia University, Teachers College, 1964.

This collection of documents deals with Catholic education in America
from 1792 to 1950. The editor provides a brief historical introduction
and sources are given, but there is no other bibliography and no index.
See also Burns (G1276-G1278) and Lee (G1345).

G1355   McHugh, John Ambrose, and Callan, Charles Jerome, trans. Catechism
of the Council of Trent, Issued by Order of Pope Pius V. New York: Joseph
F. Wagner; London: B. Herder, 1923.

Replacing earlier translations by J. Donovan and Theodore A. Buckley,
this 603 page catechetical guide is the standard source of information
on Roman Catholic religious instruction. It deals comprehensively with
basic questions on the creed, sacraments, commandments and prayer,
providing references to biblical passages and St. Thomas Aquinas in
many cases. See also Spirago (G1400) for a guide.

G1356   McKenzie, Leon. The Religious Education of Adults. Birmingham, Ala.:
Religious Education Press, c.1982.

See also Knowles (G1339).

G1357 McManis, Lester W. Handbook on Christian Education in the Inner City. New York: Seabury Press, 1966.

Prepared under the auspices of the Episcopal Church's Department of Christian Education, this handbook is designed for clergy and lay people engaged in Christian education in inner city areas. It is concise and straightforward in approach. Three main sections cover work with youth and adults, work with children, and methods, activities and resources. These offer many practical suggestions including the use of audio-visuals. An index is provided as well as the detailed table of contents.

G1358 Marthalar, Berard L. Catechetics in Context: Notes and Commentary on the "General Catechetical Directory" Issued by the Sacred Congregation for the Clergy. Huntington, Ind.: Our Sunday Visitor, 1973.

This guide seeks to relate the official General Catechetical Directory (G1284) to contemporary issues and problems in Christian catechesis.

G1359 Miller, Randolph Crump. Education for Christian Living. 2nd ed. Englewood Cliffs, N.J.: Prentice-Hall, 1963.

This provides a working guide for study and development of a program of Christian education at the local level. The first part provides a theological framework in which the significance of Christian education is seen in terms of its history, of modern secular thinking, and of theological developments. The impacts of home, school, community and church are discussed, and methods and practical problems of administration and organization are treated in detail. A basic bibliography, as well as a listing of publications keyed to the various chapters, are provided. An index facilitates use of the volume, which is designed for students, teachers, ministers and the general reader. See also Cober (G1295).

G1360 Miller, Randolph Crump. Theory of Christian Education Practice: How Theology Affects Christian Education. Birmingham, Ala.: Religious Education Press, c.1980.

See also Richards (G1385) and Schreyer (G1393).

G1361 Missionary Research Library. Schools Overseas Available for the Children of North American Missionaries. Ed. 1- . New York: Missionary Research Library, 1954- .

This was begun as part of the MRL Directory Series and has been published under variant titles.

G1362 Montessori, Maria, et al. The Child in the Church. Ed. by E.M. Standing. 2nd ed. St. Paul, Minn.: Catechetical Guild, 1965.

See also Cully (G1302) and Goldman (G1319).

G1363 Mussner, Franz. The Use of Parables in Catechetics. Trans. by Maria von Eroes. Contemporary Catechetics Series. Notre Dame, Ind.: University of Notre Dame Press, 1965.

This interpretation of twenty-three parables of Jesus is intended primarily for catechetical use. A brief preface precedes the interpretations which are given headings followed by the reference to the parable, e.g., "Who is justified by God?": the Pharisee and the Publican. The brief volume concludes with a summary.

G1364   NCEA/Ganley's Catholic Schools in America. [Ed. 1-]. Denver, Colo.: Curriculum Information Center, 1977- ; biennial.

Formerly published as Catholic Schools in the United States and Directory of Catholic Elementary Schools in the United States, this valuable handbook provides standard directory and statistical information on both primary and secondary schools. It is a useful directory for teachers and other advisers. See also Catholic Schools in America (G1289), Catholic Schools Bureau (G1288) and Official Guide to Catholic Educational Institutions (G1371).

G1365   Nash, Gerald R. Planning Better Sabbath Schools. Washington, D.C.: Review and Herald Publishing Association, 1965.

G1366   National Catholic Educational Association. Directory of Catholic Elementary Residential Schools. Washington, D.C.: National Catholic Educational Association, 1973.

This directory lists elementary boarding schools for Catholics and for each institution provides the address, tuition and other basic information.

G1367 National Conference of Catholic Charities. Catholic Day Care Centers. Washington, D.C: National Conference of Catholic Charities, 1969.

G1368 A New Catechism: Catholic Faith for Adults. Trans. by Kevin Smyth. New York: Herder and Herder; London: Burns and Oates, 1967.

This translation of a controversial Dutch work seeks to provide a Roman Catholic catechism based on the spirit and teachings of Vatican II. It is a detailed study of 510 pages for adults and covers man's place in the world, other religions, Christ and Christianity, sacraments and commandments, death and resurrection. Presented in nontechnical language, this is an admirable attempt to present a liberal interpretation of traditional teachings and is useful both for catechetical instruction and for reference purposes. See also Lawler (G1344).

G1369 Nikolaj. The Faith of the Saints: A Catechism of the Eastern Orthodox Church. [Pittsburgh, Pa.: Serbian National Federation, 1949].

See also Callinicos (G1280) and Noli (G1370).

G1370 Noli, Fan Stylian, trans. and ed. Eastern Orthodox Catechism. Boston, Mass.: Albanian Orthodox Church in America, 1954.

See also Callinicos (G1280) and Nikolaj (G1369).

G1371   Official Guide to Catholic Educational Institutions and Religious Communities in the United States. Ed. 1- . New York: Catholic Institutional Directory Company, 1959- ; annual.

Superseding the Directory of Catholic Colleges and Schools in the United States and sponsored by the United States Catholic Conference, this directory lists all universities, colleges, junior colleges, nursing schools, secondary boarding schools and religious orders of the Roman Catholic Church in the United States. It is an indispensible guide in its field, including key data on admissions, courses, costs, facilities and other pertinent topics. There is a special section on how to choose a Catholic college and how to apply for admission. See also Catholic Schools Bureau (G1288), Catholic Colleges and Universities Directory (G1286) and Catholic Schools in America (G1289).

G1372   Oldham, George Ashton. The Catechism Today: Instructions on the Church Catechism. 2nd ed. New York: Morehouse-Gorham Company, 1954.

See also Church Union (G1294), Sloyan (G1396) and Watts (G1413).

G1373   Olson, Richard Allan, ed. The Pastor's Role in Educational Ministry. Yearbooks in Christian Education, vol. 5. Philadelphia, Pa: Fortress Press, 1975.

Intended to stimulate more awareness of the role of the professional in church education and to cause pastors to reflect on views of educational ministry, this volume includes contributions by parish practitioners, religious education specialists and theologians. Editorial comment precedes each section, giving greater unity to the collection. See also Person (G1379) and Smart (G1397).

G1374   Orr, Clara E., comp. Directory of Christian Colleges in Asia, Africa, the Middle East, the Pacific, Latin America and the Caribbean. MRL Directory and Survey Series, no. 13. New York: Missionary Research Library, 1961.

This directory presents information on Protestant and Orthodox colleges in the areas of major mission activity listed in the title. Inclusion is normally on the basis of post-secondary education, although terminology varies in the areas covered. Arrangement is by region and country, with alphabetical listings of colleges under each country. The name of each institution is listed in the table of contents. Theological colleges are not included; for these see Smith and Thompson (G1398).

G1375   Otto, Gert. Handbuch des Religionsunterrichts. 3. Aufl. Hamburg: Furche-Verlag, 1967.

G1376   Paterson, J. Roy H. A Faith for the 1980's: A Guide to Membership of the Church. Edinburgh: St. Andrews Press, 1980.

Aimed primarily at prospective Church of Scotland members, this work in fact is suitable as a basic catechetical guide for other Reformed churches as well. First published as A Faith for the 1970's, Paterson covers vows, belief, worship, the Bible, money and talents, Christian living and other faiths in 88 pages of succinct and jargon-free language.

G1377   Pearce, Robin. Ideas: Handbook for Religious Education Specialists and Others Engaged in Religious Education. Worthing, West Sussex: Walter, 1973.

See also Cober (G1295).

G1378   Person, Peter Per. Introduction to Christian Education. Grand Rapids,

Mich.: Baker Book House, 1958.

This introductory textbook adequately covers the principles of Christian education at a basic level. See also Rood (G1387).

G1379 Person, Peter Per. The Minister in Christian Education. Grand Rapids, Mich.: Baker Book House, 1960.

This brief work is written in a popular style and is intended primarily for the local minister, whom it sees as a key person in local Christian education. After background chapters on the teaching ministry of the church and the minister as educator, various aspects of the minister's role in different educational groups and programs are discussed. Treatment is practical, focusing on objectives, methods and organizational aspects. See also Olson (G1373) and Smart (G1397).

G1380 Rand, Willard J. Call and Response: An Enlistment Guide for Church Occupations. New York: Abingdon Press, 1964.

See also Herrup (G1328), Landis (G1343) and Sheneman (G1395).

G1381   Reichert, Richard J. A Learning Process for Religious Education. Dayton, Ohio: Pflaum Publishers, 1974.

This straightforward guidebook is intended for professional and volunteer teachers of religion, particularly in the Roman Catholic Church. A commonsense model of the learning process, incorporating four stages, is suggested. While this work offers much practical help to church educators, it does not attempt to deal with some of the assumptions made about learning. See also Lubienska de Lenval (G1351).

G1382   Reichert, Richard J. Teaching Sacraments to Youth. New York: Paulist Press, 1975.

See also Underwood (G1407).

G1383 Reorganized Church of Jesus Christ of Latter-Day Saints. Department of Religious Education. Church School Handbook. Independence, Mo.: Herald Publishing House, 1968.

G1384   Revell's Guide to Christian Colleges. Westwood, N.J.: Fleming H. Revell Company, 1965/1966- .

See also Association of Theological Schools (G1263), Council on the Study of Religion (G1298) and White (G1417).

G1385   Richards, Lawrence O. A Theology of Christian Education. Grand Rapids, Mich.: Zondervan Publishing House, 1975.

See also Miller (G1360) and Schreyer (G1393).

G1386 Robertson, Edwin Hanton. "Take and Read": A Guide to Group Bible Study. Richmond, Va.: John Knox Press; London: SCM Press, 1961.

Intended for those wishing to undertake effective Bible study, this brief and practical guide offers suggestions on beginning a Bible study group, on groups in action and on choosing a book to study. A short bibliography and an index of biblical passages are provided. See also Hodgson (G1329) and Washburn and Cook (G1412).

G1387   Rood, Wayne R. Understanding Christian Education. Nashville, Tenn.: Abingdon Press, 1970.

This consideration of alternative approaches to the philosophy of Christian education focuses on Horace Bushnell, John Dewey, George Albert Coe and Maria Montessori and the philosophies of education which they represent. A final section is devoted to emergent principles of Christian education, their context, content, etc. An index is provided. This is a straightforward, introductory account using a biographical approach to illustrate the various philosophies. See also Burgess (G1274), Cox (G1300) and Person (G1378).

G1388   Rouch, Mark A. Competent Ministry: A Guide to Effective Continuing Education. Nashville, Tenn.: Abingdon Press, 1974.

Providing comprehensive coverage of the process and resources available in continuing education for clergy, this guide is intended as a handbook to be used by pastors to develop their own programs of continuing education. It covers theoretical and practical aspects.

G1389   Rumpf, Oscar J. The Use of Audio-Visuals in the Church. Philadelphia, Pa.: Christian Education Press, 1958.

This practical and concise presentation of the possibilities for using audio-visual materials in the local parish situation deals with background questions on the use of audio-visuals and with various techniques, their use, relevance, organization, etc. It is clearly written and illustrated. A bibliography is included. See also Getz (G1316), Harrell (G1326, G1327), Jensen and Jensen (G1335) and Waldrup (G1410, G1411).

G1390   Rusbuldt, Richard E. Basic Teacher Skills: Handbook for Church School Teachers. Valley Forge, Pa.: Judson Press, 1981.

This easy to follow handbook discusses the basic roles of the teacher, steps in planning a class session, activities to reinforce teaching content, etc. It provides a sound introduction to the practice and theory of church school teaching. See also Jeep (G1334).

G1391   Schaal, John H., comp. and ed. Feed My Sheep: A Manual for Sunday School Teachers, Superintendents and Leaders. Grand Rapids, Mich.: Baker Book House, 1972.

See also Washburn and Cook (G1412).

G1392   Schilling, Hans. Grundlagen der Religionspädagogik. Zum Verhältnis von Theologie und Erziehungsniss. Düsseldorf: Patmos Verlag, 1970.

See also Köhler (G1340).

G1393   Schreyer, George M. Christian Education in Theological Focus. Philadelphia, Pa.: Christian Education Press, 1962.

See also Little (G1350) and Richards (G1385).

G1394   Schwartz, Glenn, ed. An American Directory of Schools and Colleges Offering Missionary Courses. South Pasadena, Calif.: William Carey Library, 1973.

G1395   Sheneman, Lloyd E., et al. Careers in the Christian Ministry: An Ecumenical Guidebook. Washington, D.C.: Consortium Press, 1976.

See also Herrup (G1328), Landis (G1343) and Rand (G1380).

G1396   Sloyan, Gerard Stephen. Modern Catechetics: Message and Method in Religious Formation. New York: Macmillan Company, 1963.

See also Oldham (G1372).

G1397   Smart, Ninian. The Teacher and Christian Belief. The Religion and Education Series. London: Clarke, 1966.

This work discusses key issues in Christian belief which are relevant to those teaching religion. It examines the nature of biblical revelation, the problem of belief, science and the limits of religion, Christianity and other faiths, and other theological and philosophical issues. A bibliography is included (pp. 203-206), as well as an index. See also Olson (G1373) and Person (G1379).

G1398   Smith, Charles Stanley, and Thomson, Herbert F., comps. Protestant Theological Seminaries and Bible Schools in Asia, Africa, the Middle East, Latin America, the Caribbean and Pacific Areas: A Directory. Ed. by Frank W. Price. MRL Directory Series, no. 12. New York: Missionary Research Library, 1960.

See also Orr (G1374).

G1399   Sourcebook of Equal Educational Opportunity. Ed. 2- . Chicago, Ill.: Marquis Academic Media, 1977- ; annual.

Published in 1976 as Yearbook of Equal Educational Opportunity, this useful compendium presents a comprehensive picture of equal opportunity in education in America. A general review of the field is followed by ethnic sections devoted to Amerindian, Asian, Pacific island, black, hispanic and female sectors of the population. There are subject and geographic indexes. This is a useful work for those active in civil rights, missions and education.

G1400   Spirago, Franz. The Catechism Explained. Trans. by Richard F. Clarke. Rev. ed. by Anthony Norman Fuerst. New York: Benziger Brothers, 1961.

This 458 page guide to the Catechism of the Council of Trent (G1355) is a standard and traditional study book arranged in question and answer format. It covers a wide range of doctrinal issues from a Roman Catholic perspective and is a useful reference work for those seeking pre-Vatican II views or traditional catechetical information.

G1401   Stenzel, Anne K., and Feeney, Helen M. Volunteer Training and

Development: A Manual. Rev. ed. New York: Seabury Press, 1976.

Designed to meet needs of community groups, voluntary associations, etc. in the area of training and educational development of volunteers, this working manual discusses aspects such as the development of training programs, learning plans and evaluation of training. It provides outlines, checklists, exercises and charts adaptable to individual or group require- ments. A bibliography (pp. 217-220) and an index are included.

G1402 Stump, Joseph. An Explanation of Luther's Small Catechism. 2nd rev. ed. Philadelphia, Pa.: Muhlenberg Press, 1960.

This book aims to present an analysis of Luther's Small Catechism as well as a clear and concise explanation of its contents. It is intended for American Lutheran catechetical classes.   Each chapter is followed by a number of questions. This is a useful textbook on its specific subject. See also American Evangelical Lutheran Church (G1261).

G1403   Taylor, Marvin J., ed. Foundations for Christian Education in an Era of Change. Nashville, Tenn.: Abingdon Press, 1976.

This supplement to An Introduction to Christian Education (G1404) by the same author contains a series of useful and provocative articles on the entire field of Christian education, contributed by twenty-one specialists. It is intended primarily as an introductory volume for use in seminary and college classes, but chapter bibliographies and notes and the selected bibliography at the end of the book provide valuable guidance for further reading. There is no index but the table of contents provides adequate guidance to the various aspects discussed. See also Evenson (G1312) and Person (G1378).

G1404   Taylor, Marvin J., ed. An Introduction to Christian Education. Nash- ville, Tenn.: Abingdon Press, 1966.

This successor to the editor's previous survey of religious education (G1405) follows the same format, with essays by specialists arranged in four sections: foundations for Christian education; administration; programs, methods and materials; agencies and organizations. Similar bibliographies and indexes are provided. The volume contains thirty- two chapters.   It is intended as an introductory survey for teachers and students, local church leaders and for general reference use. See also Person (G1378).

G1405   Taylor, Marvin J., ed. Religious Education: A Comprehensive Survey. New York: Abingdon Press, 1960.

This collection of contributions by specialists is intended to serve as an introductory survey textbook for students, as a handbook for the local minister or teacher, and as a reference work for the general reader. Chapters deal with specific aspects of religious education, and are organ- ized in four main sections: principles of religious education; programs, materials and methods; administration; agencies and organizations. Each includes a bibliography, and there is a more general selected bibliography at the end of the book. A general index and a biographical index of the thirty-seven contributors are provided. While the work generally reflects a Protestant viewpoint, other denominations are included in the section on agencies and organizations. See Taylor's more recent work (G1403, G1404) for coverage of changes in this area; see also Cober (G1295) and Person (G1378).

G1406   Towns, Elmer L., ed. A History of Religious Educators. Grand Rapids, Mich.: Baker Book House, 1975.

This collection of contributions presents sections on the philosophy of education, the methodology and relationship between philosophical foundation and method of each educator discussed. Religious education is dealt with in a broad sense to include higher education, the family, theological implications of subject matter within the sciences and humanities as well as that typically dealt with in catechetical instruction. The work has been criticized in that some contributors lack experience in education, coming from other disciplines. The lack of a subject index lessens its use as a reference work. Nonetheless it may be of interest to church school teachers and other Christian educators. For the recent period (1944-1984) see Wedderspoon (G1414).

G1407   Underwood, Brian. Towards Christian Maturity: A Handbook for Teachers of Young Teenagers. London: Church Book Room Press, 1968.

See also Reichert (G1382).

G1408   United States Catholic Conference. A National Inventory of Parish Catechetical Programs Conducted by the United States Catholic Conference in Cooperation with the Boys Town Center for the Study of Youth Development, the Catholic University of America. Washington, D.C.: United States Catholic Conference, 1978.

The tables in this compilation provide detailed information on the personnel, student enrollment, finances and teaching programs of parish religious education in Catholic churches in the United States. It is a suitably detailed guide for researchers and also serves as a comparative survey for less advanced users. See also Catholic Church (G1284).

G1409   Voeltzel, R. Education et Révélation: Introduction aux Problèmes de la Pédagogie Chrétienne. Paris: Presses Universitaires de France, 1960.

G1410   Waldrup, Earl W. Teaching and Training with Audiovisuals. Nashville, Tenn.: Convention Press, 1962.

Prepared in connection with the Southern Baptist Convention church study course, this book discusses types of and purposes of audio-visuals, assesses their value in learning situations, their use in a church program and in worship, teaching and training with audio-visuals, and related aspects. Each chapter is preceded by a summary, and there are teaching suggestions at the end of the book. The presentation is clear and easy to follow. See also Getz (G1316), Harrell (G1326, G1327), Jensen and Jensen (G1335), Rumpf (G1389) and the following entry (G1411).

G1411   Waldrup, Earl W. Using Visual Aids in a Church. Nashville, Tenn.: Broadman Press, 1949.

This work discusses the nature and value of different visual aids available for church use, analyzes some problems relating to the use of such aids, and finally suggests a plan to insure the proper utilization of visual aids in a church. It is intended for church workers, especially those involved in Christian education. The book is clearly written, and an outline precedes each chapter.   There is no index, but the contents are indicated clearly in the table of contents and the outlines. See also Getz (G1316), Harrell (G1326, G1327), Jensen and Jensen (G1335), Rumpf (G1389) and the preceding entry (G1410).

G1412   Washburn, Alphonso V., and Cook, Melva. Administering the Bible Teaching Program: Sunday School Work. Nashville, Tenn.: Convention Press, 1969.

See also Shaal (G1391).

G1413   Watts, Arthur James. Ask Me Another: A Further Handbook for Teachers Based on the Revised Catechism and Agreed Syllabus. London: National Society, SPCK, 1967.

See also Oldham (G1372).

G1414   Wedderspoon, Alexander G., ed. Religious Education 1944-1984. London: Allen and Unwin, 1966.

G1415   Weld, Wayne C. The World Directory of Theological Education by Extension. South Pasadena, Calif.: William Carey Library, 1973.

This useful directory of extension programs in theology is in two main parts. The first provides background on problems of traditional education, possibilities of education by extension, growth of theological education by extension, as well as an evaluation of this educational method. The second part, the directory proper, comprises an alphabetical list of institutions and programs involved in theological education by extension, as well as regional, country, city and institution indexes, lists of supporting agencies and of relevant workshops and consultations. There is also a useful bibliography (pp. 359-374). See also the supplement (G1416).

G1416   Weld, Wayne C. The World Directory of Theological Education by Extension: 1976 Supplement. South Pasadena, Calif.: William Carey Library, 1976.

This 61 page supplement extends the 1973 compilation (G1415).

G1417   White, Alex Sandri. Guide to Religious Education: The Directory of Seminaries, Bible Colleges and Theological Schools Covering the USA and Canada. 1965-1966 ed. Allenhurst, N.J.: Aurea Publications, 1965.

This brief directory provides a comprehensive listing of schools teaching theology, divinity, religious education, church music, pastoral psychology, church administration and related subjects in the United States, Puerto Rico and Canada. All denominations offering advanced educational facilities are covered, and most institutions are of college level. Three sections list alphabetically schools and seminaries in the countries covered, and an index by denomination is provided. See also Arnhem (G1262), Council on the Study of Religion (G1298) and Revell's Guide to Christian Colleges (G1384).

G1418   The World Yearbook of Education. London: Evans in association with University of London Institute of Education and Columbia University Teachers College, 1931- .

See also Education Yearbook (G1311).

G1419   Wyckoff, D. Campbell. The Gospel and Christian Education: A Theology of Christian Education for Our Times. Philadelphia, Pa.: Westminster Press, 1958.

This introduction to the study of theory in Christian education is intended primarily for those involved in education planning and policy making. Written from a Protestant viewpoint, it discusses the rationale for a theory of Christian education and goes on to outline such a theory. Educational objectives, procedures, programs and institutions are considered in the light of the gospel. As an introductory study of the problem, the volume is most relevant to teachers and organizers of Christian education programs. An index is provided. See also Ferré (G1314) and Miller (G1360).

G1420   Wyckoff, D. Campbell. Theory and Design of Christian Education Curriculum. Philadelphia, Pa.: Westminster Press, 1961.

This book presents a framework for curriculum theory and design, based on experience in Protestant Christian education. It is clearly written and intended to stimulate further studies rather than to be dogmatic. Three parts deal with the curriculum and the task of Christian education and other background considerations, with theory and fundamental curriculum principles, and with curriculum design and development of materials. A useful bibliography (pp. 205-214) is provided, as well as an index. See also Butler (G1279).

G1421   Yearbook of Adult and Continuing Education. Ed. 1- . Chicago, Ill.: Marquis Academic Media, 1975- ; annual.

Focusing on the areas of basic, continuing and career related education for adults in the United States, this compendium presents general information and detailed statistics on a variety of opportunities, problems and achievements in this area. There are subject and geographical indexes. For clergy, counselors and teachers involved in adult education of various types this is a key source of information. S ee also Continuing Education (G1297).

Counseling

COUNSELING: BIBLIOGRAPHIES

G1422   Abortion Bibliography. Troy, N.Y.: Whitston Publishing Company, 1972- ; annual.

Covering material issued approximately two years prior to the date of compilation, this annual bibliography aims to cover all aspects of abortion treated in books, periodical articles or government documents. Each volume is in four main sections: monographs and government publications, periodical articles arranged by title, a subject listing of more than 200 key terms in which each citation is repeated in full under its relevant descriptor, an author index. This basic arrangement is supplemented by a list of periodicals covered and an index of subject headings. Originally compiled by Mary K. Floyd, this important guide to a field of growing importance now covers nearly 400 periodical titles in each volume and relies on several secondary services to supplement its data collecting procedure. The arrangement of information by periodical title is somewhat unusual, but the subject section is very useful. As a guide to the medical issues in general which surround abortion, this is very complete; the coverage of religion and ethics is more limited but still provides much useful information in each volume.

G1423 Aldous, Joan, and Hill, Reuben. International Bibliography of Research in Marriage and the Family, 1900-1972. 2 vols. Minneapolis, Minn.: University of Minnesota Press in association with the Institute of Life Insurance for the Minnesota Family Study Center, 1967-1974.

This computer produced bibliography covers 1900-1964 in volume 1 and 1965-1972 in volume 2. The most comprehensive work of its kind, this is an essential guide to more than 25,000 books and articles on all phases of marriage and family life. The two volumes are continued by Inventory of Marriage and Family Literature (G1481), of which the initial publication is designated as volume 3. See also Metz and Schlick (G1503).

G1424   Anderson, Marian P. Bibliographic, Indexing, Abstracting and Current Activity Sources: A Guide for Their Use in Mental Health Program Planning. Sacramento, Calif.: Bureau of Planning, Department of Mental Hygiene, 1964.

See also National Association for Mental Health (G1508).

G1425   Andrews, Theodora. A Bibliography of Drug Abuse, Including Alcohol and Tobacco. Littleton, Colo.: Libraries Unlimited, 1977.

Focusing primarily on English language materials published since the mid-1960s, this annotated listing of 725 items is divided into two sections. The first lists general reference sources and periodical titles; the second is a classified subject listing of materials, covering psychology, religion, education, legal aspects and medical aspects, as well as types of drugs. There are author/title and subject indexes. See also the two works by Gold (G1469, G1470), Drug Abuse Bibliography (G1460) and International Bibliography of Studies on Alcohol (G1480).

G1426   L'Année Psychologique. Vol. 1- . Paris: Presses Universitaires de France, 1884- ; semi-annual.

International in scope and usually prompt in appearing, this abstracting service includes signed resumés of periodical articles and critical book reviews. Exact references to sources are provided for each entry. Volume 26 includes author and subject indexes to vols. 1-25. Since first appearing in 1895 for 1894 materials, L'Année has been recognized as second only to Psychological Abstracts (G1514), which did not begin until 1927 and so lacks the historical breadth of this European compilation. Access to the classified entries (approximately seventeen for articles and five for reviews) is facilitated by annual author and subject indexes. See also Bulletin Signalétique (G1437), which is also prepared by the Centre National de la Recherche Scientifique.

G1427   Annual Progress in Child Psychiatry and Child Development. Vol 1- . New York: Brunner-Mazel, 1968- .

For counselors and others involved with children and their problems, this selection of the year's leading contributions to the understanding and development of both the normal and the disturbed child provides a time saving overview of the field. Each volume usually contains several dozen key articles in a number of major areas, including problems of adolescence, mental health services and similar topics. See also Child Development Abstracts and Bibliography (G1446).

G1428   The Annual Review of Psychology. Vol. 1- . Palo Alto, Calif.: Annual Reviews, 1950 .

This systematic, critical review of developments in various fields of psychology is arranged so that fields are surveyed regularly every three years at the most. Each annual compilation includes topical papers which clearly indicate the date of coverage for the literature surveyed. There are annual author and subject indexes, cumulative quinquennial and decennial indexes. There are also cumulative indexes of contributing authors and of chapter titles for vols. 13-17. See also Psychological Abstracts (G1514), Psychological Bulletin (G1515) and Contemporary Psychology (G1453).

G1429   The Annual Survey of Psychoanalysis: A Comprehensive Survey of Current Psychoanalytic Theory and Practice. Vol. 1- . New York: International Universities Press; London: Hogarth Press, 1952- .

Each annual volume contains a series of topical chapters by different authors, and at least one section deals in part with religious aspects of psychoanalysis. There is always a bibliography of text references and an analytical index. Unfortunately, there is a serious time lag in coverage (volume 8 for 1964 treated 1957 publications), but this can be marginally useful for theologically orientated counselors who do not require particularly current surveys. See also Chicago Institute for Psychoanalysis (G1444), Grinstein (G1472) and Hart (G1474).

G1430   Ansbacher, Heinz Ludwig, ed. Psychological Index: Abstract References. 2 vols. Columbus, Ohio: American Psychological Association, 1940-1941.

Compiled to serve as a backward extension of Psychological Abstracts (G1514), this set provides a list of numbers of titles from Psychological Index (G1516) for which one or more abstracts have been located in the periodicals examined. Volume 1 covers 1894-1918; volume 2, 1919-1928. In each case only numbers are given for entries, so the Index must be used with this compilation. References to abstracts appear for 45,000 titles, and some include more than one abstract. See also Quarterly Check-List of Psychology (G1517).

G1431   Astin, Helen S., ed. Sex Roles: A Research Bibliography. With the assistance of Allison Parelman and Anne Fisher. Rockville, Md.: National Institute of Mental Health, 1975.

Covering 1960-1972 publications, this bibliography of approximately 450 entries uses a classified arrangement and includes brief but detailed abstracts for each citation. Emphasis is on psychological and sociological attitudes. There are author and subject indexes. See also Indiana University (G1478, G1479).

G1432   Barnes, Dorothy L., comp. Rape: A Bibliography, 1965-1975. Troy, N.Y.: Whitston Publishing Company, 1977.

This 154 page bibliography of recent publications on rape is arranged in three sections: books arranged by author, periodical articles arranged by title, periodical articles arranged by subject. The last two sections contain the same information in a different arrangement. This work is limited to English language material, but since most writing on rape appears in this language it is an acceptable limitation. There is an author index. See also Kemmer (G1484).

G1433   Barry, Jeannette, comp. Psychiatry for the Non-Psychiatric Physician: A Bibliography. Washington, D.C.: National Library of Medicine, 1960.

See also Ennis (G1461).

G1434   Bell, James Edward. A Guide to Library Research in Psychology. Dubuque, Iowa: W.C. Brown, 1971.

This 211 page guide for undergraduates contains brief chapters on use of the library, library resources and writing of research papers. These are followed by 1900 reference sources arranged by type and including dictionaries, encyclopedias and handbooks, and by selected reading lists on various aspects of psychological science. For theological students unfamiliar with the field this can be a very helpful introductory guide.

See also Daniel (G1614) for a more advanced work which contains rather less in the way of bibliography, as does Elliott (G1621); see also Library Association (G1489).

G1435   Bibliographie Internationale de Psychologie/International Bibliography of Psychology. Vol. 1- . Paris: Comité Internationale pour la Documentation des Sciences Sociales, 1963- .

See also Psychological Index (G1516).

G1436   British Journal of Psychiatry. Ashford, Kent: Headley Brothers, 1853- ; semi-annual.

Published sporadically in what was originally The Journal of Mental Science, the "Bibliography and Epitome" section provides a contents listing of a half year's issues of some fifty journals plus abstracts of one or more important articles in these journals. It covers all aspects of psychiatry and psychology and contains some 2000 items per annum of which more than 200 are abstracted. There is an annual index of authors and an annual general index arranged by keywords. Unfortunately, the considerable delay with which many serials are covered makes this less useful than Psychological Abstracts (G1514) and similar services.

G1437   Bulletin Signalétique. 390. Psychologie - Psychopathologie - Psychiatrie. Vol. 1- . Paris: Centre National de la Recherche Scientifique, 1961- ; monthly.

Formerly issued quarterly as Bulletin Signalétique. 20. Psychologie. Pédagogie and formerly part of section 3 of Bulletin Signáletique. Philosophie. Sciences Humaines, this compilation of more than 1000 monthly abstracts is divided into two parts: psychology, psychiatry and psychopathology. It also includes a list of new periodicals, theses and books received. There are subject and author indexes. See also L'Année Psychologique (G1426) and Psychological Abstracts (G1514).

G1438   Bullough, Vern L., et al. An Annotated Bibliography of Homosexuality. 2 vols. Garland Reference Library of Social Science, vol. 22. New York: Garland Publishing Company, 1976.

This substantial bibliography of nearly 13,000 entries brings together representative material from a variety of disciplines. Citations are classified in broad categories, including behavioral sciences, education and children, law, novels, the homophile movement. There is no detailed subject index, and the annotations are very infrequent; both factors detract seriously from the quality of this work. Each volume contains an index of pseudonyms and an author index. Bullough is a helpful compilation on a topic which has aroused special concern in the churches, although this bibliography does not focus on ethical or theological issues of homosexuality. See also Parker (G1509, G1510).

G1439   Bullough, Vern L., et al., eds. A Bibliography of Prostitution. Garland Reference Library of Social Science. New York: Garland Publishing Company, 1977.

This bibliography lists more than 6400 books and periodical articles in a broad topical arrangement, including anthropology, biography, fiction, law, males and war. There is an author index but no subject index. Coverage is particularly weak in areas of concern to clergy and counselors, especially ethics and social aspects.

G1440   Buros, Oscar Krisen, ed. Personality Tests and Reviews; Including an Index to the "Mental Measurements Yearbooks". Highland Park, N.J.: Gryphon Press, 1970.

Intended to make readily available the mass of information in the first six Mental Measurements Yearbooks (G1502), this guide covers original test reviews, excerpted test reviews and references on the construction and use of specific tests. It also includes a bibliography of 513 personality tests, 7116 references dealing with the use and validity of individual tests, separate author indexes for all tests with twenty-five or more references and a scanning index to all personality tests in the present work. It also incorporates a test index to the Mental Measurements Yearbook, which is a master index to the tests, reviews and references in the first six collections. This is an essential accompaniment to the main compilation. For a more traditional bibliography plus index to the first five volumes of the Yearbook see Buros' Tests in Print (G1441).

G1441   Buros, Oscar Krisen, ed. Tests in Print: A Comprehensive Bibliography of Tests for Use in Education, Psychology and Industry. Highland Park, N.J.: Gryphon Press, 1961.

This comprehensive bibliography of standard tests lists both in print and out of print tests as of 1961; it also serves as an index and supplement to the first five editions of Mental Measurements Yearbook (G1502). Of the 2126 entries 487 are new and not included in the Yearbook. Citations for out of print materials include titles only, with cross references to additional information and reviews in the Yearbook. In print entries include bibliographic and descriptive information, Yearbook listing, citations in reviews and cross references. There is a publishers' directory and index, distributors' directory and index, name index and title index. See also Hildreth (G1476, G1477).

G1442   Capps, Donald; Rambo, Lewis; and Ransohoff, Paul. Psychology of Religion: A Guide to Information Sources. Philosophy and Religion Information Guide Series, vol. 1. Detroit, Mich.: Gale Research Company, 1976.

This compilation includes sections on myths, legends, rituals, religious experience, moral development and personality. Some entries are annotated. There is an emphasis on material published in English from 1950 to 1974. Author, subject and title indexes are provided. See also Meissner (G1493) and Vande Kempe and Malony (G1537).

G1443   Carter, Beryl, and Siegel, Sheldon. An Annotated Selective Bibliography for Social Work with the Aging. New York: Council on Social Work Education, 1968.

This 57 page compilation includes periodical articles published between 1959 and 1967. It is a classified listing without an index and is intended for use by students and practitioners. See also De Luca (G1457), Shock (G1522) and U.S. Department of Health, Education and Welfare (G1531-G1533).

G1444   Chicago Institute for Psychoanalysis. Chicago Psychoanalytic Literature Index, 1920-1970. 3 vols. Chicago, Ill.: CPL Publications, 1971.

Containing author and title entries in volume 1 and subject entries in the remaining volumes, this work is based on the Institute's index of some 100,000 cards. It is devoted to writings in English on psychoanalysis, psychosomatic medicine and related fields. Included are books, annual reviews, symposium proceedings and articles in professional journals. For pastoral counselors with a technical or research interest in psychoanalysis this is a very useful index. See also Annual Survey of Psychoanalysis (G1429), Grinstein (G1472) and Hart (G1474).

G1445   Child Abuse and Neglect Research: Projects and Publications. Springfield, Va.: National Technical Information Service for the U.S. Department of Health, Education and Welfare, Office of Human Development, Office of Child Development, Children's Bureau, National Center on Child Abuse and Neglect, 1976- ; approximately semi-annual.

Aimed at both the practitioner and the researcher, this guide regularly lists several hundred current research projects and publications selected from periodicals, books and similar sources. Projects and publications are listed in separate sections by author or investigator. Projects are indexed by investigator, organization, financial sponsor and subject; publications are indexed by author and subject.   Each entry contains a brief descriptive annotation. See also Kalisch (G1483).

G1446   Child Development Abstracts and Bibliography. Vol. 1- . Chicago, Ill.: University of Chicago Press, 1927- ; triannual.

Published under various titles by different publishers, this series contains abstracts of articles from American and foreign journals and also includes a section of book notices. The subject arrangement is supplemented by an author and subject index, which cumulates annually. This is a valuable abstracting service covering all aspects of child development and is reasonably up-to-date. See also Annual Progress in Child Psychiatry and Child Development (G1446).

G1447   Chun, Ki-Taek; Cobb, Sidney; and French, John R.P. Measures for Psychological Assessment: A Guide to 3000 Original Sources and Their Applications. Ann Arbor, Mich.: Survey Research Center, Institute for Social Research, 1975.

See also Buros (G1440, G1441).

G1448   Columbia University. Psychology Library. Author Index to "Psychological Index", 1894 to 1935, and "Psychological Abstracts", 1927 to 1958. 5 vols. Boston, Mass.: G.K. Hall and Company, 1960.

This cumulation of the author entries appearing in these two sets (G1516, G1514) combined with an earlier card file which preceded the Psychological Index is a single alphabetical file of authors writing between 1890 and 1958. As such, it is an important compilation in its own right, covering more material over a longer period than any other cumulation in psychology. See also the supplements (G1449, G1450).

G1449   Columbia University. Psychology Library. Cumulative Author Index to "Psychological Abstracts": Supplement, 1959-1963. Boston, Mass.: G.K. Hall and Company, 1965.

This supplement to the initial cumulation (G1448) covers five volumes in a single alphabetical sequence.

G1450   Columbia University. Psychology Library. Cumulative Author Index to "Psychological Abstracts": Supplement, 1964-1968. 2 vols. Boston, Mass.: G.K. Hall and Company, 1970.

This cumulation further supplements the main list (G1448), although the need to cover five years in more than one volume detracts from the overall usefulness of this collection.

G1451   Columbia University. Psychology Library. Cumulative Author Index to "Psychological Abstracts": Supplement, 1969-1971. Boston, Mass.: G.K. Hall and Company, 1973.

With this cumulation researchers have available an author index to the longest running abstracting service in psychology (Psychological Abstracts (G1514) plus its predecessor, Psychological Index (G1516)). Unlike the preceding cumulations this one covers only three years, and in general a quinquennial cumulation is adequate for most needs.

G1452   Communications/Research/Machines, Inc. PsychoSources: A Psychology Resource Catalog. New York: Bantam Books, 1973.

See also Library Association (G1489) and Harvard University (G1475).

G1453   Contemporary Psychology: A Journal of Reviews. Vol. 1- . Washington, D.C.: American Psychological Association, 1956- ; monthly.

Each issue of this major review journal is devoted to 25,000 word reviews of books and films, but it also includes short notices and a list of several hundred books received. Coverage extends to psychiatry, but only English language titles published in America appear to be discussed. This is an important and useful guide to recent publications, and the reviews are descriptive as well as critical. See also Annual Review of Psychology (G1428), Psychological Abstracts (G1514) and Psychological Bulletin (G1515).

G1454   Cumulated Subject Index to "Psychological Abstracts", 1927-1960. 2 vols. Boston, Mass.: G.K. Hall and Company, 1966.

This cumulation of the subject indexes to Psychological Abstracts (G1514) volumes 1-34 includes some revision and consolidation of headings. References are to year and abstract number only. This is a valuable time saver for those engaged in retrospective searching, as are the two supplements (G1455, G1456).

G1455   Cumulated Subject Index to "Psychological Abstracts": Supplement, 1961-1965. Boston, Mass.: G.K. Hall and   Company, 1968.

This single volume supplement cumulates the subject index to five volumes and provides the same benefits as the initial cumulation (G1454).

G1456   Cumulated Subject Index to "Psychological Abstracts": Supplement,

1966-1968. 2 vols. Boston, Mass.: G.K. Hall and Company, 1971.

Covering fewer years in more volumes than the preceding supplement (G1455), this cumulation has reached the optimum frequency for such collections. Three years in two volumes is little better than three years in three volumes; one would hope to see cumulations appearing quinquennially.

G1457   DeLuca, Lucy; McIlvaine, B.; and Mundkur, Mohini. Aging: An Annotated Guide to Government Publications. University of Connecticut Library Bibliography Series, no. 3. Storrs, Conn.: University of Connecticut Library, 1975.

This bibliography of United States federal, state, foreign and international documents provides very selective coverage of materials issued between 1960 and 1974. Arrangement is by subject, and there are title and series indexes. Although perhaps somewhat limited in the breadth of its coverage, DeLuce provides some help in tracing material which is notoriously elusive. See also Carter and Siegel (G1443), Shock (G1522-G1524) and United States. Department of Health, Education and Welfare (G1531-G1533).

G1458   Developmental Disabilities Abstracts. Vol. 1- . Washington, D.C.: United States Office of Human Development, Development Disabilities Office, 1964- ; quarterly.

Formerly Mental Retardation and Developmental Disabilities Abstracts and Mental Retardation Abstracts, each quarterly issue contains something less than 1000 informative and indicative abstracts in subject sections, including medical aspects, developmental aspects, treatment and training aspects, family and personnel. The entries are quite up-to-date and provide accurate data on the contents and scope of publication. For counselors active in mental retardation work this is an important source of current information.

G1459   Driver, Edwin D. The Sociology and Anthropology of Mental Illness: A Reference Guide. Rev. and enlarged ed. Amherst, Mass.: University of Massachusetts Press, 1972.

First published in 1965, this guide for social scientists and health workers attempts to cover the literature dealing with social and cultural aspects of mental illness throughout the world. Attention focuses on literature published between 1956 and 1968, and there are nearly 6000 entries arranged in a classified sequence. There is an author-subject index. Driver is a valuable contribution which is particularly useful for students of societal aspects of mental illness. A new edition would be most welcome. See also Favazza and Oman (G1464).

G1460   Drug Abuse Bibliography. Vol. 1- . Troy, N.Y.: Whitston Publishing Company, 1971- ; annual.

This current bibliography admirably updates Menditto (G1495), covering the preceding year's publications in each annual volume. Coverage is thus available for 1960 onwards. Material is arranged by subject, and in each section there are subdivisions according to type of publication. See also Andrews (G1425) and Gold (G1470).

G1461   Ennis, Bernice. Guide to the Literature in Psychiatry. Los Angeles, Calif.: Partridge Press, 1971.

This list covers journals, books, some audio-visual aids, government publications and a wide range of information sources (dictionaries, encyclopedias, directories, indexes, abstracting services). See also Barry (G1433).

G1462   Essertier, Daniel. Psychologie et Sociologie: Essai de Bibliographie Critique. Burt Franklin Bibliography and Reference Series, no. 199. New York: Burt Franklin, 1968.

G1463   Faberow, Norman L. Bibliography on Suicide and Suicide Prevention, 1897-1957, 1958-1970. DHEW Publications, No. HSM 72-9080. Rockville, Md.: National Institute of Mental Health, 1972.

This extension of Faberow's earlier publication covering materials through 1967 groups entries in the two periods indicated in the title. The first grouping of 2202 entries incorporates and expands the bibliography published in Faberow's The Cry for Help (New York: McGraw-Hill Book Company, 1961). The 1958-1970 section lists 2542 additional items. Foreign language titles have an English translation. The listing is by author, and there are full subject indexes for each section. See also Prentice (G1513).

G1464   Favazza, Armando R., and Oman, Mary. Anthropological and Cross Cultural Themes in Mental Health: An Annotated Bibliography, 1925-1974. University of Missouri Studies, vol. 65. Columbia, Mo.: University of Missouri Press, 1977.

This interesting compilation includes more than 3600 English language periodical articles arranged chronologically. The introduction provides a valuable survey of the cultural areas and themes related to the mental health focus of this work, which is a particularly useful introduction to the field for students and others working in the area. There are author and subject indexes. See also Driver (G1459).

G1465   Freeman, Ruth St. John, and Freeman, Harrop A. Counseling: A Bibliography (with Annotations). New York: Scarecrow Press, 1964.

This 986 page compilation uses a broad definition of counseling to gather materials under several headings: professions, religion (clergy), medicine (doctors, psychiatrists), law, social work, guidance, testing (psychologists), student counseling, marriage counseling and general. In each section entries are arranged alphabetically; references are annotated and coded or cross indexed. Bibliographical data are full and annotations are very informative. It is important to consult the introduction in order to insure best use of this guide.

G1466   Fulton, Robert L. Death, Grief and Bereavement: A Bibliography, 1845-1975. 3rd ed. Minneapolis, Minn.: Center for Death Education and Research, University of Minnesota, 1973. Reprint. New York: Arno Press, 1977.

See also Kutscher (G1488), Kutscher and Kutscher (G1487) and Poteet (G1512).

G1467   Garoogian, Andrew, and Garoogian, Rhoda. <u>Child Care Issues for Parents and Society: A Guide to Information Sources</u>. Social Issues and Social Problems Information Guide Series, vol. 2. Detroit, Mich.: Gale Research Company, 1977.

This annotated bibliography covers nontechnical books and articles, audio-visual materials, sources of free or inexpensive materials and organizations in the field of child care. The focus is on 1970-1975, and arrangement is by subject with form subdivisions. There are author, title, organization and subject indexes to this compilation which is of use to counselors, families and others active in the child care field. See also <u>Child Abuse and Neglect Research</u> (G1445) and Kalisch (G1483).

G1468   Golann, Stuart E. <u>Coordinate Index Reference Guide to Community Mental Health</u>. New York: Behavioral Publications, 1969.

This bibliography of 1510 references published between 1960 and 1967 codes each entry as to content. In addition to the glossary used to code each document, there is a multiple access coordinate index to the entries. Covering community mental health over a fairly limited period, this compilation is perhaps too specific for most counselors and researchers in the pastoral field. There is, however, a useful section on other sources of information.

G1469   Gold, Robert S.; Zimmerli, William H.; and Austin, Winnifred K. <u>Comprehensive Bibliography of Existing Literature on Alcohol, 1969 to 1974</u>. Dubuque, Iowa: Kendall/Hunt Publishing Company, 1975.

This bibliography of recent literature on alcoholism and alcohol lists both general interest and scholarly materials. It contains individual sections for periodical articles, books, pamphlets, dissertations, and within each form division a classified arrangement is used.   There is an author index and a subject index. For students unfamiliar with the field this bibliography contains many useful entries, and it is also helpful for more advanced users. See also Andrews (G1425) and <u>International Bibliography of Studies on Alcohol</u> (G1480).

G1470   Gold, Robert S.; Zimmerli, William H.; and Austin, Winnifred K. <u>Comprehensive Bibliography of Existing Literature on Drugs, 1969 to 1974</u>. Dubuque, Iowa: Kendall/Hunt Publishing Company, 1975.

See also Andrews (G1425) and <u>Drug Abuse Bibliography</u> (G1460).

G1471   Gottsegen, Gloria Behar, ed. <u>Group Behavior: A Guide to Information Sources</u>. Psychology Information Guide Series, vol. 2. Detroit, Mich.: Gale Research Company, 1979.

This guide comprises thirteen chapters, each on an aspect of group behavior or type of information source, including texts, bibliographies, persons, organizations and associations.

G1472   Grinstein, Alexander. <u>The Index of Psychoanalytic Writings</u>. 14 vols. New York: International Universities Press, 1956-1975.

This revision and updating of John Rickman's <u>Index Psychoanalyticus, 1893-1926</u> (London: Woolf, 1928) lists books, periodical articles, reviews and abstracts published between 1900 and 1969 in any language. Entries are arranged alphabetically by author in the first four volumes, and the detailed subject index in volume 4 provides highly specific access to the author entries. Titles are given in the original language, often together with an English translation. Volumes 6-9 cover 1953-1959 publications, while volumes 10-14 cover 1960-1969; volumes 9 and 14 serve as subject indexes. This provides the most comprehensive bibliography on psychoanalysis, containing more than 100,000 items. See also Chicago Institute for Psychoanalysis (G1429) and Hart (G1474).

G1473   Haley, Jay, and Glick, Ira. Psychiatry and the Family: An Annotated Bibliography of Articles Published 1960-64. Palo Alto, Calif.: Family Process, 1965.

This 162 page bibliography attempts to include all articles on family therapy and family research studies which are relevant to psychiatry and psychology. Many of the references are reprinted from the abstract section of the journal, Family Process. Entries are in a classified arrangement, and there is a full author index. For pastoral counselors and researchers interested in family therapy this is a useful, if chronologically limited, guide to articles.

G1474   Hart, Henry Harper, comp. and ed. Conceptual Index to Psychoanalytical Technique and Training. 5 vols. Croton-on-Hudson, N.Y.: North River Press, 1972.

This index covers about 300 professional monographs and more than 2500 journal articles published between 1896 and 1960. Entries are arranged according to 270 ideas and concepts, each of which is subdivided; within each subdivision entries are listed chronologically. Included are the significant ideas of Jung, Adler and others, as well as complementary works and original studies by practitioners and researchers. It is less inclusive than Grinstein (G1472) but usefully supplements this and similar works with its conceptual arrangement. See also Annual Survey of Psychoanalysis (G1429) and Chicago Institute for Psychoanalysis (G1444).

G1475   Harvard University. The Harvard List of Books in Psychology. Comp. and annotated by the psychologists of Harvard University. 4th ed. Cambridge, Mass.: Harvard University Press, 1971.

This 108 page listing of 744 titles includes items chosen for their importance and value in psychology at the present; each edition thus supersedes rather than expands its predecessor. Entries are annotated and arranged by topic, and there is an author index. New entries constitute nearly half of the list, which includes publications issued in 1970. Each edition of the Harvard List is a valuable guide to current titles in psychology for librarians, researchers and students. See also Library Association (G1489).

G1476   Hildreth, Gertrude Howell. Bibliography of Mental Tests and Rating Scales. 2nd ed. New York: Psychological Corporation, 1939.

Similar to Buros (G1440, G1441), this bibliography lists more than 4000 tests in classified arrangement. It contains both subject and author indexes to speed consultation. See also Mental Measurements Yearbook (G1502).

G1477 Hildreth, Gertrude Howell. <u>Bibliography of Mental Tests and Rating Scales. 1945 Supplement</u>. New York: Psychological Corporation, 1946.

This supplement to the second edition (G1476) lists some 1000 tests published between 1940 and 1945, as well as a few earlier tests omitted from the basic list.

G1478   Indiana University. Institute for Sex Research. Library. <u>Catalog of Periodical Literature in the Social and Behavioral Sciences Section of the Library of the Institute for Sex Research, Indiana University, Bloomington, Indiana, Including Supplement to Monographs, 1973-1975</u>. 4 vols. Boston, Mass.: G.K. Hall and Company, 1976.

The 68,800 cards in this catalog provide citations for approximately 14,000 journal articles and reprints, 200 doctoral dissertations and 1000 monographs. The dictionary arrangement utilizes subject headings from the Institute's own thesaurus. This is a significant research tool which should be used in conjunction with the main Institute catalog (G1479).

G1479   Indiana University. Institute for Sex Research. Library. <u>Catalog of the Social and Behavioral Sciences Monograph Section of the Library of the Institute for Sex Research, Indiana University, Bloomington, Indiana</u>. 4 vols. Boston, Mass.: G.K. Hall and Company, 1975.

The 30,000 books listed in this important catalog are primarily Western language materials from the nineteenth and twentieth centuries. The fields covered include sexual ethics and religion, marriage, women's rights, abortion and contraception. This guide and the supplement (G1478) are key bibliographies for researchers in these areas. See also Astin (G1431).

G1480   <u>International Bibliography of Studies on Alcohol</u>. Vol. 1- . New Brunswick, N.J.: Rutgers Center of Alcohol Studies, 1966- ; approximately decennial.

Designed as a broadly based multidisciplinary and interprofessional bibliography, this excellent work covers medical, social, legal, psychological and economic aspects of alcohol use. The first two volumes consist of a chronological listing of 25,000 book and periodical references written between 1901 and 1950 together with a full subject index (in volume 2). Subsequent decennial volumes will cover publications of a ten year period and will include indexes. This series of bibliographies should not be overlooked by counselors or researchers concerned with alcohol use or alcoholism. See also Andrews (G1425) and Gold (G1469).

G1481   <u>Inventory of Marriage and Family Literature</u>. Vol. 1- . Beverly Hills, Calif.:   Sage Publications, 1974- ; annual.

Formerly entitled <u>International Bibliography of Research in Marriage and the Family</u> (G1423), this annual listing of articles published in professional journals is an important guide to current literature on all aspects of marriage and the family, covering theory as well as practice. For researchers, academics and counselors this is a significant addition to the reference material in this field. Coverage is thorough and up-to-date. See also McKenney (G1491) and Milden (G1504).

G1482   <u>Journal of Psychology and Judaism</u>. Vol. 1- . New York: Human

Sciences Press for the Center for the Study of Psychology and Judaism, 1976- ; quarterly.

Both scholarly and pastoral in focus, this interesting serial regularly includes a section entitled "Critical Review in Psychology and Judaism". This is arranged by subject and concentrates on the interaction between psychology and religion in philosophical and clinical terms. Coverage extends to books and journal articles and does not aim to be comprehensive; nevertheless, it is a useful starting point for those new to the field or for scholars wishing to keep abreast of fairly current literature, especially from a Jewish viewpoint.

G1483   Kalisch, Beatrice J. Child Abuse and Neglect: An Annotated Bibliography. Contemporary Problems of Childhood, no. 2. Westport, Conn.: Greenwood Press, 1978.

This annotated bibliography lists more than 2000 English language works published between 1960 and 1977. The classified subject arrangement covers prediction, detection and prevention; causative factors; manifestations; treatment; sexual abuse; legal issues. There are author and subject indexes. Appendixes deal briefly with bibliographical tools and selected organizations. See also Child Abuse and Neglect Research (G1445) and Garoogian and Garoogian (G1467).

G1484   Kemmer, Elizabeth Jane. Rape and Rape-Related Issues: An Annotated Bibliography. Garland Reference Library of Social Science, vol. 39. New York: Garland Publishing Company, 1977.

This bibliography focuses on material in English published between 1965 and 1976. The basic author arrangement is supplemented by an author index. The 174 pages provide selective coverage of the social and psychological aspects of an important social problem which deserves wider study in the church. See also Barnes (G1432).

G1485   Klausner, Samuel Z. Preliminary Annotated Bibliography and Directory of Workers in the Field of Religion and Psychiatry. New York: Columbia University, Bureau of Applied Social Research, 1958.

This is a successor to Klausner's Preliminary Bibliography of Religion and Psychiatry (New York: Columbia University, Bureau of Applied Social Research, 1957).

G1486   Klausner, Samuel Z. Supplementary Bibliography of Religion and Psychiatry. New York: Columbia University, Bureau of Applied Social Research, 1958.

G1487   Kutscher, Austin H., Jr., and Kutscher, Austin H. A Bibliography of Books on Death, Bereavement, Loss and Grief: 1935-1968. New York: Health Sciences Publishing Corporation, 1969.

This guide excludes all non-English materials and is not annotated. The 1200 titles are arranged under forty-two subject headings, and there is an author index. In spite of its limitations, Kutscher is a useful guide to an important area of pastoral concern. See also Fulton (G1466), Kutscher (G1488) and Poteet (G1512).

G1488 Kutscher, Martin L., et al., eds. Comprehensive Bibliography of the Thanatology Literature. New York: MSS Information Corporation, 1975.

This author listing covers 4844 books, articles, reports, government documents and unpublished materials; many of the items are not listed elsewhere, which gives Kutscher particular value. However, the extremely broad subject terms used in the index greatly hinder use of this work. See also Miller (G1505), Poteet (G1512), Simpson (G1525).

G1489   Library Association. County Libraries Group. Readers' Guide to Books on Psychology. 2nd ed. Readers' Guides, New Series No. 69. London: Library Association, 1962.

See also Harvard University (G1475).

G1490   Louttit, Chauncey McKinley, comp. Bibliography of Bibliographies on Psychology, 1900-1927. Bulletin of the National Research Council, no. 65. Washington, D.C.: National Research Council, 1928. Reprint. Burt Franklin Bibliography and Reference Series, vol. 358. New York: Burt Franklin, 1970.

This 108 page compilation lists 2134 (8 blank) bibliographies which have appeared in books and journals between 1900 and 1927. Part 1 covers periodicals and general works searched; part 2, further bibliographical sources; part 3, list of bibliographies arranged alphabetically by author; part 4, subject index. Each entry includes an indication of the number of references provided. For older bibliographies on all aspects of psychological studies this is an indispensible collection. See also Viney (G1538).

G1491 McKenney, Mary. Divorce: A Selected Annotated Bibliography. Metuchen, N.J.: Scarecrow Press, 1975.

Limited primarily to material produced before 1972, this classified bibliography of approximately 600 items includes brief annotations in most cases. Focus is on North American publications, and coverage is broadly representative of the field. Appendixes deal with relevant organizations and state divorce laws. See also Inventory of Marriage and Family Literature (G1481) for more up-to-date coverage; see also Metz and Schlick (G1503) and Sell and Sell (G1520).

G1492   Maison des Sciences de l'Homme. Service d'Echange d'Informations Scientifiques. Liste Mondiale des Périodiques Spécialisés, Psychologie/World List of Specialized Periodicals, Psychology. Publications, Série C: Catalogues et Inventaires, 2. Paris: Mouton, 1967.

This 165 page list contains data on approximately 400 serials arranged alphabetically by country, followed by a separate section on international organizations. Entries include information on size and coverage, frequency, cost, address. There are indexes of subjects, scientific institutions, titles. Supplements appear in the International Social Sciences Council quarterly review, Social Science Information. See Tompkins and Shirley (G1530) for a more thorough guide to English language titles.

G1493 Meissner, William W. Annotated Bibliography in Religion and Psychology. New York: Academy of Religion and Mental Health, 1961.

In this 235 page guide a paragraph on each item describes the contents and conclusions reached; the notations are descriptive rather than critical. 2905 articles and books from both the scientific and theological disciplines are listed. An author index is included, but there is no detailed subject index to supplement the classified arrangement of entries. This is a valuable interdisciplinary bibliography which retains its usefulness despite being somewhat in need of revision. See also Capps (G1442) and Vande Kempe and Malony (G1537).

G1494   Melton, John Gordon. A Reader's Guide to the Church's Ministry of Healing. Evanston, Ill.: Academy of Religion and Psychical Research, 1973.

This 78 page bibliography is intended for those interested in paranormal healing within the church. Arrangement is under ten main headings, in addition to an introductory chapter, some treating a chronological period, others a topic such as spiritualism or pentecostalism. There are brief introductory comments to each section. Bibliographical data for some titles are incomplete; there are no annotations; some locations are given.

G1495   Menditto, Joseph. Drugs of Addiction and Non-Addiction, Their Use and Abuse: A Comprehensive Bibliography, 1960-1969. Troy, N.Y.: Whitston Publishing Company, 1970.

This classified listing covers both types of drugs and various social and personal problems related to them. Each subject section contains separate listings for books, articles and dissertations. There is a comprehensive author index. For ongoing information in the same field see Drug Abuse Bibliography (G1460). See also Sells (G1521), which concentrates on the treatment of narcotic addiction.

G1496   Menges, Robert J., and Dittes, James E. Psychological Studies of Clergymen: Abstracts of Research. New York: Thomas Nelson and Sons, 1965.

The 700 annotated and classified entries in this collection include books, journal articles, pamphlets and reports, most of which are dated between 1955 and 1965. There are indexes of authors, of instruments and methods, of samples and of topics.

G1497   Menninger, Karl. A Guide to Psychiatric Books in English. 3rd ed. Menninger Clinic Monograph Series, no. 7. New York: Grune and Stratton, 1972.

This successor to the editions of 1950 and 1956, both entitled A Guide to Psychiatric Books, is a checklist of books on psychiatry and closely related topics. It is arranged by subject and includes a name index. This edition does not incorporate the useful reading lists for specific groups which featured in the earlier editions. As a listing of current works, this is a useful but selective guide to more important titles (approximately 4000 items) published up to the beginning of 1971. There are no annotations. See also Menninger Foundation (G1498).

G1498   Menninger Foundation. Menninger Clinic Library. Catalog of the Menninger Clinic Library, the Menninger Foundation, Topeka, Kansas. 4 vols. Boston, Mass.: G.K. Hall and Company, 1972.

This important catalog reproduces 55,000 cards in two parts, author-title and subject. In the subject listing are many psychological and psychiatric works of importance in the more technical areas of counseling. Therefore, this collection should not be overlooked as too specialized for advanced bibliographical inquiries. See also Menninger (G1497).

G1499   Mental Health Book Review Index. Vols. 1-17. New York: Council on Research in Bibliography, 1956-1972; annual.

Issued initially on a semi-annual basis as a supplement to Psychological Newsletter, this index covers the biomedical and social sciences and humanities as they relate to mental health. Individual books range from interdisciplinary surveys to monographs on a specific topic and from technical to general treatments. Each title appears with references to three or more reviews in some 200 journals. Overall more than 5400 titles were indexed with a total of more than 34,000 references to reviews before the Index ceased publication. This guide is of value to a wide range of users. See also the following entry (G1500) and The Year Book of Psychiatry and Applied Mental Health (G1540).

G1500 Mental Health Book Review Index: Cumulative Author-Title Index, Vols. 1-12, 1956-1967. New York: Council on Research in Bibliography, 1969.

This cumulative index to the preceding title (G1499) is an important time saver and should be consulted initially for authors or titles. Unfortunately there is no similar index to the final five volumes.

G1501   Mental Health Materials Center. A Selective Guide to Materials for Mental Health and Family Life Education. 1976 ed. New York: Mental Health Materials Center, 1976.

This substantial guide reprints selected evaluations of books, pamphlets, films and plays from "IRC Recommends" in the Bulletin of the Information Resources Center for Mental Health and Family Life Education. The classified arrangement of entries is supplemented by an alphabetical index. Ordering information is included. In the field of family life education this is a valuable guide to a wide range of popular, educational and scholarly works in a variety of formats. See also United States. National Clearinghouse for Mental Health Information (G1534).

G1502   Mental Measurements Yearbook. Highland Park, N.J.: Gryphon Press, 1938- ; irregular.

Designed to help users in education, psychology and other fields where testing is important, each Yearbook supplements rather than supersedes earlier volumes. References are numbered consecutively through each volume, and they include cross references to reviews, excerpts and bibliographic citations in earlier volumes. The latest edition (7th) is in three parts: tests and reviews arranged under fifteen headings; books and reviews; indexes by periodical, publisher, book title, test title, name and test classification. Information for each entry includes title, descriptions of target groups, date, scores, availability, size, factual comments on lack of data or norms, cost, scoring, reporting services, time necessary to administer, author and publisher. Test bibliographies cover English language materials, and most of the tests included are available in the

United States. See also Buros (G1440, G1441).

G1503   Metz, René, and Schlick, Jean. Marriage and Divorce/Mariage et Divorce: International Bibliography, 1970-1972, Indexed by Computer. RIC Supplément, no. 1. Strasbourg: CERDIC Publications, 1973.

The 365 entries in this 37 page bibliography cover books and articles on the issue of marriage and divorce, focusing on ethical, theological, social and legal aspects of interest to clergy and scholars. Entries are arranged alphabetically by author, and a keyword index is provided. It is understood that RIC Suppléments 41-42 and 57-58 cover the same subject for 1975-1977 (1321 entries) and 1978-1980 (1540 entries) respectively. See also Aldous and Hill (G1423), Inventory of Marriage and Family Literature (G1481), McKenney (G1491) and Sell and Sell (G1520).

G1504   Milden, James Wallace. The Family in Past Time: A Guide to the Literature. Garland Reference Library of Social Science, vol. 32. New York: Garland Publishing Company, 1977.

Limited to English language materials published before 1976, this annotated bibliography lists books, articles, unpublished papers and theses in a classified sequence. It includes sections on methodology and theory; family in European history, in American history, in non-Western history; family history projects. There is an author index. This is a useful bibliography for students of the historical aspects of family life. See also Aldous and Hill (G1423) for a guide devoted to more current issues.

G1505   Miller, Albert Jay, and Acri, Michael James. Death: A Bibliographical Guide. Metuchen, N.J.: Scarecrow Press, 1977.

This substantial bibliography lists approximately 3850 items in a classified sequence, including general works, education, humanities, medical profession and nursing experiences, religion and theology, science, social sciences, audio-visual media. The annotations are brief and descriptive; the author and subject indexes are adequate. Much of the material listed is valuable from a pastoral or theological viewpoint. See also Poteet (G1512), Simpson (G1525), Kutscher (G1488) and Kutscher and Kutscher (G1487).

G1506   Morgan, John Henry. Death and Dying: A Resource Bibliography for Clergy and Chaplains. Wichita, Kans.: Institute on Ministry and the Elderly, 1977.

Although listing only 500 books and articles on suffering, death and closely related areas, this 30 page bibliography is useful for students and clergy unfamiliar with the field. Emphasis is on pastoral rather than theological aspects of death. See also Southwestern Baptist Theological Seminary (G1526).

G1507   Morrow, William R. Behavior Therapy Bibliography, 1950-1969; Annotated and Indexed. University of Missouri Studies, vol. 54. Columbia, Mo.: University of Missouri Press, 1971.

This author listing of 900 references includes annotations in the form of a series of abbreviations or symbols which indicate the design, setting, subject, behavior and modification procedures for each entry. Reference tables provide a classified index to each of the coded categories. Except for those interested in more experimental aspects of behavior therapy this collection is probably too specialized as a pastoral counseling bibliography.

G1508   National Association for Mental Health. Recommended Books for a Mental Health Library. 2nd rev. ed. New York: National Association for Mental Health, 1966.

This booklet lists about 200 items in three sections: background readings and general references, books on special mental health subjects, books for professional groups (including clergy). Although brief and with only a limited number of annotations, this is a useful listing for those unfamiliar with mental health literature. See also Anderson (G1424).

G1509   Parker, William. Homosexuality: A Selective Bibliography of over 3000 Items. Metuchen, N.J.: Scarecrow Press, 1971.

This compilation is intended for researchers, professional workers and laymen; it aims to include all significant items published in English to 1969. Arrangement is by type of publication, including books, articles in popular magazines, articles in legal journals, articles in medical and scientific journals. There are indexes of articles and of subjects. See also Bullough (G1438), which is more comprehensive, and Parker's supplement (G1510).

G1510   Parker, William. Homosexuality Bibliography: Supplement, 1970-1975. Metuchen, N.J.: Scarecrow Press, 1977.

This supplement to Parker's 1971 compilation (G1509) lists more than 3100 items by type: books, pamphlets and documents, theses and dissertations, and similar types of publications. Appendixes treat films, television programs, audio-visual aids, American laws on homosexuality.

G1511   Pastoral Care and Counseling Abstracts. Vol. 1- . Richmond, Va.: The Joint Council on Research in Pastoral Care and Counseling, 1972- ; annual.

This useful research tool provides abstracts of material in three sections: published research, unpublished research, research in progress. For each of these groups broad subject headings are used to classify entries, and most abstracts are listed under several headings. Each annual issue includes a list of headings and an author index. Coverage extends to all aspects of pastoral care and counseling but is limited to American work. The abstracts are based on voluntary reporting, which means that quality is variable. Both the unevenness and the broad subject categorization detract from the value of the service, but it is an up-to-date starting point for the serious researcher.

G1512   Poteet, G. Howard. Death and Dying: A Bibliography, 1950-1974. Troy, N.Y.: Whitston Publishing   Company, 1976.

Poteet concentrates almost entirely on the psychology of death and omits materials on suicide, euthanasia and legal interpretations of death. For these areas one should consult Prentice (G1513). In this bibliography books are listed in one section by author; periodical articles are listed alphabetically by subject. There is an author index. Within the limits of this specialized subject Poteet is a reasonably thorough bibliography. See also Fulton (G1466), Kutscher (G1488) and Kutscher and Kutscher (G1487).

G1513   Prentice, Ann E. Suicide: A Selective Bibliography of Over 2200 Items. Metuchen, N.J.: Scarecrow Press, 1974.

This useful bibliography contains much material of value for pastoral and ethical studies. The entries are arranged in individual sections for books, theses and dissertations, articles in religious journals, articles in medical journals, and other topical serials. There are separate author and subject indexes. See also Faberow (G1463).

G1514   Psychological Abstracts: Non-Evaluative Summaries of the World's Literature in Psychology and Related Disciplines. Vol. 1- . Washington, D.C.: American Psychological Association, 1927- ; monthly.

This important monthly index lists new books, journal articles, reports and similar documents, providing a detailed citation and abstract for each item. Nearly 15,000 items are listed in each six-monthly volume; both volumes and issues have author and subject indexes. The abstracts are arranged under seventeen major headings, which are further subdivided and include a broad range of topics relevant to religion. Data published since 1967 are in a format suitable for on-line searching, which in this case is both rapid and reasonably inexpensive. In addition to the monthly and volume indexes, there are also triennial cumulations plus more substanial subject (G1454-G1456) and author (G1448-G1451) cumulations 1927-1972. Also worth consulting is the Thesaurus of Psychological Index Terms, which can be useful in getting the most out of either on-line or hard copy searching. This is obviously an indispensible tool in its field for both students and scholars. For an important predecessor see Psychological Index (G1516), as well as Ansbacher (G1430), L'Année Psychologique (G1426), Annual Review of Psychology (G1428), Psychological Bulletin (G1515) and Contemporary Psychology (G1453).

G1515   Psychological Bulletin. Vol. 1- . Washington, D.C.: American Psychological Association, 1904- ; bi-monthly.

Like The Annual Review of Psychology (G1428), Psychological Abstracts (G1514) and Contemporary Psychology (G1453), this bulletin features extensive review articles, usually on a selected topic. Vol.68, no.3 (1968) contains a subject and author index of all reviews and summaries published between 1940 and 1966. This is widely recognized as an important aid to bibliographic research.

G1516   Psychological Index. An Annual Bibliography of the Literature of Psychology and Cognate Subjects. Vols. 1-42. Princeton, N.J.: Psychological Review Company, 1895-1936.

This classified subject listing treats books and periodical articles, in all languages, including translations and new editions in English, French, German and Italian. Each volume, which covers the preceding year, includes 5000 titles and indexes about 350 serials. The list of periodicals indexed and their abbreviations appears in volume 30, and each compilation includes an alphabetical author index. This is an important index for advanced work in psychology. For a continuation see Psychological

Abstracts (G1514). See also Ansbacher (G1430) and Quarterly Check-List of Psychology (G1517).

G1517   Quarterly Check-List of Psychology: International Index of Current Books, Monographs, Brochures and Separates. Vol. 1- . Darien, Conn.: American Bibliographic Service, 1961- .

See also Ansbacher (G1430) and Psychological Index (G1516).

G1518   Schlesinger, Benjamin. The Jewish Family: A Survey and Annotated Bibliography. Toronto: University of Toronto Press, 1971.

Following a basic survey, the bibliography (pp. 73-146) contains classified entries with annotations. Marriage and intermarriage, education and social life are among the topics considered. For those outside the Jewish tradition this is a useful guide to publications.

G1519   Schlesinger, Benjamin. The One-Parent Family: Perspectives and Annotated Bibliography. Toronto: University of Toronto Press, 1969.

Covering such topics as desertion and separation, divorce, widowhood, unmarried parents, remarriage and other aspects of single parenthood, this classified bibliography lists a wide selection of publications with informative notes on their contents. The introductory essays survey the field and include methodological considerations for research undertakings. This is an acceptable guide for those unfamiliar with the single parent family.

G1520   Sell, Kenneth D., and Sell, Betty H. Divorce in the United States, Canada and Great Britain: A Guide to Information Sources. Social Issues and Social Problems Information Guide Series, vol. 1. Detroit, Mich.: Gale Research Company, 1978.

This compendium locates bibliographies, indexes, abstracts and similar materials dealing with all aspects of divorce. Brief annotations are given, and there are name, title and subject indexes. See als McKenney (G1491) and Metz and Schlick (G1503).

G1521   Sells, Helen F., comp. A Bibliography on Drug Dependence. Fort Worth, Tex.: Texas Christian University Press, 1967.

Focusing on the treatment of narcotic addiction and the rehabilitation of addicts, this adequate bibliography (137pp.) includes some material not found in Menditto (G1495). Selected references on alcoholism have also been included. See also Andrews (G1425), Drug Abuse Bibliography (G1460) and Gold (G1470).

G1522   Shock, Nathan Wetheril. A Classified Bibliography of Gerontology and Geriatrics. Stanford, Calif.: Stanford University Press, 1951.

This 599 page bibliography and its supplements (G1523, G1524) provide the most comprehensive guide to geriatrics yet published. More than 51,000 items from around the world and on all aspects of the subject are included. See also Carter and Siegel (G1443) and United States. Department of Health, Education and Welfare (G1531-G1533) for far more selective guides.

G1523   Shock, Nathan Wetheril. A Classified Bibliography of Gerontology and Geriatrics: Supplement I, 1949-1955. Stanford, Calif.: Stanford University Press, 1957.

This 525 page supplement to the initial volume (G1522) covers works published between 1949 and 1955.

G1524   Shock, Nathan Wetheril. A Classified Bibliography of Gerontology and Geriatrics: Supplement II, 1956-1961. Stanford, Calif.: Stanford University Press, 1963.

Covering the publications for six years in 624 pages of classified entries, this second supplement to the initial volume (G1522) is continued by regular updatings in the Journal of Gerontology.

G1525   Simpson, M.A. Dying, Death and Grief: A Critically Annotated Bibliography and Source Book of Thanatology and Terminal Care. New York: Plenum Press, 1979.

See also Kutscher (G1488) and Miller (G1505).

G1526   Southwestern Baptist Theological Seminary. Fleming Library. Pastor Ministers in Time of Death: Bibliography. Fort Worth, Tex.: Southwestern Baptist Theological Seminary, Fleming Library, 1964.

This brief bibliography contains only 18 leaves. See also Morgan (G1506).

G1527   Stein, Morris Isaac, and Heinze, Shirley J. Creativity and the Individual: Summaries of Selected Literature in Psychology and Psychiatry. Glencoe, Ill.: Free Press, 1960.

This annotated bibliography of several hundred books, articles and papers provides 500 word annotations on each entry. The material is arranged in thirteen sections, and there is an index of authors and of subjects.

G1528   Strugnell, Cecile. Adjustment to Widowhood and Some Related Problems: A Selective and Annotated Bibliography. New York: Health Sciences Publishing Corporation, 1974.

This bibliography lists books, parts of books and periodical articles in English which deal with the broad areas of bereavement, widowhood, loneliness and related topics. The entries are adequately annotated, but there is no index. For both student and counselor this is a helpful compilation which lists many items of pastoral value. See also Kutscher (G1488).

G1529   Strupp, Hans H., and Bergin, Allen E. Research in Individual Psychotherapy: A Bibliography. Public Health Service Publications, no. 1944. Chevy Chase, Md.: U.S. National Institute of Mental Health, 1969.

This list of research reports pertaining to individual psychotherapy with adults as well as general references relevant to psychotherapeutic research contains 2741 entries arranged alphabetically by author. Each entry is coded by letter to one or more content categories, which indicate the major emphases of the reports. With emphasis on studies involving a research design and reporting quantitative results, this is a bibliography suitable for advanced researchers rather than practising counselors.

G1530   Tompkins, Margaret, and Shirley, Norma. <u>A Checklist of Serials in Psychology and Allied Fields</u>. 2nd ed. Troy, N.Y.: Whitston Publishing Company, 1976.

This guide to more than 800 English language periodicals (plus a few in other languages but which include English abstracts or summaries) includes for each entry a statement of objectives, indication of specific field of interest and the usual directory information for potential contributors. It is more detailed than <u>Psychologie</u> (G1492). A title and subject index plus a listing of serials by subject greatly enhance the value of this edition.

G1531   United States. Department of Health, Education and Welfare. Library. <u>More Words on Aging: Supplement</u>. Washington, D.C.: U.S. Administration on Aging, 1971.

This supplement to <u>Words on Aging</u> (G1533) carries the main volume forward by several years and again provides brief but adequate annotations. Both works should be used by those beginning research on geriatrics and requiring data on basic works.

G1532   United States. Department of Health, Education and Welfare. Library. <u>Selected References on Aging: An Annotated Bibliography Compiled for the Special Staff on Aging</u>. Washington, D.C: Government Printing Office, 1959.

This successor to earlier editions issued by the Federal Security Agency Library is a classified listing with brief annotations. The entries are highly selective and provide a reasonable guide to basic works in the field for counselors and social workers. See also Carter and Siegel (G1443) and Shock (G1522-G1524), both of which are more up-to-date.

G1533   United States. Department of Health, Education and Welfare. Library. <u>Words on Aging: A Bibliography of Selected Annotated References Compiled for the Administration on Aging</u>. Washington, D.C.: U.S. Administration on Aging, 1970.

This 190 page listing is the seventh in a series of similar listings published since 1950 (but under various titles). It provides a selective, classified list of periodical articles published between 1963 and 1967 and books published between 1900 and 1967. The annotations are brief but provide adequate information for basic user requirements. See also Carter and Siegel (G1443).

G1534   United States. National Clearinghouse for Mental Health Information. <u>Bibliography on Religion and Mental Health, 1960-64</u>. Public Health Service Publications, no. 1599. Washington, D.C.: U.S. Department of Health, Education and Welfare, Public Health Service, 1967.

This bibliography of books and journal articles concentrates on materials dealing with the theoretical and practical relationship between religion and mental health. Titles are listed under fourteen main headings such as pastoral psychology and pastoral counseling. Brief descriptive annotations are provided, as well as full bibliographical data. Only English language materials are covered unless an English translation or abstract of a foreign work was available. See also Mental Health Materials Center (G1501).

G1535   United States Catholic Conference. Education Department. Marriage Preparation Resource Book. Rev.ed. Washington, D.C.: United States Catholic Conference, 1976.

This 367 page resource manual provides up-to-date guidance on materials to be used in designing and planning a marriage preparation program. It covers theological, psychological, sexual and social aspects of marriage. See also Aldous and Hill (G1423) and Inventory of Marriage and Family Literature (G1481).

G1536   Van Why, Elizabeth Wharton, comp. Adoption Bibliography and Multi-Ethnic Sourcebook. Hartford, Conn.: Open Door Society of Connecticut, 1977.

This three part work includes a bibliography of books, articles, periodicals, bibliographies and audio-visual materials; a multi-ethnic sourcebook describing various organizations and their materials; appendixes. The rather selective bibliography is indexed by geographical locations, peoples and languages. Van Why is a practical guide geared to meet specific inquiries rather than a more general scholarly work.

G1537   Vande Kempe, Hendrika, and Malony, H. Newton. Psychology and Religion: A Bibliography of Historical Bases for the Integration of Psychology and Theology. Millwood, N.Y.: Kraus International Publications, 1982.

This bibliography focuses on the conceptual-theoretical integration of psychology and the Judeo-Christian theological tradition. The items chosen for inclusion concentrate on theoretical issues and philosophical foundations, while also providing an accurate historical overview. Topics covered include the meaning of key terms, philosophical theology, philosophical psychology, hermeneutics, biblical psychology and anthropology, pastoral counseling. Entries in each section are arranged chronologically, and full bibliographical details plus annotations are provided, as is an index of contributors and translators. See also Capps (G1442) and Meissner (G1493).

G1538   Viney, Wayne; Wertheimer, Michael; and Wertheimer, Marilyn Lou, eds. History of Psychology: A Guide to Information Sources. Psychology Information Guide Series, vol. 1. Detroit, Mich.: Gale Research Company, 1979.

This 502 page guide provides a selective but exhaustive coverage of reference materials on the history of psychology. Nearly 3000 entries, of which 1200 are annotated, are arranged in five sections: general references, references in the history of psychology, systems and schools of psychology, histories and major works in selected content areas of psychology, histories of related fields. See also Louttit (G1490).

G1539   White, Rhea A., and Dale, Laura A. Parapsychology: Sources of Information. Comp. under the auspices of the American Society for Psychical Research. Metuchen, N.J.: Scarecrow Press, 1973.

This annotated list of recent and out-of-print English language books on parapsychology and related areas includes about 300 items. In addition

to the bibliography there are sections treating parapsychology in encyclopedias, parapsychological organizations, periodicals, a chronology and
a glossary of terms.

G1540   The Year Book of Psychiatry and Applied Mental Health. Chicago,
Ill.: Yearbook Medical Publishers, 1970- ; annual.

Containing more than 400 informative abstracts with signed editorial
comments in twenty-five sections, this compilation seeks to highlight
emerging trends for practitioners and counselors involved in mental
health work. Covering such areas as alcoholism, social psychiatry and
behavior therapy, it is a useful guide to current thought in a number
of fields relevant to counseling. See also Mental Health Book Review
Index (G1499).

G1541   Zimpfer, David G. Group Work in the Helping Professions: A Bibliography. Washington, D.C.: Association for Specialists in Group Work of the
American Personnel and Guidance Association, 1976.

COUNSELING: DICTIONARIES

G1542   American Psychiatric Association. Committee on Public Information.
A Psychiatric Glossary: The Meaning of Terms Frequently Used in Psychiatry.
4th ed. New York: Basic Books, 1975.

The fourth edition of this guide contains basic and concise definitions
of approximately 1400 terms used in psychiatry. It is a useful dictionary
for those unfamiliar with the field and should be used as a starting
point rather than a detailed guide. See also Brussel (G1545).

G1543   Arnold, Wilhelm, et al., eds. Lexikon der Psychologie. 3 vols. Freiburg
im Breisgau: Herder, 1971-1972.

This alphabetically arranged series of articles is printed in double columns,
and many of the entries run to several columns. Each article includes
a short bibliography as well as numerous cross references. Brief biographies of the most significant personalities are provided. This is a standard,
German language, encyclopedic handbook. See also Dorsch (G1549),
Hehlmann (G1559) and Sury (G1571).

G1544   Beigel, Hugo G. Dictionary of Psychology and Related Fields, German-
English. New York: Frederick Ungar Publishing Company; London: Harrap,
1971.

Intended for practitioners and scholars with limited knowledge of German
but who frequently consult German language professional literature,
this dictionary contains about 10,000 entry words. Each provides the
name of originator, country of origin, gender and idiom, as well as English
equivalent. English definitions are given occasionally. A similar work
for French terms has been prepared by Castonguay (G1546).

G1545   Brussel, James Arnold, and Cantzlaar, George La Fond. The Layman's
Dictionary of Psychiatry. New York: Barnes and Noble, 1967.

This dictionary defines terms in clear, nontechnical language for the general user. Definitions are basic but accurate, providing a suitable guide for students unfamiliar with the field. Coverage is more adequate than the American Psychiatric Association guide (G1542). The British edition is entitled Chambers's Dictionary of Psychiatry (London: Chambers, 1967). See also Hinsie and Campbell (G1560).

G1546   Castonguay, Jacques. Dictionary of Psychology and Related Sciences: English-French/Dictionnaire de la Psychologie et de Sciences Connexes: Français-Anglais. St. Hyacinthe, Québec: Edisim; Paris: Maloine, 1973 [i.e. 1972].

This dictionary consists of two parts (French-English, English-French) containing about 9000 terms in each. The entries provide equivalents only and so are of value only for quick reference or in translation work. The originators of terms are indicated where known. See Piéron (G1568) for a more adequate French dictionary. Beigel (G1544) is a suitable German equivalent.

G1547   Chaplin, James Patrick. Dictionary of Psychology. Rev. ed. New York: Dell Publishing Coompany, 1975.

First published in 1968, this 576 page dictionary provides brief but accurate definitions of technical terms used in psychology. Items from the related disciplines of psychiatry, psychoanalysis and biology are included where their usage in psychology is frequent. This is a suitable work for quick reference by those needing basic definitions. See also Drever (G1550) and Harriman (G1557).

G1548   Deutsch, Albert, ed.-in-chief. Encyclopedia of Mental Health. Executive ed.: Helen Fishman. 6 vols. New York: Franklin Watts, 1963. Reprint. 6 vols. Metuchen, N.J.: Scarecrow Press, 1970.

This compendium is written for the nonspecialist by a number of recognized authorities in the field of mental health. Arranged in dictionary format, it discusses 170 topics in question-and-answer arrangement. Volume 6 contains a list of agencies, an inadequate bibliography, glossary and indexes of subjects and names. In the area of mental health this is one of the most suitable compilations for general inquiries and is admirably suited to the needs of pastoral counselors. See also Goldenson (G1555).

G1549   Dorsch, Friedrich. Psychologisches Wörterbuch. Hrsg. in Verbindung mit C. Becker-Carus. 9 Aufl. Bern: H. Huber, c.1976.

This is the standard German psychological dictionary. It defines terms concisely, clearly and accurately, including many cross references. There is also an excellent bibliography (pp. 729-773) which lists most important psychological studies, particularly continental works. See also Arnold (G1543), Hehlmann (G1559) and Sury (G1571).

G1550   Drever, James. A Dictionary of Psychology. Rev. ed. Rev. by Harvey Wallerstein. Baltimore, Md.: Penguin Books, 1964.

Initially published in 1952, this revision by Wallerstein usefully updates the original work and provides concise definitions of some 4000 psychological terms. It is accurate and reasonably detailed, serving as an excellent dictionary for a wide range of users. There are adequate cross references, and terms in German and other languages receive some attention. Biographical notes are not included, but there are entries for the various schools. See also Chaplin (G1547) and English and English (G1552).

G1551   Eidelberg, Ludwig, ed. Encyclopedia of Psychoanalysis. New York: Free Press; London: Collier-Macmillan, 1968.

In 571 pages this dictionary presents detailed definitions and interpretations of 642 terms used in psychoanalysis. Most entries include bibliographies, cross references and suggestions for further reading. The work is well indexed and provides more substantial definitions than Drever (G1550) and similar dictionaries. A bibliography of 1500 items includes all books and articles up to 1963 cited in the main entries. See also English and English (G1552) and Ryecroft (G1569).

G1552   English, Horace Bidwell, and English, Ava Champney. A Comprehensive Dictionary of Psychological and Psychoanalytical Terms: A Guide to Usage. New York: Longman, Green and Company, 1958.   Reprint. New York: McKay, 1964.

Combining terms from psychology and psychiatry, this excellent guide defines more than 12,000 terms frequently used in these fields, with emphasis on the psychological field. There are also 287 longer articles which define and compare a group of related terms or comment on terminological problems. This is a valuable dictionary which defines terms clearly and fully. Particularly helpful is the provision of one set of definitions for the nonspecialist and another for the psychologist. Probably the best compilation of its kind, this dictionary is more comprehensive than either Dreve (G1550) or Warren (G1572). See also Laplanche and Pontalis (G1564) for a French work on the subject.

G1553   Eysenck, H.J.; Arnold, W.; and Meili, R., eds. Encyclopedia of Psychology. 3 vols. New York: Herder and Herder; London: Search Press, 1972.

This important attempt to unify American and European viewpoints in psychology contains two types of entries. Concise dictionary definitions provide simple explanations of terms, while the 282 articles cover important concepts, terms and personalities in greater detail. Most articles are signed, and many include bibliographies for further reference. Some of the dictionary definitions are too brief, and there is no index. Useful for both the specialist and general user, the compilation has been published in German, French, Spanish, Italian and Portuguese editions. See English and English (G1552) for generally more adequate definitions.

G1554   Ferm, Vergilius Ture Anselm. A Dictionary of Pastoral Psychology. New York: Philosophical Library, 1955.

Wider in scope than suggested by the title, this compilation covers a range of topics of interest to those engaged in a wide variety of clerical activities.   While the focus is on the general field of psychology, it also covers such practical topics as visitation, counseling, sermon preparation and preaching. There are some longer entries in the fields of pastoral counseling and religion and mental health. Arrangement is alphabetical, and there are adequate cross references.

G1555   Goldenson, Robert M. The Encyclopedia of Human Behavior; Psychology, Psychiatry and Mental Health. 2 vols. Garden City, N.Y.: Doubleday
and Company, 1970.

Approximately 1000 entries arranged in dictionary format define and
discuss terms, theories, treatment techniques and personalities important
in the major fields of human behavior. Bibliographies are not included
with individual articles, but references are made to publications cited
in full in the bibliographical section (pp. 1384-1432). Articles on psychiatric disorders include illustrative cases, and there are numerous cross
references. There is an index plus a category index listing articles grouped
by related subject matter. See also Wolman (G1574) for a dictionary
of similar scope.

G1556   Gruenberg, Sidonie Mastner, ed. The New Encyclopedia of Child
Care and Guidance. Garden City, N.Y.: Doubleday and Company, 1968.

This revision of The Encyclopedia of Child Care and Guidance (Rev.
ed. Garden City, N.Y.: Doubleday and Company, 1963) is a substantial
(1016pp.) encyclopedic dictionary concerned with all aspects of child
development: physical, psychological, educational, emotional, cultural
and spiritual. The broadly nontechnical coverage is arranged in two
parts. The first is an encyclopedia with moderately long articles under
specific headings; this includes many cross references, agencies and
organizations, suggestions for further reading. The second part contains
a multi-chapter survey of the background to child development, and
both sections are linked by cross references. In terms of counseling
and related work the first part is most useful; the articles are succinct
and clearly written.

G1557   Harriman, Philip Lawrence, comp. and ed. Dictionary of Psychology.
3rd ed. London: Peter Owen, 1972.

Published in earlier editions as The New Dictionary of Psychology, this
basic dictionary provides brief definitions of the more common psychological terms. Where possible, the person responsible for the concept is
indicated, as is the date of origin. The definitions are clear and nontechnical but generally lack enough detail to suit advanced users. See
also Chaplin (G1547) and Harriman's Handbook (G1558).

G1558   Harriman, Philip Lawrence. Handbook of Psychological Terms. Totowa,
N.J.: Littlefield, Adams, 1965.

Similar to Drever (G1550), this work published in a first edition in 1959
is intended for undergraduates and others interested in psychology. It
offers brief definitions of some 4000 terms which have special meaning
in psychology. Technical terms are defined clearly and in nonspecialist
language. See also Harriman's Dictionary of Psychology (G1557).

G1559   Hehlmann, Wilhelm. Wörterbuch der Psychologie. 5. Aufl. Kröners
Taschenausgabe, Bd. 269. Stuttgart: A. Kröner, 1968.

This dictionary contains fairly lengthy definitions of some 4000 terms.
It includes brief biographical information on internationally recognized

psychologists with a partial listing of their works and of works about them. There is also a chronology of psychology from ancient times to the present, as well as a bibliography of standard works in psychology. For readers of German interested in fairly technical aspects of the field or in personalities this is a useful compendium. See also Arnold (G1543), Dorsch (G1549) and Sury (G1571).

G1560 Hinsie, Leland Earl, and Campbell, Robert Jean. Psychiatric Dictionary. 4th ed. New York: Oxford University Press, 1970.

This thorough revision of a standard work first published in 1940 is a multidisciplinary guide defining 9600 concepts in philosophy, science and other fields which impinge upon psychiatry, as well as standard psychiatric terms. Mental retardation, social services, occupational therapy and clinical neurology are among the areas covered. Pronunciation, explanations, illustrative quotations and bibliographic references are included. Hinsie is particularly suitable for those engaged in psychiatric counseling, as the concise definitions concentrate on practical rather than theoretical aspects. See also American Psychiatric Association (G1542) and Brussel and Cantzlaar (G1545).

G1561 Keienburg, Wolf, ed. Die Psychologie des 20. Jahrhunderts. Planung des Gesamtwerkes, Heinrich Balmer; Koordination des Gesamtwerkes, Gerhard Strube. Bd. 1- . Zürich: Kindler, 1976- .

Projected as a fifteen volume work with 1200 pages per volume, this massive encyclopedia represents an effort by European scholars to survey and condense main issues and movements of twentieth century psychology into a series of key topics. Each volume deals with a specific dimension, subdivision or allied field (e.g., Freud, Piaget, medicine, teaching); of particular interest in theological terms is volume 15 on "Imagination, Kreativitat und Transzendenz". Each volume has a separate subject and author index plus a glossary. For those willing to cope with an often heavy literary style, this reference work is a useful guide to many topics of relevance in pastoral psychology and counseling. See also Lersh (G1565).

G1562 Klein, Barry T., ed. Reference Encyclopedia of American Psychology and Psychiatry. Rye, N.Y.: Todd Publications, 1975.

See also Goldenson (G1555).

G1563 Lafon, Robert, et al. Vocabulaire de Psycho-Pédagogie et de Psychiatrie de l'Enfant. 2e éd. Paris: Presses Universitaires de France, 1969.

First published in 1964 as the work of nearly two dozen specialists, this dictionary contains signed definitions of about 2000 terms. There are numerous cross references, as well as German, English, Spanish and Italian equivalents of entry terms. Etymologies are provided, and occasionally short bibliographies are appended to articles. This is a very serviceable dictionary for those working in French.

G1564 Laplanche, Jean, and Pontalis, J.-B. Vocabulaire de la Psychoanalyse. 3e éd. Sous la direction de Daniel Lagache. Paris: Presses Universitaires de France, 1971.

First published in 1967, this vocabulary contains about 250 entries, each of which is defined in detail and discussed briefly. The German, English, Spanish, Italian and Portuguese equivalents are provided for each word, and there are French and German concept indexes.   See also English and English (G1552) for an English language work on the subject.

G1565   Lersch, Philipp, et al., eds. Handbuch der Psychologie in 12 Bänden. Vol. 1- . Göttingen: Verlag für Psychologie, C.J. Hogrefe, 1959- .

Each volume in this substantial German handbook consists of long articles on a different aspect of psychology (including general psychology, perception and learning, developmental psychology, study and theories of personality, psychological diagnosis, methods, educational psychology, industrial psychology). The articles are written by recognized authorities and include lengthy bibliographies, focusing particularly on continental literature. Each volume contains author and subject indexes. For advanced students with knowledge of German this is an important compendium. See also Dorsch (G1549), Hehlmann (G1559), Keienburg (G1561) and Sury (G1571).

G1566   Narramore, Clyde Maurice. An Encyclopedia of Psychological Problems. Grand Rapids, Mich.: Zondervan Publishing House, 1966.

This nontechnical guide covers the physical causes of psychological problems, analysis of modern psychological disorders and various factors contributing to them. It is more discursive than encyclopedic and exhibits a tendency towards theological literalism. For conservative clergy who are not familiar with the field this is an adequate guide but should not be used to the exclusion of more scientific compilations. See also Goldenson (G1555).

G1567   Nordby, Vernon J., and Hall, Calvin S. A Guide to Psychologists and Their Concepts. San Francisco, Calif.: W.H. Freeman, 1974.

This guide for the general reader presents brief biographies of forty-two psychologists whose work has been important in contemporary psychology; in addition the principal concepts developed by these individuals are set forth briefly and clearly. For very basic inquiries Nordby has some value but should not be used in place of more substantial dictionaries. See also Watson (G1573) and Zusne (G1576).

G1568   Piéron, Henri. Vocabulaire de la Psychologie. 4e éd. Remaniée et augmentée sous la direction de François Bresson et Gustave Durup. Paris: Presses Universitaires de France, 1968.

The fourth edition of this work first published in 1951 contains definitions of approximately 6000 terms used in psychology. Where there is no satisfactory French equivalent the German or English term is used. References are given to authors and dates of first use. Eleven appendixes include lists of abbreviations, symbols and related materials, and there is an index of names cited in the definitions. This work is similar to Hehlmann (G1559) in level of definitions, although biographical notes are more prominent in the German volume.

G1569   Ryecroft, Charles. A Critical Dictionary of Psychoanalysis. New York: Basic Books; London: Thomas Nelson and Sons, 1968.

Not simply a collection of definitions, this 189 page work includes an account of the origin, controversies and links of about 500 terms used in analysis. Cross references assist in establishing relationships among words. For those interested in wider aspects of selected psychoanalytic terms this is a helpful compilation, whereas a standard dictionary of psychoanalysis (such as English and English, G1552) is more suited to ordinary inquiries. Included for the assistance of beginning students are an introductory reading list and a selected bibliography (pp. 183-189).

G1570   Stone, Calvin Perry, comp. Abnormal Psychology Glossary: Technical Terms for Beginning Students in Abnormal Psychology, Mental Hygiene and Medical Social Service. Stanford, Calif.: Stanford University Press; London: Oxford University Press, 1954.

First published in 1944 as Glossary of Technical Terms, this brief (24pp.) glossary contains between 600 and 700 short definitions and biographies relevant to the field of abnormal psychology. For the beginner it is a useful dictionary with clear and nontechnical definitions.

G1571   Sury, Kurt F. von. Wörterbuch der Psychologie und Ihrer Grenz-gebiete. Unter Mitarbeit von Willy Canziani. 3. Aufl. Basel: Schwabe, 1967.

This 324 page German language dictionary contains brief definitions of key terms in psychology and closely related disciplines. A separate section covers biographical sketches of deceased psychologists who have made an important contribution to the field. Sury is helpful in defining terms which are European, and particularly German in origin. See also Arnold (G1543), Hehlmann (G1559) and Dorsch (G1549).

G1572   Warren, Howard Crosby. Dictionary of Psychology. Boston, Mass.: Houghton-Mifflin Company, 1934.

This standard dictionary contains definitions of about 7500 English lan-guage terms and foreign language concepts widely used in psychological literature. Although an older and slightly dated work, Warren remains a reliable general guide to the field. Included are eighteen tables cover-ing complexes, phobias and similar topics. There is a bibliography of technical dictionaries and vocabularies in psychology and cognate discip-lines, and useful glossaries list French and German terms with references to their English equivalents. See also English and English (G1552) and Drever (G1550).

G1573   Watson, Robert Irving, ed. Eminent Contributors to Psychology. 2 vols. New York: Springer Publishing Company, 1974-1976.

See also Nordby and Hall (G1567) and Zusne (G1576).

G1574   Wolman, Benjamin B., comp. and ed. Dictionary of Behavioral Science. New York: Van Nostrand Reinhold   Company, 1974.

This substantial volume covers all areas of psychology and closely related fields, including personality, diagnosis and treatment of mental disorders, psychiatry and psychoanalysis. Definitions are simple and concise, with cross references kept to a minimum. The unsigned entries are the work of many contributors. Appendixes treat the classification of mental disorders and ethical standards of psychologists. This is similar in coverage to Goldenson (G1555) but treats the material much more briefly.

G1575   Wolman, Benjamin B., ed. International Encyclopedia of Psychiatry, Psychology, Psychoanalysis and Neurology. 12 vols. New York: Van Nostrand Reinhold Company, 1977.

This authoritative survey of psychological and psychiatric sciences includes lengthy articles on all aspects of the field, both theoretical and applied. Brief bibliographies accompany most entries, and there are numerous cross references. Wolman is thoroughly indexed and serves as a valuable reference work for counselors actively engaged in the practice of psychology. See also Goldenson (G1555).

G1576   Zusne, Leonard. Names in the History of Psychology: A Biographical Sourcebook. Washington, D.C.: Hemisphere Publishing Corporation, 1975.

Covering the period from 540 B.C. to 1961, this chronologically arranged compilation contains biographies of 526 notable figures in the history of psychology. Each entry includes key biographical data together with details of specific contributions made to the study of psychology. Zusne is a valuable source of information for basic but somewhat detailed inquiries and is well indexed.   For a more limited biographical guide see Nordby and Hall (G1567), which treats only modern figures; see also Watson (G1573).

COUNSELING: HANDBOOKS

G1577   Adams, Jay Edward. The Christian Counselor's Casebook. Grand Rapids, Mich.: Baker Book House, 1975.

Designed for use with The Christian Counselor's Manual (G1578), this presents about 100 counseling situations with questions to help the reader decide how to deal with the case. It is intended to provide practice in identifying problems according to biblical norms, in formulating appropriate plans of action and in providing familiarity with various counseling problems.

G1578   Adams, Jay Edward. The Christian Counselor's Manual. Grand Rapids, Mich.: Baker Book House, 1973.

This sequel to Competent to Counsel (G1579) deals with the principles and techniques of pastoral counseling from a biblically oriented, conservative Protestant standpoint. Three parts deal with persons involved in the counseling process, with principles, and with specific problems and issues. The book is useful in its discussion of mechanical aspects of counseling, and stimulating in its efforts to bring scripture into the counseling process. Its rejection of psychological principles will pose problems for those wishing to use a more integrative approach to theology and psychology. See also the companion Casebook (G1577) and Crabb (G1613).

G1579   Adams, Jay Edward. Competent to Counsel. Grand Rapids, Mich.: Baker Book House, 1970.

This conservative approach to counseling uses the Bible as basic, and advocates "nouthetic counseling", involving a direct, confrontational approach in which the wrong in a person's life is indicated and an effort made to bring the person's behavior into conformity with biblical principles. The work has been criticized for rejecting Freudian and other theories only on the basis of secondary sources and without proper understanding of their nature, methodology or use. See also Crabb (G1613).

G1580   Alexander, Franz Gabriel, and Selesnick, Sheldon T. The History of Psychiatry: An Evaluation of Psychiatric Thought and Practice from Prehistoric Times to the Present. New York: Harper and Row, 1966.

This comprehensive history of 471 pages is divided into four parts: the age of psychiatry, from ancient times through the modern era, the Freudian age, recent developments. A bibliography (pp. 431-451) supplements the sources cited in notes (pp. 415-430), and the work is thoroughly indexed. The volume is well written and provides an excellent historical background to modern psychiatric practice. See also Arieti (G1584) and Nicholi (G1663).

G1581   American Psychiatric Association. Biographical Directory of Fellows and Members. Ed. 1- . New York: R.R. Bowker, 1941- ; irregular.

This compilation lists more than 20,000 American psychiatrists and overseas members of the Association. Entries provide information on training, experience, speciality, publications and similar data. Introductory material includes information on the development of the Association, and there is a geographical index.

G1582 American Psychological Association. Biographical Directory. Washington, D.C.: American Psychological Association, 1970- ; triennial.

Superseding the Association's Directory, which itself replaced the Yearbook, this compendium lists all members of the Association and gives brief biographical data for each person. There is both a geographical index and a divisional membership roster. The appendix covers psychological laws in North America, taxonomy of psychological specialties and abbreviations. Introductory material includes background information and bylaws of the Association, as well as ethical standards of psychologists. See also Duijker and Jacobson (G1620).

G1583   American Rehabilitation Foundation. Institute for Interdisciplinary Studies. Senior Centers in the United States: A Directory. Washington, D.C.: Government Printing Office, 1970.

This successor to the 1966 publication, National Directory of Senior Centers, is a state-by-state listing of more than 1200 centers which offer various programs for older people. Entries are limited to designated facilities which are open three or more days per week. This is the most complete guide of its kind and is particularly useful for counselors and clergy wishing to know what is available locally. See also National Conference of Catholic Charities (G1661).

G1584   Arieti, Silvano, ed.-in-chief. American Handbook of Psychiatry. 2nd ed. 6 vols. New York: Basic Books, 1974-1975.

These six volumes present a survey of developments, trends, techniques and problems in modern American psychiatry. Like the initial three volume collection of 1959-1966 this is an important guide to current activity. Selected bibliographies are included with individual sections. Each chapter is devoted to a single subject and provides an encyclopedic survey of activities relevant to the particular topic. Name and subject indexes are included, making Arieti a valuable reference set on psychiatric research and trends. This work usefully updates standard but older psychiatric encyclopedias and should be regarded as rather limited in the time span of material treated. S ee also Alexander and Selesnick (G1580) and Nicholi (G1663).

G1585   Arnold, William V. Introduction to Pastoral Care. Philadelphia, Pa.: Westminster Press, 1982.

This 221 page work focuses on pastoral care rather than on the narrower field of counseling. Emphasis is placed on the theological roots of pastoral duties and on the personal and professional identity of the pastor. Particularly helpful is the description of currently available pastoral resources. See also Lee (G1651).

G1586   Babbitt, Edmond H. The Pastor's Pocket Manual for Hospital and Sickroom. New York: Abingdon-Cokesbury Press, 1949.

See also Faber (G1622).

G1587   Bane, J. Donald, et al., eds. Death and Ministry: Pastoral Care of the Dying and the Bereaved. New York: Seabury Press, 1975.

Designed for clergy and other professionals in their ministry to dying and bereaved persons, this is a collection of contributions, some presented to a symposium on the subject. Papers are presented in four parts: personal perspectives; ministry to the dying; ministry to the bereaved; clergy and the medical professionals. There is no index but the titles of individual papers provide an adequate guide to content. This is a useful collection based on the experiences of many professionals involved in care of the dying and their survivors. See also Bowers (G1593) and Kübler-Ross (G1649).

G1588   Beach, Lee Roy. Psychology: Core Concepts and Special Topics. New York: Holt, Rinehart and Winston, 1973.

See also Kagan and Havemann (G1644) and Kendler (G1647).

G1589   Becker, Russell J. Family Pastoral Care. Successful Pastoral Counseling Series. Englewood Cliffs, N.J.: Prentice-Hall, 1965.

Intended as a handbook for the working pastor, this includes analysis of factors which produce special stress in the family, as well as discussion of techniques involved in family counseling. The book concentrates on the urban or suburban middle class family, and includes practical suggestions for organizing counseling sessions.

G1590   Binstock, Robert H., and Shanas, Ethel, eds. Handbook of Aging and the Social Sciences. With the assistance of associate eds. Vern L. Bengtson et al. The Handbooks of Aging. New York: Van Nostrand Reinhold, 1976.

This broad review of recent research consists of chapters by various specialists on the social aspects of aging, aging and social structure, aging and social systems, aging and interpersonal behavior, aging and social intervention. Each chapter includes an extensive and up-to-date bibliography, and author and subject indexes are provided. For advanced researchers and counselors this is a useful guide. See also Birren and Schaie (G1591).

G1591 Birren, James E., and Schaie, K. Warner, eds. Handbook of the Psychology of Aging. With the assistance of associate eds. Jack Botwinick et al. The Handbooks of Aging. New York: Van Nostrand Reinhold, 1977.

One of three handbooks on aging, this volume is intended as a basic reference work for professionals, policy makers, practitioners and others concerned with the aged, providing a review and source of scientific and professional literature on psychological and behavioral aspects of aging. Organized in four parts, with thirty subdivisions by different specialists in the field, it provides a valuable resource collection. Author and subject indexes are provided. See also Binstock and Shanas (G1590). The third volume in the collection, edited by Caleb E. Finch and Leonard Hayflick, deals with the biology of aging.

G1592 Bovet, Theodore. That They May Have Life: A Handbook on Pastoral Care for the Use of Christian Ministers and Laymen. Trans. by John A. Baker. London: Darton, Longman and Todd, 1964.

Written by a Swiss medical doctor who is also concerned with pastoral ministry, this book sets pastoral theology in a modern context, outlining the varied and complex work of the pastor. It also contains much psychological teaching. This is a useful statement of a continental viewpoint on pastoral care. See also Hiltner and Colston (G1635) and Southard (G1682).

G1593 Bowers, Margaretta K. Counseling the Dying. New York: Harper and Row, 1981.

First published in 1964, this small book provides a useful analysis of the practical, philosophical/ethical and theological issues involved in counseling the dying, as well as an evaluation of the pitfalls and opportunities for counselors. An updated bibliography is included. The work covers the viewpoints of the physician, pastor and clinical psychologist. See also Bane (G1587) and Kübler-Ross (G1649).

G1594 Brand, Ralph A. Simplified Techniques of Counseling: An Aid to Improving the Counseling Techniques of Pastors, Teachers and Christian Workers. Little Rock, Ark.: Baptist Publications Committee, 1972.

See also Drakeford (G1618).

G1595 Brett, George Sidney. A History of Psychology. 3 vols. Muirhead Library of Philosophy. London. Allen and Unwin, 1912-1921. Reprint. Cambridge, Mass.: MIT Press, 1965.

Covering ancient and patristic (vol. 1), medieval and early modern (vol. 2) and modern (vol. 3) psychology, this basic general history is a suitable introductory guide for students unfamiliar with the broad outline of psychological history. Each volume contains bibliographical notes and references; volume 3 includes a list of general works consulted. See also Woodworth (G1694) on contemporary psychology. An updated revision has been edited by R.S. Peters as Brett's History of Psychology (London: Allen and Unwin, 1962); this includes a chapter on twentieth century themes, a bibliography (pp. 769-772) and an index of proper names.

G1596   Brister,   C.W. Pastoral Care in the Church. New York: Harper and Row, 1964.

Providing the historical background for contemporary practice in the parish, this introductory work is intended primarily for theological students but is also a useful review for professionals. It builds upon scriptural understanding of the pastor's role as pastor, and brings the findings of behavioral science to bear on the pastoral task. It attempts to be comprehensive in its coverage. See also Vanderpool (G1688).

G1597   Brown, Ralph. Marriage Annulment: A Practical Guide for Roman Catholics and Others. London: Geoffrey Chapman, 1970.

G1598   Bugelski, Bergen Richard. An Introduction to the Principles of Psychology: An Essay Concerning Understanding Humans. 2nd ed. Indianapolis, Ind.: Bobbs-Merrill, 1973.

This 614 page introductory textbook includes a helpful bibliography (pp. 586-600) for further study. See also Gazzaniga (G1624).

G1599   Capps,   Donald. Pastoral Counseling and Preaching: A Quest for an Integrated Ministry. Philadelphia, Pa.: Westminster Press, 1980.

This examination of the relationship between pastoral counseling and preaching includes use of actual counseling cases and sermons as illustrations. It provides a useful treatment of concept, method and practice. See also Hamilton (G1632).

G1600   Catholic Hospital Association. Guidebook. [Ed. 1-]. St. Louis, Mo.: Catholic Hospital Association, 1974- ; irregular.

This list of Roman Catholic hospitals in the United States provides the address, telephone number, patient capacity, type of facilities provided and administrator's name. Also covered are religious orders involved in health care.

G1601   Charry, Dana. Mental Health Skills for Clergy. Valley Forge, Pa.: Judson Press, 1981.

This work discusses ways of recognizing the symptoms of the psychotic, suicidal or severely depressed person; the dynamics and techniques of referral; guidelines for dealing with drug and alcohol abuse; and the recommending of involuntary commitment. This is a useful guide for those involved in pastoral counseling and mental health care. See also Cosgrove and Mallory (G1611), Hoffmann (G1636) and O'Doherty (G1671).

G1602   Child Abuse and Neglect Programs. Alexandria, Va.: National Technical Information Service for U.S. Department of Health, Education and Welfare, Office of Human Development, Office of Child Development, National Center on Child Abuse and Neglect, 1976- ; approximately semi-annual.

This compilation regularly identifies some 2000 private and public agencies with programs in the field of child abuse and neglect. It is arranged geographically and is indexed by subject, organization and program director. See also Urban Information Interpreters (G1687).

G1603   Christensen, James L. The Pastor's Counseling Handbook. Westwood, N.J.: Fleming H. Revell Company, 1963.

Intended as an easily accessible source of practical, condensed and simplified information for the pastor, this handbook is in three main sections. It deals with resources available to the pastor as counselor, provides guidance for particular situations (psychological problems, family crises, adoption procedures, etc.), and discusses pastoral aid to the mentally ill. A bibliography (pp. 173-176) and an index are provided. As a summary guide this is a handy volume. See also Godin (G1625).

G1604   Clark, Walter Houston. The Psychology of Religion: An Introduction to Religious Behavior. New York: Macmillan Company, 1958.

This work is primarily descriptive, dealing with stages and processes in religious growth and with special topics such as mysticism, prayer, worship. It provides useful material for teachers and ministers, and contains references to other works for more specialized study. See also Oates (G1668) for a more theological approach; see also Thouless (G1684).

G1605   Clebsch, William A., and Jackle, Charles R. Pastoral Care in Historical Perspective: An Essay with Exhibits. Englewood Cliffs, N.J.: Prentice-Hall, 1964.

This comprehensive study covers various emphases in pastoral care over the years. Bibliographical footnotes are included, and historical "exhibits" (excerpts from pastoral care literature of the period under discussion) accompany the text. This is a useful work for those who wish to see pastoral care in a long term perspective.

G1606   Clinebell, Howard John, Jr. Basic Types of Pastoral Counseling. Nashville, Tenn.: Abingdon Press, 1966.

This volume provides a useful guide for ministers to developments in the fields of counseling and psychotherapy. The main part describes types of counseling appropriate to specific circumstances (family, educative, crisis, group counseling, etc.). There are practical suggestions for dealing with particular counseling needs. This is not a book for beginners, but rather a handbook for the minister on methods of applying one's theoretical knowledge in practical instances. See also Oates (G1665).

G1607   Clinebell, Howard John, Jr. Contemporary Growth Therapies: Resources for Actualizing Human Wholeness. Nashville, Tenn.: Abingdon Press, 1981.

The purpose of this survey is to highlight and make readily available the resources for personal and relational growth in several areas of psychotherapy. Clinebell summarizes the tools shaped by traditional, behavior-action, transactional, gestalt, holistic health, family systems and feminist therapies. With each summary are listed helpful suggestions for further reading. Despite the author's own preference for "creative eclecticism", this is a very sound summary of various therapies used in pastoral counseling.

G1608   Cobb, John B., Jr. Theology and Pastoral Care. Creative Pastoral Care and Counseling Series. Philadelphia, Pa.: Fortress Press, 1977.

Written primarily for ministers, but also containing useful material for seminary courses, this work is intended to stimulate innovative app-roaches to counseling. Selected theological ideas are examined and their implications for pastoral care and counseling are discussed in a straight-forward style. Notes and an annotated bibliography are included. This brings together problems of theology and of pastoral care. See also Greeves (G1628) and Thurneysen (G1685).

G1609   Cohen, Lilly; Oppedisano-Reich, Marie; and Geradi, Kathleen Hamilton, comps. and eds. Funding in Aging: Public, Private and Voluntary. 2nd ed. Garden City, N.Y.: Adelphi University Press, 1979.

Primarily of use to research workers and others seeking funding in the field of aging, this American guide is arranged in three sections: federal programs applicable to funding in this area, listed by broad subject; private philanthropic and foundation funding, by source and subject; state listings for various foundations offering program support. The work is indexed by government agency and foundation, and there are useful appendixes. For general handbooks on facilities for the aging see Norback and Nor-back (G1664) and Sourcebook on Aging (G1681).

G1610   Conway, John Donald. What They Ask about Marriage. Chicago, Ill.: Fides Publishers, 1955.

This 322 page guide to marriage and marriage instruction is written in question and answer format. See also Werth and Mihanovich (G1689).

G1611   Cosgrove, Mark P., and Mallory, James D., Jr. Mental Health: A Christian Approach. Christian Free University Curriculum: Psychology Series. Grand Rapids, Mich.: Zondervan Publishing House, 1977.

See also Charry (G1601), Hoffmann (G1636) and O'Doherty (G1671).

G1612   Crabb, Lawrence J., Jr. Basic Principles of Biblical Counseling. Grand Rapids, Mich.: Zondervan Publishing House, 1975.

See also Oates (G1667).

G1613   Crabb, Lawrence J., Jr. Effective Biblical Counseling. Grand Rapids, Mich.: Zondervan Publishing House, 1977.

This work is intended to provide a model of counseling appropriate to the functioning of the local church. It sets out the theoretical and prac-tical bases of the author's counseling approach, including useful sections on basic diagnostic factors and counseling strategy. This is a valuable discussion for those concerned with theology and psychology and the counseling process. See also Adams (G1579).

G1614   Daniel, Robert Strongman, and Louttie, Chauncey McKinley. Professional Problems in Psychology. New York: Prentice-Hall, 1953.

This revision and expansion of Louttit's Handbook of Psychological Literature (Bloomington, Ind.: Principia Press, 1932) is intended for postgraduate students, practitioners and librarians. It covers literature searching, scientific reports and problems faced by professional psychologists. Also included are an annotated bibliography of 300 reference books in psychology, a list of 300 psychological journals, sources for books and other information, a glossary of common abbreviations and indexes of names and subjects. For a less advanced and more bibliographical guide see Bell (G1434); for another related volume see Elliott (G1621).

G1615   Dember, William Norton, and Jenkins, James J. General Psychology: Modeling Behavior and Experience. Englewood Cliffs, N.J.: Prentice-Hall, 1970.

See also Wolman (G1692).

G1616   Devlin, William Joseph. Psychodynamics of Personality Development. Mental Health Series, vol. 6. Staten Island, N.Y.: Alba House, 1965.

See also Hall (G1631).

G1617   Dicks, Russell Leslie. Principles and Practices of Pastoral Care. Successful Pastoral Counseling Series. Englewood Cliffs, N.J.: Prentice- Hall, 1963.

This general introduction to the field of pastoral care is intended for the minister in the local church. The first part deals with principles, the second with practices. These offer much useful advice, and include narratives of actual pastoral encounters. However, the material is not very well organized and much of it is dated. See also Kemp (G1646) and Heasman (G1633).

G1618   Drakeford, John W. Counseling for Church Leaders. Nashville, Tenn.: Broadman Press, 1961.

See also Brand (G1594).

G1619   Draper, Edgar. Psychiatry and Pastoral Care. Successful Pastoral Counseling Series. Philadelphia, Pa.: Fortress Press, 1965.

Intended to assist pastors in making most effective use of professional and personal resources, this stimulating work contains much useful information and many helpful insights. It emphasizes the importance of pastoral diagnosis and discusses pastoral treatment in some detail. It has been criticized for not adequately translating psychiatry into either the language or mode of pastoral work. Nonetheless it provides an interesting approach to the two fields. See also Hyder (G1640) and Lake (G1650).

G1620   Duijker, Hubert C.J., and Jacobson, Eugene H., eds. International Directory of Psychologists Exclusive of the U.S.A. 2nd ed. Prepared by the Committee on Publication and Communication of the International Union of Psychological Science. Assen: Van Gorcum, 1966.

This work admirably complements the American Psychological Association compilation (G1582) and lists 8000 psychologists from seventy-nine countries. Brief biographical data are included in most cases. Arrangement is by country, and entries state specialization and background but not publications of the individual.

G1621   Elliott, Charles Kenneth. A Guide to the Documentation of Psychology. Hamden, Conn.: Linnet Books; London: Clive Bingley, 1971.

This introductory guide for students consists of eight chapters on psychology and related subjects, libraries and classification, functions of information, documentary aids (pp. 33-57), comprehensive searching procedures, current awareness, ordinary reference inquiries, miscellaneous information problems. Appendixes include a list of associations and societies connected with psychology and a selected list of psychological journals. There is an index. See also Daniel and Louttit (G1614) and Sarbin (G1677).

G1622   Faber, Heije. Pastoral Care in the Modern Hospital. Trans. by Hugo de Waal. Philadelphia, Pa.: Westminster Press, 1971.

This book is intended more for the parish minister than the hospital chaplain. It examines problems such as the size and impersonality of the modern hospital, the possible psychological problems of patients, the role of the minister in visiting patients, etc. This provides helpful insights into the particular problems created by the complex nature of the modern hospital. See also Babbitt (G1586).

G1623   Faber, Heije. Psychology of Religion. Trans. by Margaret Kohl. London: SCM Press, 1976.

This study provides a summary of the development of psychology of religion from Freud to Fromm and Erikson, and examines the phases of development described by Freud in relation to the relevance of psychoanalysis for pastoral care. This is perhaps less a handbook of psychology of religion than a psychological thesis supporting a particular theological viewpoint. See also Oates (G1668), Spinks (G1683) and Thouless (G1684).

G1624   Gazzaniga, Michael S. Fundamentals of Psychology: An Introduction. New York: Academic Press, 1973.

See also Bugelski (G1598).

G1625   Godin, André. The Pastor As Counselor. Trans. by Bernard Phillips. New York: Holt, Rinehart and Winston, 1965.

This Roman Catholic work is intended to assist the priest in using modern psychology and psychiatry in the pastoral task. It includes analyses of case studies and actual pastoral conversations, discussion of the author's method of group supervision of young priests, as well as analysis of the role of the counselor in the counseling process. See also Christensen (G1603).

G1626   Goldbrunner, Josef. Realization: Anthropology of Pastoral Care. Trans. by Paul C. Bailey and Elisabeth Reinecke. Liturgical Studies, vol. 9. Notre Dame, Ind.: University of Notre Dame Press, 1966.

Intended primarily for priests and educators, this work focuses on a doctrine of the life of the individual as an aid to evaluating different viewpoints in pastoral theology. After an introductory discussion of the pastoral task, the theory is developed and its implications discussed. An index is provided.

G1627   Greenberg, Dan. U.S. Guide to Nursing Homes. New York: Grosset and Dunlap, 1970.

Issued in three separate editions for eastern, midwestern and western states, this listing is arranged by state and then by city or town. It is a sound reference volume for counselors and clergy requiring information on nursing homes. There are useful data on points to be considered in choosing (or recommending) a home. See also Musson (G1657) and National Council on the Aging (G1662).

G1628   Greeves, Frederic. Theology and the Cure of Souls: An Introduction to Pastoral Theology. The Cato Lecture of 1960. Manhasset, N.Y.: Channel Press, 1962.

Concerned primarily with the relationship between Christian doctrine and pastoral care, this work examines particular doctrines in relation to the cure of souls, and Christian experience in this area. The role of pastors and laymen in pastoral care is discussed. See also Cobb (G1608), Thurneysen (G1685) and Williams (G1690).

G1629   Gunn, John Charles, comp. A Directory of World Psychiatry. London: World Psychiatric Association, 1971.

Covering eighty-nine countries, this compilation provides for each country data on psychiatric services, main public psychiatric hospitals, university departments and local psychiatric journals. There is also a list of national psychiatric associations and a list of materials for further reference.

G1630   Cuntrip, Henry James Samuel. Psychology for Ministers and Social Workers. 3rd ed. London: Allen and Unwin, 1971.

This 262 page standard textbook provides an introduction to pastoral and social psychology, giving ministers and social workers an indication of the possibilities in relation to their work. There are two main parts, one concerned with practical and one with theoretical issues. A brief bibliography (pp. 290-292) and an index are included. Guntrip provides a balanced approach that gives due concern to theory and practice. See also James (G1642).

G1631   Hall, Calvin Springer, and Lindzey, Gardner. Theories of Personality. New York: John Wiley and Sons, 1957.

This volume contains an excellent review of theories of personality as well as useful introductory and concluding chapters. Seventeen major theorists are considered, with biography and background information, the theorist's views on personality, representative studies and empirical techniques, current status and an evaluation of the theory provided for each. The presentations are clear and objectively written. This is a useful guide to the pastor and will provoke questions regarding the implications for Christian theology of the various viewpoints. Suggestions for further reading are included. See also Devlin (G1616).

G1632   Hamilton, James D. The Ministry of Pastoral Counseling. Source Books for Ministers. Grand Rapids, Mich.: Baker Book House, 1972.

See also Capps (G1599).

G1633   Heasman, Kathleen J. An Introduction to Pastoral Counselling for Social Workers, the Clergy and Others. London: Constable, 1969.

This introductory handbook deals both with principles and practice, examining relationships, human behavior, the person of the counselor himself, as well as specific problems of counseling the young, the mentally ill, the elderly and other groups. As an elementary work on the subject this is of interest to those seeking basic information. See also Dicks (G1617) and Kemp (G1646).

G1634   Heck, Edward T.; Gomez, Angel G.; and Adams, George L. A Guide to Mental Health Services. Pittsburgh, Pa.: University of Pittsburgh Press, 1973.

This guide presents basic but comprehensive information on mental health services, treatments and practitioners in the United States. It includes a chapter on selected sources of mental health information, which lists national agencies and suggests possible sources at both state and local levels. See also United States. National Institute of Mental Health (G1686).

G1635   Hiltner, Seward, and Colston, Lowell G. The Context of Pastoral Counseling. New York: Abingdon Press, 1961.

Designed primarily for the working pastor, this offers a useful resource book on pastoral counseling. It is based on research on counseling in church and secular settings, and includes examination of various contextual dimensions (setting, expectation, shift in relationship, relation of aims to limitations). Although some of the work is quite technical, it contains helpful insights and is instructive regarding the minister in his pastoral and counseling role. See also Bovet (G1592).

G1636   Hoffmann, Hans F. The Ministry and Mental Health. New York: Association Press, 1960.

See also Charry (G1601), Cosgrove and Mallory (G1611) and O'Doherty (G1671).

G1637   Hostie, Raymond. Pastoral Counseling. Trans. by Gilbert Barth. New York: Sheed and Ward, 1966.

Intended particularly for priests with little or no training in psychology, this work includes some useful insights and techniques for those involved in pastoral counseling. It describes the various stages of the pastoral dialogue, and gives examples and suggests procedures. The style is readable and nontechnical. See also Kemp (G1646) and O'Brien (G1670).

G1638   Hulme, William Edward. The Pastoral Care of Families: Its Theology and Practice. New York: Abingdon Press, 1962.

This work begins with an analysis of the pastoral role with regard to the ministry to individuals, and examines ways of carrying out the pastoral ministry. This is then considered in relation to the family and problems of divorce, old age, etc. While it offers a competent grasp of the ministry and its relation to family life, the book has been criticized for its efforts to give a neat theological framework to the assumptions used. See also Mitman (G1656).

G1639 Hulme, William Edward. Your Pastor's Problems: A Guide for Ministers and Laymen. Garden City, N.Y.: Doubleday and Company, 1966.

Setting out to explain to laymen the experience of being a parish minister, this brief work deals with aspects such as the layman and his view of authority, cultural pressures on a minister, personal tensions, the need to be a leader, and related questions.   This is a useful introductory work, although in places it tends to oversimplify. See also Smith (G1680).

G1640   Hyder, O. Quentin. The Christian's Handbook of Psychiatry. Old Tappan, N.J.: Fleming H. Revell Company, 1971.

This handbook sketches the development of psychiatry, then provides a detailed summary of the causes, nature and treatment of more common emotional disorders. Basic psychiatric knowledge is integrated with emphasis on the value of spiritual resources for the maintenance and restoration of psychological health. Hyder provides a clear and readable discussion from a Christian perspective of the complex field of mental disorder. See also Draper (G1619) and Lake (G1650).

G1641   Irwin, Paul B. The Care and Counseling of Youth in the Church. Creative Pastoral Counseling Series. Philadelphia, Pa.: Fortress Press, 1975.

Intended primarily for ministers, although also of interest to the lay reader, this book focuses on typical leadership concerns and situations. It is a practical handbook for those involved with youth, and deals with such aspects as the ministry of individual counseling and of interpersonal communication. An annotated bibliography is included.

G1642   James, D.E. Introduction to Psychology for Teachers, Nurses and Other Social Workers. 2nd ed. London: Constable, 1970.

See also Guntrip (G1630).

G1643   Johnson, Paul Emanuel. Person and Counselor. Nashville, Tenn.: Abingdon Press, 1967.

This work, which stresses the importance of responsive counseling, develops a pastoral model and provides guidelines for counseling from the moment help is sought.   Although the style is rather wordy, the book includes helpful material on techniques for the pastor. See also Simons and Reidy (G1679).

G1644   Kagan, Jerome, and Havemann, Ernest. Psychology: An Introduction. 2nd ed. New York: Harcourt Brace Jovanovich, 1972.

See also Beach (G1588) and Kendler (G1647).

G1645   Katz, David, and Katz, Rosa, eds. Kleines Handbuch der Psychologie. 3. Aufl. Unter Mitwerk von Albert Ackermann et al. Basel: Schwabe, 1972.

This work was published in earlier editions as Handbuch der Psychologie.

G1646   Kemp, Charles F. A Pastoral Counseling Guidebook. Nashville, Tenn.: Abingdon Press, 1971.

This is a useful handbook for the pastor who wishes to update his knowledge of pastoral counseling. It contains sections on the pastoral counselor and his people, and on principles and procedures, with discussion of more than fifty topics. Appendixes include various checklists and forms, and there is a valuable 30 page annotated bibliography. As a guide to literature and practices in this field, this is a handy work. See also Dicks (G1617) and Heasman (G1633).

G1647   Kendler, Howard Harvard. Basic Psychology. 3rd ed. Menlo Park, Calif.: W.A. Benjamin, 1974.

First published in 1963, this updated edition aims to draw a clear, comprehensive and organized picture of contemporary psychology. It is aimed at students on introductory psychology courses. It examines basic psychological processes, more complex processes such as memory, individual differences, social behavior and related issues. A bibliography and indexes are provided. See also Beach (G1588) and Kagan and Havemann (G1644).

G1648   Koch, Sigmund, ed. Psychology: A Study of a Science. Vol. 1- . New York: McGraw-Hill Book Company, 1959- .

Growing out of a 1952 decision by the American Psychological Association to encourage the preparation of a thorough and critical examination of the status and development of psychology, this encyclopedic handbook devotes each volume to a major topic. Each of these is discussed by a number of contributors from various viewpoints, offering resumés, criticisms, projections and specialized analyses. For advanced students this is a valuable compendium similar in many respects to Lersch (G1565).

G1649   Kübler-Ross, Elisabeth. On Death and Dying. New York: Macmillan Company, 1969.

Drawing on an interdisciplinary seminar conducted over several years, this work contains introductory chapters on the history of the fear of death and current attitudes towards death and dying, then explores stages through which the dying usually pass (denial, anger, bargaining for an extension of life, depression, acceptance). There are sections on helping the family of the dying, and much case material is used to illustrate the work. See also Bane (G1587) and Bowers (G1593).

G1650   Lake, Frank. Clinical Theology: A Theological and Psychiatric Basis to Clinical Pastoral Care. London: Darton, Longman and Todd, 1966.

See also Draper (G1619) and Hyder (G1640).

G1651   Lee, Roy Stewart. Principles of Pastoral Counselling. Library of Pastoral Care. London: SPCK, 1968.

This introductory work, which reflects a Freudian psychoanalytic view-point, invites readers to reexamine their theology in the light of psychological understanding. It distinguishes pastoral care from pastoral counseling and emphasizes the importance of proper training for the latter. See also Arnold (G1585).

G1652 Liebard, Odile M., comp. Love and Sexuality. Official Catholic Teachings, vol. 2. Wilmington, N.C.: Consortium Books, 1978.

Dealing with a subject of much concern in recent decades, Liebard presents official documents from various Roman Catholic sources; the volume includes papal pronouncements, conciliar decisions and related materials. These are arranged in numbered order and are indexed by subject.

G1653 McLemore, Clinton W. Clergyman's Psychological Handbook: Clinical Information for Pastoral Counseling. Grand Rapids, Mich.: William B. Eerdmans Publishing Company, 1974.

This handbook is intended to provide practical knowledge required for dealing with counseling problems. The four main sections cover modes of dysfunction, dimensions of counseling, counseling procedures, special techniques and problems. A list of references is included after each section, and there is an index. It contains much helpful guidance for the clergyman in his pastoral role. See also Narramore (G1658).

G1654 Misiak, Henryk, and Staudt, Virginia M. Catholics in Psychology: A Historical Survey. New York: McGraw-Hill Book Company, 1954.

Intended as a supplement to standard textbooks in the field, this work is a series of bio-bibliographies of Catholic psychologists of all nations. Some individuals are covered in a single chapter, others grouped in one chapter. It is a good source of information on minor psychologists not covered so thoroughly in other works.

G1655 Mitchell, Kenneth R. Hospital Chaplain. Philadelphia, Pa.: Westminster Press, 1972.

This brief, lively book reveals the typical experiences of the hospital chaplain, making clear to both clergy and the medical profession what his role is.

G1656 Mitman, John L.C. Premarital Counseling: A Manual for Clergy and Counselors. New York: Seabury Press, 1980.

This manual provides useful advice for clergy and counselors involved in premarital counseling. It is not representative of any particular denominational standpoint. See also Hulme (G1638).

G1657 Musson, Noverre. The National Directory of Retirement Residences: Best Places to Live When You Retire. Rev. ed. New York: F. Fell, 1973.

Issued in 1964 and 1968 under different titles, this 214 page guide is not intended primarily as a reference work for professionals but for use by the general public. Nevertheless, it is a helpful compendium which lists on a state-by-state basis those places judged to be suitable for retirement living. There is also information on choosing a retirement home. See also Greenberg (G1622) and National Council on the Aging (G1662).

G1658 Narramore, Clyde Maurice. The Psychology of Counseling: Professional Techniques for Pastors, Teachers, Youth Leaders and All Who Are Engaged in the Incomparable Art of Counseling.   Grand Rapids, Mich.: Zondervan Publishing Company, 1960.

Written for ministers and other Christian counselors, this book concentrates on basic concepts and techniques of counseling, giving considerable detail on the counseling process. There is also a section on special areas of counseling (marriage counseling, the mentally ill, teenagers, etc.). Appendixes include discussion of the use of scripture in counseling and references to books and recordings. There is no index, but the table of contents is quite detailed. See also McLemore (G1653).

G1659 National Conference of Catholic Charities. Directory of Residences for Unwed Mothers. Washington,   D.C.: National Conference of Catholic Charities, 1969.

G1660   National Conference of Catholic Charities. Guides for Services to Children in Catholic Institutions. Washington, D.C.: National Conference of Catholic Charities, 1964.

This is an administrative guide, with a bibliography.

G1661   National Conference of Catholic Charities. Commission on the Aging. Guides for Facilities for the Aging. Washington, D.C.: National Conference of Catholic Charities, 1969.

See also American Rehabilitation Foundation (G1583).

G1662   National Council on the Aging. A National Directory on Housing for Older People, Including a Guide for Selection. Rev. ed. New York: National Council on the Aging, 1969.

This 362 page successor to the 1965 edition is designed to help both retired persons and counselors in discovering suitable facilities. For each facility data include type, fees, location, eligibility requirements and special features. There is also a selection guide which enumerates points to consider when choosing a retirement home. More detailed than Musson (G1657), this is a valuable reference volume. See also Greenberg (G1627).

G1663 Nicholi, Armand M., Jr., ed. The Harvard Guide to Modern Psychiatry. Cambridge, Mass.: Belknap Press, 1978.

This authoritative summary of knowledge in the field of psychiatry is the work of more than thirty specialists. The signed articles are organized under six main headings such as principles of treatment and management and psychiatry and society. Historical summaries are included in several chapters.   References to the literature are included, and an index is provided. This is a technically competent, precise and valuable guide to this field for scholars, students and educators. See also Alexander and Selesnick (G1580) and Arieti (G1584).

G1664   Norback, Craig T., and Norback, Peter G. The Older American's Handbook: Practical Information and Help on Medical and Nursing Care, Housing, Recreation, Legal Services, Employment, In-Home Services, Food Associations and Organizations, Transportation, Mental Health and Counseling for Older and Retired Americans. Consulting ed.: Bernard E. Nash. New York: Van Nostrand Reinhold, 1977.

This subject listing of agencies, programs and publications on all areas of concern to the aging is intended primarily for those seeking information on self-care. It is also of some use to counselors working with older people, but there is no index to facilitate quick reference. See also Cohen (G1609) and Sourcebook on Aging (G1681).

G1665   Oates, Wayne Edward, ed. An Introduction to Pastoral Counseling. Nashville, Tenn.: Broadman Press, 1959.

This collection of papers by ten seminary professors and hospital chaplains of the Southern Baptist Convention is intended for students and for pastors involved in counseling. There are five main divisions, covering counseling in the context of the church, the personhood of the pastoral counselor, the process and procedures of pastoral counseling, pastoral counseling and the ministry of the word of God, and pastoral counseling and the educational intentions of the church. The work is particularly helpful on methods and practical suggestions. It attempts to give a comprehensive coverage of pastoral counseling and as such it is especially useful for teachers opening up this field to students or to clergy seeking a sound introduction to the field. See also Adams (G1578).

G1666   Oates, Wayne Edward. Pastoral Counseling. Philadelphia, Pa.: Westminster Press, 1974.

This volume proposes a strategy and Christian philosophy of pastoral counseling, focusing on the tensions produced by the ambiguity in the identity and function of a pastor. The first chapter asks what makes counseling pastoral, and subsequent chapters spell out eight ambiguities (institutional and personal needs, private and public ministry, etc.). This is a readable account which is not concerned with pastoral counseling techniques but with proposing a model for understanding this aspect of a pastor's work. Ssee also Crabb (G1612, G1613).

G1667   Oates, Wayne Edward. Protestant Pastoral Counseling. Philadelphia, Pa.: Westminster Press, 1962.

This work attempts to provide a theological understanding of pastoral counseling, and includes chapters on topics such as Protestant distinctiveness and pastoral counseling, and some eschatological dimensions of pastoral counseling. It offers a stimulating approach to the minister from a Protestant standpoint. See also Adams (G1578) and Crabb (G1612).

G1668   Oates, Wayne Edward. The Psychology of Religion. Waco, Tex.: Word Books, 1973.

This work contains much useful biblical, theological, philosophical and psychological material on the religious consciousness. It is primarily a textbook which draws widely upon literary and technical sources, written within the psychological context of phenomenology. Some of the material has become dated quite rapidly. See also Clark (G1604) and Pruyser (G1674).

G1669   Oates, Wayne Edward. Where to Go for Help. Rev. ed. Philadelphia, Pa.: Westminster Press, 1972.

First published in 1957, this revision is a 224 page guide for people who want to know where to go for help, for their pastors and other professional counselors. Relevant literature and addresses are listed, in addition to discussion of various problems and appropriate agencies. In two main parts different professions are presented and the main principles of selecting a counselor and finding helpful literature are put forward, and help on special problems is discussed. An index is included. See also Roe (G1675).

G1670   O'Brien, Michael J. An Introduction to Pastoral Counseling. Mental Health Series, vol. 10. Staten Island, N.Y.: Alba House, 1968.

This introductory volume, intended particularly for the parish priest, includes useful guidelines on counseling methods and approaches to be used in various situations. See also Hostie (G1637) and Kemp (G1646).

G1671   O'Doherty, Eamonn Feichin, and McGrath, S. Desmond, eds. The Priest and Mental Health. Staten Island, N.Y.: Alba House, 1963.

This collection of seventeen conference papers, contributed by medical doctors, priests and others, provides an overview of problems met by the priest in the pastoral ministry and of his role in the area of mental health. It includes chapters on personality development, emotional disorders, methods of therapy, and the priest's influence on the mental health of parishioners. Intended for the nonspecialist reader, this provides a useful summary of Roman Catholic thinking on the relationships between religion and mental health. See also Charry (G1601), Cosgrove and Mallory (G1611) and Hoffmann (G1636).

G1672   Oglesby, William B., Jr. Referral in Pastoral Counseling. Successful Pastoral Counseling Series. Philadelphia, Pa.: Fortress Press, 1968.

Discussing when, how and where to refer, this book is helpful to the pastor as counselor. It considers the kinds of problems a minister may face in dealing with special cases, offers guidelines on referral, and stresses the continuing relationship of pastor and parishioner. This is a stimulating contribution to interdisciplinary dialogue.

G1673   Pringle, Mia Lilly, et al., eds. Directory of Voluntary Organisations Concerned with Children. London: Longmans for the National Bureau for Cooperation in Child Care, 1969.

This directory is arranged in seven sections which include an alphabetical listing of voluntary organizations concerned with children and facilities administered by religious communities. A bibliography and name and subject indexes are provided. The work is British in focus. See also National Conference of Catholic Charities (G1660).

G1674   Pruyser, Paul W. A Dynamic Psychology of Religion. New York: Harper and Row, 1968.

This exploration of the full dimensions of religion uses standard psychological concepts to describe, analyze and interpret a variety of religious phenomena. The book includes analysis of how religion relates to perceptual and intellectual processes, thought organization and linguistic functions, emotional and motor processes. Case studies are used to illustrate the argument. This is a stimulating treatment for theologians, philosophers of religion or psychologists. See also Faber (G1623) and Spinks (G1683).

G1675   Roe, John E. A Consumer's Guide to Christian Counseling. Nashville, Tenn.: Abingdon Press, c.1982.

This 143 page guide analyzes dimensions of personal problems (emotional, physical, spiritual, intellectual, social) and appropriate counselors and methods. It provides advice on selecting a counselor, what to expect from a typical counseling session and costs. See also Oates (G1669).

G1676   Rudin, Josef. Psychotherapy and Religion. Trans. by Elisabeth Reinecke and Paul C. Bailey. Notre Dame, Ind.: University of Notre Dame Press, 1968.

Intended for those concerned with the apparent opposition between the insights of psychotherapy and the basic convictions of moral theology, this work deals with such matters as the concept of identification, the idea of freedom and its role in psychotherapy, and problems of defining normality and health. It concentrates on Jungian psychotherapy. The work has been criticized for not adequately meeting the needs of either pastors and pastoral counselors or psychotherapists.

G1677   Sarbin, Theodore R., and Coe, William C. The Student Psychologist's Handbook: A Guide to Sources. Cambridge, Mass.: Schenkman Publishing Company, 1969.

This brief (108pp.) outline resembles Elliott (G1621), covering similar topics in eight chapters: scope of psychological research, writing the research paper, sources of information, using the library, reading research articles, journals and handbooks (pp.53-76), glossary of statistical terms, report preparation. An appendix covers the Dewey and Library of Congress classifications in psychology.

G1678   Sharpe, William Donald. Medicine and the Ministry: A Medical Basis for Pastoral Care. New York: Appleton-Century Crofts, 1966.

This is a useful statement of a modern physician's point of view; it provides a guide for pastors with its wealth of information about physical conditions, emotional states and psychosomatic ailments. It also discusses problems of youth, young adults, sexual deviants, those with troubled marriages, the aged and the dying. As a contribution to understanding the pastor's role in the hospital and in caring for the distressed or diseased, and as an attempt at dialogue between professions, this is a stimulating work.

G1679   Simons, Joseph B., and Reidy, Jeanne. The Human Art of Counseling. New York: Herder and Herder, 1971.

Intended for anyone concerned with counseling, this work emphasizes the counselor's humanity and relationship with the client. Counseling in particular professions is discussed, as well as the counselor working in a group situation. This book does not deal with aspects such as professional preparation or particular schools of thought. See also Johnson (G1643).

G1680   Smith, Donald P. Clergy in the Cross Fire: Coping with Role Conflict in the Ministry. Philadelphia, Pa.: Westminster Press, 1973.

This monograph serves as a suitable handbook for goal setting and review, as well as offering guidance in handling role ambiguities and conflicts. There is a selective but wide ranging bibliography (pp. 223-232) for further study. The book reviews theory and research literature on the functioning of a minister in terms of roles, vocational development and organizational relationships. It contains useful information for clergy, students and others concerned with the welfare and effectiveness of the clergy. See also Hulme (G1639).

G1681   Sourcebook on Aging. Chicago, Ill.: Marquis Academic Media, 1977.

Of special value for its statistical and tabular data, this compilation reprints source materials in ten sections: general aging, health, economic status, housing, employment, education, transportation, leisure and retirement, special concerns, government programs. There are subject and geographical indexes. See also Norback and Norback (G1664).

G1682   Southard, Samuel. Training Church Members for Pastoral Care. Valley Forge, Pa.: Judson Press, 1982.

This 92 page handbook provides guidance for pastors concerned to select and train suitable persons for lay ministry, to win congregational acceptance of such a program, and so on. Bibliographical references are included. See also Vanderpool (G1688).

G1683   Spinks, George Stephens. Psychology and Religion: An Introduction to Contemporary Views. Methuen's Manuals of Modern Psychology. London: Methuen, 1963.

This study of the interrelationship of psychology and religion covers anthropology and primitive religion, the implicit psychologies of religion in Western thought, the psychologies of religion of James, Freud and Jung, and the growth of religious consciousness, prayer, worship, etc. It is primarily theoretical in approach, well supported by studies in comparative religion and nonempirical material on religious history. It is not concerned with pastoral psychology as such. It provides an adequate, brief introduction to the field. See also Clark (G1604) and Thouless (G1684).

G1684   Thouless, Robert Henry. An Introduction to the Psychology of Religion. 3rd ed. London: Cambridge University Press, 1971.

See also Clark (G1604), Faber (G1623) and Oates (G1668).

G1685   Thurneysen, Eduard. A Theology of Pastoral Care. Trans. by Jack A. Worthington and Thomas Wieser. Richmond, Va.: John Knox Press, 1962.

This application of Barthian theology to pastoral care deals with the basis of pastoral care, with its nature and practice and with implementation. It tends to neglect non-European work in this field. The absence of an index is unfortunate. See also Cobb (G1608) and Greeves (G1628).

G1686   United States. National Institute of Mental Health. Mental Health Directory. Washington, D.C.: Government Printing Office, 1977.

First published in 1964, the entries in this guide are arranged geographically by state, city and town or county. As an inventory of mental health facilities, it presents information on services provided by government, private, professional and voluntary organizations. Each entry includes name, address, telephone number and an outline of services offered. For clergy and counselors this is a useful listing of institutions in all regions of the United States. See also Heck (G1634).

G1687   Urban Information Interpreters. The National Children's Directory: An Organizational Directory and Reference Guide for Changing Conditions for Children and Youth. Ed. by Mary Lee Bundy and Rebecca Glenn Whaley. U.I.S.P. Publications, no. 16. College Park, Md.: Urban Information Interpreters, 1977.

Limited to United States coverage, this directory identifies approximately 700 national and local groups whose concern is with improving conditions for children and youth. Each entry describes the objectives, activities, publications, background and membership of the organization. There are title and subject indexes, as well as a classified bibliography of 300 titles. This is a valuable resource guide for all who are engaged in work with youth. See also National Conference of Catholic Charities (G1660) and Pringle (G1673).

G1688   Vanderpool, James A. Person to Person: A Handbook for Pastoral Counseling. Garden City, N.Y.: Doubleday and Company, 1977.

This handbook is intended as an aid to the pastor in many areas of counseling, and is concise and very readable. It examines pastoral theology and pastoral counseling and the counseling process, discusses counseling in relation to different age groups, from the child to the elderly or dying, and considers pastoral counseling and spiritual and moral values. A bibliography is included. See also Brister (G1596).

G1689   Werth, Alvin, and Mihanovich, Clement S. Papal Pronouncements on Marriage and Family from Leo XIII to Pius XII (1878-1954). Milwaukee, Wisc.: Bruce Publishing   Company, 1955.

This collection of excerpts contains material from papal pronouncements and similar documents dealing with the origin and nature of marriage, its purpose and function, the family and family life. Brief analysis of documents, references to the complete text, a general index and a bibliography are all provided to make the work more useful. See also Conway (G1610).

G1690   Williams, Daniel Day. The Minister and the Care of Souls. New York: Harper and Row, 1961.

This theological interpretation of the work of the ministry places all pastoral care in the context of the church. It is a useful blend of theology and psychology. A bibliography is included. See also Greeves (G1628).

G1691 Wolman, Benjamin, B., ed. Handbook of Developmental Psychology. Associate ed.: George Strickler. Englewood Cliffs, N.J.: Prentice-Hall, 1982.

The fifty chapters in this 960 page handbook survey the areas of major importance in developmental psychology, including research methodologies, infancy, childhood, adolescence, adulthood, aging. Each chapter is well organized and highly informative, making an excellent sourcebook and reference text in its field.

G1692 Wolman, Benjamin B., ed. Handbook of General Psychology. Englewood Cliffs, N.J.: Prentice-Hall, 1973.

See also Dember and Jenkins (G1615).

G1693 Wolman, Benjamin B., ed. Handbook of Parapsychology. New York: Van Nostrand Reinhold Company, 1977.

This handbook presents rather uneven treatment of various aspects of parapsychology in a series of thirty-four chapters by various contributors. The sections on research methods are particularly valuable, while those on parapsychological phenomena are rather unreliable and unscholarly. The frequent references to recent literature in the field are most useful, and the work is well indexed. Overall Wolman should be used with discretion by those with some understanding of parapsychology; it is not a reference work for beginners.

G1694 Woodworth, Robert Sessions, and Sheehan, Mary R. Contemporary Schools of Psychology. 3rd ed. New York: Ronald Press Company, 1964.

Dealing with schools established in the twentieth century (up to about 1960), this survey provides succinct explanations of theories and includes many cross references. Each school or movement is treated in a separate chapter, and some of these can be particularly useful for students of pastoral psychology in the broadest sense. There is an author index and an analytical subject index. For a history of psychology see Brett (G1595).

G1695 Zumbro Valley Medical Society. Medicine and Religion Committee, comp. Religious Aspects of Medical Care: A Handbook of Religious Practices of All Faiths. St. Louis, Mo.: Catholic Hospital Association, 1975.

Covering forty-three distinct religious groups, this useful guide discusses basic religious beliefs vis-à-vis medical care and treatment from a practical standpoint. Abortion, birth control, euthanasia, medical engineering, transplants are all treated at a fairly basic level. This is useful primarily to familiarize counselors with various beliefs rather than to provide detailed pastoral treatment of what religious groups teach.

Sociology

G1696   Abstracts in Anthropology. Vol. 1- . Farmingdale, N.Y.: Baywood
Publishing Company, 1971/1972- ; quarterly.

This quarterly abstracting service arranges entries under four main headings: archeology, cultural anthropology, linguistics, physical anthropology.
Cultural anthropology is subdivided into fourteen subjects, of which
one deals with religion in particular. The compilation is international
in coverage and treats som 200 journals annually (with a 50 per cent
increase proposed for volume 8). Of the nearly 4000 abstracts each
year only a small proportion deals directly with religion, but many of
the entries under cultural anthropology deal marginally with topics of
interest to Christian anthropology. The subject index in each issue lists
many of these entries not found under the religion subdivision. There
is also an author index and a list of periodicals covered in each issue.
The coverage of each volume is limited to that particular year, and
the abstracts themselves are not only very concise but also include
full bibliographical details. Abstracts in Anthropology provides much
useful information of a scholarly nature on anthropological aspects of
all religions.

G1697 L'Année Sociologique. Vol. 1- . Paris: Presses Universitaires de France,
1948- ; annual.

Covering 1896-1925 in the 1948 edition and gradually bringing coverage
more up-to-date in each annual volume, this serial consists largely of
a selective survey of significant sociological literature arranged in several
sections (including sociology of religion). Each issue contains 200-300
reviews of varying length, and there is an author index. As an abstracting/
review service devoted to current literature, this is a reasonably helpful
guide for those trying to keep abreast of publications in sociology. See
also International Bibliography of Sociology (G1733).

G1698   Annual Review of Anthropology. Vol. 1- . Palo Alto, Calif.: Annual
Reviews, 1972- .

This successor to the Biennial Review of Anthropology (G1704) describes and evaluates a wide range of recent anthropological publications. Each chapter covers a specific topic of current interest in physical, social and cultural anthropology and includes a full bibliography of the works discussed. Although the focus is on works in English, coverage is international, and there are both subject and author indexes.   This is an important service for researchers and advanced students, discussing topics of some interest to various aspects of the anthropology of religion. It is much more useful in this area than Abstracts in Anthropology (G1696), which is concerned mainly with physical and ethnological aspects of anthropology. See also Reviews in Anthropology (G1765).

G1699   Astin, Helen S.; Suniewick, Nancy; and Dweck, Susan. Women : A Bibliography on Their Education and Careers. Washington, D.C.: Human Service Press, 1971. Reprint. New York: Behavioral Publications, 1974.

The 352 items in this classified bibliography include books, periodical articles, theses and pamphlets.   Entries are annotated clearly and adequately, and there author and subject indexes.   For more general bibliographies on women one should consult Krichmar (G1736) and Wheeler (G1786).

G1700 Baatz, Wilmer. The Black Family and the Black Woman. [Bloomington, Ind.: Indiana University, Afro-American Institute], 1981.

This 129 page annotated bibliography is available only in photocopy. See also Davis (G1714, G1715).

G1701   Bahr, Howard M. Disaffiliated Man: Essays and Bibliography on Skid Row, Vagrancy and Outsiders. Toronto: University of Toronto Press, 1970; London: Oxford University Press, 1971.

The annotated bibliography in this guide (pp. 94-394) is arranged by topics. Coverage is extensive, indicating most of the key works in each field, and the annotations are adequately descriptive. For clergy and counselors engaged in a wide range of social service activities this is a useful reference bibliography; for researchers it is a sound starting point but should not be used in place of more up-to-date indexes. See also Hoerder (G1727) and Miller (G1749).

G1702   Bell, Gwen; Randall, Edwina; and Roeder, Judith E.R. Urban Environments and Human Behavior: An Annotated Bibliography. Community Development Series, vol. 2. Stroudsburg, Pa.: Dowden, Hutchinson and Ross, 1973.

For students of urbanization and attendant social problems this is a suitable bibliography, although concentrating primarily on environmental rather than social aspects. The three main sections cover design approaches to the urban environment, social science approaches to the urban environment and framework of the urban environment; each of these is further subdivided into several sections, and there are author and subject indexes. Some entries related to the social sciences may be of interest in the theological context, although social concerns are largely ignored. See also Meyer (G1748), Hoover (G1728, Ross (G1767) and Sage Urban Studies Abstracts (G1769).

G1703 Bienen, Henry. Violence and Social Change: A Review of Current Literature. Chicago, Ill.: University of Chicago Press for the Adlai Stevenson Institute of International Affairs, 1968.

This descriptive bibliography of approximately 150 references is arranged by subject, the most useful of which for clergy and counselors deals with violence in the ghetto. Although only representative of the field, this is a useful starting point for study and research on violence as related to society. See also Dunmore (G1717) and Hoerder (G1727).

G1704 Biennial Review of Anthropology. Vol. 1-Vol. 7. Stanford, Calif.: Stanford University Press, 1959-1971.

Now replaced by the Annual Review of Anthropology (G1698), this international biennial survey is arranged in chapters dealing with the various fields of interest. Each specialist chapter describes and evaluates recent papers and monographs and includes a bibliography. Individual volumes are indexed by subject. See also Reviews in Anthropology (G1765).

G1705 Bonjean, Charles M.; Hill, Richard J.; and McLemore, S. Dale. Sociological Measurement: An Inventory of Scales and Indices. Chandler Publications in Anthropology and Sociology. San Francisco, Calif.: Chandler Publishing Company, 1967.

See also Simonis and Simonis (G1772).

G1706 Boorer, David R., and Murgatroyd, Stephen J. Adolescence: A Select Bibliography. Caerphilly: MTM Publishing House, 1972.

This bibliography consists of approximately 1000 unannotated entries in six sections, including youth work and welfare, advice and sociology. There is no index, and without annotations the work is of limited use. It is suitable as a starting point for research on various aspects of youth and adolescent behavior. See also National College for Training of Youth Leaders (G1752).

G1707 Cameron, Colin, comp. Attitudes of the Poor and Attitudes toward the Poor: An Annotated Bibliography. Madison, Wisc.: University of Wisconsin-Madison, Institute for Research on Poverty, 1975.

Focusing on 1965-1973 publications, this bibliography uses a classified arrangement for entries and includes author and subject indexes. For those concerned with social and societal aspects of poverty this is an interesting, if somewhat limited, compilation. See also Medical and Health Research Association of New York City (G1746) and Schlesinger (G1771).

G1708 Carrier, Hervé, and Pin, Emile. Sociologie du Christianisme: Bibliographie Internationale, 1900-1961/Sociology of Christianity: International Bibliography, 1900-1961. Studia Socialia, 8. Rome: Presses de l'Université Grégorienne, 1964.

This is a bilingual, unannotated, alphabetical bibliography of books and articles in the field of sociology dealing with the Christian religion. Geographical and subject indexes are provided. See Carrier (G1709) for an updating; see also Instituto Fe y Secularidad (G1731).

G1709   Carrier, Hervé; Pin, Emile; and Fasola-Bologna, Alfred. Sociologie du Christianisme: Supplément, 1962-1966/Sociology of Christianity: Supplement, 1962-1966. Studia Socialia, 8. Rome: Presses de l'Université Grégorienne, 1968.

This updates Carrier and Pin (G1708), covering the period January 1962-December 1966 and following the principles of the previous publication. Some new subject headings have been added in both the geographical and the analytical subject indexes. Several titles for the previous period have also been added.

G1710   Chambers, Merritt Madison, and Exton, Elaine. Youth, Key to America's Future: An Annotated Bibliography. Washington, D.C.: American Council on Education, 1949.

This sequel to Menefee (G1747) is a classifed and annotated bibliography of materials on all aspects of youth in America.   For a more current bibliography see Gottlieb (G1724).

G1711   Council on Social Work Education. Building a Social Work Library: A Guide to the Selection of Books, Periodicals and Reference Tools. New York: Council on Social Work Education, 1962.

This classifed listing includes a representative selection of books considered basic for a social work library. There is no index, and the coverage is now quite dated. See also Li (G1737), Social Work Research and Abstracts (G1774) and Tighe (G1780).

G1712   Council on Social Work Education. Committee on International Social Welfare Education. Selected Bibliography of North American Social Welfare Literature. New York: Council on Social Work Education, 1958.

G1713   Current Literature on Community Health and Personal Social Services. No. 1- . London: Department of Health and Social Security Library, 1966?- ; monthly.

This mimeographed listing covers such areas as family planning, health services, youth and public administration. Some entries include brief annotations. It is British in coverage and does not include housing or probation. See also National Council of Social Service (G1754-G1756).

G1714   Davis, Lenwood G. The Black Family in the United States: A Selected Bibliography of Annotated Books,   Articles and Dissertations on Black Families in America. With the assistance of Janet Sims. Westport,   Conn.: Greenwood Press, 1978.

Davis contains more than 380 annotated entries which are grouped by form (books, articles, dissertations) and subdivided by subject (slavery, poverty, economic status, religion, health, education, sex). There are author and keyword indexes to this useful but highly selective bibliography. See also Baatz (G1700) and Dunmore (G1716).

G1715   Davis, Lenwood G. The Black Woman in American Society: A Selected Annotated Bibliography. Boston, Mass.: G.K. Hall and Company, 1975.

This bibliographic survey of black women is arranged by form of material,

including books, articles and general reference works. It includes a directory of black periodicals, a list of relevant national organizations, elected
officials and similar information. There is an author and subject index.
See also Baatz (G1700).

G1716   Dunmore,   Charlotte. Black Children and Their Families: A Bibliography. San Francisco, Calif.: R and E Research Associates, 1976.

This list of publications on the black American child is arranged by
topic, covering adoption, education, health, family life, ghetto life,
mental health, sex and family planning. Separate sections treat bibliographies and reference works, periodicals, sources for films and filmstrips,
selected library collections. This is a carefully prepared guide to resources
and meets a variety of reference needs for students, counselors and
laymen. See also Davis (G1714).

G1717   Dunmore,   Charlotte. Poverty, Participation, Protest, Power and
Black Americans: A Selected Bibliography for Use in Social Work Education.
New York: Council on Social Work Education, 1970.

Although aimed specifically at the needs of social work educators, this
bibliography provides valuable data for others engaged in work with
or study of black Americans. Items are listed by main entry and include
marginal code letters to indicate the subject focus. Most entries are
annotated and reflect a post-1954 concentration. See also Hoerder (G1727).

G1718   Een, JoAnn Delores, and Rosenberg-Dishman, Marie Barovic. Women
and Society, Citations 3601 to 6000: An Annotated Bibliography. Beverly
Hills, Calif.: Sage Publications, 1978.

This 275 page follow-up to Rosenberg (G1766) retains the main organization of the initial volume but omits the sections on women's collections
and libraries and women's periodicals and newspapers. It adds sections
on the political status of women and women's handbooks and almanacs.
Een is indexed by authors, places and topics and includes a special index
of journal issues of sections devoted to women. This is a very useful
updating of the basic work and should be consulted by all those interested
in the field. See also Haber (G1725).

G1719   Ethnic Studies Bibliography. Vol. 1- . Pittsburgh, Pa.: University
of Pittsburgh, University Center for International Studies, 1977- ; annual.

This abstracting service covers articles which have appeared two years
prior to the date of compilation. Each issue contains approximately
600 articles from nearly 400 social science journals published in America.
The abstracts are quite detailed, and there are indexes of authors, subjects, geographical areas, proper names, journal titles. See also Miller
(G1751), Oaks (G1762) and Sage Race Relations Abstracts (G1768).

G1720   Fischer, Clare B., comp. Breaking Through: A Bibliography of Women
and Religion.   Berkeley, Calif.: Graduate Theological Union Library, 1980.

G1721   Furstenberg, Friedrich, ed. Religionsoziologie. Neuwied am Rhein:
H. Luchterhand Verlag, 1964.

See also Goldschmidt and Matthes (G1723).

G1722 Glenn, Norval D.; Alston, Jon P.; and Weiner, David. Social Stratification: A Research Bibliography. Berkeley, Calif.: Glendessary, 1970.

Covering publications in English written between 1940 and 1968, this classified bibliography lists books and journal articles from many fields with a bearing on social stratification. There is an author index but no title or detailed subject index.

G1723 Goldschmidt, Dietrich, and Matthes, Joachim, eds. Probleme der Religionssoziologie. Kölner Zeitschrift für Soziologie und Sozialpsychologie, Sonderheft 6. Cologne: Westdeutscher Verlag, 1962.

See also Furstenberg (G1721).

G1724 Gottlieb, David; Reeves, Jon; and TenHouten, Warren D. The Emergence of Youth Societies: A Cross-Cultural Approach. New York: Free Press, 1966.

Most of this 416 page volume is devoted to a wide ranging bibliography of materials on adolescent behavior and training of youth. Coverage is international, and entries are arranged by country. Many items are annotated briefly but succinctly. This is a very full guide to a subject which has assumed significant proportions in the last two decades. For earlier and less adequate works see Menefee (G1747) and Chambers and Exton (G1710).

G1725 Haber, Barbara. Women in America: A Guide to Books, 1963-1975. Boston, Mass.: G.K. Hall and Company, 1978.

Intended primarily for university teachers unfamiliar with recent literature on women's issues, this work surveys the field under broad subject categories but does not include reference materials. All entries are annotated and provide useful notes not only for teachers but also for librarians and students. There is an index of authors and titles. Haber is suitable for students at several levels who wish to read more widely on women's issues. See also Hughes (G1729) and Rosenberg (G1734).

G1726 Harvard University. Library. Sociology. Widener Library Shelflist, no. 45-46. 2 vols. Cambridge, Mass.: Harvard University Library, 1973.

This comprehensive catalog lists 49,000 titles on social theory and history, social groups and institutions, social problems and reform and social psychology. Volume 1 contains the classification schedule, a classified listing of entries by call number and a chronological listing. Volume 2 contains the author and title listing. This is a valuable guide for those requiring a relatively complete list of titles in sociology. See also International Bibliography of Sociology (G1733).

G1727 Hoerder, Dirk. Protest, Direct Action, Repression: Dissent in American Society from Colonial Times to the Present; A Bibliography. Munich: Verlag Dokumentation, 1977.

Similar to the same author's Violence in the United States: Riots, Strikes, Protest and Suppression; A Working Bibliography for Teachers and Students (Materialen John F. Kennedy-Institut für Nordamerikastudien, 2. Berlin: Freie Universität Berlin, John F. Kennedy-Institut für Nordamerikastudien,

1973), this 434 page compilation is a classified bibliography of English language books, periodical articles and dissertations. It is arranged in three parts, each of which is subdivided by topic and chronology: general literature on direct action and social change, social protest and repression in American history, minorities in the United States and their rebellion against discrimination and oppression. There is a chronological register of events cited with references to bibliographic citations, as well as an author index. See also Bahr (G1701), Bienen (G1703), Dunmore (G1717) and Miller (G1749).

G1728   Hoover, Dwight W. Cities. Bibliographic Guides for Contemporary Collections. New York: R.R. Bowker, 1976.

Limited to contemporary materials of wide availability, this bibliography lists more than 1000 books, films, filmstrips and other media in a classified arrangement with basic annotations. There are author and title indexes. For students new to the fields of urban studies and urban society this is a useful bibliography, although it is weak on aspects of socio-ethical issues. See also Bell (G1702), Ross (G1767) and Sage Urban Studies Abstracts (G1769).

G1729 Hughes, Maruja Matich. The Sexual Barrier: Legal, Medical, Economic and Social Aspects of Sex Discrimination. Rev. ed. Washington, D.C.: Hughes Press, 1977.

This revision of the 1970 edition and its supplements groups more than 8000 books, articles, pamphlets and documents in English published between 1960 and 1975 into seventeen chapters. Each of these is further subdivided by specific topic and geographical region, and there are numerous brief annotations. Of particular value are the listings which deal with legal issues and with specific occupations. This is an important bibliography which is complemented by Jacobs (G1734) and Rosenberg (G1766).

G1730   Human Resources Abstracts: An International Information Service. Vol. 1- . Beverly Hills, Calif.: Sage Publications, 1966- ; quarterly.

Entitled Poverty and Human Resources Abstracts until 1974, this abstracting service covers books and articles on human and social problems. The abstracts are grouped by topic, and the author and subject indexes in each issue cumulate annually. Although perhaps too broad in coverage for many users, this is nevertheless a helpfully up-to-date survey for those seeking information on a variety of social issues.

G1731   Instituto Fe y Secularidad. Sociologia de la Religion y Teologia: Estudio Bibliographico/Sociology of Religion and Theology: A Bibliography. Madrid: Editorial Cuadernos para el Diálogo, 1975.

See also Carrier and Pin (G1708, G1709).

G1732 International Bibliography of Social and Cultural Anthropology/Bibliographie Internationale d'Anthropologie Sociale et Culturelle. Vol. 1- . International Bibliography of the Social Sciences. London: Tavistock Publications, 1958- ; irregular.

Prepared by the International Committee for Social Science Information and Documentation in cooperation with the International Congress of Anthropological and Ethnological Sciences, this irregularly produced annual lists publications in various languages from any country on all aspects of anthropology. It includes books, periodical articles, government publications and reports of various types. Entries are listed in a classified arrangement, and there are author and subject indexes in English and French. The main drawback of this bibliography is its late appearance (three years or more after the year covered). Otherwise it is a useful tool for locating anthropological literature.

G1733   International Bibliography of Sociology/Bibliographie Internationale de Sociologie. Vol. 1- . International Bibliography of the Social Sciences. London: Tavistock Publications, 1952- ; irregular.

This extensive classified listing of books, articles, reports and other documents in many languages is prepared as part of the International Bibliography of the Social Sciences by the International Committee for Social Science Information and Documentation. It is indexed by author and subject, providing researchers with the most complete international guide to recent literature in all fields of sociology. Unfortunately, the volumes appear irregularly and very much later than the year covered, which gives them more of a retrospective function than current awareness use. See also L'Année Sociologique (G1697) and Harvard University (G1726).

G1734   Jacobs, Sue Ellen. Women in Perspective: A Guide for Cross Cultural Studies. Urbana, Ill.: University of Illinois Press, 1974.

This extensive bibliography of books, articles, dissertations and similar materials is arranged in two main sections. The first, geographical topics, is subdivided by country region; the second, subject topics, is subdivided by specific subjects. There is an author index and a detailed table of contents, but the lack of a subject index detracts from the usefulness of this volume. See also Hughes (G1729) and Rosenberg (G1766).

G1735   Kehr, Helen, comp. and ed. Prejudice: Racist - Religious - Nationalist. Wiener Library, Catalogue Series, no. 5. London: Valentine, Mitchell for the Institute of Contemporary History, 1971.

Particularly rich in German materials and antisemitism, this collection of 4511 items without annotations is arranged in four sections: reference books, general works, individual countries, newspapers and periodicals dealing with racism and arranged by country. There are numerous cross references and an author and anonymous title index. For background studies on racism and race relations this is a valuable bibliography. See also Sage Race Relations Abstracts (G1768) and Thompson and Thompson (G1779).

G1736   Krichmar, Albert. The Women's Rights Movement in the United States, 1848-1970: A Bibliography and Sourcebook. Metuchen, N.J.: Scarecrow Press, 1972.

This topically arranged bibliography covers the political, economic, legal, religious, educational and professional status of women in America since 1848. There are more than 5100 references to books, periodical articles and pamphlets, many with annotations. There are additional sections on manuscript sources and women's liberation serials. The work is adequately indexed and provides a good starting point for research and study in the field of women's rights. See also Astin (G1699) and Wheeler (G1786).

G1737   Li, Hong-Chan. Social Work Education: A Bibliography. Metuchen, N.J.: Scarecrow Press, 1978.

This classified bibliography lists more than 3000 books, periodicals, proceedings, reports, government documents and dissertations on social work education. It is limited to English language materials produced primarily since 1960 but is international in scope. For teachers of Christian social work this is a substantial guide to professional literature. See also Council on Social Work Education (G1711).

G1738   Library. Anthropology Resource Group. Serial Publications in Anthropology. Ed. by Sol Tax and Francis X. Grollig. Chicago, Ill.: University of Chicago Press, 1973.

This list of serials in anthropology is arranged alphabetically by title and provides information on publisher and frequency for each title. There are no annotations or data on contents, so this compilation is of limited bibliographical or evaluative value.

G1739   Litman, Theodor James. Sociology of Medicine and Health Care: A Research Bibliography. San Francisco, Calif.: Boyd and Fraser, 1976.

This 664 page bibliography is arranged by broad topics and specific sub-divisions. It includes English language books, periodicals and dissertations from the early 1920s to 1971. Although drug addiction, family planning, gerontology, sexual deviancy and mental illness are not covered, Litman does treat a number of currently important topics. There are author and subject indexes. This is a valuable bibliography for researchers and practitioners. See also Medical and Health Research Association of New York City (G1746).

G1740   Lunday, G. Albert. Sociology Dissertations in American Universities, 1893-1966. Commerce, Tex.: East Texas State University, 1969.

See also Mark (G1744).

G1741   McKee, Kathleen Burke. Women's Studies: A Guide to Reference Sources. With a supplement on feminist serials in the University of Connecticut's Alternative Press Collection by Joanne V. Akeroyd. Bibliography Series, no. 6. Storrs, Conn.: University of Connecticut Library, 1977.

This 112 page guide is arranged by type of material, including guides, library catalogs, handbooks, directories, statistics, indexes, abstracts and bibliographies; there are topical subdivisions where necessary. The 364 annotated items are all of direct use in feminist studies, and the author, title and subject indexes greatly assist retrieval of data. McKee is a particularly useful compilation which should be more widely available. See also Lynn (G1834), Haber (G1725) and Women's Work and Women's Studies (G1788).

G1742   McPherson, James M., et al. Blacks in America: Bibliographical

<u>Essays</u>. Garden City, N.Y.: Doubleday, 1971.

This 430 page work attempts to combine narrative, interpretation and bibliography in a chronological and topical framework suitable for teachers, students and interested readers. Material is organized under 100 topics (from Africa and the slave trade to lifestyles in urban ghettos of 1970). Introductory paragraphs summarize factual data and interpretive questions and discuss major sources for each topic. More than 4000 titles are covered in the bibliographical sections. A detailed table of contents and index facilitate access to this valuable work which forms a basis for black studies courses at various levels, including postgraduate. See also Miller (G1750).

G1743   Marien, Michael. <u>Societal Directions and Alternatives: A Critical Guide to the Literature</u>. La Fayette, N.Y.: Information for Policy Design, 1976.

This classified bibliography focuses on English language books and articles which deal with the future of society and with alternative societies. The more than 1000 entries include lengthy and critical annotations which indicate level of readership. There are nine indexes: author, organization, chronological book title, titles for present society, evolutionary stage theory, alternative societies, selected proposals, selected criticism, selected subjects and ideas. See also World Future Society (G1789).

G1744   Mark, Charles. <u>Sociology of America: A Guide to Information Sources</u>. American Studies Information Guide Series, vol. 1. Detroit, Mich.: Gale Research Company, 1976.

This classified listing of approximately 1900 items on the sociology of American life published primarily since 1960 begins with three general chapters on bibliographic resources, general reference works and journals. Succeeding chapters list empirical studies on selected topics important in the American milieu; these sections are useful for students beginning detailed study of various aspects of American society. There are indexes of authors, titles, subjects and periodical titles. See also Lunday (G1740).

G1745   Meadows, Paul, <u>et al</u>. <u>Recent Immigration to the United States: The Literature of the Social Sciences</u>. Prepared for the Research Institute on Immigration and Ethnic Studies, Smithsonian Institution. RIIES Bibliographic Series, no. 1. Washington, D.C.: Smithsonian Institution Press, 1976.

This bibliography of post-1945 immigration to the United States focuses on the themes of general migration theory, world immigration trends, the impact of immigration on both the sending country and the United States, immigration policy in countries of origin and settlement, the settlement process and comparison of old and new immigrants. There is no index to this 112 page work.

G1746 Medical and Health Research Association of New York City. <u>Poverty and Health in the United States: A Bibliography with Abstracts</u>. New York: Medical and Health Research Association of New York City, 1967.

This is a selective list of studies on the health status of the poor, on health services, on medical deprivation and on programs for improving the health care of the disadvantaged. Author and subject indexes are provided. Semi-annual supplements were issued in 1968. See also Cameron (G1707), Litman (G1739) and Schlesinger (G1771).

G1747   Menefee, Louise Arnold, and Chambers, Merritt Madison. American Youth: An Annotated Bibliography Prepared for the American Youth Commission. Washington, D.C.: American Council on Education, 1938.

This annotated and classified bibliography on youth in America is a standard older guide which is valuable chiefly for historical study of the topic. There is an alphabetical index. See Chambers and Exton (G1710) for a supplementary work and Gottlieb (G1724) for a much newer compilation.

G1748   Meyer, Jon K. Bibliography on the Urban Crisis: The Behavioral, Psychological and Sociological Aspects of the Urban Crisis. Public Health Service Publications, no. 1948. Chevy Chase, Md.: National Institute of Mental Health, 1969.

With emphasis on materials published between 1954 and 1968, this guide attempts to provide a comprehensive listing of academic and popular literature on causes, effects and responses related to urban disorders. Items are listed in reverse chronological order within broad subject categories, and there are author and keyword indexes. See also Bell (G1702) and Sage Urban Studies Abstracts (G1769).

G1749   Miller, Albert Jay. Confrontation, Conflict and Dissent: A Bibliography of a Decade of Controversy, 1960-1970. Metuchen, N.J.: S carecrow Press, 1972.

This interesting compilation contains approximately 5400 entries on a variety of topics relevant to the 1960s in particular. Dissent, generation gap, drugs and similar areas are covered under a variety of subject headings. There are many references from underground or alternative publications, which is an unusual feature in such a guide. Author and subject indexes permit quick access to entries. See also Bahr (G1701) and Hoerder (G1727).

G1750   Miller, Elizabeth Williams, comp. The Negro in America: A Bibliography. 2nd rev. and enlarged ed.   Comp. by Mary L. Fisher. Cambridge, Mass.: Harvard University Press, 1970.

Compiled for the American Academy of Arts and Sciences, this 351 page bibliography on black Americans concentrates on materials published since 1954. Both books and periodical articles are listed under a variety of subjects, many of them relevant to various aspects of social theology (urban problems, intergroup relations, employment, education, political rights). Of the many general bibliographies on blacks in America this is one of the most useful. An author index is included.   See also McPherson (G1742) and Union Theological Seminary (G1781).

G1751   Miller, Wayne Charles, et al. A Comprehensive Bibliography for the Study of American Minorities. 2 vols. New York: New York University Press, 1976.

This excellent bibliography contains more than 29,000 entries listed in a classified sequence and with brief annotations. Focus is on monographs, although articles and pamphlets are included for ethnic groups which have received less coverage in the published literature. Miller covers bibliographies, periodicals and indexes, works in the social sciences and humanities. Historical-bibliographical essays precede each group; these are reprinted in Handbook of American Minorities (G1839). There are author and title indexes. This is a major contribution to the field and provides very thorough coverage of minority groups in America, including many not treated elsewhere. See also Ethnic Studies Bibliography (G1719), Oaks (G1762) and Schlachter (G1770).

G1752   National College for Training of Youth Leaders. Youth Service Information Centre. A Select List of Research, Surveys and Theses in Youth Work, Adolescence and Allied Educational and Social Fields. Leicester: Youth Service Information Centre, 1960-1968.

This looseleaf compendium is intended primarily to advise youth workers on research undertaken largely since 1960. The subject arrangement covers both educational and social services for youth, and there are indexes of research topics, research agencies and resources. Now dated, this remains a useful retrospective bibliography of British research on youth work. See also Boorer and Murgatroyd (G1706).

G1753   National College for Training of Youth Leaders. Youth Service Training Centre. Annotated Youth Work Book List. Leicester: Youth Service Book Centre, 1966- ; irregular.

This looseleaf bibliography and its irregular supplements (fifth published in 1971) contains more than 1000 annotated entries arranged by subject. Topics include social work, the handicapped, voluntary organizations and other useful fields. There are subject and author indexes to this useful, if somewhat limited, complement to primarily North American guides to youth work.

G1754   National Council of Social Service. More Books on the Social Services: List of Classified Selected Books by British Publishers. London: National Council of Social Service, 1973.

This bibliography supplements the Council's earlier listings (G1755, G1756), again concentrating mainly on the British context.

G1755   National Council of Social Service. Some Books on the Social Services: Statutory and Voluntary Services, Family and Children, Social Policy, Housing, Delinquency, Health and Welfare, Social Work, Methods, Race Relations, Social History, Old People. London: National Council of Social Service, 1969.

Intended for students, teachers, librarians and social workers, this bibliography lists some 1000 items in fourteen sections. Although British in orientation, it is an excellent corrective to the American bias of similar compilations and provides a useful starting point for research on a wide range of topics. Entries are not annotated, and there is no index. See also the Council's two related works (G1754, G1756) and Current Literature on Community Health and Personal Social Services (G1713).

G1756   National Council of Social Service. Some Books on the Social Services: Statutory and Voluntary Services, Family and Children, Social Policy, Housing,

Delinquency, Health and Welfare, Social Work Methods, Race Relations, Social History, Old People. 1970 Supplement. Additions and Amendments. London: National Council of Social Service, 1970.

This compilation updates and corrects the 1969 publication (G1755). See also More Books on the Social Services (G1754).

G1757   New York Public Library. Schomburg Center for Research and Black Culture. Bibliographic Guide to Black Studies. Boston, Mass.: G.K. Hall and Company, 1976- ; annual.

This valuable sequel to the Schomburg Collection catalogs (G1758-G1761) lists material acquired during the preceding year and also includes some entries from Library of Congress MARC tapes. A dictionary catalog arrangement is followed, using some subject headings developed specifically for the Schomburg Collection. For serious students of black life and culture this is an indispensible guide to publications.

G1758   New York Public Library. Schomburg Collection of Negro Literature and History. Dictionary Catalog. 9 vols. Boston, Mass.: G.K. Hall and Company, 1962.

This important catalog and its supplements (G1759-G1761) list published and archive materials on black American life and history. Coverage is international in scope and includes books by authors of African descent regardless of subject matter or language and all significant materials about people of African descent. The more than 36,000 volumes in the main catalog include many items of importance in advanced studies of black society. See also New York Public Library. Schomburg Center (G1757).

G1759   New York Public Library. Schomburg Collection of Negro Literature and History. Dictionary Catalog. Supplement 1. 2 vols. Boston, Mass.: G.K. Hall and Company, 1967.

This supplement adds substantially to the main work (G1758). See also the 1972 and 1974 supplements (G1760, G1761).

G1760   New York Public Library. Schomburg Collection of Negro Literature and History. Dictionary Catalog. Supplement 2. 4 vols. Boston, Mass.: G.K. Hall and Company, 1972.

See the main volumes (G1758) and earlier supplement (G1759) for which this is an updating.

G1761   New York Public Library. Schomburg Collection of Negro Literature and History. Dictionary Catalog. Supplement 3. Boston, Mass.: G.K. Hall and Company, 1974.

Providing bibliographic data for materials acquired between January 1972 and September 1974, this supplement retains the dictionary format for entries but no longer reproduces catalog cards as in previous supplements (G1759, G1760). Materials processed after September 1974 are listed in Bibliographic Guide to Black Studies (G1757).

G1762   Oaks, Priscilla. Minority Studies: A Selective Annotated Bibliiography.

Boston, Mass.: G.K. Hall and Company, 1975.

> This bibliography of 1800 items begins with a section on general studies, followed by appropriately subdivided sections on native Americans, Spanish Americans, Afro-Americans and Asian Americans. Both popular and scholarly materials are covered, and there is an author/title index. The annotations are brief and descriptive. See also Miller (G1751) and Schlachter (G1770).

G1763   Odubho, Constance E. Black-White Racial Attitudes: An Annotated Bibliography. Westport, Conn.: Greenwood Press, 1976.

> Odubho deals with the crucial issues of attitude formation, attitude change and associated factors of importance in social understanding. The annotated, classified bibliography covers books, articles and dissertations published between 1950 and 1974 dealing with conditions in the United States. There are author and subject indexes. See also West (G1783) and Peebles (G1764) for more thorough coverage of dissertations; see also Thompson and Thompson (G1779).

G1764   Peebles, Joan B. A Bibliography of Doctoral Research on the Negro, 1967-1977. Ann Arbor, Mich.: University Microfilms International, 1978.

> This complement to West (G1783) and updating of a 1967-1969 supplement uses a classified arrangement to list several hundred dissertations on black Americans in all fields. The author index provides references to Dissertation Abstracts, University Microfilms order numbers and prices.

G1765   Reviews in Anthropology. Vol. 1- . Pleasantville, N.Y.: Redgrave Publishing Company, 1974- ; quarterly.

> Covering publications for 1972-1973 in the first issue, this quarterly serial publishes lengthy and extremely detailed reviews of books in all fields of anthropology. For researchers interested in social and cultural topics this is a useful source of relatively current data. See also Annual Review of Anthropology (G1698).

G1766 Rosenberg, Marie Barovic, and Bergstrom, Len V. Women and Society: A Critical Review of the Literature with a Selected Annotated Bibliography. Beverly Hills, Calif.: Sage Publications, 1975.

> This valuable literature survey and bibliography begins with an introductory review of classic works on women in history, women at work and women in politics. The bulk of the work lists 3600 books, articles, periodicals, newspapers and documents plus women's library collections grouped into broad subject areas. Most chapters include more specific topical subdivisions, and there are brief annotations of materials cited. Rosenberg is indexed by authors, persons, places, subjects and journal issues devoted to women. Een (G1718) contains an additional 2400 entries arranged along the same lines. See also Haber (G1725), Hughes (G1729) and Jacobs (G1734).

G1767 Ross, Bernard H., and Fritschler, A. Lee. Urban Affairs Bibliography: An Annotated Guide to the Literature in the Field. 3rd ed. Washington, D.C.: American University, College of Public Affairs, School of Government and Public Administration, 1974.

> Prepared by Fritschler in earlier editions, this brief (85pp.) classified bibliography is limited to books and does not contain an index. The annotations are brief but descriptive, and entries deal specifically with urban arrairs rather than the urban environment. For those interested in the political and social aspects of urban studies Ross can be of some use. See also Bell (G1702), Hoover (G1728), Meyer (G1748) and Sage Urban Studies Abstracts (G1769).

G1768   Sage Race Relations Abstracts. Vol. 1- . London: Sage Publications for the Institute of Race Relations, 1976- ; quarterly.

> Better than Ethnic Studies Bibliography (G1719) in the sense that it appears more frequently and covers material published in the preceding year, this service supersedes Race Relations Abstracts. It covers both American and European periodical literature on immigration and race relations; some books, essays and "fugitive" publications are also included. The abstracts are reasonably detailed, and there are author and subject indexes. A geographical index would be a welcome addition. There is some British focus in this serial, which generally begins each issue with a substantial bibliographical essay on a particular topic. See also Kehr (G1735), Odubho (G1763) and Thompson and Thompson (G1779).

G1769   Sage Urban Studies Abstracts. Vol. 1- . Beverly Hills, Calif.: Sage Publications, 1973- ; quarterly.

> This valuable abstracting service provides abstracts of approximately 250 English language books, articles, reports and documents in each issue. There is a section of related citations in ancillary fields without annotations. The abstracts are detailed and descriptive, and there are author and subject indexes in each issue. For students of urban affairs as viewed through the social sciences this is a usefully up-to-date and reasonably comprehensive guide. For related bibliographies see Bell (G1702), Hoover (G1728) and Ross (1767).

G1770   Schlachter, Gail A., and Belli, Donna. Minorities and Women: A Guide to Reference Literature in the Social Sciences. Los Angeles, Calif.: Reference Services Press, 1977.

> Limited to English language materials dealing with minorities and women in America, this 349 page listing of more than 800 reference sources is divided into two main sections: information sources, including fact books, biographies, documentary sources, directories, statistical materials; citation sources, including bibliographies, indexes and abstracts. Each section is subdivided by group (minorities, American Indians, Asian Americans, black Americans, Spanish Americans, women. There are author, title and subject indexes. For those interested in both minorities and the issue of feminism this is a useful bibliography. The annotations are particularly lucid and adequately descriptive. See also Ethnic Studies Bibliography (G1719), Miller (G1751) and Oaks (G1762).

G1771   Schlesinger, Benjamin. Poverty in Canada and the United States; Overview and Annotated Bibliography. Toronto: University of Toronto Press, 1966.

Arranged by subject, the bibliography in this compilation follows general introductory essays on poverty in North America. The annotations are brief and judicious, although the materials included are perhaps too selective for any but the beginning student. See also Cameron (G1707) and Medical and Health Research Association of New York City (G1746).

G1772   Simonis, Heide, and Simonis, Udo E. Lebensqualität: Zielgewinnung und Zielbestimmung/Quality of Life: Methods and Measurement. Kieler Schrifttumskunden zu Wirtschaft und Gesellschaft, Bd. 21. Kiel: Bibliothek des Instituts für Weltwirtschaft, 1976.

Dealing with an area of increasing concern to the church, this bibliography lists 2064 published and unpublished materials on the quality of life and social indicators. The first part treats items located at the Kiel Institute for World Economy; the second covers items not in this library. In each of these sections citations are arranged alphabetically by author, and there are personal and corporate author indexes. The lack of a subject arrangement or subject index greatly hampers use of this potentially valuable compilation. The introductory matter is in both German and English. See also Bonjean (G1705).

G1773   Social Compass: International Review of the Sociology of Religion. Vol. 1- . Ottignies-Louvain-la-Neuve: Social Compass, 1953- ; quarterly.

Containing the "International Bibliography of Sociology of Religion" in the second number of each volume, this annual service surveys some 125 European and American journals for material on the sociology of religion. Each issue of the bibliography presents up-to-date coverage of information by subject; within each field items are arranged alphabetically by author, and entries include only basic bibliographical data. In its field this is a useful guide primarily because it provides a specific subject focus for information which may be gleaned from more general sociological or theological indexes.

G1774   Social Work Research and Abstracts. Vol. 1- . New York: National Association of Social Workers, 1965- ; quarterly.

Originally entitled Abstracts for Social Workers, this quarterly compilation regularly presents approximately six substantial research papers, followed by abstracts of published articles in six main sections: fields of service, social policy and action, service methods, the profession, history, related fields of knowledge. There are quarterly author and subject indexes which cumulate annually. This is a reasonably thorough abstracting service for educators and practitioners and should be consulted by advanced students as well. See also Council on Social Work Education (G1711).

G1775   Sociological Abstracts. Vol. 1- ; San Diego, Calif.: Sociological Abstracts, 1952- ; five per annum.

Covering the full range of sociological topics, this abstracting service lists some 8000 items annually in a classified subject sequence. Entries are arranged alphabetically by author within each subject, and full bibliographical details and abstracts accompany every item. Each issue includes subject, author and periodical indexes, while the sixth number of a volume is an index issue providing cumulative subject, author and periodical indexes (the last with full publishing details). Religious and theological topics related to sociology are well represented in this service, which is an up-to-date, comprehensive international guide to this discipline. The abstracts are particularly clear and succinct; those dealing with religious topics provide just enough information to permit rapid evaluation. See also International Bibliography of Sociology (G1733).

G1776   Spitz, Allan A. Developmental Change: An Annotated Bibliography. Lexington, Ky.: University of Kentucky Press, 1969.

This classified and annotated bibliography of approximately 2500 articles from journals, symposia and conference reports since 1960 covers several aspects of modernization and development, including political, social and economic factors. Relevant books are listed without annotations in an appendix. This is a suitable starting point for research in social and related change, although a new edition is required to take account of the substantial recent literature in this subject. See also Task Force on Alternative Books in Print (G1778).

G1777   Sussman, Marvin B., ed. Author's Guide to Journals in Sociology and Related Fields. Author's Guide to Journals Series. New York: Haworth Press, 1978.

This guide to more than 350 journals provides for each entry the manuscript and subscription addresses, price, frequency, indexing and abstracting sources, general interest areas, appropriate topics, style sheet, review period, publication lag, acceptance rates. There is a subject, title and keyword index. Sussman is of most use to scholars wishing to submit material for publication; it is also useful for librarians.

G1778   Task Force on Alternative Books in Print. Alternatives in Print: An Index and Listing of Some Movement Publications Reflecting Today's Social Change Activities. 2nd ed. Columbus, Ohio: Office of Educational Services, Ohio State University Libraries, 1972.

See also Spitz (G1776).

G1779   Thompson, Edgar Tristram, and Thompson, Alma Mary. Race and Religion: A Descriptive Bibliography, Compiled with Special Reference to the Relations between Whites and Negroes in the United States. Chapel Hill, N.C.: University of North Carolina Press, 1949. Reprint. New York: Kraus Reprint Company, 1971.

See also Kehr (G1735) and Odubho (G1763).

G1780   Tighe, Leo W. A Classified Bibliography for the Field of Social Work. Santa Clara, Calif.: Premier Publications, 1959.

This 235 page bibliography lists approximately 5500 books, articles, documents and dissertations in the areas of counseling, guidance and social work. Although now dated, it is a useful starting point for basic research requirements. See also Council on Social Work Education (G1711).

G1781   Union Theological Seminary. Library. Urban Education Collection. The Negro in American History and Culture: A List of Resources for Teaching. New York: Union Theological Seminary, 1965.

See also McPherson (G1742) and Miller (G1750).

G1782   United States. Department of Health, Education and Welfare. <u>Cata-</u>
<u>logs of the Departmental Library</u>. 49 vols. Boston, Mass.: G.K. Hall and
Company, 1966.

Comprising twenty-nine volumes on the author/title catalog and twenty
on the subject catalog, this publication reproduces the approximately
850,000 cards for books, pamphlets, congress proceedings and federal,
state and local documents held by the Department Library.

G1783   West, Earl H. <u>A Bibliography of Doctoral Research on the Negro,</u>
<u>1933-1966</u>. Ann Arbor, Mich.: Xerox University Microfilms, 1969.

This bibliography lists 1452 dissertations on the black American experience
in classified order. There is an author index which includes references
to <u>Dissertation Abstracts</u> and ordering information. See also Peebles
(G1764) for a useful updating.

G1784   Westergaard, John H.; Weyman, Anne; and Wiles, Paul. <u>Modern British</u>
<u>Society: A Bibliography</u>. Rev. ed. New York: St. Martin's Press, 1977.

This revision of a work first published in Britain (London: Frances Pinter,
1974) uses a classified arrangement for books and a few periodical articles
dealing with all aspects of society in Britain. There is a detailed table
of contents, an author index but no subject index. For students of British
society and social problems this bibliography is a basic starting point
for serious study.

G1785   Westmoreland, Guy T. <u>An Annotated Guide to Basic Reference Books</u>
<u>on the Black American Experience</u>. Wilmington, Del.: Scholarly Resources,
1974.

This 98 page compilation is a classified and annotated guide to reference
works which deal primarily with the black American experience. There
are author, title and subject indexes. Where more complete bibliographies are available, Westmoreland need not be consulted. See also McPherson (G1742) and Miller (G1750).

G1786   Wheeler, Helen Rippier. <u>Womanhood Media: Current Resources about</u>
<u>Women</u>. Metuchen, N.J.: Scarecrow Press, 1972.

This wide ranging compilation includes sections on reference works,
a basic book collection (annotated), women's movement periodicals,
audio-visual materials and a directory of sources. It is a useful complement to Krichmar (G1736). See also Astin (G1699).

G1787   <u>Women Studies Abstracts</u>. Vol. 1- . Rush, N.Y.: Rush Publishing
Company, 1971- ; quarterly.

This guide to periodical articles on women is a classified subject listing
of publications in all disciplines. The subject coverage includes religion,
and the table of contents provides an outline of the classification scheme.
Each entry lists author, title and other bibliographical details together
with an analytical abstract in most cases. There is a full subject index
annually. <u>Women Studies Abstracts</u> is international and up-to-date in

its coverage of relevant literature; it provides a good guide to current writings on women from a religious standpoint and should be regularly consulted by those interested in feminism, women in the church and related topics. See also McKee (G1741) and Women's Work and Women's Studies (G1788).

G1788   Women's Work and Women's Studies. New York: Women's Center, Barnard College, 1972- ; annual.

Published annually to cover work in the preceding year, this interdisciplinary bibliography deals with published research, research in progress and dissertations. It includes some pamphlet material but omits articles in the popular press. Entries are classified under major headings, and some materials are briefly annotated. There is an author index. This is a valuable scholarly tool for researchers. See also McKee (G1741) and Women's Studies Abstracts (G1787).

G1789   World Future Society. Information Sources for the Study of the Future. Resources Directory for America's Third Century, vol. 2. Washington, D.C.: World Future Society, 1977.

This directory provides information on approximately 450 individuals, 230 organizations, 116 research projects, 400 books and reports, 107 periodicals, 354 films and various other audio-visual resources and more than 200 courses and programs offered by educational institutions on future research. Less international than McHale (G1837), this guide usefully covers a wide range of information and should not be ignored by students interested in this field. It includes a glossary, a geographical index and a subject index. See also Marien (G1743).

SOCIOLOGY: DICTIONARIES

G1790   Bernsdorf, Wilhelm. Wörterbuch der Soziologie. 2. Aufl. unter bearatender Mitwirkung von Theodor W. Adorno et al. et unter Mitarbeit von Horst Knospe. Stuttgart: F. Enke Verlag, 1969.

This encyclopedic dictionary of 1317 pages contains long definitions provided by some 165 contributors. The articles are detailed and complete, and most include brief bibliographies. For readers of German this is one of the best single volume guides to sociological concepts and terminology. See also Fuchs (G1795).

G1791   Clegg, Joan, comp. Dictionary of Social Services: Policy and Practice. London: Bedford Square Press, 1971.

This work defines about 500 technical terms used in social work practice, relating to health and welfare, social work, child care, housing, etc. There are numerous cross references, a note on official sources and on reports relevant to the social services. See also Romanofsky (G1802).

G1792   Encyclopedia of Sociology. Guildford, Conn.: Dushkin Publishing Group, 1974.

This dictionary contains more than 1300 articles on the language, theories, institutions and leading figures in sociology. Most of the entries consist of brief definitions or descriptions, but some are more substantial. A classified bibliography of some 700 recent titles is aimed primarily at the nonprofessional. This work is suitable for basic reference inquiries by less advanced students. See also Fuchs (G1795) for a comparable but larger German work.

G1793   Fairchild, Henry Pratt, ed. Dictionary of Sociology. New York: Philosophical Library, 1944. New ed. Transatlantic Book Service, 1962.

Brief, signed articles provide definitions and some lengthier comments on some 500 sociological terms. There are many cross references. Biographies are not included. The dictionary attempts to establish greater precision in sociological language by emphasizing a particular meaning currently assigned to a given word or phrase. See also Mitchell (G1800).

G1794   Fappani, Antonio. Dizionario Sociale. Ed. riv. ed. ampliata. Rome: Edizioni ACLI, 1960.

This accurate, although not exhaustive, Christian encyclopedia of sociology contains brief entries. It does not include bibliography. See also Jacquemet (G1798).

G1795   Fuchs, Werner, et al., eds. Lexikon zur Soziologie. Opladen: Westdeutscher Verlag, 1973.

This 783 page dictionary contains brief definitions of several thousand sociological and related terms. For many entries the equivalent English terms are provided, which is of particular value when translating or reading German language works. The entries are concise and thorough, providing reasonable data for inquiries at various levels. See also Sussman (G1777) for a comparable English language dictionary; see also Bernsdorf (G1790).

G1796   Hoult, Thomas Ford. Dictionary of Modern Sociology. Totowa, N.J.: Littlefield, Adams, 1969.

Hoult emphasizes the modern aspect of sociology by focusing on current concept usage as found in sociological literature. The definitions are clear and concise, and many include examples of usage. There is an extensive bibliography of works and authors cited. This work is more advanced than Mitchell (G1800) and similar to Theodorson (G1803).

G1797   Hunter, David E., and Whitten, Phillip, eds. Encyclopedia of Anthropology. New York: Harper and Row, [1976].

Intended for the student and teacher, this 411 page dictionary contains approximately 1400 entries, some of which are very detailed. Main concepts and terms as well as significant individuals are treated concisely and clearly, and brief bibliographies accompany some articles. This is a useful reference work for those requiring basic and nontechnical information on all aspects of anthropology (with the exception of ethnography, which is not treated).

G1798   Jacquemet, G., ed. Dictionnaire de Sociologie Familiale, Politique, Economique, Spirituelle, Générale. Vol. 1- . Paris. Letouzey et Ané, 1933- .

This dictionary covers all aspects of sociology from a Catholic viewpoint in long, scholarly articles with bibliographical references throughout and lists at the end of each article. See also Fappani (G1794) and Willems (G1804).

G1799   Lingemann, Elfriede. Glossary of Social Work Terms in English, French, German. 2nd ed. Schriften des Deutschen Vereins für Offentliche und Private Fürsorge. Cologne: C. Heymann Verlag, 1958.

This successor to the 1956 compilation by Angela Lorenzi is a useful glossary of 2500 social work terms arranged in three sequences: German-English-French, English-French-German, French-English-German. Only equivalents are provided, making Lingemann a handy reference glossary for readers unfamiliar with terminology of the major foreign languages often quoted in English social work studies. See also National Association of Social Workers (G1801) and Zapf (G1806).

G1800   Mitchell, Geoffrey Duncan, ed. A Dictionary of Sociology. Chicago, Ill.: Aldine Publishing Company; London: Routledge and Kegan Paul, 1968.

Containing only about 300 entries, this guide for the beginner provides substantial definitions of key sociological terms in clear and nontechnical language. See Hoult (G1796) or Theodorson (G1803) for more advanced dictionaries.

G1801   National Association of Social Workers. Encyclopedia of Social Work. Vol. 1- . New York: National Association of Social Workers, 1929- ; irregular, approximately every six years.

Formerly the Social Work Year Book, this encyclopedia described organizational activities in social work and related fields with emphasis on recent or current affairs. It comprises two parts, the first containing topical articles plus biographies of social workers and bibliographies, the second containing directory data and statistical tables. The articles, which are fairly long and detailed, are grouped together in order to stress interrelationships. A detailed subject index complements the alphabetical arrangement of articles. This is an important guide to current social work thinking for more advanced inquiries, and the detailed index makes consultation very easy. See also Lingemann (G1799) and Zapf (G1806).

G1802   Romanofsky, Peter, ed.-in-chief. Social Service Organizations. Advisory ed.: Clarke A. Chambers. 2 vols. The Greenwood Encyclopedia of American Institutions. Westport, Conn.: Greenwood Press, 1978.

This dictionary presents substantial historical sketches of approximately 200 national and local voluntary social service agencies in the United States, particularly those listed in the Encyclopedia of Social Work and the Social Work Year Book. Each sketch is approximately 3-5 pages in length and discusses archives, publications and scholarly secondary sources. A particularly valuable appendix lists social service organizations affiliated with religious bodies; other appendixes provide a chronology of founding dates, a subject index of agency functions and a list of name changes and institutional mergers and dissolutions. See also Clegg (G1791).

G1803   Theodorson, George A., and Theodorson, Achilles G. A Modern Dictionary of Sociology. New York: Thomas Y. Crowell, 1969; London: Methuen, 1970.

This 469 page dictionary contains brief definitions of terms drawn from all areas of sociology. It is intended for students, general readers and professional workers in related fields. Definitions are concise and non-technical, providing adequate but not extensive information on about 2500 entry words. See also Fairchild (G1793) and Mitchell (G1800).

G1804   Willems, Emilio. Dictionnaire de Sociologie. Adaptation Française par Armand Cuvillier. Paris. Marcel Rivière, 1961.

Originally published in 1950 as Diccionário de Sociologia, this French translation is a revised and updated version of the Portuguese original. The alphabetically arranged entries provide definitions of sociological terms and concepts together with biographical sketches of internationally known social scientists. Nearly half of the entries are biographical, which detracts somewhat from the definitional value of Willems. In many respects the work is similar to Hoult (G1796); see also Jacquemet (G1798).

G1805   Young, Erle Fisk. Dictionary of Social Welfare. New York: Social Sciences Publications, 1948.

Brief definitions are provided of technical, psychological and slang terms. Although dated, Young can be a useful source of information, particularly in the last category of terms.

G1806   Zapf, Karl. Wörterbuch der Sozialarbeit. Dictionary of Social Work. Schriften des Deutschen Vereins für Offentliche und Privat Fürsorge, 217. Cologne: C. Heymann Verlag, 1961.

Like Lingemann (G1799) this work provides equivalents of social work terms in various languages, including German, English, Dutch, French, Italian and Spanish. Part 1 gives the German entry word followed by terms in the various languages. Genders are listed with the terms, which is helpful for more detailed translating, and there are indexes for all but German words. See also National Association of Social Workers (G1801).

SOCIOLOGY: HANDBOOKS

G1807   Alberione, Giacomo Giuseppe. Fundamentals of Christian Sociology. Boston, Mass.: St. Paul Editions, 1962.

See also Demant (G1816) and Höffner (G1828).

G1808   Birou, Alain. Sociologie et Religion. Collection de Sociologie Religieuse, tome 5. Paris: Economie et Humanisme, Les Editions Ouvrières, 1959.

See also Carrier (G1812), Crofts (G1815) and Laloux (G1833).

G1809   Bonhoeffer, Dietrich. The Communion of Saints: A Dogmatic Inquiry into the Sociology of the Church. New York: Harper and Row, 1963.

Also published as Sanctorum Communio: A Dogmatic Inquiry into the Sociology of the Church (London: William Collins Sons, 1963), this study recognizes the need to study the church both theologically and sociologically and to relate the two. Although the language and style are complicated, and the sociological approach follows that of the formalistic school, this work is rich with insights into the nature of the church. See also Fallding (G1818).

G1810   Budd, Susan. Sociologists and Religion. Themes and Issues in Modern Sociology. London: Collier-Macmillan, 1973.

See also Towler (G1864).

G1811   Burke, Joan Martin. Civil Rights: A Current Guide to the People, Organizations and Events. 2nd ed. New York: R.R. Bowker Company, 1974.

This successor to the 1970 edition by A. John Adams and Joan Martin Burke is an invaluable reference work on civil rights. The main alphabetical section provides information on individuals and organizations concerned with civil rights. This is followed by several excellent appendixes: lists of congressional voting records on civil rights acts, a list of federal and state agencies with civil rights responsibilities, a civil rights chronology, a list of elected black officials, a directory of civil rights resources, a selected bibliography and an index. The range of information thus provided is of value for counselors, political activists, welfare workers and others involved in civil rights in the United States. See also Dollen (G1817).

G1812   Carrier, Hervé. The Sociology of Religious Belonging. Trans. by Arthur J. Arrieri in cooperation with the author. New York: Herder and Herder; London: Darton, Longman and Todd, 1965.

See also Birou (G1808) and Crofts (G1815).

G1813   Catholic Social Guild. Central Executive, ed. The Catholic Social Year Book. Vol. 1- . Oxford: Catholic Social Guild, 1910- ; annual.

The first six volumes of this annual contained essays on activities of the Guild and other charitable organizations in Britain and the United States, as well as a diary of events of the previous year. In 1916 the work was transformed into volumes on single themes such as Catholic social action in Britain, 1909-1959 (1960). See also National Conference of Catholic Charities (G1843-G1845).

G1814   Charities Digest; Being a Classified List of Charities. Vol. 1- . London: Family Welfare Association and Butterworth, 1882- ; irregular.

First published in 1882 as The Annual Charities Register and Digest, this detailed directory contains thirty-four sections on charitable trusts and associations for special and general classes such as family, maternity and child welfare and the blind. A detailed index is provided. For social workers and counselors this is a valuable guide to British charities. See also National Conference of Catholic Charities (G1843-G1845).

G1815   Crofts, Ambrose M. Catholic Sociology: A Text Book for Beginners. Dublin: M.H. Gill, 1960.

See also Birou (G1808) and Carrier (G1812).

G1816   Demant, Vigo Auguste. God, Man, and Society: An Introduction to Christian Sociology. Milwaukee, Wisc.: Morehouse Publishing Company, 1934.

This introductory work is representative of the "Christendom" Group and the Anglican tradition in twentieth century moral theology. It indicates ways in which the Christian religion illuminates social life and its problems. The first section contains a discussion of Christian sociology, the second considers issues of international politics, national politics and economics in the light of the Christian approach. The book is written in a straightforward style. A detailed table of contents is provided, but there is no index. See also Alberione (G1807) and Höffner (G1828).

G1817   Dollen, Charles, ed. Civil Rights: A Source Book. Boston, Mass.: St. Paul Editions, 1964.

See also Burke (G1811).

G1818   Fallding, Harold. The Sociology of Religion: An Explanation of the Unity and Diversity in Religion. New York: McGraw-Hill Book Company, 1974.

This book is intended for those interested in a sociological approach which is basically Durkheimian. The first part treats the unity of religion, the second its diversity, explaining the general role of religion as a force of social unification and fitting many religions into a sociological framework. It contains some useful material on mythology as a social phenomenon, on Marxism and religion, and some statistical tables. It has been criticized for too superficial treatment of some traditions, for example, Buddhism. See also Bonhoeffer (G1809).

G1819   Family Welfare Association. Guide to the Social Services: A Book of Information Regarding the Statutory and Voluntary Services. Vol. 1- . London: Family Welfare Association, 1882- ; annual.

First published in 1882 as part of the Charities Digest, this annual guide contains more than seventy sections on social work; employment and industry; marriage, separation and divorce; children; charities, etc. in Britain. Useful addresses and an index are included. See also Social Services Year Book (G1860).

G1820   Federation of Protestant Welfare Agencies. Directory: A Manual for Benefactors and Their Advisors. 1st ed.- . New York: Federation of Protestant Welfare Agencies, 1935- ; irregular.

Published under various titles since its first appearance, this guide provides directory and descriptive information on a wide range of Protestant agencies. There is an index of types of services listed in the directory. See also National Conference of Catholic Charities (G1843-G1845).

G1821   Ferguson, Elizabeth A. Social Work: An Introduction. 2nd ed. Philadelphia, Pa.: Lippincott, 1969.

See also Friedlander (G1823) and Stroup (G1863).

G1822   Frantz, Charles. <u>The Student Anthropologist's Handbook: A Guide to Research, Training and Career</u>. Cambridge, Mass.: Schenkman, 1972.

Following introductory chapters on the nature of anthropology and the field as a profession, there are sections on field and laboratory research, use of libraries and museums, reference works and aids to library research, a consideration of cultural areas and regional studies. This is not a useful bibliographic guide but otherwise is a helpful source of information for theological students working in social anthropology for the first time.

G1823   Friedlander, Walter A., ed. <u>Concepts and Methods of Social Work</u>. Prentice-Hall Sociology Series. Englewood Cliffs, N.J.: Prentice-Hall, 1958.

This work describes and provides case illustrations of three methods of social work practice: casework, group work, community organization for social welfare. Theoretical discussion is included. Indexes of authors and of subjects are provided. The book is intended for the experienced practitioner as well as the concerned layman. See also Ferguson (G1821) and Stroup (G1863).

G1824   Hargrove, Barbara W. <u>Reformation of the Holy: A Sociology of Religion</u>. Philadelphia, Pa.: F.A. Davis Company, 1971.

This work displays a thorough grasp of much of the classical and contemporary material in the sociology of religion. It treats issues such as the nature and function of religion, religion as a social institution, religion and social class, religion and social change. In some cases a more thorough exposition of theory would have produced a sounder treatment, but as an overview of the field this is adequate. See also Nottingham (G1848) and O'Dea (G1849, G1850).

G1825   Hart, Pauline, and Frankel, Linda. <u>The Student Sociologist's Handbook</u>. 2nd ed. Morristown, N.J.: General Learning Press, 1976.

This 264 page guide is an ideal starting point for students unfamiliar with the discipline of sociology and who wish to understand the basic research skills and tools. Hart begins with brief notes on the study of sociology and then presents sections on writing a sociology paper, doing library research, using periodical literature, the various types of reference sources, data sources, a glossary of statistical terms. The work is adequately indexed for basic reference needs.

G1826   Heasman, Kathleen J. <u>Christians and Social Work</u>. London: SCM Press, 1965.

See also Schultejann (G1858).

G1827   Hill, Michael. <u>A Sociology of Religion</u>. New York: Basic Books, 1974.

First published in Britain (London: Heinemann, 1973), this 285 page introductory textbook locates the sociology of religion within the framework of classical sociological theory. It includes consideration of Weber's thesis on Protestantism and capitalism, of the relationship of religion and socio-political change, secularization, etc. The focus is on Christianity (with limited discussion of primitive religion). Extensive bibliographies are provided after each chapter, and at the end of the book. This is a useful textbook for sociology and theology students and for the interested layman. See also O'Dea (G1849, G1850) and Vernon (G1866).

G1828   Höffner, Joseph. Fundamentals of Christian Sociology. Trans. by Geoffrey Stevens. Westminster, Md.: Newman Press, 1965.

See also Alberione(G1807) and Demant (G1816).

G1829   Houtart, François. Sociology and Pastoral Care. Trans. by Malachy Carroll. Chicago, Ill.: Franciscan Herald Press, 1965.

G1830   Internationales Jahrbuch für Religionssoziologie. Vol. 1- . Wiesbaden: Westdeutscher Verlag, 1966- ; annual.

See also Mensching (G1836).

G1831   Kertzer, Morris Norman, ed. The Rabbi and the Jewish Social Worker. New York: Commission on Synagogue Relations, Federation of Jewish Philanthropies, 1964(?).

G1832   Labbens, Jean. La Sociologie Religieuse. Encyclopédie du Catholique au XXème Siècle. 9 ptie: Les Problèmes du Monde et de l'Eglise, 100. Paris: A. Fayard, 1959.

This brief work on the sociology of religion defines the field, provides relevant statistics, and considers aspects such as the social function of religion. The section on the application of statistics in this area contains some interesting material, but on the whole the approach is rather narrow, neglecting some topics which might have been considered. See also Laloux (G1833).

G1833   Laloux, Joseph. Manuel d'Initiation à la Sociologie Religieuse. Collection FERES. Paris: Editions Universitaires, 1967.

See also Birou (G1808) and Labbens (G1832).

G1834   Lynn, Naomi B.; Matasar, Ann B.; and Rosenberg, Marie Barovic. Research Guide in Women's Studies. Morristown, N.J.: General Learning Press, 1974.

This basic guide of 194 pages is aimed primarily at the undergraduate and contains only four chapters specifically on women's studies. The other six chapters deal with general reference works, writing of research results, use of statistics and other basic topics. For students beyond the very basic level Lynn is not recommended; McKee (G1741) is a more suitable guide in this field.

G1835   Mehl, Roger. The Sociology of Protestantism. Trans. by James H. Farley. Philadelphia, Pa.: Westminster Press; London: SPCK, 1970.

This 324 page translation of Traité de Sociologie du Protestantisme (Neuchâtel: Editions Delachaux et Niestlé, 1965) attempts to provide an overall theoretical perspective on the sociology of religion. It covers topics such as religious practice, development of religious structures, secularization and ecumenism, but has been criticized for inadequate coverage of British and American works, and for failing to set the sociology of religion firmly within general sociological theory. For a study of the sociology of American religion, particularly Protestant groups, see Moberg (G1840).

G1836   Mensching, Gustav. Soziologie der Religion. 2. Aufl. Bonn: Röhrscheid, 1968.

See also Internationales Jahrbuch für Religionssoziologie (G1830).

G1837   McHale, John, and McHale, Magda Cordell, comps. The Futures Directory: An International Listing and Description of Organizations and Individuals Active in Future Studies and Long Range Planning. With Guy Streatfield and Laurence Tobias. Boulder, Colo.: Westview Press; Guildford, Surrey: IPC Science and Technology Press, 1977.

Usefully complementing the World Future Society's less international guide to the same subject (G1789), McHale provides data on a wide range of organizations and individuals actively engaged in future research. It presents information on orientation of work, methods used, time range of work, sources of funding, sponsors and related points. The compilation is separately indexed for organizations and individuals by geographical location, method and subject. For advanced researchers this is a valuable guide to an important field.

G1838   Miller, Haskell M. Compassion and Community: An Appraisal of the Church's Changing Role in Social Welfare. New York: Association Press, 1961.

This work presents brief factual accounts of charity in the past and of recent developments in welfare work, and considers the role of the social worker and special areas of concern such as aging, alcoholism, juvenile delinquency, child welfare and urban housing. Questions for discussion and follow-up projects are included in each of the eight chapters. This provides useful material for clergy, social workers, theological students and others concerned with social welfare.

G1839   Miller, Wayne Charles. A Handbook of American Minorities. New York: New York University Press, 1976.

This work reprints the introductory essays from Miller's Comprehensive Bibliography (G1751); these are intended to provide basic historical overviews of various American minorities and to present bibliographical introductions to useful sources of information. The minorities are treated according to country or region of origin in six main sections: from Africa and the Middle East, from Europe, from Eastern Europe and the Balkans, from Asia, from the Pacific islands, native Americans. There is no index, and this guide is most suitable in its fuller version. See also Wasserman and Morgan (G1868).

G1840   Moberg, David O. The Church as a Social Institution: The Sociology of American Religion. Prentice-Hall Sociology Series. Englewood Cliffs, N.J.: Prentice-Hall, 1962.

This broad ranging work includes some theoretical analysis with emphasis on empirical research. It covers most recent sociological research on American religious institutions, tending to give more adequate treatment to major Protestant groups than to Catholicism or to Judaism. There are numerous footnote references, annotated bibliographies after each of the nineteen chapters and a very thorough index, making this particularly useful as a survey of the literature on this area. For a more European focus on the sociology of religion, especially Protestantism, see Mehl (G1835).

G1841   Mol, J.J., et al., eds. Western Religion: A Country by Country Socio-logical Enquiry. In collaboration with Margaret Hetherton and Margaret Henty. Religion and Reason, vol. 2. The Hague: Mouton, 1972.

This volume contains sections on almost thirty countries, arranged alpha-betically with tables and bibliography appended. It is intended primarily to provide undergraduates with material about the sociology of religion in various Western countries, and data to enable interaction between theory and generalization on a cross cultural basis. Each section includes a brief historical introduction, a demographic section, studies of religious beliefs and practices, relations between religious institutions and politics, class, economy, etc. Although neglecting South and Central America this work is otherwise a valuable information reference containing much useful material. See also Stark (G1862), Weber (G1869) and Wilson (G1871).

G1842   Muthard, John E.; Rogers, Kurt B.; and Crocker, Linda M. Guide to Information Centers for Workers in the Social Services. Gainesville, Fla.: University of Florida, 1972.

In 72 pages this brief guide presents directory information and descriptive statements on a wide range of social services, including education and training, rehabilitation, therapy and medical services. See also Pinson (G1851).

G1843   National Conference of Catholic Charities. Annual Survey, National Conference of Catholic Charities. Vol. 1- . Washington, D.C.: National Conference of Catholic Charities, 1978- .

See also Charities Digest (G1814) and Federation of Protestant Welfare Agencies (G1820).

G1844   National Conference of Catholic Charities. Directory of Catholic Institutions in the United States, 1960. 2nd ed. Washington, D.C.: National Conference of Catholic Charities, 1960.

Basic information, including statistics, is provided on homes for the aged, mothers and children; protective institutions; schools for exceptional children. Geographical arrangement is used, with an index. See also Federation of Protestant Welfare Agencies (G1820).

G1845   National Conference of Catholic Charities. Directory of Diocesan Agencies of Catholic Charities in the United States and Canada. Washington, D.C.: National Conference of Catholic Charities, 1964.

This successor to John O'Grady's Directory of Catholic Charities in the United States (Washington, D.C.: National Conference of Catholic Charities, 1922) lists in geographical arrangement the names, addresses and telephone numbers of local Catholic charities and their staff. Schools of social work are also included. See also Federation of Protestant Welfare Agencies (G1820).

G1846   National Council of Social Service. Voluntary Social Services: Direc-tory of Organisations and Handbook of Information. New ed. London: Bedford Square Press, 1975.

This British directory provides the name and address, name of secretary, date of foundation, objectives, activities and titles of publications for approximately 500 voluntary organizations. Also provided are classified lists of voluntary social service organizations, an alphabetical list of professional and occupational organizations and a list of addresses. The Directory includes an index. It is an indispensible compendium for those requiring information on British social service agencies in the voluntary sector. See also the following entry (G1847) and Willmott (G1870).

G1847   National Directory of Private Social Agencies. Queen's Village, N.Y.: Social Service Publications, 1964- ; irregular, with monthly supplements.

This compilation of information on private social service agencies in the United States lists about 10,000 homes, organizations and other agencies which provide direct assistance to individual applicants or which refer them to appropriate channels. The monthly amendments are essential in keeping this work up-to-date. Many services provided by churches and other religious organizations are included. For a guide to public assistance see Public Welfare Directory (G1853). See also Federa-tion of Protestant Welfare Agencies (G1820) and the preceding entry (G1846).

G1848   Nottingham, Elizabeth Kristine. Religion: A Sociological View. New York: Random House, 1971.

This introductory study of the sociology of religion relies heavily on the classical theorists such as Durkheim and Weber. The approach is functional analysis by societal type, beginning with systems of belief and religious organization in preliterate, preindustrial and industrial-secular societies, and ranging over issues such as the functions of religion with respect to social change. As an introductory work this is useful for its comparative approach, and contains a helpful overview of major theoretical and survey research studies as an appendix. See also Hill (G1827).

G1849   O'Dea, Thomas F. Sociology and the Study of Religion: Theory, Research, Interpretation. New York: Basic Books, 1970.

This 370 page book includes four essays concerned with Catholicism and a section containing O'Dea's "Mormon" work, all concerned with the sociology of religion. The first four essays are somewhat dated. Nonetheless this is an interesting collection of the work of a prominent figure in this field. See also Hill (G1827) and Vernon (G1866).

G1850   O'Dea, Thomas F. The Sociology of Religion. Foundations of Modern Sociology Series. Englewood Cliffs, N.J.: Prentice-Hall, 1966.

This introductory text admirably reviews contributions of important theorists and defines central concepts both in their work and in the field as a whole. It focuses on historical issues, emphasizing this dimension of contemporary sociology of religion. The book is intended primarily for undergraduates. See also Hill (G1827) and Vernon (G1866).

G1851   Pinson, William M. Resource Guide to Current Social Issues. Waco, Tex.: Word Books, 1968.

This 272 page guide includes sections on approximately forty topics of widespread current concern to Christians and others interested in social issues. It lists agencies, organizations and printed sources of information relevant to the various issues. See also Muthard (G1842).

G1852   Ploski, Harry A., and Marr, Warren, II, comps. and eds. The Negro Almanac: A Reference Work on the Afro-American. 3rd ed. New York: Bellwether Company, 1976.

This substantial revision of the 1971 edition follows a similar arrangement and covers a wide range of topics in the social sciences which illustrate various aspects of black life, history and culture. See also Smythe (G1859), which is a guide of similar scope and usefulness.

G1853   Public Welfare Directory. Vol. 1- . Washington, D.C.: American Public Welfare Association, 1940- ; annual.

This important directory lists federal, state and local public assistance and welfare agencies. It includes mental health, social services and other agencies of value to social workers, clergy and counselors. For each state there is an introduction to its public welfare system and a guide to sources of information. See also Federation of Protestant Welfare Agencies (G1820) and National Directory of Private Social Agencies (G1847).

G1854   Rj Associates. Asian American Reference Data Directory. Washington, D.C.: U.S. Department of Health, Education and Welfare, Office of Special Concerns, Office for Asian American Affairs, 1976.

Focusing on topics relevant to the Department of Health, Education and Welfare, this guide covers data developed by government agencies, universities and individuals. Particular attention is paid to the current health, education and social welfare of Asian Americans. There are 480 abstracts on material produced since 1970. Author, ethnic group and subject indexes are provided.

G1855   Robertson, Roland. The Sociological Interpretation of Religion. Introductions to Sociology. New York: Schocken Books, 1970.

Also published in Blackwell's Sociology Series (Oxford: Basil Blackwell, 1970), this 256 page introduction is a helpful guide for students and others new to the field.   Robertson clearly and adequately covers the principles of typological construction in sociology and the main viewpoints relevant to a sociological interpretation of religion. Secularization, the place of the church and related topics are touched upon briefly. Bibliographical references are particularly helpful for the student seeking further information. As a reference volume, Robertson provides adequate data on the theories, concepts and main viewpoints of the field. See also Scharf (G1856) and Schneider (G1857).

G1856   Scharf, Betty R. The Sociological Study of Religion. New York: Harper and Row, 1971.

This study summarizes a wide range of material relevant to the socio-logical study of religion in a critical and ordered manner. Topics such as definitions of religion and of secularization; functional theories of religion; church, sect and denomination; church and state; and religion in industrial societies are examined. This provides a good overview of the field, and is particularly useful in its summaries of theories in the sociology of religion. See also Robertson (G1855) and Schneider (G1857).

G1857   Schneider, Louis. Sociological Approach to Religion. New York: John Wiley and Sons, 1970.

This work sets out to give a more comprehensive account of structural-functional analysis and to suggest the importance of historical and com-parative materials in the study of the sociology of religion. It is suitable for the graduate seminar rather than as an undergraduate introduction to this field. It has been criticized for lacking unity, and resembling a varied collection of essays rather than a unified work. See also Robert-son (G1855) and Scharf (G1856).

G1858   Schultejann, Marie. Ministry of Service: A Manual of Social Involve-ment. New York: Paulist Press, 1976.

See also Heasman (G1826).

G1859   Smythe, Mabel M., ed. The Black American Reference Book. Sponsor-ed by the Phelps-Stokes Fund. Englewood Cliffs, N.J.: Prentice-Hall, 1976.

This substantial revision of John P. Davis' The American Negro Refer-ence Book (Yonkers, N.Y.: Educational Heritage, 1966) contains more than two dozen chapters which summarize current information on the main aspects of black life in America. Some chapters include bibliograph-ical footnotes or bibliographies. Although the presentation varies greatly in quality, this is a useful source of information on black American life and culture. See also Ploski (G1852).

G1860   Social Services Year Book. No. 1- . London: Councils and Education Press, 1972- .

In thirty sections this yearbook provides information on regional services, on voluntary children's homes, on education and training, etc. A digest of statistics and a list of relevant journals are supplied. There is no general index. See also Family Welfare Association (G1819).

G1861   A Sociological Yearbook of Religion in Britain. 8 vols. London: SCM Press, 1968-1975.

During its brief lifetime, this yearbook carried a series of articles dealing with theoretical, empirical and methodological aspects of religion in Britain. Particularly useful for the sociologist interested in recent devel-opments are the empirical studies of religious attitudes, church member-ship and the like.

G1862   Stark, Werner. The Sociology of Religion: A Study of Christendom. 3 vols. New York: Fordham University Press, 1966-1967.

Also published in London by Routledge and Kegan Paul as part of the International Library of Sociology and Social Reconstruction, this is not an account of the concepts, theories and techniques of the sociology of religion. Rather it is an interpretation of evolving Christendom, a "macro-sociology of religion" involving exploration of the relation between religious bodies and the societies in which they exist. A threefold typology is used, corresponding with the three volumes: established religion; sectarian religion; the universal church. The work has been criticized for superficial treatment, broad generalizations, and inadequate reference to other research in this area. See also Mol (G1841).

G1863   Stroup, Herbert Hewitt. Social Work: An Introduction to the Field. 2nd ed. American Sociology Series. New York: American Book Company, 1960.

This work is designed as a basic text for an introductory course, and emphasis is on the structure of social work. Historical material on social work in the United States is included. There is extended treatment of government services and of group work and community organization. Types of social work (medical, psychiatric, etc.) and social work with particular groups (children, delinquents, etc.) are discussed. The work is nontechnical. Indexes of authors and subjects are provided, and relevant periodicals and professional schools are listed in appendixes. See also Ferguson (G1821) and Friedlander (G1823).

G1864   Towler, Robert. Homo Religiosus: Sociological Problems in the Study of Religion. New York: St. Martin's Press, 1974.

See also Budd (G1810).

G1865   Trecker, Audrey R., and Trecker, Harleigh B. Handbook of Community Service Projects. New York: Association Press, 1960.

G1866   Vernon, Glenn M. Sociology of Religion. McGraw-Hill Series in Sociology. New York: McGraw-Hill Book Company, 1962.

This introductory text in the sociology of religion clearly and adequately treats the major conceptual and empirical problems of the field in early chapters, while later sections deal competently with the relationship between religion and several major institutions of society. Sociologically Vernon is an acceptable treatment of the field, but in terms of religion too little is said by way of background detail, empirical evidence or comparison. For this reason this textbook is most useful for those with some knowledge of religion and none of sociology. It is a useful guide to the terminology. See also Hill (G1827) and O'Dea (G1849, G1850).

G1867   Wasserman, Clare Sedacca, and Wasserman, Paul, eds. Health Organizations of the United States, Canada and Internationally: A Directory of Voluntary Associations, Professional Societies and Other Groups Concerned with Health and Related Fields. 2nd ed. Ithaca, N.Y.: Cornell University, Graduate School of Business and Public Administration, 1965.

First published in 1961, this directory contains a fully annotated alphabetical listing of voluntary and unofficial bodies. A subject index is provided.

G1868   Wasserman, Paul, and Morgan, Jean, eds. Ethnic Information Sources of the United States: A Guide to Organizations, Agencies, Foundations, Institutions, Media, Commercial and Trade Bodies, Government Programs, Research Institutes, Libraries and Museums, Religious Organizations, Banking Firms, Festivals and Fairs, Travel and Tourist Offices, Airlines and Ship Lines, Bookdealers and Publishers' Representatives, and Books, Pamphlets and Audiovisuals on Specific Ethnic Groups. Detroit, Mich.: Gale Research Company, 1976.

This extremely comprehensive guide contains sections on more than 100 ethnic groups arranged alphabetically by group. Information sources are indicated in subtitles grouped under twenty-six major headings within each section. Blacks, native Americans and Eskimos are not included. There are indexes of organizations and publications. The data on religious bodies and on other publications are especially useful, and overall Wasserman is a most valuable resource guide to many American minorities. See also Miller (G1839), Ploski (G1852) and Smythe (G1859).

G1869   Weber, Max. The Sociology of Religion. Trans. by Ephraim Fischoff. Boston, Mass.: Beacon Press, 1963.

This volume provides the first English translation of the chapter entitled "Religionssoziologie (Typen religiöser Vergemeinschaftlung)" in Wirtschaft und Gesellschaft. It summarizes and systematizes studies of Confucius and Lao-tun in China, the ancient Vedic and Buddhist literature in India, and the Old Testament prophets of ancient Judaism. The chapter is of book length and provides a summary of Weber's comparative analysis of world religions. See also Mol (G1841).

G1870   Willmott, Phyllis, ed. Public Social Services: Handbook of Information. 13th ed. London: Bedford Square Press, 1973.

This companion to the Council's directory of voluntary social services (G1846) includes chapters on social security, housing and the administration of justice. A detailed nonanalytical index is provided. This is an indispensible guide to public social services in Britain.

G1871   Wilson, Bryan. Religion in Sociological Perspective. Oxford: Oxford University Press, 1982.

This somewhat eclectic study seeks to trace the dominant contours of religion as perceived by the sociologist. Wilson is not as systematic as O'Dea (G1849, G1850) but ranges from the study of sectarianism to relations between religion and culture in modern Eastern and Western societies. On the topics treated this is a useful work, as it provides more detail than is possible in introductory textbooks; the latter, however, provide a better overview of the entire field. See also Mol (G1841).

G1872   Winston, Eric V.A., and Trezise, Marilyn, comps. Directory of Urban Affairs Information and Research Centers. Metuchen, N.J.: Scarecrow Press, 1970.

This 175 page listing provides information on more than 250 organizations, agencies and institutions engaged in activities concerned with solving urban problems. Arrangement is alphabetical with geographical and subject indexes. For sociologists and others engaged in urban studies, as well as for practitioners in various fields, this is a useful but increasingly dated guide to resources.

G1873 Women's Organizations and Leaders. Washington, D.C.: Today Publications and News Service, 1973- ; annual (?).

This comprehensive directory and guide to more than 8000 women's organizations and their leaders includes individuals active in the women's movement through their actions and writings; it also covers those individuals of importance through their institutional affiliations, thereby providing a broadly comprehensive guide. It is most useful for those who wish to contact feminists in key positions or those with particular expertise. For a guide on women's studies see Lynn (G1834).

Author Index

Seminariis et Studiorum, G1283

Catholic Church. Congregatio pro Clericis, G1284, G1358

Catholic Church. Congregatio Sacrorum Rituum, G0901

Catholic Church. International Committee on English in the Liturgy, G0516, G0519

Catholic Church. National Conference of Catholic Bishops, G1285

Catholic College Bureau, G1286, G1288

Catholic Education Council for England and Wales, G1287

Catholic Hospital Association, G1600

Catholic Library Association, G0081

Catholic Schools Bureau, G1288

Catholic Social Guild, G1813

Cavarnos, C., G0902

Center for Applied Research in the Apostolate, G1290

Center for Parish Development, G0082

Centre Documentaire Catechetique, G1173

Chamberlin, M.W., G0272

Chambers, C.A., G1802

Chambers, M.M., G1710, G1747

Chambers, R., G1056

Champlin, J.D., Jr., G0403

Chapin, J., G1130

Chaplin, J.P., G1547

Chappell, P., G0903

Charry, D., G1601

Chevalier, C.U.J., G0261, G0273

Chevalier, J., G0404

Chicago Institute for Psychoanalysis, G1444

Child, H., G0810

Christ-Janer, A., G0811

Christensen, J.L., G0524-G0527, G1603

Christian Science Publishing Society, G0904

Christie, Y., G0812

Chrysostom, J., G0754

Chun, Ki-Taek, G1447

Church of England, G0083, G0312, G0313, G0419, G0458, G0484, G0491, G0528, G0584, G0585, G0782, G0884, G0907, G0996

Church of England. Central Council of Diocesan Advisory Committees, G0084

Church of England. Liturgical Commission, G0529-G0532

Church of Scotland, G0533, G0905, G0963

Church of Scotland. Committee on Public Worship and Aids to Devotion, G0534, G0535

Church of South India, G0536

Church of the Brethren, G0537

Church of the Nazarene, G0085

Church Union, G1294

Church Ushers Association of New York, G0538

Churchill, J., G0908

Cirlot, J.E., G0405

Clark, H.G., G0086

Clark, K.C., G0274

Clark, W.H., G1604

Clarke, R.F., G1400

Clarke, W.K.L., G0539

Cleary, J.W., G1027

Clebsch, W.A., G1605

Clegg, J., G1791

Clinard, H.G., G1054

Clinebell, H.J., Jr., G1606, G1607

Cobb, J.B., Jr., G1608

Cobb, S., G1447

Cober, K.L., G1295, G1296

Coe, W.C., G1677

Coffin, H.S., G0540

Cohen, L., G1609

Colles, D., G0810

Collins, K.T., G1236

Colquhoun, F., G0541

Colston, C.G., G1635

Columbia University. Psychology Library, G1448-G1451

Columbia University. Teachers' College Library, G1174

Communaute de Taize, G0542

Communications/Research/Machines, Inc., G1452

Congregational Union of England and Wales, G0543, G0909

Conlay, I., G0813

Connelly, J., G0910

Conway, J.D., G1610

Coogan, D.F., Jr., G0704

Cook, M., G1412

Cooke, B.J., G0088

Cornish, G.P., G0275

Corrigan, J.T., G0089, G1175

Corwin, E.T., G0090

Cosgrove, M.P., G1611

Couch, H.F., G0544

Council for the Care of Churches, G0276

Council on Social Work Education,

Title Index

tion, G1117

Fundamentals of the Liturgy, G0666

Funding in Aging: Public, Private and Voluntary, G1609

Funeral Customs, Their Origin and Development, G0712

Funeral Encyclopedia, a Source Book, G0784

Funeral Handbook, G0723

Funeral Service, G0297

Funeral Services, G0525

Funeral Source Book, G0647

Futures Directory, G1837

Ganley's Catholic Schools in the United States, G1364

Gauging Sermon Effectiveness, G1087

General Catalogue of Printed Books. Liturgies, G0267

General Catechetical Directory, G1284, G1358

General Intercessions, G0679

General Menaion, G0695

General Psychology: Modeling Behavior and Experience, G1615

George Pullen Jackson Collection of Southern Hymnody, G0346

Geschichte der Auflosung der Alten Gottesdienstlichen Formen, G0592

Geschichte der Evangelischen Kirchenmusik, G0887

Geschichte der Quellen und Literatur des Canonischen Rechts, G0034

Geschichte der Quellen und Literatur des Evangelischen Kirchenrichts, G0035

Glossary of Ecclesiastical Ornament and Costume, G0713

Glossary of Liturgical and Ecclesiastical Terms, G0432

Glossary of Social Work Terms in English, French, German, G1799

Glossary of Technical Terms, G1570

God, Man, and Society, G1816

God's Party, G0719

God's Word Today, G1281

Gospel and Christian Education, G1419

Gospel in Hymns, G0880

Gottesdienstliche Predigt, G1113

Gradual Romain, G0931

Grammar of Plainsong, G0932

Granger's Index to Poetry, G1133

Greek Orthodox Catechism, G1280

Gregorian Chant, G0877

Gregorianisch, G0265

Group Behavior: A Guide to Information Sources, G1471

Group Work in the Helping Professions, G1541

Growth and Development of the Catholic School System in the U.S., G1276

Grundlagen der Religionspadagogik, G1392

Grundlegung der Pastoraltheologie als Praktische Theologie, G0200

Grundriss der Praktischen Theologie, G0119

Grundsatzfragen des Offentlichen Lebens, G0039

Guidance and Counseling in Schools, G1349

Guide Book for Catholic Church Choirmasters, G0994

Guide for the Christian Assembly, G0658

Guide for the Organization and Operation of a Religious Resource Center, G0089

Guide for the Priest during Parish Services, G0634

Guide in the Selection of a Catholic School, G1288

Guide to American Educational Directories, G1192

Guide to Art Reference Books, G0272

Guide to Basic Information Sources in the Visual Arts, G0327

Guide to Church Furniture, G0816

Guide to Church Ushering, G0567

Guide to Effective Hymn Playing, G0876

Guide to Hymn Study, G1015

Guide to Information Centers for Workers in the Social Services, G1842

Guide to Library Research in Psychology, G1434

Guide to Mental Health Services, G1634

Guide to Music for the Church Year, G0256

Guide to Music in Worship, G0326

Guide to Pastoral Care, G0242

Guide to Periodicals in Education, G1171

Guide to Periodicals in Education and Its Academic Disciplines, G1171

Handbook of Psychological Literature, G1614

Handbook of Psychological Terms, G1558

Handbook of Public Prayer, G0590

Handbook of Research Design and Social Measurement, G0175

Handbook of Stewardship Procedures, G0229

Handbook of Symbols in Christian Art, G0859

Handbook of the Liturgy, G0707

Handbook of the Psychology of Aging, G1591

Handbook on Christian Education in the Inner City, G1357

Handbook on the Principles of Church Building, G0823

Handbook to the Church Hymnary, G0963

Handbook to the "Church Hymnary": Supplement, G0972

Handbuch der Katholischen Kirchenmusik, G0948

Handbuch der Musikgeschichte, G0871

Handbuch der Pastoraltheologie, G0062

Handbuch der Psychologie, G1645

Handbuch der Psychologie in 12 Banden, G1565

Handbuch des Religionsunterrichts, G1375

Handbuch zum Evangelischen Kirchengesangbuch, G0956

Handling the Church's Money, G0195

Handworterbuch der Sozialwissenschaften, G0043

Handworterbuch der Staatswissenschaften, G0043

Harper's Dictionary of Music, G0383

Harper's Encyclopedia of Art, G0420

Harvard Dictionary of Music, G0384

Harvard Guide to Modern Psychiatry, G1663

Harvard List of Books in Psychology, G1475

Health Organizations of the United States, Canada and Internationally, G1867

Hiscox Guide for Baptist Churches, G0127

Hiscox Standard Baptist Manual, G0127

Histoire de l'Art Depuis les Premiers Temps Chretians, G0846

Histoire de la Musique Religieuse des Origines a Nos Jours, G0941

Histoire du Breviaire Romain, G0477

Historia Iuris Canonici Latini Institutiones Academicae, G0223

Historical Companion to Hymns Ancient and Modern, G0927

History of Anglican Liturgy, G0547

History of Architectural Development, G0860

History of Art: A Survey of the Major Visual Arts, G0838

History of Byzantine Music and Hymnography, G1020

History of Catholic Church Music, G0923

History of Catholic Education in the United States, G1278

History of Christian Worship, G0763

History of Church Music [Appleby], G0878

History of Church Music [Weinmann], G1019

History of Our Lord As Exemplified in Works of Art, G0834

History of Preaching, G1058

History of Preaching: From the Close of the Nineteenth Century, G1112

History of Psychiatry, G1580

History of Psychology, G1595

History of Psychology: A Guide to Information Sources, G1538

History of Religious Education, G1406

History of the Cure of Souls, G0242

History of the Roman Breviary, G0477

History of Western Education, G1270

History of Western Music, G0934

Holy Orthodox Church, G0549

Holy See at Work, G0158

Holy-Days and Holidays, G1060

Home Book of Bible Quotations, G1152

Home Book of Proverbs, Maxims and Familiar Phrases, G1153

Home Book of Quotations, Classical and Modern, G1154

Homiletics: A Manual of the Theory and Practice of Preaching, G1099

Missale Romanum, ex Decreto Sacrosancti Concilii Tridentini, G0505

Missale Romanum, ex Decreto Sacrosancti Concilii Tridentini Restitutum, G0520

Models of Teaching, G1337

Modern Architecture and Christian Celebration, G0815

Modern British Society, G1784

Modern Catechetics: Message and Method in Religious Formation, G1396

Modern Church Architecture, G0811

Modern Dictionary of Sociology, G1803

Modern Liturgical Bibliography, G0367

Modern Liturgical Texts, G0531

Modern Liturgy Handbook, G0670

Modern Practice of Adult Education, G1339

Monitor Ecclesiasticus, G0025

Monumenta Eucharistica et Liturgica Vetustissima Collegit, G0715

More Books on the Social Services, G1754

More Parish Liturgies, G0488

More Words on Aging: Supplement, G1531

Morning Sacrifice, G0602

Multiple Staff Ministry, G0144

Music and Worship in the Anglican Church, 597-1967, G0903

Music and Worship in the Church, G0953

Music for the Church Year, G0937

Music for the Protestant CHurch Choir, G0365

Music in England before 1800, G0293

Music in Protestant Worship, G1007

Music in the Church, G0898

Music in the History of the Western Church, G0913

Music in the Life of the Church [Foote], G0924

Music in the Life of the Church [Sydnor], G1008

Music in the Pentecostal Church, G0874

Music Index, G0328

Music of the English Church, G0950

Music of the English Parish Church, G1011

Music of the Methodist Hymn-Book, G0949

Music Reference and Research Materials, G0283

Musica Divina, G0977

Musical Periodical Literature, G0322

Musicalia, G0279

Musician's Guide to Church Music, G0947

Musicological Works in Progress, G0248

Musik in Geschichte und Gegenwart, G0394

Musikhandschriften des Ansbacher Inventars von 1686, G0360

Musique Religieuse, G0872

Myth and Religion in European Painting, 1270-1700, G0391

NCEA/Ganley's Catholic Schools in America, G1364

NICEM Update of Nonbook Media, G1213

Names in the History of Psychology, G1576

National Children's Directory, G1687

National Directory of Private Social Agencies, G1847

National Directory of Retirement Residences, G1657

National Directory of Senior Centers, G1538

National Directory on Housing for Older People, G1662

National Inventory of Parish Catechetical Programs, G1408

Negro Almanac, G1852

Negro in America, G1750

Negro in American History and Culture, G1781

Neues Glaubensbuch, G1313

New Baptist Song Book 1971, G0979

New Catechetical Methods, G1318

New Catechism: Catholic Faith for Adults, G1368

New Concept Guide to Reference in Education, G1216

New Congregational Hymn Book, G0909

New Dictionary of Psychology, G1557

New Dictionary of the Liturgy, G0450

New Directory for Baptist Churches, G0127

New Educator's Library, G1257

New Encyclopedia of Child Care

Pastor and Community Resources, G0147

Pastor and His Library, G0178

Pastor and His Ministry, G0072

Pastor and the People, G0209

Pastor As Counselor, G1625

Pastor As Worship Leader, G0744

Pastor at Work, G0077

Pastor Ministers in Time of Death, G1526

Pastoral Administration, G0058

Pastoral Care and Counseling Abstracts, G1511

Pastoral Care in Historical Perspective, G1605

Pastoral Care in the Church, G1596

Pastoral Care in the Modern Hospital, G1622

Pastoral Care of Families, G1638

Pastoral Catechetics, G1330

Pastoral Companion, G0171

Pastoral Counseling [Hostie], G1637

Pastoral Counseling [Oates], G1666

Pastoral Counseling and Preaching, G1599

Pastoral Counseling Guidebook, G1646

Pastoral Preaching, G1075

Pastor's Counseling Handbook, G1603

Pastor's Handbook, G0201

Pastor's Manual, G0129

Pastor's Pocket Manual for Hospital and Sickroom, G1586

Pastor's Prayerbook, Selected and Arranged for Various Occasions, G0730

Pastor's Public Relations, G0098

Pastor's Role in Educational Ministry, G1373

Pelican History of Art, G0847

Penguin Dictionary of Architecture, G0447

People Worship, G0752

Periodicals for Religious Education Resource Centers, G1175

Person and Counselor, G1643

Person to Person, G1688

Personal Finance for Clergymen, G0071

Personality Tests and Reviews, G1440

Philosophy of Education: A Select Bibliography, G1219

Philosophy of Education: An Organization of Topics [Broudy], G1168

Philosophy of Education: An Organization of Topics [Smith], G1226

Piccolo Dizionario Liturgico, G0433

Pilgrim Hymnal, G0976, G0986

Place of Christ in Liturgical Prayer, G0623

Planning a Christian Funeral, G0711

Planning and Furnishing the Church Library, G0139

Planning Better Sabbath Schools, G1365

Planning Christian Education in Your Church, G1269

Planning for Church Music, G1009

Planning the Church Bulletin for Effective Worship, G0125

Pocket Primer of Parliamentary Procedure, G0222

Polity and Practice in Baptist Churches, G0168

Polyglot Dictionary of Musical Terms, G0435

Pontifical Romain, G0714

Pontificale Romanum, G0513, G0521

Poverty and Health in the United States, G1746

Poverty and Human Resources Abstracts, G1730

Poverty in Canada and the United States, G1771

Poverty, Participation, Protest, Power and Black Americans, G1717

Power in Preaching, G1105

Practical Church Administration Handbook, G0185

Practical Commentary on the Code of Canon Law, G0246

Practical Studies in the Liturgy, G0790

Practical Theology: Bibliography for Graduate Studies, G0019

Praktisch-Theologisches Handbuch, G0187

Praktisches Worterbuch der Religionspadagogik und Katechetik, G1246

Praxis der Verkundigung, G1093

Prayer, G0553

Prayer Book Dictionary [Harford], G0419

Prayer Book Dictionary [Tatlock], G0458

Prayer for Every Meeting, G0733

Prayer of Christians, G0510

Sacristan's Manual, G0675

Sacristy Manual, G0593

Sage Race Relations Abstracts, G1768

Sage Urban Studies Abstracts, G1769

Sainte Vierge, G0856

Saints and Their Attributes, G0852

Saints and Their Emblems, G0412

Saints in Season, G0581

Saints, Signs and Symbols, G0849

Sayings and Sentences for Church Bulletins, G1135

School Question, G1182

Schools Overseas Available for the Children of North American Missionaries, G1361

Schwenkfelder Hymnology and the Sources of the First Schwenkfelder Hymn-Book Printed in America, G0997

Scriptores Ecclesiastici de Musica Sacra Potissimum, G0277, G0295

Scriptorum de Musica Medii Aevi Novam Seriem, G0277

Select List of Research, Surveys and Theses in Youth Work, G1752

Select Liturgical Lexicon, G0409

Selected Bibliography of North American Social Welfare Literature, G1712

Selected List of Choruses for Women's Voices, G0314

Selected List of Church Music Recordings, G0355

Selected References on Aging, G1532

Selective Bibliography for the Study of Hymns, G0274

Selective Bibliography of Existenitalism in Education, G1203

Selective Guide to Materials for Mental Health and Family Life, G1501

Seminaria Ecclesiae Catholicae, G1283

Senior Centers in the United States, G1583

Serial Publications in Anthropology, G1738

Sermon Suggestions in Outline, G1120

Servant of the Word, G1066

Service Book and Hymnal of the Lutheran Church in America, G0316, G0317, G0648

Service Book for Ministers, G0649

Service Book of the Holy Orthodox-Catholic Apostolic Church, G0698

Service Explained for Use in Church Bulletins, G0636

Service Manual for Ministers, G0721

Service Manual for Ministers of Non-Liturgical Churches, G0616

Service Music and Anthems for the Nonprofessional Choir, G0288

Services for Trial Use [Episcopal Church], G0575, G0746

Sex Roles, G1431

Sexual Barrier, G1729

Shape of Religious Instruction, G1348

Shape of the Liturgy, G0562

Shaping the Church's Educational Ministry, G1296

Short Baptist Manual of Polity and Practice, G0169

Short Bibliography for the Study of Hymns, G0274

Short Titles of Books Relating to or Illustrating the History and Practice of Psalmody in the United States, 1620-1820, G0374

Signs and Symbols in Christian Art, G0820

Simplified Techniques of Counseling, G1594

Singing Church [Brown], G0895

Singing Church [Phillips], G0975

Small Catechism, G1402

Small Liturgical Dictionary, G0433

Social Compass, G1773

Social Science Research Handbook, G0166

Social Sciences and Humanities Index, G0038

Social Sciences Citation Index, G0037

Social Sciences Index, G0038

Social Scientific Studies of Religion, G0004

Social Service Organizations, G1802

Social Services Year Book, G1860

Social Stratification, G1722

Social Work: An Introduction [Ferguson], G1821

Social Work: An Introduction to the Field, G1863

Social Work Education: A Bibliography, G1737

Social Work Research and Abstracts, G1774

Social Work Year Book, G1801

Subject Index

architecture
see also art; church architecture
dictionaries, G0380, G0382, G0397,
G0420, G0439, G0447, G0454
handbooks, G0860
indexes, G0251
periodicals, G0251
art
see also archeology; architecture
bibliographies, G0249, G0254,
G0255, G0272, G0286, G0327,
G0349
dictionaries, G0380, G0382, G0388,
G0389, G0391, G0403, G0406,
G0414, G0416, G0418, G0420,
G0426, G0437, G0439-G0442,
G0446, G0459, G0466
handbooks, G0800-G0869
indexes, G0253
  Byzantine
    bibliography, G0249
    dictionary, G0466
  classical
    dictionary, G0414
  Medieval
    dictionary, G0391
  religious
    see also iconography; symbolism
    bibliography, G0341
    dictionaries, G0391, G0443
    handbooks, G0802, G0803,
    G0812, G0813, G0818, G0821,
    G0825, G0830, G0831, G0833-
    G0837, G0846, G0858
    index, G0342
  Renaissance
    dictionary, G0391
audio-visual resources
see also education, audio-visual
resources for; religious education,
audio-visual resources for
bibliographies, G1159, G1160,
G1163
authority
in the church
bibliography, G0021

baptism
see also sacraments
bibliography, G0338
documents, G0795
handbooks, G0617
Baptist Church
handbook, G0218
  associations of the
    handbook, G0116

and church government
  handbooks, G0092, G0106,
  G0114, G0127, G0128, G0163,
  G0168, G0169, G0181, G0191
hymns of the
  see hymns, Baptist
and religious education
  handbook, G1296
worship in the
  handbooks, G0605, G0721
behavior therapy
see also psychotherapy
bibliography, G1507
bereavement
see death
Bible
and preaching
  see preaching, and the Bible
Bible colleges
see also theological schools
directories, G1260, G1398, G1417
blacks
see also minority groups
bibliographies, G1700, G1714-
G1717, G1742, G1750, G1757,
G1758-G1761, G1764, G1781,
G1783, G1785
Book of Common Prayer, G0528,
G0571, G0748
see also prayer books; Proposed
Book of Common Prayer
concordance, G0611
dictionaries, G0419, G0458
handbooks, G0484, G0491, G0539,
G0585, G0599, G0633, G0676,
G0748, G0755, G0782
indexes, G0619, G0708
Book of Worship, The
handbook, G0564
books of hours
see also breviaries
bibliographies, G0263, G0264,
G0300, G0309
breviaries, G0503, G0514, G0518,
G0608, G0678
see also books of hours; prayers
bibliographies, G0262
handbooks, G0477, G0703, G0750,
G0893, G0899

canon law
see also church administration
Eastern Orthodox
  dictionary, G0050
  documents, G0196
  handbook, G0196

canon law, cont.
  Protestant
    bibliography, G0035
    handbooks, G0083, G0177
  Roman Catholic
    abstracts, G0007
    bibliographies, G0001, G0002,
      G0009, G0012, G0025, G0034,
      G0036, G0042
    concordance, G0154
    dictionaries, G0047, G0048,
      G0050, G0054
    documents, G0069, G0078-G0080,
      G0110
    handbooks, G0057, G0069, G0078,
      G0134, G0171, G0196, G0204,
      G0206, G0223, G0233, G0240,
      G0246
careers guidance
  see vocational guidance
catechetics
  see also religious education
  documents, G1308, G1355
  handbooks, G1273, G1280-G1282,
    G1284, G1294, G1313, G1318,
    G1322, G1325, G1330, G1331,
    G1344, G1352, G1358, G1362,
    G1363, G1368-G1370, G1372,
    G1376, G1382, G1396, G1400,
    G1402, G1408, G1413
    Anglican
      handbooks, G1294, G1372,
        G1413
    Church of Scotland
      handbook, G1376
    Eastern Orthodox
      handbooks, G1280, G1369, G1370
    Lutheran
      handbook, G1402
    Roman Catholic
      handbooks, G1281, G1282, G1284,
        G1308, G1318, G1325, G1330,
        G1344, G1355, G1358, G1368,
        G1400, G1408
cathedrals
  see also church architecture
  English
    handbooks, G0827, G0862
chaplains
  see also campus chaplains; hospital
  chaplains
  Roman Catholic
    directory, G1304
charities
  see also voluntary organizations
  directories, G1814, G1843-G1845

child abuse
  see also child care; family
  bibliographies, G1445, G1483
  handbook, G1602
child care
  see also adoption; child abuse;
  children; family
  bibliography, G1467
  dictionary, G1556
child development
  abstracts, G1446
  bibliographies, G1427, G1446
child psychiatry
  bibliography, G1427
  dictionary, G1563
children
  see also child care; family
  services to
    directories, G1660, G1673, G1687
choral music
  see also Gregorian chant; hymns;
  liturgy; music; plainsong; solo
  voice; worship
  bibliographies, G0270, G0288,
    G0314, G0320, G0330, G0331,
    G0365
  handbooks, G0891, G0892, G0895,
    G0908, G0921, G0937, G0969,
    G0974, G0975, G0994, G1007,
    G1024
Christian colleges
  see church-related colleges
Christian Reformed Church
  and church government
    handbook, G0220
Christian Science
  and hymns
    see hymns, Christian Science
Christmas
  see also church festivals
  handbooks, G0474, G0545, G0556,
    G0603
church administration
  see also church government;
  church organizations; laity;
  parish development; worship
  handbooks, G0058, G0061, G0067,
    G0068, G0082, G0095-G0097,
    G0100, G0104, G0105, G0107,
    G0117, G0118, G0120, G0122,
    G0130, G0138, G0143, G0155,
    G0156, G0159, G0180, G0185,
    G0188, G0193, G0197, G0205,
    G0208, G0210, G0243, G0244,
    G0247
church architecture

church architecture, cont.
see also church monuments
handbooks, G0800, G0805, G0807,
G0811, G0815, G0821-G0823,
G0826, G0828, G0829, G0839,
G0841, G0844, G0858, G0861,
G0867
Byzantine
handbook, G0839
early Christian
handbook, G0821
English
handbook, G0805
Irish
handbook, G0841
Scottish
handbooks, G0828, G0844
church archives
see also church libraries
handbooks, G0060, G0228
church buildings
see church property
church festivals
see also Christmas; Easter
handbooks, G0467, G0499, G0563,
G0583, G0595, G0597, G0598,
G0601, G0657, G0660, G0693-
G0695, G0762, G0767, G0774,
G0775, G0787, G0789, G0792,
G0808, G1056, G1060, G1084,
G1096
church finance
see also fund raising
handbooks, G0093, G0102, G0111,
G0123, G0131, G0132, G0153,
G0189, G0195, G0229, G0237,
G0238
church furnishings
see also vestments; worship
handbooks, G0816, G0823, G0829,
G0832, G0833, G0842, G0851,
G0864
church government
see also canon law; church admin-
istration; church organizations;
laity; and entries under specific
denominations
handbooks, G0064, G0066, G0085,
G0090, G0092, G0101, G0106,
G0109, G0114, G0127, G0128,
G0146, G0158, G0161, G0163,
G0168, G0169, G0181, G0198,
G0199, G0211, G0220, G0221,
G0247
church libraries
see also church archives

directories, G0081
handbooks, G0059, G0065, G0073,
G0075, G0089, G0103, G0124,
G0137, G0139, G0140, G0150,
G0151, G0167, G0170, G0174,
G0178, G0182, G0183, G0212,
G0213, G0216, G0217, G0219,
G0226, G0230, G0231, G0236,
G0241
church management
see church administration
church monuments
see also church architecture
handbooks, G0809, G0814, G0819
church music
see also choral music, Gregorian
chant; hymnology; hymns; liturgy;
plainsong; worship
bibliographies, G0256, G0271,
G0277, G0278, G0288, G0295,
G0296, G0298, G0299, G0304,
G0305, G0325, G0344, G0352,
G0356, G0361, G0376-G0378
dictionaries, G0402, G0407, G0423,
G0431, G0443-G0445, G0451,
G0457, G0465
dissertations, G0298
handbooks, G0872, G0874, G0878,
G0883, G0887, G0889, G0895,
G0898, G0901-G0903, G0906,
G0908, G0913, G0915, G0918,
G0922-G0924, G0930, G0937-
G0942, G0945-G0948, G0950,
G0953, G0959, G0964, G0966,
G0968, G0973, G0975, G0977,
G0983-G0985, G0987, G0992,
G0993, G0995, G1000-G1006,
G1008, G1009, G1011, G1012,
G1013, G1016, G1017, G1019,
G1020, G1021, G1025, G1026
recordings, G0302, G0355
Afro-American
bibliography, G0305
American
handbooks, G0918, G0959,
G1006
Anglican
bibliographies, G0278, G0288
handbooks, G0903, G0950,
G0975
Byzantine
handbooks, G0902, G0995,
G1016, G1020
English
bibliographies, G0278, G0377,
G0378

church music, cont.
  Jewish
    bibliographies,   G0361,   G0376
    dictionary, G0444
  Moravian
    bibliographies, G0296,   G0344
  Pentecostal
    handbook, G0874
  Protestant
    dictionary, G0407
    handbooks,   G0887,   G0889,
    G0922, G0942, G1005, G1006,
    G1012, G1017
  Roman Catholic
    dictionaries,   G0431,   G0465
    handbooks,   G0901,   G0923,
    G0938, G0940, G0946, G0948,
    G0964,   G0966,   G0968,   G1003
  Spanish
    bibliography, G0299
  and theology
    handbooks,   G0987,   G1004
Church of England
  see Anglican Church
Church of Jesus Christ of Latter-
Day Saints
  worship in
    handbook, G0600
Church of Scotland
  and religious education
    handbook, G1376
  worship in the, G0533-G0535
Church of South India
  worship in the
    handbook, G0536
Church of the Brethren
  worship in the
    handbook, G0537
Church of the Nazarene
  handbooks, G0085, G0190
church organizations
  see   also   church   administration;
  church government; laity; parish
  activities; voluntary organizations
  handbooks, G0074, G0108, G0152,
  G0207
    Baptist
      handbook, G0116
    Roman Catholic
      handbook, G0165
church polity
  see church government
church property
  see   also   church   administration;
  churchyards
  handbooks, G0063, G0084, G0115,
  G0224

  conservation of
    bibliography, G0276
church-related colleges
  directories, G1263, G1286, G1298,
  G1371,   G1374,   G1384,   G1398
church-related universities
  directories, G1286, G1371
church renewal
  see parish development
church schools
  directories, G1292, G1293
    Jewish
      directory, G1336
    Protestant
      handbooks,   G1268,   G1390
    Reorganized   Church   of   Jesus
    Christ   of   Latter-Day   Saints
      handbook, G1383
    Roman Catholic
      directories,   G1287-G1289,
      G1305, G1364, G1366, G1367,
      G1371
      handbooks,   G1276-G1278,
      G1341, G1342, G1345, G1354
    Seventh-Day Adventist
      handbook, G1365
church-state relations
  and education
    bibliography, G1182
churchyards
  see also church property
  handbook, G0809
civil law
  in Germany
    bibliography, G0002
civil rights
  see also minority groups
  handbooks, G1811, G1817
clergy
  problems of
    handbooks, G1639, G1680
  psychological studies of
    abstracts, G1496
communication
  see   also   homiletics;   public   relations; rhetoric
  bibliographies,   G1028,   G1029
  handbooks, G0125, G1035, G1048,
  G1049,   G1077,   G1080,   G1081,
  G1101, G1117
Communion
  see eucharist
conference centers
  directory, G1310
confirmation
  see also sacraments
  handbook, G0617

Congregational Union of England and Wales
  worship in the
    handbook, G0543
continuing education
  see also adult education
  directory, G1297
  handbook, G1388
  yearbook, G1421
counseling
  see also pastoral care
  bibliographies, G1422-G1541
  dictionaries, G1542-G1576
  handbooks, G1577-G1695

death
  bibliographies, G1466, G1487, G1488,
    G1505, G1506, G1512, G1525,
    G1526, G1528
  handbooks, G1587, G1593, G1649
dedication services
  see also worship
  handbooks, G0613,   G0639, G0650
devotional literature
  see also prayer
  bibliographies,   G0260,   G0282,
    G0358, G0362
devotional programs
  see also worship
  dictionary, G0400
dissent
  see also violence
  bibliographies,   G1701,   G1727,
    G1749
divorce
  see also family; marriage
  bibliographies,   G1491,   G1503,
    G1520
  handbook, G1597
drama
  bibliography, G0275
drug abuse
  see also alcoholism
  bibliographies, G1425,   G1460,
    G1470, G1495, G1521
dying
  see death

Easter
  see also church festivals
  handbooks, G0485, G0785
Eastern Orthodoxy
  hymns of
    see hymns, Eastern Orthodox
  liturgies of, G0692-G0698, G0706
  handbooks, G0483, G0549, G0550,

    G0557,   G0580,   G0602,   G0628,
    G0640,   G0641,   G0643,   G0685,
    G0717,   G0735,   G0753,   G0760,
    G0761, G0774
  prayers of, G0777
    see also Eastern   Orthodoxy,
    liturgies of
  handbook, G0747
  and religious education
    handbooks, G1280, G1369, G1370
  vestments of
    handbook, G0625
education
  see also adult education; church-
  related colleges; church-related
  schools; church-related universities; continuing education; religious
  education
  abstracts, G1229
  bibliographies,   G1159-G1233
  biographies, G1244, G1251
  dictionaries, G1234-G1257
  directories, G1192, G1193
  handbooks, G1258-G1421
  indexes, G1167, G1178, G1184,
    G1185, G1221
  yearbooks, G1311, G1418
    audio-visual resources for
      see also religious education;
      audio-visual   resources   for
    bibliographies,   G1159,   G1163,
      G1164, G1194, G1225
    indexes,   G1185,   G1205-G1213
  and equal opportunity
    yearbook, G1399
  and evaluation
    dictionary, G1234
  philosophy of
    bibliographies,   G1168,   G1219,
      G1226
  sociology of
    abstracts, G1227
  statistics on
    bibliography, G1187
  and values
    handbooks,   G1323,   G1324
Eglise Reforme de France
  see Reformed   Church   of   France
English   Catholic   Prayer   Book,
  G0569
English Hymnal, The
  index, G0280
episcopal ceremonies
  see also worship
  Roman Catholic
    handbook, G0765

hymns, Roman Catholic, cont.
    handbooks, G0569, G0604, G0882, G0893, G0899, G0909, G0910
    Scottish
      bibliography, G0353
      handbook, G0926
    Schwenkfelder
      handbook, G0997
    Welsh
      bibliography, G0369

iconography
  see also art, religious; symbolism
  bibliography, G0259
  dictionaries, G0386, G0429
  handbooks, G0817, G0824, G0840, G0845, G0848, G0850, G0854-G0857
imagery
  see iconography; symbolism
immigration
  see also minority groups
  bibliography, G1745

John Chrysostom, St
  see also Eastern Orthodoxy
  liturgy of, G0692, G0697, G0753
Judaism
  quotations, G1124
    and the family
      bibliography, G1518
    and psychology
      bibliography, G1482
    and religious education
      directory, G1336

laity
  see also church administration; church government; church organizations
  bibliographies, G0023, G0041
  handbooks, G0099, G0133, G0144, G0157, G0164, G0173, G0203, G0209, G0244
    and attitudes to preaching
      handbook, G1071
    and liturgy
      handbook, G0630
Latin
  handbooks, G0558
    liturgical
      dictionaries, G0392, G0410
leadership
  see also church administration; church government

and the church
  handbooks, G0100, G0118, G0152, G0164, G0173
lectionary
  see also prayer books; Psalter
  Protestant
    handbook, G0468
  Roman Catholic, G0507-G0509
    handbooks, G0581, G0758
libraries
  see church libraries
liturgics
  see also homiletics; worship
  bibliographies, G0248-G0379
  dictionaries, G0380-G0466
  handbooks, G0125, G0467-G0799
liturgy
  see also church music; eucharist; hymns; pontifical; prayer books; sacraments; worship
  Benedictine
    bibliography, G0307
  theology of
    handbooks, G0469, G0552, G0555, G0607, G0734, G0742, G0776, G0779
Lord's Supper
  see eucharist
love
  and sexuality
    handbook, G1652
Lutheran Church
  and church government
    handbooks, G0120, G0161
  hymns of the
    see hymns, Lutheran
  and religious education
    handbooks, G1261, G1402
  worship in the, G0648, G0778
    handbooks, G0472, G0579, G0592, G0672, G0720, G0766

marriage
  see also divorce; family
  bibliographies, G1423, G1481, G1503, G1535
  handbooks, G0526, G0615, G0637, G0701, G1610, G1656, G1689
martyrology
  see also hagiography; symbolism
  dictionary, G0452
  handbooks, G0511, G0560, G0688
mass
  see eucharist
media centers
  see church libraries

religious research, cont.
directory, G1262
religious work
see also vocational guidance
careers guidance for
handbooks, G1328, G1343, G1380,
G1395
Reorganized Church of Jesus Christ
of Latter-Day Saints
handbooks, G0201, G0202
schools of
handbook, G1383
Rerum Novarum
bibliography, G0020
retirement residences
see nursing homes
rhetoric
see also homiletics; preaching
bibliography, G1027
Roman Catholic Church
and adult education
handbooks, G1344, G1368
altar manuals of, G0470, G0471
breviaries of, G0503, G0514, G0518,
G0608, G0678
handbooks, G0477, G0703, G0750
and campus chaplains
directory, G1304
and church government
see also canon law
handbooks, G0158, G0211
and church-related colleges
directories, G1286, G1305, G1371
and day care centers
directory, G1367
and diocesan priesthood
directory, G1353
and diocesan seminaries
directories, G1283, G1290
and episcopal ceremonies
handbook, G0765
and "etiquette"
handbooks, G0493, G0577
and eucharist, G0506, G0512, G0523
see also missals
handbooks, G0546, G0591, G0622,
G0642, G0655, G0658, G0669,
G0687, G0705, G0731
hymns of the
see hymns, Roman Catholic
and lectionary, G0507-G0509
handbooks, G0581, G0758
liturgy of the, G0504, G0510,
G0512, G0516, G0517, G0519,
G0624, G0626, G0663, G0683,
G0740, G0793

handbooks, G0481, G0495,
G0499, G0501, G0502, G0519,
G0555, G0566, G0582, G0627,
G0630, G0644, G0645, G0654,
G0655, G0659, G0666, G0668,
G0670, G0681, G0691, G0700,
G0704, G0707, G0716, G0728,
G0736, G0737, G0751, G0752,
G0768, G0769, G0776, G0779,
G0798
and martyrology, G0511, G0560,
G0688
mass of the
see Roman Catholic Church,
and eucharist
missals of the, G0505, G0520,
G0593
see also Roman Catholic Church,
and eucharist
handbooks, G0687, G0739
pontifical of the, G0513, G0521
handbook, G0714
prayers of the, G0470, G0471,
G0486, G0497, G0506, G0514,
G0515, G0569, G0679
see also Roman Catholic Church,
breviaries of
handbooks, G0498, G0553,
G0623, G0659, G0669, G0794
and quotations, G1130
and religious education
handbooks, G1281, G1282,
G1284, G1285, G1308, G1318,
G1322, G1325, G1330, G1331,
G1341, G1342, G1345, G1351,
G1354, G1355, G1358, G1362,
G1400, G1408
and religious orders
directory, G1371
and Rerum Novarum
bibliography, G0020
and sacramentary
see Roman Catholic Church,
and eucharist; Roman Catholic
Church, missals of the
and sacristy
handbooks, G0675, G0686
and schools
directories, G1287-G1289,
G1305, G1364, G1366, G1371
handbooks, G1276-G1278,
G1349
and social sciences
bibliographies, G0020, G0039
vestments of the
handbooks, G0651, G0677,

About the Authors

THE REVEREND G. E. GORMAN, formerly Chaplain of St. Hugh's College (Oxford) and Lecturer in Librarianship at the Ballarat College of Advanced Education (Australia), is currently Lecturer in Library Science and in Religious Studies at Riverina-Murray Institute of Higher Education (Australia). He is the author of *The South African Novel in English, Guide to Current National Bibliographies in the Third World, Theological and Religious Reference Materials: General Resources and Biblical Studies, Theological and Religious Reference Materials: Systematic Theology and Church History*, and an editor of *Library Acquisitions: Practice and Theory* as well as other journals and book series. His articles have appeared in *Communio Viatorum, Journal of Religious History, Modern Churchman, International Social Science Journal, International Library Review*, and elsewhere.

DR. LYN GORMAN has been a tutor or administrator at the University of New England (Australia), the Institute of Development Studies at the University of Sussex, and Brighton Polytechnic. She is the coauthor of *Theological and Religious Reference Materials: General Resources and Biblical Studies* and *Theological and Religious Reference Materials: Systematic Theology and Church History*, and her articles have appeared in the *Army Journal, European Studies Review, International Social Science Journal*, and *Die Dritte Welt*. She is coeditor of *The Second Enlargement of the EEC*, cofounder of Library Information and Publishing Consultants, and currently works as a freelance editor and information consultant.